Regulating Investor Protection under EU Law

AF823323

Antonio Marcacci

Regulating Investor Protection under EU Law

The Unbridgeable Gaps with the U.S. and the Way Forward

palgrave
macmillan

Antonio Marcacci
European University Institute Alumnus -
Compliance Professional at a Global Systemically
Important Bank
Milan, Italy

ISBN 978-3-030-07985-7 ISBN 978-3-319-90297-5 (eBook)
https://doi.org/10.1007/978-3-319-90297-5

© The Editor(s) (if applicable) and The Author(s) 2018
Softcover re-print of the Hardcover 1st edition 2018
This work is subject to copyright. All rights are solely and exclusively licensed by the Publisher, whether the whole or part of the material is concerned, specifically the rights of translation, reprinting, reuse of illustrations, recitation, broadcasting, reproduction on microfilms or in any other physical way, and transmission or information storage and retrieval, electronic adaptation, computer software, or by similar or dissimilar methodology now known or hereafter developed.
The use of general descriptive names, registered names, trademarks, service marks, etc. in this publication does not imply, even in the absence of a specific statement, that such names are exempt from the relevant protective laws and regulations and therefore free for general use.
The publisher, the authors, and the editors are safe to assume that the advice and information in this book are believed to be true and accurate at the date of publication. Neither the publisher nor the authors or the editors give a warranty, express or implied, with respect to the material contained herein or for any errors or omissions that may have been made. The publisher remains neutral with regard to jurisdictional claims in published maps and institutional affiliations.

Cover illustration: MariaTkach, iStock / Getty Images Plus

Printed on acid-free paper

This Palgrave Macmillan imprint is published by the registered company Springer International Publishing AG part of Springer Nature.
The registered company address is: Gewerbestrasse 11, 6330 Cham, Switzerland

To Valentina, in her loving memory.

Preface

This book analyzes the legal system for the protection of retail investors under the European Union law of investment services. It identifies the regulatory leitmotiv driving the EU lawmaker and ascertains whether and to what extent such a system is self-sufficient, using a set of EU-made and EU-enforced rules essentially different and autonomous from the Member States' legal orders.

The book takes a double perspective: comparative and intra-firm. Given the federal dimension of the US legal system and, thus, the "role-model" it plays vis-à-vis the EU, the book compares the two systems. The *Union/Federal* level as such— that is, detached from the national (in EU terms) and state (in US terms) level—is taken into account in order to fully highlight the existing gaps and measure the completeness/self-sufficiency of the EU system against its American counterpart. Alongside this, the book brings to the table the unique perspective of a European investment firm and analyzes how EU-produced public-law conduct-of-business[1] rules become a set of compliance requirements for investment services providers. This "within-the-firm" perspective is taken into account to gauge the completeness/self-sufficiency of the EU system of retail investor protection from the standpoint of an EU-regulated entity.

The book opens by positing the hypothesis, namely, that the EU lawmaker—interested in morphing the traditionally bank-based financial market of Continental Europe into a market-based financial system like that of the United States—uses public-law conduct-of-business rules to adapt relationships traditionally regulated by private law to the new market infrastructure without, anyhow, paying enough attention to the private enforcement of such rules. The analysis leverages on the European Regulatory Private Law theory which makes it possible to highlight the regulatory nature of EU law and the current path leading toward a formal Americanization of the law and, at the same time, to a substantial centralization of regulatory and enforcement powers at EU level.

After setting the scene, the book is shaped into two main pillars: *the law-on-the-books,* that is, investor protection in the texts; and *the law-in-action*, that is, the enforcement[2] of investor protection rules on the part of public and private actors, and the practice of transposition of such rules into investment firms[3] for which the internal Compliance Function is in charge. The first Part provides the reader with an illustrative breakdown and an evolutionary analysis of the European statutes dealing with financial services. The aim is twofold: on the one hand, it highlights the functional role that the retail investor plays in the EU Law of financial services within the context of the construction of an EU-wide market-based financial system and the related introduction of specific—increasingly detailing—public-law rules. On the other hand, it flags—by giving concrete examples—how the *law-on-the-books* becomes a set of regulatory requirements for investment firms with the result of making the Compliance Function a central figure within the firms (overcoming/mitigating inefficiencies at the *micro* level with a broader view of contributing to market efficiency at the *macro* level). The first Part subsequently compares the client-service provider relationship under the EU and US laws in order to test to what extent the two systems share similar patterns and verify whether and to what extent the US blueprint may be reproducible in Europe.

Subsequently, the first two chapters of the second Part analyze the legal tools provided by Union/Federal law for public and private enforcement and draw the attention to the fashion public and private mechanisms interact with one another. The purpose is not to examine the procedural elements of enforcement processes, but to assess whether the EU law-maker prefers one set of tools over the other (private *vs.* public), to ascertain to what extent the American enforcement framework may be reproducible in Europe, and to identify the current trend of centralization at the European level. The conclusive chapter, by taking a within-the-firm approach, is devoted to analyzing the role played by the Compliance Function, designed to fill the vacuum between the law-on-the-books and the law-in-action directly *within* a firm. This Function has emerged as the "embedder" of public-law rules into an investment firm and as a "frontliner" of enforcement of such public-law rules, due to its activities of regulatory advice, internal monitoring and reporting, and oversight of complaints-handling procedures, particularly relevant for very minor infringements that can be solved *within* the firm.

The conclusions show how the choice made by the EU lawmakers—that is, preference of the market-based over the bank-based financial system—(in)directly leads to a formal Americanization of the regulatory leitmotif of the EU law of investor protection. However, the EU system is incomplete when being compared to the US one due to the fact that the EU has neither a single common-law contract tradition nor a federal system of public (but a process of public enforcement centralization has been kicked off) and, in particular, private enforcement (where only national-based remedies and procedures can be employed). Despite that, when viewed through the lenses of a European investment firm and, in particular, its Compliance Function, the EU law of investor protection already fully develops its norms and quasi-independently enforces such norms through mechanisms it has itself provided (intra-firm complaints-handling; extra-judicial mechanisms; centralized enforcement powers). The result is the emergence of a European *Regulatory Investor Protection Law* that imposes a full set of regulatory requirements on financial firms to resemble—without, anyhow, yet gaining the full structure of—a self-sufficient system.

The book takes into account legislation as of July 2017. The views expressed in the book are those of the author and do not necessarily represent the views of his current and/or past employers.

Milan, Italy Antonio Marcacci

Notes

1. Conduct-of-business regulation "governs the conduct of financial intermediaries in providing financial products and services". Andrew Tuch, "Conduct of Business Regulation," in *The Oxford Handbook of Financial Regulation*, ed. Niamh Moloney, Eilís Ferran, and Jennifer Payne (Oxford: Oxford University Press, 2015). At 538. In their seminal book, Professors Grundmann and Glasow also define this as *Best Practice Rules for Intermediaries*. Stefan Grundmann and Falko Glasow, *European Company Law: Organization, Finance and Capital Markets—2nd Edition* (Cambridge: Intersentia, 2012). At 525–540.

   Prudential regulation, instead, deals with financial stability: "Micro prudential regulation concerns itself with the stability of each individual institution. Macro-prudential regulation concerns itself with the stability of the financial system as a whole." Centre for Economic Policy Research, "The Fundamental Principles of Financial Regulation—Geneva Reports on the World Economy 11," ed. International Center for Monetary and Banking Studies (2009). At xvi.
2. Within the context of this book, "private enforcement mechanisms" englobe the enforcement actions brought by private parties—either individually or collectively—before civil courts and Alternative Dispute Resolution schemes such as arbitration. On the other side of the spectrum, "public enforcement mechanisms" englobe the enforcement actions brought by public supervisory authorities. The word "supervision" stands for the public activity of authorizing and monitoring private market players, which very often englobes enforcement actions to sanction supervisees for their wrongdoings.
3. The "transposition of rules into investment firms" means the transformation of extra-firm rules (legal norms produced by the public rulemakers) into intra-firm rules (internal compliance requirements).

Acknowledgments

Firstly, I would like to express my open gratitude to Professor Hans-Wolfgang Micklitz for his guiding knowledge and precious advice, which I have received even after defending my PhD thesis. His guidance helped me deepen my research and gave me the tools to frame my "in-action" professional activity into a broader theoretical picture.

Sincere thanks go to my academic fellows—Dr. Marta Cantero-Gamito, Dr. Federico Della Negra, Dr. Heikki Marjosola, and Dr. Paul Verbruggen—for spending time going through the preliminary versions of this book. I will never forget your generous help. I would also like to thank Professor Yane Svetiev, Mr. Rodrigo Vallejo, and Dr. Barbara Warwas for their very useful comments on my MiFID presentations at the Conference and Workshops held between Helsinki and Florence since 2015, which I used to ameliorate this book.

Special thanks go to my industry fellows Craig Roberts, Francesco Martiniello, and Chiara Cassarà for sharing with me technical and professional opinions on topics crossing investment services laws and the daily activity of an investment firm. Your inputs, expertise, and teachings helped me a lot when pouring my "in-action" experience into the book.

Last but, definitely, not the least, deepest heartfelt thanks go to Flavia for her tenacious help, continuous support, and wise advice on the often-unclear academic world, and to Antoine, who smartly persuaded me not to give up and to set the bar much higher than I had ever dared. I would have not achieved this point without such persistent and brave encouragements. Thank you.

All mistakes are, of course, my responsibility only.

Contents

List of Abbreviations

ADR	Alternative Dispute Resolution
CONSOB	Commissione Nazionale per le Società e la Borsa
EBA	European Banking Authority
ECJ	Court of Justice of the European Union
EIOPA	European Insurance and Occupational Pensions Authority
ESMA	European Securities and Markets Authority
EU	European Union
FIN-NET	Consumer Complaints Network for Financial Services
FINRA	Financial Industry Regulatory Authority
IAA	Investment Advisers Act
MiFID I	Markets in Financial Instruments Directive I
MiFID II	Markets in Financial Instruments Directive II
MiFIR	Markets in Financial Instruments Regulation
PG	Product Governance
SA	Securities Act
SEA	Securities Exchange Act
SEC	Securities and Exchange Commission
UCITS	Undertakings for Collective Investment in Transferable Securities
US	United States

List of Tables

1

Introduction

The book revolves around the legal protection of retail investors under the European Union law. Although it originally stems from the "on-the-books" studies of the author, it has been enhanced by his subsequent "in-action" professional experience as Compliance Professional in the European banking and financial industry. For this reason, the book is intended for both Compliance Professionals and academic scholars interested in this topic, and the language and jargon employed are meant to adapt to both audiences.

The main argument of the book is that the EU lawmaker has been building a European Regulatory Investor Protection Law which, on the one hand, apparently reproduces the American approach on investor protection, and, on the other hand, is increasingly self-sufficient. The Americanization feature is particularly enshrined in the "rational investor/disclosure" paradigm, whereas the self-sufficiency implies a set of EU-made and EU-enforced rules that is essentially different and autonomous from the Member States' legal orders. The driver of the EU lawmaker is the policy goal to morph the traditionally bank-based financial markets of Continental Europe into a single market-based financial system like that of the United States. In order to do so, the EU lawmaker uses public-law rules to adapt relationships traditionally regulated by

© The Author(s) 2018

A. Marcacci, *Regulating Investor Protection under EU Law*,
https://doi.org/10.1007/978-3-319-90297-5_1

private law to the new financial markets infrastructure without, anyhow, paying enough attention to the private enforcement of such rules. The analysis leverages on the European Regulatory Private Law (ERPL) theory[1] which makes it possible to highlight the regulatory nature of the EU law and the current trend toward self-sufficiency through centralization of regulatory and enforcement powers at EU level.

The methodology employed is a balance between the author's "on-the-books" studies and his "in-action" experience as Compliance Professional. The book is divided into two main parts: *the law-on-the-books*, that is, investor protection in the texts; and *the law-in-action*, that is, the enforcement[2] of investor protection rules on the part of public and private actors, and the embedding of such rules into investment firms,[3] for which the internal Compliance Function is in charge.

The methodological choice lets the monograph take a double perspective: comparative and intra-firm. Given the federal dimension of the US legal system and the "role-model" it plays vis-à-vis the EU, the book compares the two systems. In order to fully highlight the existing differences and measure the completeness of the EU system against its American counterpart, the *Union/Federal* level as such— that is, autonomous from the domestic (in EU terms) and State (in US terms) level—is taken into account. The intra-firm perspective unfolds through the eyes of a European investment firm and analyzes how EU-produced public-law rules become a set of compliance requirements for investment services providers. This in-action standpoint is essential to gauge the completeness of the EU system of retail investor protection for an EU-regulated firm. The word "compliance" is, then, used in the organizational context of an investment firm and is related to the tasks carried out by a firm's internal Compliance Function.

The book opens by drawing up the boundaries of its normative scope. Chapter 2 starts by briefly explaining the key differences of the two traditional patterns of financial systems and the gradual shift—from bank-based toward market-based—which has been occurring in Europe over the last decades. It, then, gives an account of the ERPL theory and embeds the EU law of investor protection into the margins of such theory. The claim is that the EU law of investor protection is actually a

"European Regulatory Investor Protection Law". The following chapters are meant to provide footing for this assertion.

The first Part of the book concerns the above-defined "law-on-the-books". Chapter 3 provides the reader with an illustrative breakdown and an evolutionary analysis of the European statutes dealing with financial services. The aim is twofold: on the one hand, it highlights the functional role that the retail investor plays in the EU law of financial services within the context of the construction of an EU-wide market-based financial system and the related introduction of specific—increasingly detailing—public-law rules.

An integrated and liberalized financial services market requires proactive and rational retail investors, directly involved in market operations and capable of making good investment decisions. To this end, the disclosure paradigm was at the outset used as the cornerstone of retail investor protection. Under it, retail investors were considered rational market participants, and their protection would ultimately work as an ancillary tool to the general goal of market efficiency. However, over time, the regulatory approach has become increasingly sensitive toward *less-rational* retail investors and has required firms to proceduralize consumer protection tools previously handled mostly through contracts. The post-crisis legislative wave has intensified such an approach.

On the other hand, the chapter flags—by giving concrete examples—how the EU *law-on-the-books* has become a detailed set of regulatory requirements for investment firms. This is the intra-firm proceduralization of conduct-of-business duties set forth by EU law. Through proceduralization, the Compliance Function has become a central figure within the firms, pursuing the purpose of overcoming/mitigating inefficiencies at *micro* level with a broader view of contributing to market efficiency at *macro* level.

Subsequently, Chap. 4 compares the single features of the client-service provider relationship under the EU and US laws in order to test to what extent the two systems share similar patterns and verify whether and to what extent the US blueprint may be reproducible in Europe. The result of the comparison highlights the structural difference between the two systems: whereas the United States rests on a common-law contract law, the European Union arrangement for investor protection relies on public-law duties.

The second part of the book concerns the above-defined "law-in-action". Chapter 5 covers public regulators and their regulatory and enforcement powers, while Chap. 6 describes private enforcement mechanisms. The analysis is not carried out from a procedural law perspective but, rather, with a view to discovering to what extent public and private mechanisms interact with each other (in both the EU and the United States), and whether Europe prefers one set of tools over the other.

The findings of the two chapters reveal that the enforcement of EU law of investor protection is very much—if only entirely!—public driven/regulatory. This is so because the EU law is substantially public even when it touches upon (and penetrates) private-law norms. Due to its public nature, EU investor protection norms are used by public authorities to monitor and gauge service providers' compliance with the law and become regulatory requirements for investment firms (embedded and monitored by the Compliance Function).

Against this backdrop, the EU agency devoted to securities markets—the European Securities and Markets Authority (ESMA)—has been slowly acquiring enforcement powers. Although such powers still massively rest on the shoulders of domestic authorities, local supervisors are more and more under the influence of ESMA's activity for the convergence of interpretative and enforcement practices at EU level. Civil procedural rules, instead, are firmly in the hands of the Member States and the only tool the EU has in this area is the establishment of fast and reliable Alternative Dispute Resolution mechanisms, harmonized at European level.

When being read together, Chaps. 5 and 6 offer a comparative account of the EU vis-à-vis the US system. Not only does the EU still lack a truly, single ("federal", in the American language) law enforcer (but recent reforms may change this status in the mid-run), but the absence of any sort of private enforcement at European level renders it impossible to contemplate an EU version of the US federal interplay between private and public enforcement mechanisms. The result is that the European system still looks incomplete.

Finally, Chap. 7 concerns the Compliance Function and its activity as rule-embedder and enforcement frontliner, with the aim to give the reader an account of how the "law-in-action within an EU firm" unfolds. Since its establishment under Market in Financial Instrument Directive (MiFID) I, the Compliance Function has been gaining importance vis-à-vis the traditional Legal Department, and this phenomenon consolidates the finding that the EU system is public-law lopsided.

Importantly, when the European system of investor protection is being viewed through the lenses of a European investment firm, then its degree of self-sufficiency looks far less incomplete than the vision gained from the formal comparison with the United States. The regulatory production has substantially—if not entirely—shifted toward the European level, with ESMA (and, formally, the European Commission) adopting most of the norms directly affecting and directly applicable to investment firms. The result is that EU-produced norms by now automatically become regulatory requirements that have to be complied with by regulated entities under the rule-embedding and monitoring of the internal Compliance Function. In addition, public enforcement has been enhanced with emergency investor protection powers not only for domestic supervisors but even for ESMA (under certain circumstances). Private enforcement procedures are still under the full responsibility of the Member States, but extra-judicial mechanisms and intra-firm complaints-handling procedures (which cross private and public enforcement) are being harmonized by EU law (and more so in the future through ESMA supervisory convergence activity).

The result of the combination of the two parts of the books is twofold. On the one hand, the book shows that the rational investor paradigm has been progressively dimmed in favor of a more paternalistic approach that shifts investment decision responsibility onto the shoulders of service providers (and their internal Compliance Function). Nevertheless, the US system still works as a blueprint, and the comparison shows how the US interplay between private and public enforcement mechanisms simply does not exist in Europe and it is not even reproducible. When being compared with the United States, the EU system of investor protection seems irreparably incomplete.

On the other hand, however, the European law of investment services now provides for a full set of public-law conduct-of-business rules. Not only does such a set affect traditional private-law relationships and is being used as supervisory and enforcement tools (European supervision private law), but its level of details makes it directly applicable to firms.

The outcome is that the EU normative production automatically becomes regulatory requirements for investment firms, with the Compliance Function playing the increasingly important role of rule-embedder and internal enforcer, in charge of overseeing intra-firm complaints-handling procedures (for very minor infringements). On top of this, the new emergency enforcement powers granted to ESMA and the harmonization of extra-judicial mechanisms (significantly, the Compliance Function copes with both) give the EU system a new layer of completeness. The result is that from the lenses of a European investment firm, the EU system of investor protection increasingly resembles a self-sufficient system.

Notes

1. The European Regulatory Private Law theory has been developed over the years by Professor Hans-Wolfgang Micklitz. Among the theory's founding texts, the following is to be mentioned: Hans-Wolfgang Micklitz, "The Visible Hand of European Regulatory Private Law—the Transformation of European Private Law from Autonomy to Functionalism in Competition and Regulation," *Yearbook of European Law* 28, no. 1 (2009).
2. Within the context of this book, "private enforcement mechanisms" englobe the enforcement actions brought by private parties—either individually or collectively—before civil courts and Alternative Dispute Resolution schemes such as arbitration. On the other side of the spectrum, "public enforcement mechanisms" englobe the enforcement actions brought by public supervisory authorities.
3. The "embedding of rules into investment firms" means the transformation of extra-firm rules (legal norms produced by public rulemakers) into intra-firm rules (internal compliance requirements).

Bibliography

Centre for Economic Policy Research. "The Fundamental Principles of Financial Regulation – Geneva Reports on the World Economy 11." International Center for Monetary and Banking Studies, 2009.

Grundmann, Stefan, and Falko Glasow. *European Company Law: Organization, Finance and Capital Markets.* 2nd ed. Cambridge: Intersentia, 2012.

Micklitz, Hans-Wolfgang. "The Visible Hand of European Regulatory Private Law – The Transformation of European Private Law from Autonomy to Functionalism in Competition and Regulation." *Yearbook of European Law* 28, no. 1 (2009): 3–59.

Tuch, Andrew. "Conduct of Business Regulation." In *The Oxford Handbook of Financial Regulation*, edited by Niamh Moloney, Eilís Ferran and Jennifer Payne. Oxford: Oxford University Press, 2015.

2

Toward a European Regulatory Investor Protection Law

2.1 Bank-Based Financial Systems versus Market-Based Financial Systems

Financial systems are usually divided into two main categories: market-based and bank-based financial systems. The former are characterized by the fact that "securities markets share center stage with banks in terms of getting society's savings to firms, exerting corporate control, and easing risk management,"[1] whereas in the latter "banks play a leading role in mobilizing savings, allocating capital, overseeing the investment decisions of corporate managers, and in providing risk management vehicles."[2]

Theoretically speaking, in a market-based financial system, firms directly raise funds through securities markets and disclose information concerning their soundness and, to a lesser extent, their business strategies, so that investors can assess the economic and financial value of the firm and price its assets and liabilities.[3] Investment banks are key players in a market-based financial system as they perform highly sophisticated activities such as underwriting of debt and equity securities issues, merger advisory, and other securities-related services aimed at helping companies (and governments) raise funds in capital markets.[4]

© The Author(s) 2018

A. Marcacci, *Regulating Investor Protection under EU Law*,
https://doi.org/10.1007/978-3-319-90297-5_2

Bank-based financial systems differ from the market-based alternative because the former tends to establish long-term relationships between banks and borrowers (both businesses and households), while the latter creates financial instruments whereby firms can raise liquidity.[5] Commercial banks are key players in a bank-based financial system as their traditional core business areas are deposit-taking, cash management, payment services, and fund lending—such as loans and home mortgages.[6]

Importantly, the potential control held by the creditors diverges: on the one hand, in a bank-based financial system, banks are very often the key (in some countries, the only) entities providing a firm with funds and they have a close monitoring of the borrowers. On the other hand, in a market-based financial system, (a potentially large amount of) investors fund a firm by relying on the information disclosed by the undertaking.[7]

The United States has been traditionally labeled as a prototype of the market-based financial system.[8] On the contrary, Continental Europe—whose economy is largely based on small-medium firms—is usually categorized as a bank-based financial system.[9] More specifically, the German banking system has been traditionally based on a three-pillar structure, the so-called *Drei Säulen Struktur.*[10] This is made up of three kinds of banking undertakings: commercial banks, the so-called *Kreditbanken*; publicly run banks, the so-called *Sparkassen* and *Landesbanken*; and Credit Unions, the so-called *Genossenschaftsbanken*. Similarly, the Spanish banking and financial system has been traditionally made up of three major categories of credit institutions, *los bancos*, *las cajas de ahorro*, and *las cooperativas de crédito*.[11]

In France and in Italy there have traditionally been general credit institutions, like commercial banks, saving banks (*caisses d'épargne/casse di risparmio*), people's banks (*banques populaires/banco popolare*), and cooperative banks (like *caisses de crédit agricole/banche di credito cooperativo*), and their corporate governance has many similarities to that of the twin firms existing in Germany and Spain. Importantly, a typical feature of the French credit industry is "universal banking",[12] which was reformed in 1984[13] and allows bank to conduct retail and investment businesses at the same time—thus directly connecting retail financial services to wholesale markets. As regards the Italian banking law, a revolution took place in 1990 with the Act n. 218 of 1990, the so-called *Legge Amato*.[14] This important piece of legislation was meant to roll back the frontiers of the government by starting the transformation of publicly owned credit institutions into privately run banking companies.

The traditional feature of the financial systems of Continental Europe is the classic central role given to deposit-taking credit institutions. The soundness of such institutions has always been the indirect protection of depositors,[15] with the purpose of avoiding bank-runs.[16] In this system, the retail level has always been characterized by the so-called prudent banking saver,[17] a term—*saver*—also originally used by 1977 Commission Recommendation on a European code of conduct for transactions in transferable securities.[18] The saver is someone who receives an annual return on the money deposited with a credit institution and/or invests their savings in (allegedly) low-risk instruments, in particular sovereign bonds. The transformation has occurred in the last thirty years for several economic and political reasons, and it has been partnered with the EEC/EC/EU law of financial markets and services[19] that, by escorting traditional bank-based systems toward the market-based style, contributed to morphing traditional banking institutions into investment service providers.

In their seminal contribution from 1999, Demirguc-Kunt and Ross highlighted the existence of an important globally generalized trend that had been taking place for some years. This trend revolved around the fact that the national financial systems of richer countries were increasingly market-oriented as they became wealthier,[20] and securities markets were becoming larger and more efficient in relation to banks over time.[21] Leaving aside the economic reasoning and statistical data that led the two authors to this conclusion, what matters for this book is the evolution of the EU law of financial services in that it "has long been struggling to embed market finance in the single market by deploying a range of mechanisms, including regulatory tools".[22] In doing so, the European bank-based financial systems have increasingly assimilated a US-patterned market-oriented approach with the idea that the latter model was far more efficient than the former.[23]

2.2 The EU Investor Protection Law: Its Completeness (Self-Sufficiency) and the Role of the Retail Investor

The regulatory changes employed at the European level to contribute to driving the shift from a bank-based financial model toward a much more market-leaning system can be read and examined through the lenses of the ERPL theory.[24] This analyzes the relationship between private law and market regulation and posits that existing European private law is a *regulatory private law*. Such regulatory private law provides for mandatory and default rules and—when looking at the financial market sector—follows the regulatory goal of the establishment of a new market order, while taking into its remit specific protective (protection of retail investors) and political integration aims (the opening up of the retail financial services markets).[25]

For this, ERPL theory provides for a unique approach to investor protection that helps understand the ancillary role the legal protection of retail investors plays[26] in the current macro framework of financial markets legislation. Against this backdrop, the retail investor is "a very hard character or set of characters to pin down [... since] investors are incredibly diverse, and often a rather vague and ill-defined group".[27] However, for the sake of clarity, retail investors can be defined as the "most vulnerable customers [...] who may lack the sophistication and knowledge necessary to protect themselves from fraud, market abuse, or misleading advice and must rely on financial institutions and the representatives of those financial institutions to protect their interests".[28] Under the EU law, indeed, the "investor protection regime applies to a set of retail investors who are largely inexperienced with market investments".[29]

Historically speaking, the relationship between market regulation and private law was not invented by the EU law, but it has been evolving throughout the twentieth century. It is particularly important to flag how the Freiburg School of Law and Economics, the so-called Ordoliberalism,[30] elaborated a highly sophisticated conceptual structure for such a relationship[31] already in the 1930s, above all within the realm of antitrust market regulation with a view of creating "the order of the economy"[32] based on the principle of "competition order" (*Wettbewerbsordnung*). Notably,

Ordoliberalism had a strong influence in the post-war European integration project and its blossoming competition law.[33]

Positive regulation of private law can, by and large, be split into two main venues: the social wave—from the end of the nineteenth century up to the 1960s—and the liberalization and privatization wave—from the 1970s onward.[34] The first phase is characterized for using social regulation to limit contract freedom and private autonomy in order to protect the weaker party (usually the worker, the tenant, and, later, the consumer).[35] The second phase fosters the privatization of formerly publicly owned enterprises—to open up key markets like those of telecommunication and postal services[36]—and it is characterized by two, seemingly contradictory directions: freedom of contract is enlarged but, simultaneously, the law restricts it.[37]

Although such regulatory phases took place and unfolded well before the European Union was endowed with the necessary regulatory powers, the EU has progressively become the main regulator, for the social area before and, then, for the market field.[38] As Professor Micklitz rightly states, "The decline of the welfare state model in the Member States and the transfer of regulatory competences to the EU are parallel developments. [...] Matters of social justice via regulation have been substituted through a new model of European justice, called access justice."[39] The outcome of this trend has been the creation of an ERPL.

Unlike the Ordoliberalism, which keeps private and public laws firmly separated, the ERPL analyzes the functional convergence of the two spheres, in particular the instrumental use of private law to achieve public policy goals. What the ERPL theory does is to highlight how and to what extent private law has been used and is still being used to "give shape to the Internal Market", a process that Professor Micklitz has labeled as "economization" (*Ökonomisierung*).[40] The functional use of private law turns it into an instrumental device needed to constitute (1) an efficient Internal Market (regulatory nature of European private law) which is also a (2) competitive market (*competition* as a grounding principle) meant to make Europe fit for a globalized world.[41]

Against this backdrop, the ERPL must be interpreted as (the emergence of) a self-sufficient European private law.[42] This is, by and large, distinct and independent from national private legal orders, where rules are created and enforced at EU level,[43] and where the "private" denotes the goal to foster private relationships, and the "regulatory" implies the determination to realize objectives of public policy.[44] Foremost, the ERPL "focusses on private law beyond the boundaries of traditional private law and on the role of EU legal intervention in the transformation of private law".[45]

The ERPL covers many fields traditionally governed by national private laws.[46] In particular, when looking at the law of financial services and markets, such an effort is symbolized by the legislative activity of the European Union to regulate the EU wholesale financial market and to drive the integration of the local retail financial services markets toward a single retail market. More specifically, here the process of economization is substantially embodied by the shift from a bank-based to a market-based financial system.

To push for the establishment of a market-based financial system, the ERPL has so far used two different—often perceived in contrast to each another—tools: traditional private-law rules (like mandatory contractual terms) and public (administrative)-law rules.[47] The clash lies in the roles that private and public laws traditionally play, that is, individual autonomy enshrined in contract freedom versus public regulation symbolizing heteronomy.[48]

Against this backdrop, the ERPL uses public-law normative measures to penetrate national private laws,[49] with the two systems coexisting alongside. And in doing so, the ERPL can play in two opposite games: negative regulation—that is, the abrogation of barriers built up by national laws that inhibit the integration of the internal financial markets; active regulation—that is, the adoption of European rules that, first, harmonize local rules and, then, directly replace them.[50] This is the shift from minimum to full harmonization Directives, to pan-EU single rules established through Regulations, as the EU law of financial markets clearly shows.

Professor Micklitz, while highlighting the instrumental use of private law as a regulatory tool to shape the EU Internal Market, points out that the ERPL develops through several parameters/devices/principles.[51] These parameters highlight the ERPL's functional role toward the market as grounding principle—efficiency—and the changing paradigm of justice—from social justice to fair access to the market.

First, the ERPL provides for a protective instrumental device. The addressees of the ERPL are the weaker parties of a transaction, such as retail investors. However, such a protection is granted on the basis of the *economic function* played by the weaker party, instead of being linked to a traditional meaning of social justice (see the parameter on justice below).

Subsequently, the "merging" of advertising, pre-contractual information, and contract conclusion indirectly empowers the weaker party. A network of disclosure informational duties, inverting the traditional approach followed by national private laws, is crafted in order to inform the weaker party about the terms of the contract, necessary for the conclusion of the contract itself. To the same wavelength, post-contractual cancellation/rescission/termination rights are introduced in order to give the weaker party the possibility to rescind a contract with either zero or low cost, enhancing competition among services providers.

Within this framework, a competitive and contractual transparency emerges. The former aims at putting contractual parties in a position to compare a specific contract against other prospective contracts on the basis of the information provided. The latter aims at putting contractual parties in a position to understand the reciprocal rights and duties.

Comparison and understanding of contractual terms are increased via standardized contract rules and contract-making. Standardized contracts do not only ease information exchange (propaedeutic to market efficiency) but also reduce negotiation timing: the purpose is not granting autonomy to the parties, but, rather, improving market functioning (functional role of private law). By the same token, the EU law introduces mandatory contract rules directly imposed by the law and statutory black and gray lists of contractual clauses with an invalidating effect.

All this brings about a sea change in the pattern of justice: fairness as market clearance and market access replaces the social justice paradigm enshrined into national private-law traditions of Continental Europe, which is conventionally understood as distributive justice,[52] where contract laws revolve around a system of rights and entitlements like freedom of contract.[53] The objective pursued by the ERPL differs from the one pursued by traditional private law, and it concerns the creation of the internal market,[54] and, for this, "the *acquis communautaire* in the field of private law is therefore regulatory in nature."[55] As a result, it resembles the evolution of the Anglo-American legal system where "commercial law was needed to manage English trade internationally",[56] market fairness is a leading value, and the way of looking at the "role and function of law is much more economic (ökonomischer) in its basic assumptions as opposed to"[57] the Continental legal traditions.[58]

The EU model of justice diverges from social justice conceived as distributive justice in that it consists in the idea of fairness and market access, where the point is granting access to both businesses and consumers: access justice/*Zugangsgerechtigkeit*[59] (meaning justice through nondiscriminated access, not access to justice). The EU is bound to make sure that "those who are excluded from the market or […] those who face difficulties in making use of the market freedoms"[60] can enter the market and become full-fledged market players. Rules of European private law must be efficient in that they must ensure "that the weaker parties have and maintain access to the market—and to the European society insofar as this exists".[61] It goes without saying that such an approach on justice chimes with the economic efficiency doctrine (also highlighted by the ERPL).

Finally, the need for fast (and, sometimes, even quick-and-dirty) redress of rights pushes, on the one hand, toward an increased role of public enforcement mechanisms and, on the other hand, toward the establishment of Alternative Dispute Resolution (ADR) mechanisms. The EU law views enforcement—in particular public—as a tool to regulate market players' behavior (even overcoming separation between substantive and procedural law typical of Continental private legal orders).[62]

When investor protection is at stake, the EU lawmaker is committed to crafting protective instrumental devices for the weaker party, who suffers from a lopsided relationship vis-à-vis the investment service provider. A key goal the EU lawmaker pursues is the mitigation and limitation of the information asymmetry between the average retail investor and investment firms, since providers (are supposed to) know what they sell much better than their customers:

> "Information asymmetry" refers to the client's limited knowledge vis-à-vis the intermediary with regard to the investment activity (e.g., the mechanics of buying and selling security products), the information surrounding

> the investment product in which the client may be interested (e.g., corporate information and execution information), and the intermediary's self-interest in the client's activity (i.e., whether there may be any conflict of interest). Such information asymmetries, in the absence of regulation, may result in the intermediary abusing its position of superior knowledge.[63]

Information asymmetry hampers the confidence[64] of less-sophisticated investors in the basic mechanism of financial market, with the ultimate consequence of decelerating (or even stopping) its functioning.[65] Retail market regulation is employed to address this market failure.[66] Investors are provided with mandatory disclosure[67] as if it were the best way to make them feel "confident",[68] without impairing "two of the most deeply rooted principles of Western societies: namely, the idea of free markets and the autonomy principle".[69]

Since the policy goal of the EU lawmaker is to morph the European traditionally bank-centered financial system into a market-driven system, the role tailored for the retail investor must be coherent with this aim. The retail investor is, thus, "cuddled" through information disclosure, as s/he is perceived as the weaker contractual party[70] that would be able to make fully rational investment decisions when being provided with the necessary information. This is the so-called rational expectations investor model—very much employed in the United States under the influence of the Law and Economics school[71]—that views investors behaving "like members of the species *homo economicus*: they are cool, calculating, and purely self-interested actors".[72] Within this context, the EU law provides for mandatory information disclosure and conduct-of-business rules based on contract-connected duties, from which not only contractual liability but even administrative sanctions may stem: traditional contract-law relationships are, indeed, used as public enforcement tool[73] (administrative enforcement of private law).[74]

The functional image—instrumental for market-building—of the "confident consumer" has a normative implication for what seems to be an "infiltration of the Anglo-American understanding of the role and function of law".[75] In particular, the "reasonable consumer/investor" is directly linked to the "changing paradigm of justice and the increasing importance of economic efficiency".[76] The contract-law role of the consumer/investor is not handled on the basis of party autonomy and mutual contractual justice (distributive justice), but it is, instead, crafted around its market-driven rationality (access justice—fairness/*Zugangsgerechtigk eit*).[77] However, as the comparison between the US and the EU systems of investor protection shows, "Americanization" blurs away when it comes to the coherent construction of the body of law and to procedural law.

By leveraging on the ERPL theory, the book unfolds by pursuing the two following goals. First, showing that the role played by the retail investor under the EU law of investor protection is functional to the policy goal of market construction.[78] To this aim, the book describes the substance of the EU law on investor protection, by paying attention to the evolution of the regulatory instruments employed over time, and to the degree of "Americanization" of the regulatory *leitmotif.* Second, testing the self-sufficiency of the EU law on investor protection. To this aim, the book takes into account the level of details of the rules produced through the EU legislative procedures[79] and by the EU regulatory agencies[80]; the fashion in which such rules are enforced (taking into account both private and public enforcement mechanisms); a comparison with the US federal system of investor protection, given the "role-model" it plays vis-à-vis the EU; and, finally, the perspective of a European investment firm and how it is affected by the EU law of financial services.

Conclusions show that the EU law of retail investor protection suits the parameters of the ERPL theory, and it is functional to pursue the general economization aim—that is, the shift from a bank-based to a market-based financial system (the philosophy underpinning the *law-on-the-book*). The result is a Regulatory Investor Protection Law whose degree of self-sufficiency depends on the perspective standpoint. When compared to a full-fledged federal system of investor protection like that of the United States, the EU Regulatory Investor Protection Law shows visible gaps (both on substantial—the EU lacks of a single contract law—and procedural law—lack of an interplay of private and public enforcement mechanisms at EU level). However, when viewed through the lenses of a European investment firm, the EU Regulatory Investor Protection Law gains a substantial degree of self-sufficiency, being its public-law rules entirely made and potentially enforced via public enforcement at the European level. In this regard, self-sufficiency is still incomplete, but it is quite likely that the recently boosted centralization trend will keep strengthening.

Notes

1. Asli Demirguc-Kunt and Ross Levine, "Bank-Based and Market-Based Financial Systems: Cross-Country Comparisons," *The World Bank - Policy Research Working Paper no. WPS 2143* (1999). At 1.
2. Ibid. At 2. Professors Moloney, Ferran, and Payne state that: "Bank-based intermediation manages this process by means of maturity transformation: the provision by banks of long-term loan assets to capital seekers, based on the short-term bank deposit liabilities which provide returns for capital suppliers. Market-based intermediation is based on the raising of funds by capital seekers through marketable instruments (such as shares and bonds) which provide capital suppliers with a return." Niamh Moloney, Eilís Ferran, and Jennifer Payne, "Introduction," in *The Oxford Handbook of Financial Regulation*, ed. Niamh Moloney, Eilís Ferran, and Jennifer Payne (Oxford: Oxford University Press, 2015). At 4. As regards studies concerning the different kinds of financial systems, see: Raymond W. Goldsmith, *Financial Structure and Development* (New Haven: Yale University Press, 1969); Franklin Allen and Douglas Gale, "A Welfare Comparison of Intermediaries and Financial Markets in Germany and the U.S.," *American Economic Review* 39 (1995); *Comparing Financial Systems* (Cambridge, MA: MIT Press, 2000); Asli Demirgüç-Kunt and Ross Levine, eds., *Financial Structure and Economic Growth: A Cross-Country Comparison of Banks, Markets, and Development* (Cambridge, MA: MIT Press, 2001), in particular: Sergio Schmukler and Esteban Vesperoni, "Firms' Financing Choices in Bank-Based and Market-Based Economies," in *Financial Structure and Economic Growth: A Cross-Country Comparison of Banks, Markets, and Development*, ed. Asli Demirgüç-Kunt and Ross Levine (Cambridge, MA: MIT Press, 2001); Sigurt Vitols, "The Origins of Bank-Based and Market-Based Financial Systems: Germany, Japan, and the United States," ed. Wissenschaftszentrum Berlin für Sozialforschung - Discussion Paper FS I 01 - 302 (Berlin, 2001); Ross Levine, "Bank-Based or Market-Based Financial Systems: Which Is Better?," ed. National Bureau of Economic Research Working Paper

Series - WP No. 9138 (Cambridge, MA, 2002); Iain Hardie and David Howarth, "Market-Based Banking and the Financial Crisis," ed. University of Edinburg Working Paper (Edinburgh, 2011).
3. In the words of R. Barry Johnston, Liliana Schumacher, Jingqing Chai: "public disclosure [... is] a key concern under market-based financial systems". R. Barry Johnston, Liliana Schumacher, and Jingqing Chai, "Assessing Financial System Vulnerabilities," *International Monetary Fund - Working Paper No. 00/76* (2006). At 10.
4. Casu, Girardone, and Molyneux give a clear account of the difference between commercial banking and investment banking: Barbara Casu, Claudia Girardone, and Philip Molyneux, *Introduction to Banking*, vol. 10 (Pearson Education, 2006). At 69–71.
5. Sergio Schmukler and Esteban Vesperoni, "Firms' Financing Choices in Bank-Based and Market-Based Economies," in *Financial Structure and Economic Growth*, ed. Asli Demirguc-Kunt and Ross Levine (MIT Press, 2001). At 349.
6. Casu, Girardone, and Molyneux, 10. At 70–71. On the role of banks, Bart DeMeester, *Liberalisation of Trade in Banking Services: An International and European Perspective* (Cambridge: Cambridge University Press, 2014). At 13.
7. Schmukler and Vesperoni, "Firms' Financing Choices in Bank-Based and Market-Based Economies." At 349–350. In particular, the authors highlight how: "Bank-based systems may encourage long-term relationships between borrowers and lenders. During a crisis, banks' inside information allows them to continue lending to sound firms". At 350.
8. The World Bank, "Financial Structures – Bank-Based Vs. Market-Based Financial System," http://go.worldbank.org/R6XUIEOF40.
9. Ibid. Furthermore, in the words of Kern Alexander, Rahul Dhumale, John Eatwell: "The United States was classified as a financial system that relies to a large extent on capital-market finance, whereas Germany was classified as a financial system that relies, by and large, on bank-led finance." Kern Alexander, Rahul Dhumale, and John Eatwell, *Global Governance of Financial Systems: The International Regulation of Systemic Risk* (New York: Oxford University Press, 2006). At 19.
10. Ginevra Cerrina Feroni and Ettore Andreani, "Il Sistema Delle Sparkassen in Germania Tra Frammentazione Del Mercato, Processi Di Privatizzazione E Fondazioni Di Emanazione Bancaria," in *Fondazione E Banche. Modelli Ed Esperienze in Europa E Negli Stati Uniti*, ed. Ginevra Cerrina Feroni (Torino: Giappichelli, 2011). At 75.

11. On the traditional Spanish credit system: Gianluca Mancuso, "Le Cajas De Ahorro Quali Enti Fondazionali Del Sistema Creditizio Spagnolo," ibid., ed. Ginevra Cerrina-Feroni. At 107.
12. Christophe Blot et al., "Structural Evolutions and Reforms of the French Banking and Financial System since the 1980s: Relationship with the Legal Process of European Integration," in *FESSUD Working Paper Series No. 66*, ed. FESSUD Project (2014). At 7.
13. *Loi N°84-46 Du 24 Janvier 1984.*
14. *Legge N. 218 Del 30 Luglio 1990.* The Act was officially named *disposizioni in materia di ristrutturazione e integrazione patrimoniale degli Istituti di credito di diritto pubblico* (provisions on the capital restructuring and consolidation of credit institutions of public law), and informally named "Amato Act", after the then Minister of the Treasury, Professor Giuliano Amato.
15. See Filippo Zatti, "La Dimensione Costituzionale Della Tutela Del Risparmio. Dalla Tutela Del Risparmio Alla Protezione Dei Risparmiatori/Investitori E Ritorno?," in *Studi in Onore Di Vincenzo Atripaldi*, ed. Marco Benvenuti et al. (Naples: Jovene, 2010).
16. A bank-run "occurs when depositors suspect that a bank may go bankrupt and, therefore, "run" to the bank to withdraw their deposits". N. Gregory Mankiw, *Principles of Macroeconomics* (Mason: Cengage Learning, 2008). At 353.
17. The term "prudent saver" is used by the 2008 Optem Report in opposition to "gamblers": both invest their funds in securities markets but the latter are "more likely to take and accept risks" than the former [European Commission, "Optem Report - Study on Pre-Contractual Information for Financial Services" (2008), at 8]. In this book the term "prudent banking saver" is, however, mostly referred to the traditional banking-deposit savers, namely, someone who deposits their money in low-return saving accounts and invest in "zero-risk" instruments. This meaning is used by Professor Zatti in his article "La dimensione costituzione della tutela del risparmio". Zatti. At 1472. Professor Zatti mentions the seminal work of Professor Costi: *tutela dei depositanti e tutela del risparmio tendenzialmente coincidono, nel senso che entrambi si riconducono alla solvibilità dell'impresa bancaria e (...) quest'ultima deve essere perseguita nell'interesse dello sviluppo dell'economia reale* [Author's translation: "depositor protection and savings protection tend to coincide, since both refer to the solvency of the banking entity and (...) solvency shall be pursued in the interests of the development of the real economy"] Renzo Costi, *L'ordinamento Bancario* (Bologna: Il Mulino, 2007). At 39.

18. *Commission Recommendation 77/534/Eec of 25 July 1977 Concerning a European Code of Conduct Relating to Transactions in Transferable Securities*. Commission Recommendation 1977/534/EEC, OJ L 212/37, 20.08.1977.
19. In her seminal work, Eilís Ferran carries out an analysis on the law's role in building an integrated securities market. In particular, Professor Ferran points out: "The recent shift in Continental Europe towards securities market-based financing can be attributed to a range of factors, some of which affected securities markets around the world, some of which were exclusively, or particularly, EU-orientated. [...] The evolving EU processes of political and economic integration also played a significant part in fostering the development of securities market-based financing." Eilís Ferran, *Building an EU Securities Market* (Cambridge: Cambridge University Press, 2004). At 22–23.
20. Demirguc-Kunt and Levine. At 4.
21. Ibid. At 37. A similar conclusion was achieved by Hardie and Howarth in 2011: "It is now clear that banking in developed world economies, to varying but significant degrees, underwent profound changes in the early years of this century. Amongst the casualties of this change is the distinction, central to the varieties of financial capitalism literature, between 'bank-based' and 'capital market-based' capitalism. Banking, this special edition argues, has, increasingly but to varying degrees across the countries studied, become 'market-based banking'." Hardie and Howarth. At 2.
22. Moloney, Ferran, and Payne. At 6.
23. As it is evident from the parallels drawn in the Lamfalussy Committee's Final Report. The Committee of Wise Men - Lamfalussy Committee, "Final Report of the Committee of Wise Men on the Regulation of European Securities Markets" (2001).
24. Some parts of this section have been previously published in Antonio Marcacci, "European Regulatory Private Law Going Global? The Case of Product Governance," *European Business Organization Law Review* 18, no. 2 (2017).
25. Hans-Wolfgang Micklitz, "The Transformation of Enforcement in European Private Law: Preliminary Considerations," *European Review of Private Law* 4 (2015). At 496.
26. In the words of Professor Moloney: "investor protection regime is ultimately a creature of political compromise and is closely tied to market integration priorities." Niamh Moloney, *How to Protect Investors: Lessons from the EC and the UK* (Cambridge: Cambridge University Press, 2010). At 45.

27. Julia Black, "Involving Consumers in Securities Regulation: Research Study for the Taskforce to Modernize Securities Legislation in Canada," ed. Task force to Modernize Securities Regulation in Canada (2006). At 28.
28. Eric Pan, "Organizing Regional Systems: The Us Example," in *The Oxford Handbook of Financial Regulation*, ed. Niamh Moloney, Eilís Ferran, and Jennifer Payne (Oxford: Oxford University Press, 2015). At 192.
29. Moloney. At 32.
30. Grounding publications of the School of Freiburg are: Franz Böhm, "Die Idee Des Ordo Im Denken Walter Euckens. Dem Freund Und Mitherausgeber Zum Gedächtnis," in *Ordo - Jahrbuch Fuer Die Ordnung Von Wirtschaft Und Gesellschaft* (1959); Walter Eucken, *Grundsätze Der Wirtschaftspolitik* (Tübingen: Mohr Siebeck, 2004); *Die Grundlagen Der Nationalökonomie* (Berlin: Springer, 2013); Leonhard Miksch, *Wettbewerb Als Aufgabe* (Stuttgart: Kohlhammer, 1937). For more recent analyses: Manfred E. Streit, "Economic Order, Private Law and Public Policy the Freiburg School of Law and Economics in Perspective," *Journal of Institutional and Theoretical Economics* 148, no. 4 (1992); Viktor Vanberg, "Freiburg School of Law and Economics," in *The New Palgrave Dictionary of Economics and the Law*, ed. Peter Newman (London: Palgrave Macmillan, 1998).
31. The author would like to thank Professor Hans Micklitz for his advice on Ordoliberalism.
32. As mentioned in: Oliver Budzinski, "Monoculture Versus Diversity in Competition Economics," *Cambridge Journal of Economics* 32, no. 2 (2007). At 305.
33. Christian Joerges, "The European Economic Constitution and Its Transformation through the financial Crisis," in *A Companion to European Union Law and International Law*, ed. Dennis Patterson and Anna Södersten (New York: Wiley, 2016). At 245.
34. Hans-Wolfgang Micklitz, "The Internal Vs. The External Dimension of European Private Law—a Conceptual Design and a Research Agenda," in *EUI Working Paper Law 2015/35*, ed. European University Institute (Florence, 2015). At 2 mentioning Duncan Kennedy, "Three Globalizations of Law and Legal Thought: 1850–2000," in *The New Law and Economic Development - a Critical Appraisal*, ed. David M. Trubek and Alvaro Santos (Cambridge: Cambridge University Press, 2006).
35. Micklitz, "The Internal Vs. The External Dimension of European Private Law—a Conceptual Design and a Research Agenda." At 2.

36. Ibid. At 2.
37. Ibid. At 2.
38. Ibid. At 2.
39. Ibid. At 2. Mentioning: “Social Justice and Access Justice in Private Law,” in *EUI Working Paper Law 2011/2*, ed. European University Institute (Florence, 2011). At 3.
40. “The Visible Hand of European Regulatory Private Law—the Transformation of European Private Law from Autonomy to Functionalism in Competition and Regulation,” *Yearbook of European Law* 28, no. 1 (2009). At 7.
41. Ibid. At 8–10.
42. Hans-Wolfgang Micklitz, Yane Svetiev, and Guido Comparato, “European Regulatory Private Law—the Paradigms Tested,” in *EUI Working Paper Law 2014/04*, ed. European University Institute (Florence, 2014). At 5, as also mentioned by Vanessa Mak, “The Consumer in European Regulatory Private Law,” in *Tilburg Private Law Working Paper Series No. 05/2015*, ed. Tilburg University (Tilburg, 2015).
43. Olha O. Cherednychenko, “Financial Consumer Protection in the Eu: Towards a Self-Sufficient European Contract Law for Consumer Financial Services?,” *European Review of Contract Law* 10, no. 4 (2014). At 478.
44. On this point: Mak.
45. Hans-Wolfgang Micklitz, “The Public and the Private – European Regulatory Private Law and Financial Services,” *European Review of Contract Law* 10, no. 4 (2014).
46. For the telecommunication sector, see the exhaustive analysis of Marta Cantero-Gamito, “Towards the Self-Sufficiency in European Regulatory Private Law (I) the Case of European Telecommunications Services Law,” in *A Self-Sufficient European Private Law – a Viable Concept?*, ed. Hans-Wolfgang Micklitz and Yane Svetiev (EUI Working Papers, LAW 2012/31: European University Institute, 2012). For the energy sector, see the comprehensive analysis of Lucila DeAlmeida, “Integration through Self-Standing European Private Law: Insights from the Internal Point of View to Harmonization in the Energy Market” (PhD Thesis, European University Institute, 2017).
47. Micklitz, “The Visible Hand of European Regulatory Private Law—the Transformation of European Private Law from Autonomy to Functionalism in Competition and Regulation.”

48. Giudo Comparato, "Private Autonomy and Regulation in the Eu Case-Law," in *European Regulatory Private Law-the Paradigms Tested*, ed. Hans-Wolfgang Micklitz, Yane Svetiev, and Guido Comparato (EUI Working Paper Law 2014/04: European University Institute, 2014).
49. As Professor Mak says: "inroads into party autonomy in private law can be explained, or even justified, in the light of the EU's internal market policy," Mak. At 4.
50. Ibid.
51. Micklitz, "The Visible Hand of European Regulatory Private Law—the Transformation of European Private Law from Autonomy to Functionalism in Competition and Regulation." At 33.
52. "Most, not all, continental private legal orders enshrine the idea of social justice, understood as distributive justice, which has to be preserved in private law matters, both in contract and in tort law," ibid. At 9. In addition: "Social Justice and Access Justice in Private Law."
53. Cherednychenko. At 477. In the words of Professor Cherednychenko: "Traditionally, private law has been concerned with doing justice between the two private parties in an individual case and not with the attainment of external political, social, or economic goals." "Public Supervision over Private Relationships: Towards European Supervision Private Law?," *European Review of Private Law* 22, no. 1 (2014). At 51.
54. In the words of Professor Cherednychenko: "national private laws have been primarily concerned with justice between market participants rather than the pursuance of specific public goals, the EU has viewed private law, in particular contract law, as an instrument for achieving the collective objectives of European integration" "Public Supervision over Private Relationships: Towards European Supervision Private Law?." At 38.
55. Ibid. At 38. See also: "Financial Consumer Protection in the EU: Towards a Self-Sufficient European Contract Law for Consumer Financial Services?." At 478.
56. Micklitz, "Social Justice and Access Justice in Private Law." At 6.
57. Ibid. At 6.
58. Professor Micklitz compares the English pragmatism with the German Idealism and the French Rationalism. Ibid.
59. Ibid.
60. Ibid. At 2.
61. Ibid. At 2.

62. Micklitz, "The Visible Hand of European Regulatory Private Law—the Transformation of European Private Law from Autonomy to Functionalism in Competition and Regulation." At 34.
63. Iris H-Y Chiu, "Securities Intermediaries in the Internet Age and the Traditional Principal-Agent Model of Regulation: Some Observations from European Union Securities Regulation," *Virginia Law & Business Review* 2, no. 2 (2007). At 309–310.
64. Keeping investors' confidence in financial markets has been also highlighted by the ECJ: *Alpine Investments Bv V Minister Van Financiën* (1995).
65. Professor Haar highlights "a close interdependence between market efficiency and investor confidence". Brigitte Haar, "Organizing Regional Systems: The Eu Example," in *The Oxford Handbook of Financial Regulation*, ed. Niamh Moloney, Eilís Ferran, and Jennifer Payne (Oxford: Oxford University Press, 2015). At 168.
66. "Retail market regulation has, from the outset, been concerned with addressing market failures arising from the gaping information asymmetry between retail investors and professional market actors". Niamh Moloney, "Regulating the Retail Markets," ibid. At 739.
67. In the words of Professors Enriques and Gilotta: "The core function of MD [*mandatory disclosure*] in financial market regulation is to provide economic agents with information to help them make better decisions. Its rationale, in turn, is grounded on the belief that in the absence of MD there would be less information available for such choices than it would be optimal or (which is largely the same) that higher production and dissemination costs would lead to its undersupply." Alongside investor protection and market functioning concerns, Enriques and Gilotta rightly claim that mandatory disclosure also "addresses the agency problems affecting large corporations, thus supporting their ability to serve as a means of organizing, financing and operating today's large entrepreneurial ventures; and […] ensures that prices fully reflect all value-relevant information, so as to help financial markets in their fundamental function of efficiently allocating scarce financial resources across the economy". Luca Enriques and Sergio Gilotta, "Disclosure and Financial Market Regulation," ibid. At 513–514.
68. In the words of Professor Micklitz: "The concept of the confident consumer now becomes a legal normative prerogative which changes the outlook of consumer law". Micklitz, "The Visible Hand of European Regulatory Private Law—the Transformation of European Private Law from Autonomy to Functionalism in Competition and Regulation." At 10.

69. Enriques and Gilotta. At 513.
70. On the weaker consumer: Mak.
71. Professor Lynn A. Stout explains that the rational expectations investor model is strongly interconnected with the law and economics school: "legal scholars who specialize in securities regulation have been strongly influenced over the past two decades by the "law and economics" school of analysis. The law and economics school, in turn, relies on a model of investor behavior that I will call the "rational expectations" investor model." Lynn A. Stout, "The Investor Confidence Game," *Brooklyn Law Review* 68, no. 2 (2002). At 6–7.
72. Ibid. At 7.
73. "Conduct of Business Rules as Supervision Standards" Olha O. Cherednychenko, "The Regulation of Retail Investment Services in the Eu: Towards the Improvement of Investor Rights?," *Journal of Consumer Policy* 33, no. 4 (2010). At 410.
74. In the words of Professor Micklitz: "Regulatory agencies, designed for securing the functioning of the respective market, are confronted with the need to either instrumentalise private law rules for public enforcement and/or to delegate the enforcement of private law rules in regulated markets to the parties concerned, and thus to the judiciary as the traditional form of conflict resolution." Hans-Wolfgang Micklitz, "Administrative Enforcement of European Private Law," in *The Foundations of European Private Law*, ed. Roger Brownsword et al. (Oxford-Portland: Hart Publishing, 2011). At 564.
75. "The Visible Hand of European Regulatory Private Law—the Transformation of European Private Law from Autonomy to Functionalism in Competition and Regulation." At 12.
76. Ibid. At 13.
77. Ibid. At 13.
78. Although in a different specific context, this is also claimed by Professor Enriques: "Investor Protection is just an instrumental end, something to the pursued in order to attain market integration." Luca Enriques, "Conflicts of Interest in Investment Services: The Price and Uncertain Impact of Mifid's Regulatory Framework," in *Investor Protection in Europe*, ed. Guido Ferrarini and Eddy Wymeersch (New York: Oxford University Press, 2006). At 338.
79. I am referring here to the Lamfalussy procedure.
80. I am referring here to the ESMA.

Bibliography

Alexander, Kern, Rahul Dhumale, and John Eatwell. *Global Governance of Financial Systems: The International Regulation of Systemic Risk*. New York: Oxford University Press, 2006.

Allen, Franklin, and Douglas Gale. "A Welfare Comparison of Intermediaries and Financial Markets in Germany and the U.S." *American Economic Review* 39 (1995): 179–209.

———. *Comparing Financial Systems*. Cambridge, MA: MIT Press, 2000.

Alpine Investments Bv V Minister Van Financiën. 1995.

Black, Julia. "Involving Consumers in Securities Regulation: Research Study for the Taskforce to Modernize Securities Legislation in Canada." Edited by Task force to Modernize Securities Regulation in Canada, 2006.

Blot, Christophe, Jérôme Creel, Anne-Laure Delatte, Fabien Labondance, and Sandrine Levasseur. "Structural Evolutions and Reforms of the French Banking and Financial System since the 1980s: Relationship with the Legal Process of European Integration." In *FESSUD Working Paper Series No. 66*, edited by FESSUD Project, 2014.

Böhm, Franz. "Die Idee Des Ordo Im Denken Walter Euckens. Dem Freund Und Mitherausgeber Zum Gedächtnis." In *Ordo - Jahrbuch Fuer Die Ordnung Von Wirtschaft Und Gesellschaft*, 1959.

Budzinski, Oliver. "Monoculture Versus Diversity in Competition Economics." *Cambridge Journal of Economics* 32, no. 2 (2007): 295–324.

Cantero-Gamito, Marta. "Towards the Self-Sufficiency in European Regulatory Private Law (I) the Case of European Telecommunications Services Law." In *A Self-Sufficient European Private Law – a Viable Concept?*, edited by Hans-Wolfgang Micklitz and Yane Svetiev. EUI Working Papers, LAW 2012/31: European University Institute, 2012.

Casu, Barbara, Claudia Girardone, and Philip Molyneux. *Introduction to Banking*. Vol. 10. Essex: Pearson Education, 2006.

Cherednychenko, Olha O. "The Regulation of Retail Investment Services in the Eu: Towards the Improvement of Investor Rights?" *Journal of Consumer Policy* 33, no. 4 (2010): 403–24.

———. "Financial Consumer Protection in the Eu: Towards a Self-Sufficient European Contract Law for Consumer Financial Services?" *European Review of Contract Law* 10, no. 4 (2014a): 476–95.

———. "Public Supervision over Private Relationships: Towards European Supervision Private Law?" *European Review of Private Law* 22, no. 1 (2014b): 37–68.

Chiu, Iris H-Y. "Securities Intermediaries in the Internet Age and the Traditional Principal-Agent Model of Regulation: Some Observations from European Union Securities Regulation." *Virginia Law & Business Review* 2, no. 2 (2007): 307–61.

Commission Recommendation 77/534/Eec of 25 July 1977 Concerning a European Code of Conduct Relating to Transactions in Transferable Securities.

Comparato, Giudo. "Private Autonomy and Regulation in the Eu Case-Law." In *European Regulatory Private Law-the Paradigms Tested*, edited by Hans-Wolfgang Micklitz, Yane Svetiev, and Guido Comparato. EUI Working Paper Law 2014/04: European University Institute, 2014.

Costi, Renzo. *L'ordinamento Bancario.* Bologna: Il Mulino, 2007.

DeAlmeida, Lucila. "Integration through Self-Standing European Private Law: Insights from the Internal Point of View to Harmonization in the Energy Market." PhD Thesis, European University Institute, 2017.

DeMeester, Bart. *Liberalisation of Trade in Banking Services: An International and European Perspective.* Cambridge: Cambridge University Press, 2014.

Demirguc-Kunt, Asli, and Ross Levine. "Bank-Based and Market-Based Financial Systems: Cross-Country Comparisons." The World Bank - Policy Research Working Paper No. WPS 2143, 1999.

Demirgüç-Kunt, Asli, and Ross Levine, eds. *Financial Structure and Economic Growth: A Cross-Country Comparison of Banks, Markets, and Development.* Cambridge, MA: MIT Press, 2001.

Enriques, Luca. "Conflicts of Interest in Investment Services: The Price and Uncertain Impact of Mifid's Regulatory Framework." In *Investor Protection in Europe*, edited by Guido Ferrarini and Eddy Wymeersch. New York: Oxford University Press, 2006.

Enriques, Luca, and Sergio Gilotta. "Disclosure and Financial Market Regulation." In *The Oxford Handbook of Financial Regulation*, edited by Niamh Moloney, Eilís Ferran, and Jennifer Payne. Oxford: Oxford University Press, 2015.

Eucken, Walter. *Grundsätze Der Wirtschaftspolitik.* Tübingen: Mohr Siebeck, 2004.

———. *Die Grundlagen Der Nationalökonomie.* Berlin: Springer, 2013.

European Commission. "Optem Report - Study on Pre-contractual Information for Financial Services." 2008.

Feroni, Ginevra Cerrina, and Ettore Andreani. "Il Sistema Delle Sparkassen in Germania Tra Frammentazione Del Mercato, Processi Di Privatizzazione E Fondazioni Di Emanazione Bancaria." In *Fondazione E Banche. Modelli Ed Esperienze in Europa E Negli Stati Uniti*, edited by Ginevra Cerrina Feroni. Torino: Giappichelli, 2011.

Ferran, Eilís. *Building an Eu Securities Market*. Cambridge: Cambridge University Press, 2004.

Goldsmith, Raymond W. *Financial Structure and Development*. New Haven: Yale University Press, 1969.

Haar, Brigitte. "Organizing Regional Systems: The Eu Example." In *The Oxford Handbook of Financial Regulation*, edited by Niamh Moloney, Eilís Ferran, and Jennifer Payne. Oxford: Oxford University Press, 2015.

Hardie, Iain, and David Howarth. "Market-Based Banking and the Financial Crisis." Edited by University of Edinburg Working Paper. Edinburgh, 2011.

Joerges, Christian. "The European Economic Constitution and Its Transformation through the financial Crisis." In *A Companion to European Union Law and International Law*, edited by Dennis Patterson and Anna Södersten. New York: Wiley, 2016.

Johnston, R. Barry, Liliana Schumacher, and Jingqing Chai. "Assessing Financial System Vulnerabilities." International Monetary Fund - Working Paper No. 00/76, 2006.

Kennedy, Duncan. "Three Globalizations of Law and Legal Thought: 1850–2000." In *The New Law and Economic Development - a Critical Appraisal*, edited by David M. Trubek and Alvaro Santos. Cambridge: Cambridge University Press, 2006.

Legge N. *218 Del 30 Luglio*, 1990.

Levine, Ross. "Bank-Based or Market-Based Financial Systems: Which Is Better?" National Bureau of Economic Research Working Paper Series - Wp No. 9138. Cambridge, MA, 2002.

Loi N°84-46 Du 24 Janvier 1984.

Mak, Vanessa. "The Consumer in European Regulatory Private Law." In *Tilburg Private Law Working Paper Series No. 05/2015*, edited by Tilburg University. Tilburg, 2015.

Mancuso, Gianluca. "Le Cajas De Ahorro Quali Enti Fondazionali Del Sistema Creditizio Spagnolo." In *Fondazione E Banche. Modelli Ed Esperienze in Europa E Negli Stati Uniti*, edited by Ginevra Cerrina-Feroni. Torino: Giappichelli, 2011.

Mankiw, N. Gregory. *Principles of Macroeconomics*. Mason: Cengage Learning, 2008.

Marcacci, Antonio. "European Regulatory Private Law Going Global? The Case of Product Governance." *European Business Organization Law Review* 18, no. 2 (2017): 305–32.

Micklitz, Hans-Wolfgang. "The Visible Hand of European Regulatory Private Law—the Transformation of European Private Law from Autonomy to

Functionalism in Competition and Regulation." *Yearbook of European Law* 28, no. 1 (2009): 3–59.

———. "Administrative Enforcement of European Private Law." In *The Foundations of European Private Law*, edited by Roger Brownsword, Hans-Wolfgang Micklitz, Leone Niglia, and Stephen Weatherill, 563–92. Oxford-Portland: Hart Publishing, 2011a.

———. "Social Justice and Access Justice in Private Law." In *EUI Working Paper Law 2011/2*, edited by European University Institute. Florence, 2011b.

———. "The Public and the Private – European Regulatory Private Law and Financial Services." *European Review of Contract Law* 10, no. 4 (2014).

———. "The Internal Vs. The External Dimension of European Private Law—a Conceptual Design and a Research Agenda." In *EUI Working Paper Law 2015/35*, edited by European University Institute. Florence, 2015a.

———. "The Transformation of Enforcement in European Private Law: Preliminary Considerations." *European Review of Private Law* 4 (2015b): 491–524.

Micklitz, Hans-Wolfgang, Yane Svetiev, and Guido Comparato. "European Regulatory Private Law—the Paradigms Tested." In *EUI Working Paper Law 2014/04*, edited by European University Institute. Florence, 2014.

Miksch, Leonhard. *Wettbewerb Als Aufgabe*. Stuttgart: Kohlhammer, 1937.

Moloney, Niamh. *How to Protect Investors: Lessons from the Ec and the Uk*. Cambridge: Cambridge University Press, 2010.

———. "Regulating the Retail Markets." In *The Oxford Handbook of Financial Regulation*, edited by Niamh Moloney, Eilís Ferran, and Jennifer Payne. Oxford: Oxford University Press, 2015.

Moloney, Niamh, Eilís Ferran, and Jennifer Payne. "Introduction." In *The Oxford Handbook of Financial Regulation*, edited by Niamh Moloney, Eilís Ferran, and Jennifer Payne. Oxford: Oxford University Press, 2015.

Pan, Eric. "Organizing Regional Systems: The US Example." In *The Oxford Handbook of Financial Regulation*, edited by Niamh Moloney, Eilís Ferran, and Jennifer Payne. Oxford: Oxford University Press, 2015.

Schmukler, Sergio, and Esteban Vesperoni. "Firms' Financing Choices in Bank-Based and Market-Based Economies." In *Financial Structure and Economic Growth: A Cross-Country Comparison of Banks, Markets, and Development*, edited by Asli Demirgüç-Kunt and Ross Levine, 347–75. Cambridge, MA: MIT Press, 2001a.

———. "Firms' Financing Choices in Bank-Based and Market-Based Economies." In *Financial Structure and Economic Growth*, edited by Asli Demirguc-Kunt and Ross Levine, 347–75: MIT Press, 2001b.

Stout, Lynn A. "The Investor Confidence Game." *Brooklyn Law Review* 68, no. 2 (2002): 407–37.

Streit, Manfred E. "Economic Order, Private Law and Public Policy the Freiburg School of Law and Economics in Perspective." *Journal of Institutional and Theoretical Economics* 148, no. 4 (1992): 675–704.

The Committee of Wise Men - Lamfalussy Committee. "Final Report of the Committee of Wise Men on the Regulation of European Securities Markets." 2001.

The World Bank. "Financial Structures – Bank-Based Vs. Market-Based Financial System." http://go.worldbank.org/R6XUIEOF40.

Vanberg, Viktor. "Freiburg School of Law and Economics." In *The New Palgrave Dictionary of Economics and the Law*, edited by Peter Newman. London: Palgrave Macmillan, 1998.

Vitols, Sigurt. "The Origins of Bank-Based and Market-Based Financial Systems: Germany, Japan, and the United States." Wissenschaftszentrum Berlin für Sozialforschung - Discussion Paper FS I 01 - 302. Berlin, 2001.

Zatti, Filippo. "La Dimensione Costituzionale Della Tutela Del Risparmio. Dalla Tutela Del Risparmio Alla Protezione Dei Risparmiatori/Investitori E Ritorno?" In *Studi in Onore Di Vincenzo Atripaldi*, edited by Marco Benvenuti et al., 1469–94. Naples: Jovene, 2010.

Part I

The Law-on-the-Books

3

The Evolution of the EU Law of Financial Markets

3.1 The Legal Bases of the EU Law of Financial Markets

The EEC Treaty and its successors do not provide the Community/Union with a patent, clear, and exclusive competence in the financial markets domain[1]—contrary, for instance, to that granted for the Common Commercial Policy.[2] This implies that the EU law for financial markets must be grounded on more general legal bases, like that concerning the internal market. In this context, the legal *lender of last resort* was Article 2 ECT,[3] largely replaced by Article 3 TEU, which holds that "The Union shall establish an internal market" and "an economic and monetary union". More concretely, the EC/EU law of financial markets is entrenched in the so-called free movement of capital, free provision of services, and freedom of establishment, as provided by Article 14 TEC,[4] now Article 26 TFEU, whose second paragraph states that:

Some parts of this chapter have been previously published in: Antonio Marcacci, "European Regulatory Private Law Going Global? The Case of Product Governance," *European Business Organization Law Review* 18, no. 2 (2017), p. 305–332, DOI: 10.1007/s40804-017-0068-0.

© The Author(s) 2018

A. Marcacci, *Regulating Investor Protection under EU Law*,
https://doi.org/10.1007/978-3-319-90297-5_3

> The internal market shall comprise an area without internal frontiers in which the free movement of goods, persons, services and capital is ensured in accordance with the provisions of the Treaties.

When it is not possible to establish a single European financial market through the four freedoms, Professor Moloney points out that "the harmonization process steps in by providing for the adoption of harmonized securities-regulation rules which are designed to remove the remaining regulatory obstacles to integration by putting common standards in place."[5]

Specifically speaking, practically all legislation concerning financial markets enacted over the years has been widely backed by three articles. Article 50 TFEU (former Article 44 TEC) on freedom of establishment, Article 53 TFEU (former Article 47 TEC) on the taking up and pursuing of activities by self-employed persons, and Article 114 TFEU (former Article 95 TEC) on the measures for the approximation of Member States' rules. An important role has also been played by Article 62 TFEU (former Article 55 TEC) on services and Article 115 TFEU (former Article 94 TEC) on approximation measures.[6] Importantly, legislation dealing with the issuance and the trade of securities and products is generally based on Articles 50 TFEU[7] and 114 TFEU,[8] while legislation dealing with financial intermediaries and their investment services and activities is usually based on Article 53 TFEU.[9]

3.2 The Birth of the EC/EU Law of Financial Markets and Investment Services: The 1970s and the Early 1980s

Professor Moloney identifies five eras that mark the evolution of the EU Securities and Markets Regulation.[10] This book follows Moloney's path[11] and outlines three (increasingly dense) regulatory waves affecting the legal protection of retail investors. The first one starts with the 1985 Commission's Internal Market White Paper and the 1986 Single European Act; the second one is characterized by the normative production springing from the 1999 Financial Services Action Plan (FSAP); and the last wave relates to the current post-crisis reforms.

Regarding the beginning, the European integration process concerning the financial sector was quite slow. Skepticism was strong across Europe, as it is perfectly expressed in the words of Sir George Blunden[12]:

> The banking system of a country is central to the management and efficiency of its economy; its supervision will inevitably be a jealously guarded national prerogative. Its subordination to an international authority is a highly unlikely development, which would require a degree of political commitment which neither exists nor is conceivable in the foreseeable future.[13]

If this was the general feeling toward the hypothetical supranational overseeing of domestic banks and financial intuitions, it is of no small significance that the EEC Treaty was signed within[14] the international political framework of the Bretton Woods agreements, which restricted movements of capital worldwide and established a fixed rate system for domestic currencies. All this implies that a sudden liberalization of capital flows in Europe was at least at odds with the public sentiment of the day.

The first steps toward what nowadays is "EU law of financial markets and services" date from the 1970s. Pieces of legislation of this époque are entrenched[15] in the 1974 European Court of Justice (ECJ) judgments which recognized the direct effect of Article 52 on the right of establishment[16] (current Article 49 and ex-Article 43) and Article 59 on services[17] (current Article 56 and ex-Article 49). First legislation[18] is based on abolishing the legal restrictions on authorization and capital ratios set forth by national banking laws—given the bank-based system of Continental Europe. Public enforcement was already given a key role (the Banking Advisory Committee [BAC]—replaced by the European Banking Committee [EBC] in 2003—was established in 1977),[19] due to the role played by public authorities on monitoring on the access side to the banking market (license/authorization).

The first steps toward European securities regulations were taken at the end of the 1970s. The first policy measure was the 1977 Commission Recommendation on a European code of conduct relating to transactions in transferable securities.[20] This Recommendation aimed at paving the way for the slow establishment of a common European set of securities regulations. However, more than ten years before, in 1966, the ECC Commission's

Group of Experts headed by Claudio Segré[21] had already adopted the "The Development of a European Capital Market"[22] Report. The Report had concluded that certain prohibitions imposed by Member States were hindering the flow of funds throughout the Community and, therefore, a process of harmonization of the laws was highly recommendable.[23]

The late 1970s/early 1980s securities directives[24] aimed to give a minimum harmonization of the conditions under which securities were admitted to official stock exchanges (now "regulated markets" under the MiFID regime). Furthermore, they introduced disclosure requirements, such as the publication of information sheets, defined as "listing particulars", meant to increase market transparency and put parties in the position to understand the reciprocal rights and duties, and to "enable investors and their investment advisers to make an informed assessment".[25]

National public authorities were in charge of monitoring the admission of securities and were required to cooperate (exchange of information). Interestingly, Article 20 of Council Directive 79/279/EEC established the new "Contact Committee" tasked with facilitating the harmonization process, advising the Commission, and easing the establishment of a "concerted attitude" (which sounds like the ancestor of the current *supervisory convergence*—see below and Chap. 5) between the Member States.

It is worth noting that, even in this very first phase, we can detect two different approaches toward the banking and securities regulation. The first is substantially concentrated on prudential and capital requirement rules, in order to make domestic banking systems more stable. The second, instead, mainly focuses on mandatory information disclosure (and, later on, conduct of business) on the reliability of the securities issuer, with the main aim of protecting investors and facilitating new firms in entering securities markets.[26]

By looking at this division from a retail investor perspective, it can be said that as long as banking savers "invest" their money in banking products, like savings accounts or banking certificates, product disclosure is relatively *less* important since the investment is protected by the bank's capital (and prudential regulations). The entire backdrop changes if the same actor becomes a retail investor and switches from savings accounts or zero-risk sovereign bonds to financial instruments issued by listed companies. In the latter context, information disclosure plays a key role, and the pieces of legislation of late 1970s to early 1980s show that the information disclosure paradigm (governed through public enforcement) was already enshrined.

A fortiori, in the 1977 Commission Recommendation,[27] the European Executive stresses the importance of "fair, accurate, clear, adequate" information and uses the words "saver" and "investor" interchangeably.[28] In this historical phase, the leap from the banking saver to the retail investor—to be protected as the weaker party of a transaction—is still vague, but it will be progressively clearer as securities markets become increasingly open and the EU law of investment services takes root.

In this époque, the European lawmaker was already perceiving the need to overcome the negative approach—that is, the abolition of barriers to the integration of the internal market by means of national laws—and adopt a more active regulatory role. As highlighted by the ERPL theory, the idea of a competitive market transparency based on standardized criteria replacing old local rules hindering the efficient functioning of financial market forces was emerging.

3.3 The First European Regulatory Wave: The 1985 White Paper and the 1986 Single European Act

This period is characterized by the application to the European policy on financial services of the seminal judgment of the ECJ *Cassis de Dijon*[29] on mutual recognition. This is reflected[30] in the Commission's White Paper on the completion of the internal market (adopted on 14 June 1985)[31] which shaped financial market regulation through the principles of mutual recognition and home country control[32] (although mitigated by public interest reasons)[33] and set the schedule for the measures necessary for the completion of the single market by 31 December 1992. From a *constitutional* viewpoint, the 1986 Single European Act was the great leap forward of the new regulatory area, marking the watershed between negative market integration and positive market regulation.[34]

In this phase the scope of the European financial markets law widens and consolidates by including collective investment schemes (1985, the first UCITS Directive, *see below*); mandatory information disclosure on the acquisition of major holdings (1988)[35]; information prospectuses on public offerings (1989)[36]; investment services (1993)[37]; and, finally, deposit-guarantee (1994)[38] and investor-compensation (1997)[39] schemes.

3.3.1 The 1985 Undertakings for Collective Investment in Transferable Securities (UCITS) Directive and Its Subsequent Amendments

UCITS is not a simple single directive, but a set of directives enacted in Europe since 1985. The first piece was Directive 85/611/EEC,[40] the so-called UCITS I. An attempt to reform UCITS I was made in the early 1990s, but it failed (the so-called UCITS II proposal). In 2001, Directive 2001/107/EC[41] and Directive 2001/108/EC[42] were enacted (the so-called UCITS III), ensued in 2009 by Directive 2009/65/EC,[43] the so-called UCITS IV, followed by two implementing Commission Recommendations (583/2010[44] and 584/2010[45]) and two Commission Directives (2010/42/EU[46] and 2010/43/EU[47]). Finally, the UCITS package was reformed in 2014 with the adoption of Directive 2014/91/EU.[48] This set of directives regulates Collective Investment Schemes (CIS), and it principally aims at creating a European single market by allowing funds to be managed on a cross-border basis through a system of mutual recognition and authorization.[49]

Through the lenses of the ERPL Theory, it is under UCITS that the strategy for opening up retail financial markets through harmonization of product regulation alongside competitive and contractual transparency is concretely tested for the first time. In particular, regulatory contractual transparency is exemplified by the Key Information Investor Document (KIID), introduced by UCITS IV to replace the simplified prospectus.

Concerned with information disclosure, the EU lawmaker introduced the simplified prospectus in 2001.[50] In 2004 the Commission adopted a Recommendation[51] meant to clarify "some of the elements of information which have to be included into the simplified prospectus".[52] The Recommendation specified that this document was "designed to provide clear information about the essentials the investor should know before investing in a fund, and be easily understood by the *average* retail investor"[53] [*our emphasis*], and it was "also designed to facilitate the cross-border marketing of units of UCITS, and be used as a single marketing tool throughout the Community".[54] Therefore, the two key elements of this Recommendation were: disclosure for the average retail investor and the opening up of domestic retail markets.

However, the simplified prospectus proved to be ineffective due to several problems. Implementation was inconsistent and harmonization was insufficient,[55] and the tool itself was unnecessarily costly for the industry and of very limited use to investors.[56] Furthermore, the legal instrument—a recommendation—was too weak to clarify the components of the simplified prospectus; the content was investor-unfriendly (too long and complex, not meaningful and hard to grasp for the *average* retail investor); and the format/design did not allow different funds to be compared.[57]

To overcome these issues, the simplified prospectus was replaced by a stand-alone, pre-contractual document: the KIID. This document was designed to provide retail investors with "lucid and succinct"[58] disclosure; more comprehensible content to avoid information overload[59]; and clear and appealing layouts that facilitate and "grab readers' attention".[60] Coherently, the KIID must contain the investment objectives and policy of the UCITS, its risk-reward profile, fees and charges, past performances, and, finally, a range of practical information.[61] The KIID must be written in plain language, avoiding jargon, complex concepts and specialist language; words with different meanings in normal usage which could be misleading; legalistic or foreign words.[62] Furthermore, it must contain only the essential pre-defined information; complex information needs to be presented clearly using short sentences with no more than twenty-five words.[63]

The KIID is intended to be an optimized, investor-friendly version of the simplified prospectus. Indeed, UCITS IV Recital 59 affirms that: "A single document of limited length presenting the information in a specified sequence is the most appropriate manner in which to achieve the clarity and simplicity of presentation that is required by retail investors, and should allow for useful comparisons, notably of costs and risk profile, relevant to the investment decision." Thus, Article 78(5) states that the KIID must "be presented in a way that is likely to be understood by retail investors". All this aims at reinforcing retail investors' confidence through providing them with more comprehensible information.

In 2015, ESMA adopted a Q&A on the KIID.[64] Like any other ESMA Q&A documents, also this one is "a practical convergence tool"[65] enacted under Article 29.2 of ESMA Regulation[66] and aims at answering particular questions to improve the market's comprehension of the KIID instrument and, above all, "promote common supervisory approaches and practices in the application of the UCITS Directive and its implementing measures".[67] As it will be shown in Chap. 5, supervisory convergence is an important point for ESMA.

What deserves to be put into question here is the legal nature of such an information document. This is introduced by a statute (in this case, a European Directive) as a disclosure tool to make the weaker contractual counterparty aware of the basic characteristics of a CIS. The KIID can alternatively be seen as a public-law tool introduced into a contractual relationship and used for public enforcement reasons or as a mandatory step of a private-law-based relationship from which contractual liability may raise: a very good example of European supervision private law.[68] As it will be showed in MiFID, the dispute on the public versus private-law nature of EU investor protection rules is not that easy to disentangle.

UCITS IV has been amended by (without replacing)[69] 2014 UCITS V.[70] The new Directive very much focuses on the role played by the depositary—such as harmonization of duties for asset-keeping, segregation requirements for assets held in custody, and the prohibition of multiple depositaries (now a UCITS can only have one single depositary). Furthermore, it focuses on remuneration policies for fund managers to manage conflicts of interests; and, on the harmonization of administrative sanctioning powers available to competent authorities (coherently with the pro-public enforcement approach of the EU law of investment services). The theme of investor protection is, then, treated indirectly, by making the custody of financial instruments safer and reducing the risk of investors' losses of gains due to intra-firm conflicts of interests.

3.3.2 The 1994 Deposit-Guarantee Schemes Directive and the 1997 Investment Compensation Scheme Directive

The 1994 Deposit-Guarantee Schemes Directive[71]—reformed in 2014[72]—is an anti-bank-runs device that gives European banking clients a guarantee on their deposit. The threshold provided by the Directive is €100,000 (Article 6, 2014 Directive) and the timing for the payout is set for seven days (Article 8, 2014 Directive). Not all kinds of deposits are covered by the Directive: for instance, bonds like those prescribed in Article 22 (4) of Directive 85/611/EEC[73] are not considered covered deposits. Credit institutions must disclose their membership to a particular scheme by using a Depositor Information Template provided by Annex I of the 2014 reform Directive.

The leitmotiv of the Directive is to protect average banking clients who do not know, and are not in a position to learn, the soundness of their credit intermediary.[74] For this reason, those supposed to be highly sophisticated in financial terms—like financial institutions and insurance companies—and have access to further information are excluded from the scheme (Article 5, 2014 Directive).

Very importantly, in 2004, the ECJ clarified the relationship between the European banking directives and the role played by national banking supervisors. As a result of bankruptcy and the consequent loss of deposit, the plaintiff claimed damages from the national banking authority for not properly delivering on their supervisory duties. Given the complexity of banking supervision, the Court understandably ruled that the Directive does not confer upon individuals a right to claim "compensation for damage resulting from defective supervision on the part of that authority"[75] and affirmed that the only direct individual right granted under EU law was the deposit insurance under the Deposit-Guarantee Schemes Directive.[76]

The Investment Compensation Scheme Directive, Directive 97/9/EC,[77] was adopted to give European (retail) investors the guarantee that a system of minimum safeguards would operate in the case of a bankruptcy of an investment firm. This guarantee covers both traditional banks and other kinds of investment firms, and it would activate when a firm is no longer able to reimburse its customers the securities they own. Importantly, the Directive provides a system of "home country control" over the investor-compensation arrangements since the home banking and financial regulators also supervise these schemes.

Directive 97/9/EC is a minimum harmonization directive and the fund threshold differs from Member State to Member State, with the minimum coverage being €20,000. In 2010, the European Commission had proposed to increase this ceiling up to €50,000 and make it "a fixed amount in order to avoid arbitrage and investors' choice to be influenced by any different coverage granted in different Member States".[78] Unfortunately, due to political disagreements, the Commission eventually withdrew its proposal in March 2015.[79]

3.4 The Second European Regulatory Wave: The 1999 Financial Service Action Plan and the Lamfalussy Procedure

This phase is kicked off by the adoption of the FSAP[80] in 1999 and is culturally characterized by a growing support for "financialization".[81] The FSAP was a series of specific measures to improve the Single Market for financial services.[82] It had a harmonization and liberalization strategy[83] and pursued three objectives: "establishing a single market in wholesale financial services, making retail markets open and secure and strengthening the rules on prudential supervision."[84] With the approval of the FSAP, the EC financial markets legislation achieved a high level of complexity and became "a discrete and far-reaching regulatory regime [—so strong as to effectively determine] Member States' regulatory policy".[85]

Important pieces of legislation, such as MiFID or the Prospectus Directive, were adopted during this phase. Probably, the most important feature of the FSAP legislation is its harmonization level goal, with a stronger emphasis on full harmonization: at first glance, this might look less important than it really is, but such qualitative leap implies a much stronger role of the EU in regulating investment services, even affecting private-law relationships.[86]

Soon after the adoption of the FSAP, the Council of Economic and Finance Ministers created the Committee of Wise Men on the Regulation of European Securities Markets, on 17 July 2000.[87] The official reason to establish this Committee was that, given "the existing institutional framework [... there was] the need to respond effectively to the challenges of integrating the financial markets [... rendering] it necessary to set up a committee of independent persons".[88] This was chaired by Alexandre Lamfalussy and came to be better known as the "Lamfalussy Committee". It was tasked with focusing on the following areas: "the listing of enterprises, the public offer of securities and requirements relating to reporting by issuers, the conduct of cross-border financial operations, the day-to-day operation of the regulated markets, the protection of consumers and investors in the provision of investment services, and the integrity of the market."[89]

The Lamfalussy Committee had to: evaluate the "conditions for implementation of the regulation of the securities markets in the European Union [...]; assess how the mechanism for regulating the securities markets in the European Union can best respond to developments under way on the securities markets [...]; in order to eliminate barriers and obstacles, propose as a result scenarios for adapting current practices in order to ensure greater convergence and co-operation in day-to-day implementation and take into account new developments on the markets."[90] Prudential supervision was set aside.

Importantly, the Lamfalussy Committee established the so-called Lamfalussy Procedure.[91] This is a scheme used for the development and adoption of European legislation concerning financial services, designed with the aim of creating a more efficient rulemaking procedure capable of keeping pace with the constantly changing financial environment.[92] The Lamfalussy Procedure splits the lawmaking process into different steps where the main lawmakers, namely, the Council and the Parliament, restrict themselves to defining a kind of broader regulatory frame.[93] This outline is, then, completed through the input of experts from the national regulators[94] in the framework of the so-called comitology procedure, whereby committees assist the Commission in determining "(more technical) implementing measures".[95] The Lamfalussy steps[96] can be summarized as follows:

1. Framework legislation: Namely Directives and Regulations adopted by the Council and the European Parliament through the ordinary legislative procedure. These pieces of legislation contain quite broad rules to be further specified by the II Level measures.
2. Implementing measures: Commission Delegated and Implementing Acts adopted under Articles 290 and 291 TFEU. These Acts are adopted by the Commission aided by specific committees, such as the European Banking Committee (EBC),[97] the European Securities Committee (ESC),[98] and the European Insurance and Occupational Pensions Committee (EIOPC).[99] Significantly, the members of these committees are representatives of national Governments. Furthermore, do not only the three European Supervisory Authorities (ESAs) (*see point 3 below*) provide technical advice to the Commission for its delegated acts, but they may adopt regulatory and implementing standards (attuned with II Level delegated and implementing acts)[100] which must be endorsed by the Commission.
3. Regulatory convergence: At this level, the three ESAs—namely the European Securities and Markets Authority (ESMA), the European Banking Authority (EBA), and the European Insurance and Occupational Pensions Authority (EIOPA)[101]—work to achieve convergence on the interpretation and implementation of the EU legislation, particularly through common positions and opinions, and interpretative guidelines (very important for the industry

	because they ease the interpretation effort of the Compliance Function).
4. Enforcement:	At this level the European Commission watches over the Member States to make sure they enforce the legislation adopted at the first and second levels and comply with the convergence lead set at the third level.

Traditional regulatory instruments normally consist of legislative interventions which set mandatory open-ended contract-law rules, while the Lamfalussy Procedure constitutes a shift toward less traditional regulatory instruments which provide for public-law conduct-of-business rules alongside soft-law rules (such as guidance and interpretations) and inputs from self-regulation and co-regulation.[102] Under this approach, rules are increasingly concretized over the second and third levels of the procedure, where the Commission and the three ESAs are deeply involved. During the procedure, stakeholders—particularly consumers and market participants[103]—can be heard during consultations held by the ESAs, thus making the picture more complete. Given the regulatory nature of the topics under debate, the voices from the industry usually convey views of the firms' internal Compliance Functions.

Significantly, the Lamfalussy Procedure is an essential step toward the centralization at the European level of a regulatory function previously scattered among different nation states.[104] In particular, it is a key brick in the wall of the ERPL in that it represents the governance tool through which the European normative production affecting private-law rules tries to compensate "for the lack of traditional regulatory approaches".[105]

3.4.1 The Legislative Output of the Financial Service Action Plan

As regards the legislative output that took place after the adoption of the 1999 FSAP in 2001 or a full sixteen years after its original proposal,[106] the Directive on the Reorganization and Winding up of Credit Institutions[107] was finally adopted. Its aim was to avoid country-based discriminations between creditors of a bankrupt bank and, for this, affirms the illegality of the "ring fencing" practice, which happens when assets are separated in a fashion that causes discrimination between creditors.[108]

The Stock Exchange Law Directive[109] was also promulgated in 2001. It is a codification of four previous directives[110] dealing with the admission of securities to official stock exchanges and the information that must be providing upon the public offer. Need for clarification drove the unification of the four different pieces of legislation, but the content was left unchanged.[111] The Directive allowed company whose securities are admitted to the official stock exchange of its home country to also be simultaneously admitted to any other Member States' stock exchange.[112] The Stock Exchange Law Directive was later amended by the Market Abuse Directive (MAD),[113] the Prospectus Directive,[114] and the Transparency Directive.[115] Disclosure is the tool provided by the law to protect (all kinds of) investors with a view of making opening the markets (access justice, in ERPL terms).

In 2002, the Financial Conglomerate Directive[116] was adopted to provide national financial supervisors with additional powers and tools to supervise financial conglomerates on a group-wide basis, especially the very big companies providing cross-sector financial services and operating in more than one Member State.[117] In particular, this Directive compels domestic public enforcers to carry out supplementary supervision on financial conglomerates, which amounts to a supervisory activity beyond the classical sectorial supervision.[118] Stricter cooperation between public authorities carrying supplementary supervision is provided.[119] The movement in favor of public enforcement as heralded by the ERPL is, thus, confirmed by this Directive as well.

Moreover, this Directive also confirms the changing landscape of the Continental European financial markets. As already occurred in the United States, European financial players that had traditionally operated in one single financial sector (i.e., banking or insurance) have become increasingly involved in other financial sectors[120] and voices for unified regulators have surged over time.[121] This new phenomenon was made legally possible by the opening up of traditionally split financial sectors and by allowing financial operators to conduct business cross-sectorially: a clear example of *access justice* on the supply side.

A year later, in 2003, another important piece of European legislation was promulgated: the MAD.[122] This piece of European legislation aimed at strengthening the integrity of European securities markets by fighting insider trading (dealing) and market manipulation,[123] and pushing for closer cooperation among national authorities, even facilitating procedures for the exchange of information (Article 16). The MAD was classified as a minimum harmonization measure.[124]

Alike other pieces of legislation adopted under the FSAP, the MAD relied on disclosure of (price-sensitive) information and on public enforcement. Interestingly, due to the necessity to keep European legislation up to date with a constantly changing financial market, the statutory definitions of insider dealing and market manipulation were not provided by the first-level directive (2003/6/EC) but were given by the second-level directive (2003/124/EC). Interestingly, as regards inside information, Directive 2003/124/EC affirms that "'information which, if it were made public, would be likely to have a significant effect on the prices of financial instruments or related derivative financial instruments' shall mean information a *reasonable investor*[125] [our emphasis] would be likely to use as part of the basis of his investment decisions."[126]

Finally, another very important FSAP directive should be included: the 2004 Transparency Directive,[127] revised in 2013.[128] This piece of European legislation focuses on disclosure requirements to be provided by firms whose securities are traded in a regulated market with the purpose of increasing the market efficiency and improving investor protection.[129] Apart from a very complex set of harmonizing rules regarding information requirements, the Directive is built on the "home country principle".[130] This aims to encourage capital mobility throughout the Union by opening up access to markets and it is coherent with a strategy focused on creating an increasingly efficient market where information disclosure plays a leading role.

3.4.1.1 The 2003 Prospectus Directive

Directive 2003/71/EC,[131] the so-called Prospectus Directive—recently repealed and replaced by a brand-new Regulation 2017/1129 adopted in June 2017 (*see below*)—has been the European legal cornerstone for securities prospectuses for more than fifteen years and, for this reason, deserves a more in-depth description and analysis.

First and foremost, the aim pursued is single-market construction and market liberalization. The tool provided to protect investors is disclosure, perceived (again) as the best instrument to combine investor protection needs with the underlying policy objectives (access to market). However, disclosure has been over time readapted to a changing regulatory environment, increasingly sensitive toward more incisive investor protection solutions.

Directive 2003/71/EC, revised in 2010,[132] was, like the Market in Financial Instrument Directive—MiFID (*see below*), a full harmonization directive.[133] This Directive applied to all firms that issued their securities on securities markets of a Member State, no matter in which State the firm was incorporated. Implementing Commission Regulation 809/2004[134]—reformed over time[135]—and Commission Delegated Regulation 1392/2014[136] completed the legal framework provided by the Directive.

The 2004 Commission Regulation quite in detail defined the information included in a prospectus and that incorporated by reference. The predecessor of the ESMA—Committee of European Securities Regulators (CESR)—played a significant role in defining the information included in a prospectus, and, indeed, its technical advice was used as the basis for the first regulation.[137] ESMA took the torch and kept playing the same key role all over the regulatory reform exercise. The 2014 Commission Delegated Regulation, instead, directly integrated the first-level legislation by defining detailed regulatory technical standards for publication of supplements to the prospectus. This increasing regulatory splinter of the EU rulemaker is clear in the evolution of the EU Prospectus legislation.

The core aim of the Prospectus Directive was (and still is) the creation of a single passport for issuers (like MiFID does for investment services providers—*see below*). Investor protection through market transparency is ancillary, even though essential, to the key objective of the creation of a single market, and it was explicitly mentioned in Recitals 12, 16, 18, 19, 20, 21, 29 and in Articles 21.3, 21.4, and 23.2.2, of the Directive.

The implementing Regulations were more technical but they followed the same drift: material information "must be included in a prospectus in order to enable investors to understand the financial position of the issuer"[138] and put her/him in a position to "make an informed assessment of the issuer's financial position and prospects".[139] All in all, the implementing Regulations confirmed that regulated disclosure regimes must be proportionate and designed in a way to improve investor protection without establishing useless red tape, thus letting firms leverage on the information already disclosed to and available on the markets.[140] As a matter of experience, excessive disclosure can easily turn into an unnecessary burden for firms, which might even limit the issuance of financial instruments.

Directive 2010/73/EC,[141] amending the Prospectus Directive, introduced a categorization of clients by way of overhauling the original "one size fits all" approach: "qualified investors" were aligned with the "professional client" and "eligible counterparties" as provided by MiFID (*see below*). However, those securities offers that were addressed only to "qualified investors" did not have to be accompanied by a prospectus: this was to reduce the costs on the side of the issuers. Moreover, as of 2010 the intermediaries could use the categorization already built for MiFID in order to easily and quickly identify those clients who were "qualified".[142]

Recital 21 of the Prospectus Directive required a prospectus to have a summary of no more 2500 words. Directive 2010/73/EU, instead, required the summary to convey the so-called key information, namely, those elements which describe "the essential characteristics of, and risks associated with, the issuer, any guarantor, and the securities offered or admitted to trading on a regulated market".[143] Moreover, the summary had to "be drawn up in a common format in order to facilitate comparability of the summaries of similar securities".[144] All this was done "in order to aid investors when considering whether to invest in [...] securities".[145] The Commission Delegated Regulation 486/2012/EU[146] helped to better define the content of the summary and it indicated that the "summary shall be drafted in clear language, presenting the key information in an easily accessible and understandable way" (Article 1.10).

Domestic public authorities carried out the ex ante enforcement of the Prospectus Directive necessary to permit market operators to issue securities. The Directive provided that prospectuses were to be approved in advance of publication by the competent authority of the home Member State. The national regulator's approval simply entailed a "positive act at the outcome of the scrutiny of the completeness of the prospectus by the home Member State's competent authority including the consistency of the information given and its comprehensibility".[147] While public authorities must control the prospectus' compliance with requirements established by the Prospectus Directive (and domestic implementing legislation), the approval could not imply a guarantee for a successful investment.

The ex post enforcement of the Prospectus Directive was largely left to domestic tools: "Member States shall ensure that their laws, regulation and administrative provisions on civil liability apply to those persons responsible for the information given in a prospectus."[148] Moreover, it was stated that "without prejudice to the right of Member States to impose criminal sanctions and without prejudice to their civil liability regime, Member States shall ensure, in conformity with their national law, that the appropriate administrative measures can be taken or administrative sanctions be imposed against the persons responsible, where the provisions adopted in the implementation of this Directive have not been complied with".[149] However, the Directive provided quite clear rules concerning the persons subject to civil liability.[150]

3.4.1.2 The Retail Investor Enters the Scene: The 2004 Markets in Financial Instruments Directive—MiFID

The 2004 Markets in Financial Instruments Directive—MiFID I[151]—was the most important regulatory outcome of the 1998 FSAP.[152] It was based on Article 47 TEC (now Article 53 TFEU) and focused on firms providing investment services and executing investment activities, on the nature of such services and activities, and how such services and activities are carried out (rights and duties of counterparties, conduct-of-business rules). Due to the fact that a "new" MiFID was adopted in 2014, the 2004 piece is commonly labeled "MiFID I".

MiFID I replaced the Investment Services Directive (so-called ISD), 93/22/EEC,[153] which had governed European investment services market for more than a decade, but it is much broader than its predecessor, by dealing with more issues and in greater depth. The ISD was a minimum harmonization law,[154] whereas MiFID I was grounded on full harmonization[155] of national legislation[156] which prohibits the so-called gold plating,[157] and promotes the use of the single passport.[158] MiFID I was welcome "as a milestone for the integration of a European securities market and investor protection".[159]

Importantly, the full harmonization feature goes deep to the very core of MiFID itself, namely, whether it concerns not only public-law but also private-law rules. In this regard, it can be argued that MiFID is a public-law statute that indirectly interferes with private law[160] and such indirectness would allow Member States to both introduce new rules of private law and keep the old ones.[161] On the other side of the spectrum, instead, it has been affirmed that the full harmonization character does not leave any leeway to Member States to introduce new or maintain old rules which are covered by the Directive, regardless of whether these are public- or private-law rules, due to the fact that MiFID is sufficiently adequate to protect investors.[162]

The picture is even more puzzled if we consider that MiFID conduct-of-business rules have been ranked by some as norms with a dual legal nature[163] (both regulatory and private law)[164]; while some scholars have suggested that MiFID public-law duties would overtake private law[165]: in this case MiFID might be seen as an EU-wide (proto-)codification of national private laws.[166] However, what cannot be overlooked is the outright reliance of MiFID on public, rather than private, enforcement. This denotes the basic public nature of the MiFID duties of care expressed in Article 19(1) and leads to the explanation of why this Directive was implemented by the Member States in their public-law supervisory legislation and not in the civil codes or consumer protection legislation.[167]

Furthermore, a confirmation of the MiFID substantial public nature can be found in the establishment of the Compliance Function under the 2006 MiFID I Implementing Directive.[168] Under MiFID, the Compliance

Function is tasked with handling the compliance risk of the investment firm. The compliance risk is basically connected to the risk of a firm being sanctioned due to the non-observance of the applicable regulations on investment services. Civil liability is handled through litigation risk and is usually looked after by the Legal Department. The fact that MiFID places so much importance on the Compliance Function rather than on the Legal Department should be interpreted as a mark of its public-law nature. Chapter 7 is devoted to analyzing the Compliance Function and the related risks.

MiFID I follows a sector-related vertical legislative approach by regulating one specific sector, that of investment services. It officially aimed to create a level playing field for service providers and, thereby, a more competitive cross-border financial market[169] with the objective to reduce costs for raising capital[170]—by, for instance, abrogating the concentration rule for equity instruments introduced by the ISD[171] which had preserved for more than a decade the status quo ante.[172] For this reason, a key aspect of MiFID I was the establishment of alternative trading venues (Multilateral Trading Facilities [MTFs] and Systematic Internalizers) alongside Regulated Markets. Furthermore, MiFID passport let investment firms[173]—authorized by their home country authority—operate throughout the Union by providing investment services and carrying out investment activities when a financial instrument is involved.

Significantly, MiFID I did not provide for a clear-cut definition of "financial instrument" but it *merely* listed in Annex I—Section C those contracts that are considered financial instruments. This is coherent with the fact that, on the one hand, the European Union does not enjoy any competences in determining the terms and conditions of a contract, leaving such duty to the Member States. On the other hand, an ex ante determination of contracts generated in fast-evolving markets would have made this piece of legislation old on the very day of its adoption.[174]

Article 4 MiFID I defines the following services and activities governed by MiFID[175]:

- *Execution of orders on behalf of clients*: when an investment firm acts to conclude agreements to buy or sell one or more financial instruments on behalf of its clients. The firm providing this service must have in place an execution policy that lists the execution venues (i.e., the selected trading venues) that can be used to execute the clients' orders. Very importantly, MiFID I introduced the so-called Best Execution, which, put it simply, is about investors "receiving the most favorable terms available for their trades"[176] and, contractually speaking, it can be described as "an obligation of means"[177] from the service provider vis-à-vis its client. The Best Execution requires firms to verify the negotiation conditions of the execution venues and choose the best one for their customers. It has, thus, a twofold knitted aim: increasing competition among trading venues and improving investor protection. Importantly, both MiFID I and II exempt firms from applying the best execution to clients classified as eligible counterparties,[178] thus conceiving it as a tool for less-sophisticated investors.

- *Reception and transmission of orders in relation to one or more financial instruments (RTO)*: when a firm receives an order to buy/sell a financial instrument from a client and transmits it in order to have it executed on a trading venue. When a firm only offers the RTO service, then it must transmit its orders to an executor, that is, another firm providing the service of execution of orders on behalf of clients.
- *Investment advice*: this is the first of the so-called advisory services, and it concerns the provision of personal recommendations to a client, either upon her/his request or at the initiative of the service provider, in respect of one or more transactions relating to financial instruments. Given the delicate nature of the service that implies a high degree of discretion, a suitability test for the client is mandatory (see Chap. 4).
- *Portfolio management*: this service too can be labeled as "advisory" and, alike the investment advice, is covered by the suitability test. The service concerns the management on the part of the investment firm of a client's portfolio of financial instruments in accordance with a discretionary mandate given by the client. The management is individually[179] carried out on a client-by-client basis within the remit defined by the discretionary mandate.
- *Underwriting and/or placing of financial instruments on or without a firm commitment basis*. Underwriting and placing concern the combined services offered by an investment firm to an issuer of financial instruments: as a first thing, the investment firm underwrites the

newly issued instruments, and, subsequently, sells (*places*) such instruments to investors (either/both institutional or/and professional/retail). A commitment basis implies that the investment firm has a duty to buy the unsold financial instruments (those not bought by the investors).[180]

- *Dealing on own account*: when a firm trades as *principal* with its counterparties against the firm's own proprietary capital to conclude transactions in one or more financial instruments. Dealing on own account has been considered an activity rather than a service, which implies that when a firm carries out this activity it "has virtually no obligation"[181] in terms of investor protection. However, it is a daunting task to draw a line between a simple counterparty and a client, and such a decision is very often on the shoulders of the Compliance Function. Confusion can be generated when a client—who has, thus, entered into a contract for the provision of investment services—asks for a specific, bespoke financial instrument not available in a secondary market and, in order to execute such a request, the investment firm becomes the client's counterparty for that specific financial instrument. This could be the case, for instance, of derivatives tailored on a client's business needs. Conversely, when a firm uses its own proprietary capital to conclude a financial instrument with a counterparty that is *not* a client—without a standing contract for the provision of investment services—then the firm might claim that MiFID investor protection rules do not apply. As shown below, the possibility to use the "dealing on own account" feature has been reduced by MiFID II.
- *Operation of MTFs*: an MTF is a trading platform run—on non-discretionary basis—by an investment firm or a market operator,[182] which brings together (institutional) investors to buy and sell financial instruments. It is quite similar to a traditional stock exchange, but it has less stringent transparency rules and it can be run by an investment firm (whereas regulated markets can only be managed by market operators).

Within this framework, the regulation of the relationship between retail investors and investment firms is an important element (even though the protection of the retail investor is "certainly not at the heart of this Directive"[183]), necessary for the efficient provision of regulated services and, thus, the correct functioning of the market. The dominant topic driving the regulation of investor protection is the existence of an information asymmetry between the customer and the service provider. In order to tame the effects of this asymmetry, Article 19(1) MiFID I provides for a general obligation of fair dealing:

> [W]hen providing investment services and/or, where appropriate, ancillary services to clients, an investment firm act honestly, fairly and professionally in accordance with the best interests of its clients.[184]

Very importantly, the first time in the EU law of investment services, disclosure is not the only tool envisaged to protect retail investors and the disclosure paradigm is mitigated by public-law conduct-of-business rules. MiFID I and its implementing Directive 2006/73 provided for conduct-of-business measures to be applied when financial investment services are being provided. Such rules require investment firms to obtain information *from* their own customers concerning their financial knowledge and needs, and to give them information on the characteristics of the instruments offered and the services supplied, which must take place before a contract is concluded, at the point of sale and even after it, depending on the nature of the contract.[185]

The key features of the MiFID conduct-of-business regime are the suitability and appropriateness tests, which were introduced by Article 19.4/5. These tests originate from the *know your customer* rules and aim to disclose a client's knowledge and experience, her/his inclination to risk, and her/his financial situation, so that investment firms can assess whether a service is suitable and appropriate for their customers.[186] While the suitability test is more intrusive and applies only to so-called advisory tests (advice and portfolio management), the appropriateness test applies to all services when complex products are involved.[187]

Such conduct-of-business rules have a public-law nature but are embedded into the contract governing the provision of investment services. This implies that a breach of these duties for sure leads to administrative sanctions but also to contractual liability, even if this depends on the Member States' civil liability regimes.[188] MiFID strongly relies on the role of public law in designing a retail investor fit for a full-fledged and fully opened single European investment services market,[189] and, above all, on public rather than private (collective) enforcement.

Viewed from within a European investment firm, the public nature of MiFID suitability is proved by the greater impact it has on the Compliance Function rather than on the Legal Department. The Legal Department is usually concerned with drafting pre-determined, standardized contract terms and conditions, and its main responsibility is the incorporation of the gist of the suitability into a firm's agreement for the provision of investment services. The Compliance Function, instead, is usually tasked with writing the internal Suitability Policy, crafting the internal processes and procedures connected to the regulatory requirement, designing first-level controls, and running second-level controls, with the purpose of meeting the domestic supervisor's expectations.

Under the MiFID regime, public-law conduct-of-business rules conveyed through contracts are used by public oversight agencies to test whether and to what extent an investment firm has complied with the law when performing a regulated activity, a phenomenon defined by Professor Cherednychenko as "European supervision private law".[190] Such an approach was implicitly confirmed by the "Background Note on the Draft Commission Directive implementing MiFID" where the Commission stated that the "detailed disclosure requirements [...] are designed to give regulators and investors the necessary tools to be able to discern and punish inefficiency and unprincipled conduct by firms."[191] MiFID I, thus, openly favored public enforcement, with Articles 48–51 giving supervisory administrative bodies clear and certain powers. On the other side of the spectrum, Article 52(2) only offered a "rather cryptic provision on collective enforcement"[192] without giving a strong position to stakeholders.

Article 48 of the MiFID I provided that each Member State is to designate one public authority to carry out all the duties provided for under the different provisions of MiFID. A potential delegation of powers is allowed; however, this must be done in a way that it does not "involve either the exercise of public authority or the use of discretionary powers of judgment".

Even if it is somewhat hidden in the text, it is crystal clear that MiFID I strongly privileged public supervisors and regulators over privately run organizations, like the American Financial Industry Regulatory Authority (FINRA). This is quite evident in Article 48.2, which provides that, in case of delegation, the designated public authority takes "all reasonable steps to ensure that the entity to which tasks are to be delegated has the capacity and resources to effectively execute"[193] them. In particular, the paragraph continues by stating that "a clause obliging the entity in question to act and be organised in such a manner as to avoid conflict of interest and so that information obtained from carrying out the delegated tasks is not used unfairly or to prevent competition."[194] Here it is evident how the European lawmakers are inclined to believe that privately run organizations are much more likely—compared to public supervisors and regulators—to be subject to conflicts of interests capable of hampering the functioning of financial markets.

Interestingly, given the usual coordination and accountability problems generated by situations in which administrative powers are not conferred upon a single entity, but are instead divided between two or more bodies, Article 49 provided that where there are multiple competent authorities "their respective roles shall be clearly defined and they shall cooperate closely". Moreover, it maintains that Member States must require "that competent authorities exchange any information which is essential or relevant to the exercise of their functions and duties".

Articles 50 and 51 of MiFID I were of utmost importance because they attempted to harmonize domestic administrative laws by providing a whole range of supervisory, investigatory, and, although to a lesser extent, sanctioning powers that had to be made available to competent authorities. These include the power to access any document in any form whatsoever, and to obtain copies thereof, to carry out on-site inspections, to request the freezing and/or the sequestration of assets, to request temporary prohibitions of professional activity, to require the suspension of trading in a financial instrument, and to adopt any type of measure to ensure that investment firms and regulated markets comply with legal requirements. In other words, these are the powers deemed necessary in order to put a supervisor in a position to be able to effectively carry out its monitoring tasks.

3.5 The Third European Regulatory Wave: The Legislative Response to the Financial Crisis

The period spanning from 2005 to 2008 covers the time between the adoption of the MiFID and the outbreak of the global financial crisis in September 2008.[195] It is characterized by how the existing legislation was revised, updated, or, more simply, implemented through further Commission directives, as was the case for the MiFID implementing Directive or the Directive implementing the provisions of the Transparency Directive.[196] The EU law of investment services goes more in depth, and the more generic norms conveyed by the Lamfalussy first-level legislation become more detailed at the second level.

Since "[r]egulation is usually advocated as a corrective response to market failure",[197] as the crisis burst, a new legislative époque started. Economically speaking, this period is characterized by a seemingly endless financial crisis that started in 2008 as a private debt emergency and, then, turned into a sovereign debt catastrophe. During this tormented period, many directives were revised and updated (like the already examined Directive 2009/65/EC[198] [so-called UCITS IV] and Directive 2010/73/EU[199] amending the Prospectus Directive) and consensus was finally achieved on the necessity to establish a "Single Rulebook"[200] for financial markets.

Interestingly, Regulation 596/2014/EU[201] replaced the MAD. The new Market Abuse Regulation (MAR) marks another step of the increasingly penetrating approach of the EU law: from minimum harmonization directives to regulations. Concerning investor protection, the MAR directly employs the "reasonable investor" notion (Recital 14, Article 7) and confirms an approach adopted by the ECJ took in the *Spector* case on the presumption of use of inside information.[202] Furthermore, the Regulation extends the duty of public disclosure of inside information: not only for financial instruments traded (or going to be traded) on Regulated Markets but also for financial instruments only negotiated (or going to be negotiated) on other trading venues such as MTFs and Organized Trading Facilities (OTFs; Article 2). Furthermore, the issuer is now not only prohibited from combining the disclosure of inside information with the marketing of its activities, but it also must maintain all the inside information to be publicly disclosed on its website for at least five years (Article 17). The result is that the MAR reiterates the disclosure/rational-investor/efficient-market-functioning paradigm combined with a philosophy of *access justice*.

Alongside revision of existing pieces of legislation, the EU lawmaker adopted new laws either directly or indirectly affecting investor protection. Such new pieces of legislation concern the EU supervisory framework (see Chap. 5 on Public Enforcement); Credit Rating Agencies[203] (due to the importance of their ratings on the flux of financial information); OTC Derivatives[204] (given the alleged contribution these instruments had on the crisis); Financial Benchmarks[205] (since they play a key role for the pricing of credit agreements—such as home mortgages and personal loans—and financial instruments—as the Libor scandal[206] clearly proved); Short Selling and Credit Default Swaps[207] (to reduce speculation on sovereign bonds). As already forecast by the ERPL theory, Regulations rather than Directives have been the legislative tool employed, thus leading to an increased solidification of the EU law. Coherently, the detailing character of the Lamfalussy second- and third-level normative production has strongly increased, with the EU-made rules resembling technical standards previously adopted by domestic authorities.

Significantly, in September 2015[208] the European Commission launched the so-called Capital Markets Union (CMU), which is supposed to be the sister legislative infrastructure of the already existing (but incomplete)[209] Banking Union. However, unlike the Single Supervisory Mechanism under the Banking Union, the Capital Markets Union does not foresee the creation of a new, all-mighty single supervisor. This is mainly due to the *constitutional* constraints under current Article 127 TFEU, which provides for the conferral of specific prudential supervisory tasks on credit institutions and other financial institutions to the European Central Bank without mentioning the supervision of conduct of business.[210] On the contrary, ESMA has been endowed with more powers to push for stronger supervisory convergence among national competent authorities (NCAs) under its own auspices (a problem—that of supervision differences—already highlighted by the 2009 Larosière Report).[211]

The CMU plan focuses on legislative initiatives indirectly affecting the welfare of retail investors, such as business insolvency, small-medium enterprises' fund raising, securities ownership, clearing and settlement of cross-border securities transactions. Indeed, within the CMU framework, the Commission is committed to undertaking a wide-ranging assessment of the "markets for retail investment products, including distribution channels and investment advice".[212] Particular attention will be paid to the benefits stemming from the new possibilities offered by online-based services and FinTech,[213] as very recently reaffirmed in the Commission's Action Plan on Consumer Financial Services, meant to set "out further steps towards a genuine technology-enabled Single Market for retail financial services".[214] Nevertheless, when it comes to investment services, it is yet to be seen how the digital distance selling market (Action 12) for this sector will be coped with in statutory terms.[215]

Concerning the protection of (retail) investors, in 2009 the Commission committed itself "to developing legislative proposals for raising standards of investor protection and improving the consistency of existing measures across the different sectors making up the retail investment market".[216] The 2008 Optem Report[217]—focused on the disclosure regimes for the Financial Services sector of twenty-seven Member States (including investment services)—had already found that disclosure could not be of great help to less experienced and more conservative investors,[218] who tended to reveal "widespread distrust and dissatisfaction" about "financial institutions and the information they provide on their services".[219] The next section will show how the mitigation of the disclosure paradigm opened by the Commission through MiFID I has been strongly boosted by MiFID II.

As a result of the Commission's post-crisis legislative effort,[220] three pieces of legislation are particularly worthy to be analyzed: the 2014 Regulation on key information documents (KIDs) for packaged retail and insurance-based investment products (PRIIPs), the new Directive on Markets in Financial Instruments (MiFID II) which replaced MiFID I, and the brand-new Prospectus Regulation. All three pieces of legislation are characterized by the fact that they strongly mitigate (and, in some circumstances, overcome) the sic-*et-simpliciter* disclosure paradigm. In this regard, the Product Governance (PG) regime introduced under MiFID II is further analyzed in Chap. 4.

3.5.1 The PRIIPs Regulation

As the crisis unfolded, the EU lawmaker realized that consumer confidence had been undermined,[221] that existing disclosure mechanisms "often do not help retail investors to compare different products, or understand their features",[222] and that the existence of diverging national rules for retail products "create an unlevel playing field between different products and distribution channels, erecting additional barriers".[223] In order to revive confidence, improve transparency, and help investors make better investment decisions, the PRIIPs Regulation[224] was enacted in 2014 to establish uniform norms, common for the entire EU, on KIDs for retail investment products. Significantly, PRIIPs Regulation is meant to be "complementary to measures on distribution in"[225] MiFID II.

The term PRIIP is a merger between "packaged retail investment product" (PRIP) and "insurance-based investment product". The former is defined as an investment "where, regardless of the legal form of the investment, the amount repayable to the retail investor is subject to fluctuations because of exposure to reference values or to the performance of one or more assets which are not directly purchased by the retail investor" (Article 4.1). The latter is defined as an "insurance product which offers a maturity or surrender value and where that maturity or surrender value is wholly or partially exposed, directly or indirectly, to market fluctuations" (Article 4.2). Being connected to market fluctuations, thus having a structured form, is the key characteristic of PRIIPs.

The core feature of this Regulation is the KID. The KID is defined, designed, organized, and standardized[226] by the Regulation itself in terms of content (sections such as "What is this product?" guide investors through the product's characteristics), timing of provision (before investors are contractually bound), layout (three sides of A4-sized paper when printed), medium (durable), and even general *disclaimers* for consumers.[227] Article 8 provides for strict details on how to craft a KID. Due to the legal nature of this piece of law—a Regulation—the provided rules uniformly apply throughout the EU, unlike what happens for other similar information documents envisaged by Directives that must be transposed into national legal systems and whose details are developed by NCAs under the aegis of the ESAs.

The choice made by the EU lawmaker is to introduce a uniformed standard, with the purpose of overcoming any potential discrepancies that may lead to market distortion, consumer detriment, and regulatory arbitrage.[228] Very hard to figure out in a pre-crisis world, the Commission Delegated Regulation 2017/653[229] sets forth detailed technical standards concerning the presentation, the content, the review and the revision of KIDs, and the conditions for meeting the requirement to provide it to the customers. Annex I of the Delegated Regulation even depicts a standardized template breaking down all of the information a KID must contain and indicates the layout firms may use to craft their KIDs (!).

The PRIIPs' first- and second-level legislation prove that the level of details achieved by the European normative production is so deep to make the domestic transposition of EU-made rules substantially redundant (if not pointless from the viewpoint of regulated entities). Investment firms and securities issuers now view their PRIIPs-related compliance risk stemming *directly* from EU-produced norms as if they were concluded and directly applicable (which is, actually, the case for Delegated Regulations such as 2017/653). In this framework, the role and overall responsibility of the internal Compliance Functions is magnified and its Compliance Risk Assessment (see Chap. 7) is critical for the firm's business model.

The level of detail is astonishing and this is particularly true for the KID. This is defined as a stand-alone, *pre-contractual* information document, clearly separated from marketing materials (Article 6). It must avoid financial jargon and terminology that is not immediately understandable to retail investors (Recital 14), be easy to read (through the use of characters of readable size) (Article 6.4), state where and how more detailed pre-contractual information can be found (Article 6.3), and "be clearly expressed and written in language and a style that communicate in a way that facilitates the understanding of the information, in particular, in language that is clear, succinct and comprehensible" (Article 6.4c).

Those manufacturing— that is, creating and issuing—a PRIIP must produce and update the KID which must be provided to retail clients by the investment firm selling or advising the PRIIP (Article 13). Those making changes to an existing PRIIP, such as altering the risk and reward profile or the costs associated, are also considered manufacturers (Article 4.4).

Interestingly, the PRIIPs Regulation adopts a jargon and a conceptual framework also employed by MiFID II PG, such as the distinction between manufacturers and distributors/sellers of products.

Both PRIIP manufacturers and PRIIP sellers/advisers—that is, those selling and/or recommending a PRIIP manufactured by others—must meet the requirements imposed by the Regulation, but these do not equate. Article 11 explicitly establishes a civil liability for PRIIP manufacturers in case the KID is "misleading, inaccurate or inconsistent with the relevant parts of legally binding pre-contractual and contractual documents or with the requirements laid down" by the Regulation. The burden of proof rests on the shoulders of the retail investor, who can claim damages from the PRIIP manufacturer for losses resulting from reliance on the KID.

Significantly, on the one hand, the Regulation recognizes the Union's limitation of competences in civil-law matters by stating that terms such as "loss" and "damages" are to be interpreted and applied in accordance with the national laws. On the other hand, in case of cross-border sales, the applicable national laws are channeled through the Europeanized[230] rules of private international law, in order to overcome conflicts of jurisdictions within the Union[231] and as an attempt to reduce divergences in national interpretations. This is a clear case of *European* civil liability with the interpretation of core elements still reverting to the national legal systems, which may diverge and, thus, eventually weaken the attempted civil liability "standard" for PRIIP manufacturers.

PRIIP sellers and advisers are responsible for the (free-of-charge) handover of the KID, which must be done in "good time" before the retail investor is contractually bound (Article 13). The definition of the civil liability stemming from this duty is left to domestic jurisdictions. Even if the KID is defined as a pre-contractual information document, the Regulation only refers to the importance of "establishing appropriate administrative sanctions and measures" (Article 22.1).

Article 10 digs into a manufacturer's internal processes and procedures. It provides for the establishment of internal programs finalized to review on a regular basis—which is likely to be, at least, annual—the information conveyed through a PRIIP and the revision of the KIDs in case the review's outcome so requires. To make the EU regulatory splinter more penetrating into intra-firm internal processes and procedures, the ESAs are requested to issue regulatory technical standards detailing the conditions for reviewing and—where necessary—revising the information contained in a KID, and the circumstances under which a firm's retail investors must be informed of a revised KID related to a PRIIP they have already bought. This implies the setting up of new process involving not only a firm's Compliance Function and Processes Function, but also the Business divisions, first of all, the Retail Distribution Network. Moreover, such requirements have a strong impact on the existing plans of manufacturers' Product Committees and on the seller-manufacturer information-sharing agreements, since a PRIIP seller/advisor must be promptly informed of the review's outcomes conducted by the manufacturer.

Similarly, Article 19 requires both manufacturers and sellers/advisers to establish appropriate complaints-handling internal schemes and procedures. Such intra-firm arrangements play a key role in a twofold meaning: first—consistently with the new MiFID II PG regime (see Chap. 4)—they contribute to addressing mis-selling cases in the post-crisis era and helping a firm keep its clients by offering them alternative solutions (in particular, in case the complaint's outcome proves the firm's shenanigan). Second, robust complaints-handling procedures either can work as the frontline of defense before a public supervisor's inquiries, proving a firm's best effort to comply with investor protection rules; or can be used to avoid a customer referring to an ADR or—in the worst-case scenario—to a court. The Compliance Function is usually asked to play a role on drafting and monitoring complaints-handling internal schemes and procedures that are mainly conceived to address minor infringements.

Interestingly, the PRIIPs Regulation leaves the door opens to Member States for deciding the balance between administrative and criminal liability, as it states that "Member States may decide not to lay down rules for administrative sanctions […] for infringements which are subject to criminal sanctions under their national law" (Article 22.1). This is particularly important for those Member States with a stricter approach on the *ne bis in idem* principle.[232] Nevertheless, the Regulation still leans toward administrative enforcement as Recital 31 warns that in case a Member State chooses criminal over administrative penalties, this "should not reduce or otherwise affect the ability of competent authorities to cooperate, access and exchange information in a timely way".

The key role agreed to public enforcement is visibly clear. Not only does Article 5 provide for the possibility of an ex ante notification of the KID by the manufacturer to the NCA. But the entire Chapter V of the Regulation is devoted to regulating administrative penalties and other measures, with articles specifying the powers that must be granted to NCAs, the amount of fines, the circumstances where public sanctions must be applied, the publicity of sanctions, and the right of appeal.

Even more importantly, national insurance authorities are now allowed to restrict or even prohibit an activity or practice, or the marketing, distribution, or sale of insurance-based investment products. This is possible if the restrictive action is proportionate, does not have a discriminatory effects, and when existing applicable regulatory requirements would not be better addressed by improved supervision or enforcement. Furthermore, the authority can act only when there is a significant investor protection concern or such a product/activity/practice "poses a threat to the orderly functioning and integrity of financial markets or the stability of whole or part of the financial system within at least one Member State" (Article 17). MiFIR provides for the same kind of product intervention powers for financial instruments and structured deposits,[233] which are active only in case of *very* major infringements—that diverge from minor infringement in that the former concerns the management of "emergency" type of risks, whereas the latter regards the management of "normal" risks.[234]

Alongside a more traditional facilitation and coordination role between competent authorities (Article 18), Article 16 grants the EIOPA the power to temporarily prohibit or restrict an insurance activity or practice, or the marketing, distribution, or sale of insurance-based investment products, when all of the following conditions occur:

(a) There is a "significant investor protection concern or a threat to the orderly functioning and integrity of financial markets or to the stability of the whole or part of the financial system in the Union".
(b) The applicable regulatory requirements do not address the threat.
(c) The NCA has not taken action to address the threat or the actions taken do not adequately address the threat.

To avoid misuse of intervention powers vis-à-vis market operators and investors, and to protect the NCAs' remit of autonomy, EIOPA is allowed to act only when its action does not have a detrimental effect on the markets efficiency or on investors which is disproportionate to the benefits of the action itself; or generate a risk of regulatory arbitrage.

3.5.2 The MiFID II Package: Requirements for Firms and Powers for ESMA

The MiFID II package[235] is a post-financial and post-sovereign-debt crises legislation package made up of a Directive[236] and a Regulation[237] (MiFIR), very much focused on what the EU lawmakers thought the European Union needed to avoid its home financial system breaking down. Although the core objective is unchanged, the MiFID II package is bigger, deeper, and broader than MiFID I.[238] Furthermore, the plethora of implementing rules hammered out by the Commission and the related technical standards issued by the ESMA[239] is incommensurably larger than the second-level measures adopted under MiFID I. The outcome is an unpreceded move of detailed normative production from the domestic to the European level,[240] which de facto turns domestic regulators in "regulatory branches" of the European rulemaker, ESMA.

The MiFID II package modifies MiFID I investor protection regime in several crucial points (some of which are further explained in Chap. 4):

- Inclusion of *structured deposits* into the MiFID's scope. Although deposits are banking products, structured deposits are treated like financial instruments due to their complexity. Such deposits are defined as products that are "fully repayable at maturity on terms under which interest or a premium will be paid or is at risk, according to a formula" which involves several factors such as an index or a combination of indices. For this, Article 41 of MiFIR gives the EBA—and not the ESMA—the temporary intervention powers on structured deposits (*see later*).
- Introduction of the independent investment advice, which compels—inter alia—the firm not to accept/retain fees, commissions, or any monetary/non-monetary benefits connected to the provision of the service.

- More and (allegedly) clearer information and reporting to clients, with particular emphasis on costs and charges.
- More coherent rules on suitability and best execution.
- Organizational requirements such as PG and the related responsibilities of the Compliance Function and the senior management.
- Broadening of the execution of orders on behalf of clients' service (Table 3.1).

The outcome of the new definition is the inclusion of the so-called self-placement—when firms distribute products they issue themselves—into the remit of MiFID. Self-placement is a particularly sensitive area where the two extremes of business values may clash: maximization of shareholder value versus commitment and trust toward clients.[241] Under MiFID I self-placement was in a limbo due to the fact the service of placing of financial instruments is connected to instruments issued by third parties and, for this reason, is very often linked to the service of underwriting. The instruments—such as share and bonds—issued by an investment firm and directly sold to its own clients could be classified neither as placing (since the instruments are not being issued by third parties) nor as execution of orders (due to the fact that the buyer was the direct counterparty of the firm). In Italy, for instance, to fill this gap, article 25-bis of Consolidated Law on Financial Intermediation extended MiFID rules to self-placement (alongside insurance policies, which are not financial instruments) but other Member States did not treat self-placement as an investment service.[242] The clear inclusion of self-placement within the remit of MiFID grants wider protection in particular to

Table 3.1 Execution of orders on behalf of clients: MiFID I versus MiFID II

MiFID I	MiFID II
"Execution of orders on behalf of clients" means acting to conclude agreements to buy or sell one or more financial instruments on behalf of clients.	"Execution of orders on behalf of clients" means acting to conclude agreements to buy or sell one or more financial instruments on behalf of clients and includes the conclusion of agreements to sell financial instruments issued by an investment firm or a credit institution at the moment of their issuance.

retail clients buying bonds issued by commercial banks, which has become a politically sensitive topic[243] after the entry into force of the Bank Recovery and Resolution Directive[244] that has introduced the so-called bail-in tool.

- Establishment of *OTFs*,[245] which have been conceived as exchange platforms for non-equity instruments, with the aim to increase market transparency. OTFs have been created with the purpose of using them as trading venues for those sufficiently liquid[246] derivatives—subject to the clearing obligation provided by EMIR[247]—which fall within the trading obligation introduced by Article 28 of MiFIR.
- *Trading obligation* of derivatives: this requirement consists in the mandatory duty to negotiate certain classes of derivatives on trading venues (in particular, OTFs) and it is meant to bring further transparency in market for the benefit of all investors, including retail investors interested in and having an investment profile suitable for such instruments. Interestingly, MiFIR trading obligation alongside EMIR clearing obligation for OTC derivatives clearly shows a trend toward centralization and standardization[248] aimed at improving market monitoring and reducing systemic risk.
- Introduction of the so-called *Transaction Reporting* of financial operations: Article 26 of MiFIR provides that investment firms executing transactions in financial instruments are required to report complete and accurate details of such transactions to their home competent supervisory authority. Among the reportable information, firms must communicate the identifier codes of their clients: the legal entity identifier code—LEI—for client legal persons, and the national client identifier code—NIC—for client natural persons (to be determined on basis of the client's citizenship, not on her/his country of residence). The LEI Code—to be yearly renewed—is released against remuneration by Local Operating Units, and investment firms may choose to pay it for and on behalf of their clients as part of the services offered. In any case, firms are required to obtain the LEI/NIC codes from their customers in order to avoid incomplete reporting and, for this, prospective administrative fines. A way to obtain such codes might be the contractualization of the

customers' duty to communicate their codes: a clause—in existing and future investment services contracts—which states that in case the client does not communicate the necessary code, the provision of some investment services may be interrupted and the firm may exercise the right to withdraw and terminate the contract. Leaving aside the significant costs of repapering existing contracts, investment firms would also be squeezed between the threat of public sanctions imposed by home authorities for improper reporting and the risk of losing business in case customers are slow in communicating their codes. This looks like a case where market transparency is enhanced at the expenses of both retail/professional investors (in particular legal persons that pay for their own LEI code) and financial intermediaries.

Single features of investor protection will be examined in Chap. 4. What should be flagged here is the step forward taken by MiFID II in mitigating the disclosure paradigm through the new PG, and the confirmation of the privileged importance given to public over private enforcement when it comes to sanctioning (major) infringements (alongside a centralization trend which shifts enforcement from the domestic to the European level).

3.5.2.1 Product Governance

PG is a brand-new feature introduced by MiFID II that deserves particular attention due to its innovative nature that de facto overcomes the disclosure paradigm.[249] PG is an investor protection tool provided by public law and it is arranged as an intra-firm process instead of being conceived as a mandatory contract-related rule, as it happens for the "traditional" transparency and conduct-of-business obligations. Indeed, PG enhances the regulatory focus by adding to the fashion a product is being distributed (conduct-of-business) the duty to control the product itself allover its life-cycle[250] in order to avoid mis-selling. Such control is both internal—basically run by the internal Compliance Function—and external—as the below-described product intervention powers under MiFIR show.

The PG is introduced by Recital 71, Articles 9, 16(3), and 24 of MiFID II and is, then, further developed by Articles 9 and 10 of the implementing Delegated Directive.[251] Recital 71 spells out the basic principles upon which PG is built: acting in line with the best interests of clients (fiduciary duty); obligation to "establish and review effective policies and arrangements to identify the category of clients to whom products and services are to be provided"[252] ("know your customer"), through the understanding of the characteristics of the products recommended and offered[253] ("know the security"[254]). Nevertheless, unlike the suitability and appropriateness tests (see above on MiFID I and below in Chap. 4) which stem from and are embedded into an investment services contract, the PG develops as an intra-firm procedure which precedes and accompanies a service provision contract and self-adjusts its outputs on the basis of the outcomes of the provider-client relationship.

MiFID I already established requirements affecting intra-firm processes when carrying out clients' orders, such as client order-handling and best execution. However, order-handling and best execution only cover the execution of an order concerning a specific financial instrument, it thus concerns the conditions at which that purchase/sale is executed over a trading venue and the order is treated internally within the firm. PG, instead, is a systemic regulatory framework governing intra-firm processes and arrangements with the aim to protect investors before the conclusion of a contract for the provision of investment services (*ex ante product testing*) and during the performance of such an agreement (*ongoing product testing*). The objective is to avoid the sale of unfit products to (a pre-determined category of) clients (remedial actions to address mis-selling).[255]

All obligations related to PG must be proceduralized into formal intra-firm practices and tracked all the way through. Such proceduralization is to be done proportionally, taking into account the complexity of services and product supplied by the investment firm. The Compliance Function inevitably plays a key role in establishing and monitoring the necessary arrangements, even if the formal accountability for the correct functioning of the PG process is officially in the hands of a firm's management body—which is usually the Board—as it must have "effective control over the firm's product governance process".[256] Firms failing to establish such processes and procedures may incur administrative fines and related reputational risks and costs. Both manufacturers and distributors must adopt a written internal policy—usually drafted by the Compliance Function—which formalizes the whole process. From the identification criteria for client targeting to product testing to the potential remedial actions in case of mis-selling[257] and the related feeding-back of information into product design, including a proceduralization of information-sharing agreement between manufacturers and distributors. All these steps are intra-firm proceduralization of contract-law principles of investor protection,[258] with the protection starting at the very moment a product is crafted. For this reason, PG is going to have an impact on an investment firm's business model and the Compliance Risk Assessment of the entire PG process is going to affect such model. Similarly, the role of the Risk Management Function in assessing (and periodically reassessing) the risk profile of a product is also crucial.

The PG strongly mitigates (or it even overcomes at all) the disclosure/rational-investor paradigm by de facto shifting a great deal of the responsibility to make *right investment decisions* from the shoulders of the retail investors to that of the firm[259] and, in particular, of the Compliance Function tasked with designing and monitoring the PG internal processes and procedures. The PG marks a clear move from a *pure* access justice through ex ante regulated contract-based disclosure toward a *paternalistic*[260] access justice through the proceduralization of public-law conduct-of-business duties, where an allegedly less-rational[261] investor is nudged[262] by the accountable service provider to enter the market and make their own decisions. The shift from contract-based disclosure to intra-firm processes also explains the increasing importance of the Compliance Function—in charge of shielding the firm from administrative sanctions (key aspect of the compliance risk)—at the expenses of the Legal Department—traditionally tasked with counseling on and drafting service contracts in a way to dim the litigation risk (lawsuits before civil courts).[263]

Another key takeaway of PG is that it tries to overcome and/or mitigate inefficiencies at *micro* level—client-provider relationship—with a broader view of contributing to market efficiency at *macro* level.[264] To this aim, the *micro* level is monitored by the firm itself—in particular, again, through the control activity of the internal Compliance Function—whereas the *macro* level is under the auspices of domestic public enforcers and ESMA (which can wield emergency product intervention powers granted by MiFIR).

3.5.2.2 Enforcement Under MiFID II: Product Intervention Powers

Compared to MiFID I, MiFID II Articles 69–74 have a clearer approach on administrative sanctions for infringements.[265] Member States are, indeed, required to endow their competent authorities with stronger and more sophisticated supervisory and investigatory powers.[266] Good examples are the power to require existing data traffic records held by a telecommunication operator (but only when this is allowed under national law), and the possibility to request any person to take steps to reduce the size of their position or exposure (Article 69).

Article 70 provides for a detailed account of provisions whose transgression must necessary lead to the enactment of administrative sanctions, while Article 72 lays down the way supervisory and sanctioning powers must be wielded. Furthermore, Article 71 envisages mandatory publication of enforcement decisions through the authorities' official website without undue delay, unless the decision's publication would be "disproportionate following a case-by-case assessment" of data or, above all, this would endanger the financial markets stability or an ongoing investigation. In these cases, the authority has the power to postpone publication, anonymize it, or not publish the sanctioning decision at all.

All in all, public enforcement and supervision of investment services is viewed by MiFID II as a crucial step to grant the efficient functioning of financial markets. The accurate list of enforcement and sanctioning powers ensured to and the procedural duties imposed upon public authorities clearly prove so. Domestic public authorities are requested to simultaneously ponder two different objectives—investor protection and integrity/stability of financial markets—without overlooking the competitiveness of their home financial markets.

To overcome possible disruptions *within* the single financial market, ESMA is endowed with emergency intervention powers (grounded on emergency powers under Article 9.5 of ESMA Regulation—see Chap. 5) and the power to settle disputes between domestic authorities. Concerning the former, MiFIR pushes for a centralization at the European level by introducing product intervention powers for ESMA[267] (alongside national securities authorities[268]) like the one the PRIIPs Regulation confers on the EIOPA (and national insurance authorities). Article 40 of MiFIR grants

ESMA the same power to temporarily prohibit or restrict (1) dangerous financial activities or practices and (2) the marketing, distribution, or sale of certain financial instruments. Conditions under which ESMA can exercise these powers trace those already showed for the PRIIPs Regulation.[269] Key for the activation of such powers is the existence of a significant investor protection concern or a threat to the orderly functioning and integrity of financial markets or to the stability of the whole or part of the European financial system (Article 40, 2a). This combination confirms how the objectives of investor protection and the safeguard of the functioning and stability of the financial markets go hand in hand.

The Commission Delegated Regulation supplementing MiFIR[270] lists criteria and factors that ESMA, EBA, and the NCAs must take into account when using emergency product intervention powers for very major infringements. Examples of these criteria are the degree of complexity of the financial instrument (or structured deposit) under scrutiny, the type of investors involved (whether retail or professional, and if retail, what kind of sub-category), pricing and associated costs, the selling practices employed by the industry or the single investment firm, the financial and business situation of the issuer, the case in which the characteristics of the financial instrument (or structured deposit) make it particularly susceptible to being used for the purposes of financial crime, and so on and so forth.

Product intervention powers[271] are particularly important because, for the very first time in the history of the European financial law, an EU authority is endowed with direct supervisory and enforcement powers on investor protection issues (other emergency powers, like those under the Short Selling Regulation, do not concern investor protection directly—see Chap. 5). Even if such powers are *parallel* and *secondary*[272] to those wielded by national authorities since ESMA can step in only in case domestic "competent authorities have not taken action to address the threat or the actions that have been taken do not adequately address the threat" (Article 40, 2c), such "emergency powers" are anyhow *hierarchically superior*[273] as the measures adopted by ESMA "prevail over any previous action taken by a competent authority" (Article 40, 7). Product intervention powers under MiFIR clearly mark a trend opened with the Short Selling Regulation: the centralization of enforcement powers at European level, at least for emergency cases. The trend is: the bigger the emergency, the hierarchically higher the enforcement responsibility.

The path already opened by MiFID I has been definitely confirmed by MiFID II: private enforcement is (still) left behind, with some—yet important—attention paid to extrajudicial mechanisms for consumer complaints (Article 75). Against the background of MiFID I/II, (public-law) conduct-of-business rules are used by public authorities as tools to monitor over and sanction market players for their wrongdoings, thus indirectly affecting the private-law relationship between retail investors and investment services providers. A leading example is provided by the suitability rule that MiFID II does not cover with any pan-European private remedies (which are still left to domestic courts), thus primarily conceiving it as a tool for public enforcement in that it is "directed at ensuring the effective supervision over the compliance by investment service providers".[274] The contract stemming from the provision of the investment service eventually turns from a *negotium juridicum* (*das Rechtsgeschäft*) into a tool for public enforcement.

The idea of an internal Compliance Function within a financial institution established in order to constantly advise and monitor on the obedience to the applicable laws and regulations was born out of this context, increasingly inclined toward public, rather than private, enforcement. Here the law is employed with the purpose of "achieving, fostering or managing of particular markets or particular policy objectives".[275] An internal control Function designed to fill the vacuum between the law-on-the-books (public regulation) and the law-in-action[276] *within* the firm: for this reason, the Compliance Function is squeezed between the business needs of its own firm and the tasks of regulatory advice and monitoring directly provided by the law. As regulations become increasingly detailed, the Function's role inexorably grows in importance. Chapter 7 is fully devoted to analyzing such an internal Function.

3.5.3 The Prospectus Regulation

The brand-new Prospectus Regulation[277] (out in June 2017) is one of the first pieces of legislation hammered out under the umbrella of the Capital Market Union.[278] The core objective of the new Regulation is to "ensure investor protection and market efficiency, while enhancing the internal market for capital",[279] and it unfolds through the following prongs:

1. To help small- and medium-sized enterprises raise capital at lower costs,[280] being the Regulation applicable only to issuances more than one billion Euros, calculated over a period of twelve months.[281]
2. To simplify and rationalize the information to be provided for all kinds of securities, by focusing on specific and material risk-factors.[282]
3. To allow a lighter prospectus for secondary issuances and the use of already published information.[283]
4. To make prospectuses more understandable for investors by means of a summary of key information, focused on information concretely relevant for them.[284]

Point 4 is the most important one for retail investors. Article 7 of the Prospectus Regulation sets forth that prospectuses must include a summary[285] providing the key information that investors need to receive in order to be able to understand[286] the nature, the warnings related to and the risks of the issuer, of the guarantor and of the securities being offered/admitted to trading on a regulated market.[287] Furthermore, this summary should be read as an introduction to the prospectus and be crafted in a way to guide the investor through the body of the prospectus itself (Article 7.2). Significantly, the summary can be omitted when the security can be bought only by qualified investors (i.e., eligible counterparties and professional clients), thus making it an EU-wide, single disclosure instrument particularly designed for those retail investors allegedly able to understand a prospectus if helped through easier-to-read information sheets.

3.6 An Increasingly More "Regulatory" EU Law of Investor Protection and the Resulting Growing Importance of the Compliance Function

This chapter has given an account of the evolution of the EU law of financial services and markets through the lenses of the investor protection topic. The legislative history of this branch of EU law looks like a slow but inevitable evolution from negative intervention—through minimum harmonization—to positive intervention—through maximum/full harmonization—and, finally, to regulatory standardization—through Regulations. The Prospectus legislation clearly represents the combination of the move from Directives to Regulations with the move from harmonizing rules to a set of uniform standards. Coherently, implementing rules move from the domestic to the European dimension (second and third Lamfalussy level) and the border with detailed technical standards blurs. One of the outcomes of such a trend is the increased, direct thrust of the EU normative production on the regulatory compliance of European investment firms: the more Europeanized the norms by means of the Single Rulebook and the stronger the supervisory convergence fostered by ESMA[288] (see Chap. 5), the closer the practices of firms' Compliance Functions throughout the Union.

This evolution has been driven by the policy goal of turning traditionally domestic bank-based systems characterized by the "prudent banking saver" (see Chap. 2) into a single-market-based system characterized by the "rational retail investor".[289] The objective and leitmotiv of this movement is the assumption that a market-based system is a better mechanism and that the law should be employed to help market's efficiency and stability.[290]

Legislation moves from the domestic dimensions toward the European one. At the national level, the prudent banking saver was protected by the stability and solidity of the domestic banking system.[291] At the European level, investors become investment service consumers who contribute to the completion of the single market. The "rational retail investor" has, indeed, its origins from the "average consumer", that is, the "reasonably well informed and reasonably observant and circumspect"[292] buyer, as crafted by the European consumer law. This "is inherently bound to making the consumer fit for the market, to eliminating access barriers to the market and to guaranteeing equal treatment of all citizen-consumers in the market."[293]

Within this framework, the disclosure paradigm[294] is dominant[295] and is the crucial tool to empower[296] the rational (retail) investor and increase her/his confidence in the market.[297] Coherently, retail investors are provided (through harmonized, mandatory [public-law] rules) with all the information necessary to fully understand the product or service they undertake as if they were "rational maximisers of their own utility".[298] Disclosure as competitive transparency, which has always been the protection tool granted to institutional investors (supposed to be) able to make rational investment decisions when they are properly informed, is gradually extended to reach the retail level.

Within this model,[299] investor protection is an ancillary tool[300] devised in order to establish an efficient market: "There is no room for social justice as an eminent expression of a social welfare obligation. Social distributive justice, which constituted the trigger point for the rise of consumer policy as social policy, is replaced by [...] 'access justice'—*Zugangsgerechtigkeit*—and a materialized anti-discrimination principle."[301]

This chapter has shown that up until the end of the 1970s, national legislation was very scarcely (actually, not at all) harmonized. The situation started changing in the early 1980s, but the decisive legislative input was given by the adoption of the Single European Act[302] and the Commission 1985 White Paper,[303] which opened the path toward the stronger integration of domestic financial markets in a unified European market. The first pieces of EU law of financial market, although very general, already had the basic features of this branch of EU law: competitive market transparency based on standardizing criteria and disclosure duties to grant fair market access, and coordinated public enforcement activities to monitor market access and cross-border operations. The security prospectus, in this regard, can be viewed as "prototype of the disclosure mechanism"[304]: rational professional and institutional investors can read a prospectus, and on the basis of that, they can choose one security over another.[305] These investors have the skills and knowledge to read a prospectus—full of technical terms and concepts—understand the content and, on that basis, make an informed (economically efficient) decision.

With a view of building the single market, the disclosure paradigm became harmonized through EU public law, used as supervisory tool, and progressively applied to retail investors, with the main difference with institutional investors being disclosure's accuracy and understandability. The evolution of the UCITS Directives—from the simplified prospectus to the KIID—proves an increased interest toward less-sophisticated investors and their understanding of products through comparison by means of standardization.[306] Similarly, the 2010 amendment to the 2003 Prospectus Directive introduced the difference between retail investors and qualified investors, and added some nuance to the "one-size-fits-all" scheme.

Until the 2004 MiFID I, information disclosure conveyed through contractual material—rather than selling restrictions on unsuitable products—was practically the only instrument conceived by the EU law to protect retail investors.[307] MiFID I marks a change due to the fact that, even if its conduct-of-business rules follow the same drift (indirect public harmonization of private laws and instrumental use of the contract), the disclosure paradigm is partnered with the suitability and appropriateness tests meant to promote investors' engagement. These compel investment service providers to take into account the knowledge, experience, and risk inclination of their client, in order to promote and accompany an investor's (more or less autonomous) ability to make investment decisions.[308] Not only are MiFID I conduct rules meant to make investors aware of an investment-related actual and potential risks, but in the case of suitability, they even refrain an investment operation from being executed. Significantly, with MiFID I the rational retail investor becomes *slightly less* rational. Within this context of progressively decreased rationality, MiFID differentiates between:

1. Advisory services (advice and portfolio management)—where the investment-decision-making is strongly influenced by the service provider—which are grounded on a fiduciary mandate from the investor to the provider and governed by the suitability test which shifts much of the responsibility on the provider's shoulders.

2. Execution non-advisory services (such as reception and transmission of orders)—where the retail investor makes autonomous investment decisions and is responsible for such decisions—which are governed by the appropriateness test (meant to warn the investor about the investment-connected risks) and disclosure plays its traditional empowerment role.[309]

3. Execution-only services on non-complex instruments,[310] where the appropriateness test can be skipped. This third category symbolizes the *non-plus ultra* of the responsible consumer and it is probably the last example of caveat emptor[311] regulation in the EU law of investment services.[312] However, not only does the MiFID general duty of care (having its roots in traditional contract law) apply to all of the

circumstances, but it clearly emerges under Best Execution (and, even more, under MiFID II PG) that applies to all services.

Ten years after MiFID I, the PRIIPs Regulation thrusts the EU splinter even deeper into national private laws. Uniform, standardized pre-contractual (public) rules raising civil liability on the part of the service provider are established to protect the weaker parties, make them confident to access the market, and create a level playing field where products are easily comparable through competitive (between products) and contractual (on counterparties reciprocal rights, in particular the duties of the stronger party) transparency. The nature of the EU penetration is public and this is reflected by the assignment of intra-firm responsibilities to the Compliance Function rather than the Legal Department. It is usually up (1) to the manufacturer's Compliance Function to ensure that the PRIIPs' KID is drafted according to the regulatory requirements (Compliance's advisory task) and (2) to the distributor's Compliance Function to ensure that the KID is accurately distributed (Compliance's monitoring task).

On the same wavelength, MiFID II increases ex ante and ex post sales information disclosure on the total costs and charges (one-off and ongoing) and on the cumulative effect of such costs on the return of the investment, for both the service and product provided. Unlike PRIIPs, MiFID II does not prescribe any standardized formats (yet), although it clarifies which information must be provided. Alike in PRIIPs, the Compliance Function plays the king role in advising on the correct content of the disclosure material and in monitoring the related procedures.

The result of this trend is that investment firms must comply with regulatory, public-law conduct-of-business rules stemming from EU law—what professor Cherednychenko labels as "European supervision private law".[313] To do that, firms are in strong need of internal guidance in order to correctly embed and monitor the new, multiple EU legal requirements into their internal processes and procedures. This is why the Compliance Function has become critically important: it is the defense frontline[314] of a firm vis-à-vis the competent public enforcer, and its mission is to avoid or reduce the risk of administrative actions (a key component of the compliance risk) by correctly embedding the applicable regulatory requirements of EU origin.

The main redress under EU law is, indeed, public. Public enforcers can use PRIIPs pre-contractual documents and MiFID-harmonized disclosure documents to impinge administrative sanctions and fines on distributors, manufacturers, and investment service providers. However, unlike MiFID I whose reference to private enforcement was "rather cryptic",[315] the PRIIPs Regulation introduces a civil liability to be applied throughout Europe, even if the interpretation of its borders still depends on the principles of national private laws.[316]

The role granted since the very beginning to administrative authorities has been further strengthened, and so has been the internal role of the Compliance Function. The first pieces of legislation already focused on administrative enforcement and coordination of national supervisory agencies. This trend was corroborated over time with the UCITS Directives, Prospectus Directive, and, in particular, MiFID I and its detailed list of powers and duties. In lawmaking terms, the input of regulatory bodies has been crystallized in the Lamfalussy procedure. The result is that the harder the law (from minimum to full harmonization to regulations), the more intrusive the norms on public enforcement, the more important the role played by the Compliance Function on the obedience of such norms vis-à-vis that of the Legal Department.

Viewed through the lenses of a European investment firm, MiFID suitability rule has a greater impact on the Compliance Function's daily work than on that of the Legal Function. Indeed, the Compliance Function is usually tasked with writing the internal Suitability Policy, crafting the internal processes and procedures connected to the regulatory requirement, designing first-level controls, and running second-level controls, with the purpose of meeting the domestic Competent Authority's expectations. The quality of the job done by the Compliance Function is then subject to prospective enforcement actions from public authorities. The Legal department is, instead, usually concerned with drafting predetermined, standardized contract terms and conditions, and its main responsibility relates to litigation risk by incorporating the gist of the suitability rule into a firm's agreement for the provision of investment services (depending on the national civil-law circumstances).

The leap forward brought by MiFIR and PRIIPs in enforcement terms is represented by the product intervention powers. Such new powers are conceived and designed as an investor confidence and financial stability tool. Administrative authorities are (reasonably) lifted by the responsibility of pre-authorizing, pre-approving, or licensing financial products[317] as this would imply an ex ante control of the market and a potential shift of (civil) responsibility from the product manufacturers/sellers to public authorities. This would clearly deprive the market of its core nature, suffocate financial innovation, and encourage moral hazard.[318] Public supervisors are, instead, asked to step in and limit private autonomy (firms' practices, activities, and product selling), when this is necessary to shield a higher principle, namely, market survival (with consumer confidence being a corner stone). Such intervention powers mark a clear step in the centralization of enforcement powers at the European level since they are also attributed to ESMA, EBA, and EIOPA in temporary emergency situations.

For the time being, however, it is left to be seen how to gauge financial instability and threats to the orderly functioning and integrity of the markets provided under MiFIR. Public rulemakers are asked to provide standards to be employed in order to measure risks (banking law already does so), but the yardstick on how to interpret and apply those standards is still entrenched into administrative authorities' margin for discretion.[319]

The Commission Delegated Regulation 2017/567 supplementing MiFIR[320] provides for a list of non-quantitative factors and criteria to take into account when using intervention powers. It also clarifies that ESMA/EBA/NCAs have the power to "determine the existence of a significant investor protection concern or a threat to the orderly functioning and integrity of financial markets [...] or to the stability of the whole or part of the financial system of the Union based on one or more of those factors and criteria".[321] Article 16(8) of the PRIIPs Regulation does the same for the EIOPA and insurance-based investment products.

In addition, it is yet to be seen is whether, how, and to what extent public authorities will actually wield these powers. Much will depend on the supervisory culture that will evolve in the coming years under the auspices of ESMA. Such new powers have grown out of the general acceptance of the fact that financial market forces cannot heal themselves[322] and they need strong public guardians to avoid wreaking havoc on the overall economic system.

Rules on PG and those on Product Intervention powers work as a bridge between intra-firm investor protection and extra-firm market stability.[323] In both cases, the Compliance Function is fully engaged (advice on product crafting and distribution; internal monitoring; liaison with public enforcers). When PG and Product Intervention are viewed together, then "libertarian paternalism"[324] seems to have gained definitive ground vis-à-vis pure deregulation. The lawmaker's expectations are that the financial industry should be able to refrain itself from designing and selling unfit products to its own customers under the threat of (strong) public intervention. If expressed in ERPL terms this can be translated into *paternalistic*[325] access justice.

The regulatory grip on private law on the part of the EU law of investment services has been increasing over time alongside the consolidation of lawmaker's preference for the market-based over the bank-based financial system. Professor Cherednychenko rightly points out that the combination of an intra-firm process-based PG regime alongside product-banning powers in the hands of European and domestic public authorities "has the potential to have a profound impact on the main subject matter of contracts concluded between investment firms and consumers".[326]

Alongside this, provisions of European origins have become increasingly more detailed and larger in quantitative terms. This is proved by the number of legislative delegations to ESMA and the European Commission under MiFID II[327] and qualitative details of second-level measures which leave less and less leeway to national private-law traditional solutions. A clear example is provided by Article 54.11 of Commission Delegated Regulation 2017/565 which sets forth the duty for investment firms to ensure that investment switching is always suitable for the client. To prove so, firms must carry out an analysis of the costs and benefits of the switching and make sure that the benefits exceed the costs. Through the eyes of a private lawyer, such a duty should have been already implied in the duty of care of the investment service provider (and handled through national private-law legislation). The new EU-made public-law rule prospectively imposes administrative sanctions on the firm in case of non-compliance with the investment switching provision,[328] a liability that is to be enforced by NCAs (i.e., the members of ESMA).

The consolidation trend of the EU regulatory law has pushed for the emergence and consolidation of the Compliance Function in European investment firms. Coherently, the combination within ESMA of a wider regulatory production alongside the new intervention powers[329] will very likely lead to an intensified role of the EU contract-related public-law business-of-conduct rules.[330] As a matter of fact (as a *law-in-action* consequence), this is because EU harmonizing rules are likely to be viewed by the industry Compliance Function as standards from which it is dangerous to depart for fear of administrative sanctions imposed by enforcement agencies. Conservative interpretations of EU harmonizing rules are seen as "safe harbors", with the result of pushing the regulatory thrust of the EU law even deeper and—as implicitly forecast by the ERPL theory—definitely turning investor protection law into regulatory investor protection law. Table 3.2 gives a graphic vision of this conclusion:

Table 3.2 Evolution of the EU system of investor protection

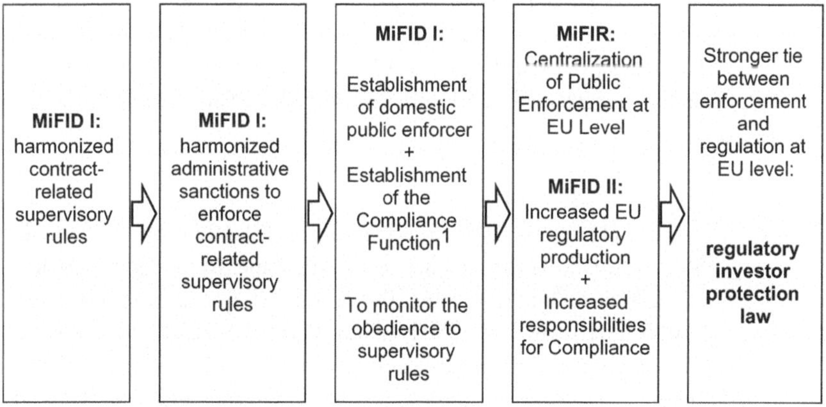

Notes

1. Article 67.1 of the Treaty of Rome simply stated that "during the transitional period and to the extent necessary to ensure the proper functioning of the common market, Member States shall progressively abolish between themselves all restrictions on the movement of capital belonging to persons resident in Member States and any discrimination based on the nationality or on the nationality or on the place of residence of the parties or on the place where such capital is invested".
2. Article 207 TFEU, ex-Article 133 TEC.
3. Niamh Moloney, *EC Securities Regulation, 2nd Ed.*, Oxford EC Law Library (Oxford: Oxford University Press, 2008). At 6.
4. Ibid. At 6.
5. Ibid. At 8. Professor Moloney maintains: "Article 3(h) EC provides that the approximation of Member States' laws to the extent required for the functioning of the common market is an activity of the Community." Note that former art. 3(1)h TEC was substantially replaced by art. 3 and 6 TFUE.
6. Ibid. At 8.
7. As it is the case for the Prospectus Directive 2003/71/EC which was based on then Articles 44 and 95.
8. As it is the case for Regulation 648/2012 on OTC derivatives, central counterparties and trade repositories (EMIR); Regulation 2016/1011 on indices used as benchmarks in financial instruments and financial contracts (FBMR); Regulation 600/2014 on markets in financial instruments (MiFIR); Regulation 1286/2014 on key information documents for packaged retail and insurance-based investment products (PRIIPs).
9. As it is the case for Directive 2014/65/EU on markets in financial instruments (MiFID II).
10. These are: (1) 1960s–1985, the beginning; (2) 1985–1999, from the 1985 Commission's Internal Market White Paper to the 1999 Financial Services Action Plan; (3) 1999–2004, the FSAP normative production; (4) 2005–2010, the post-FSAP pause; (5) 2010–2014, the crisis and post-crisis normative production (two waves of reforms). Niamh Moloney, *EU Securities and Financial Markets Regulation* (Oxford: Oxford University Press, 2014). At 22–47.

11. By also considering Moloney's approach on the development of a retail market agenda at European level in her seminal 2010 book: *How to Protect Investors: Lessons from the EC and the UK* (Cambridge: Cambridge University Press, 2010). At 5–12.
12. Sir George Blunden was the Chairman of Committee on Banking Regulations and Supervisory Practices (now called the Basel Committee on Banking Supervision) from 1974 to 1977. He was also the Executive Director of the Bank of England. Source: Basel Committee on Banking Supervision, "Basel Committee Organisation and Governance," https://www.bis.org/bcbs/organ_and_gov.htm.
13. Bank of England, "Bank of England Quarterly Bulletin" (1977).
14. The preposition "within" does not imply a direct legal connection between the ECC Treaty and the Bretton Woods agreement but, more modestly, it remarks that the ECC Treaty was not operating outside the international financial structure created by the Bretton Woods agreements.
15. On these judgments and the first Directives: Martijn Van Empel, "Financial Services in the EU: Harmonization and Liberalization "in *Financial Services in Europe: An Introductory Overview*, ed. Martijn van Empel (Boston Kluwer, 2008). At 28.
16. *Reyners V Belgium*, ECR 00631 (1974).
17. *Van Binsbergen V Bedrijfsvereniging Metaalnijverheid*, ECR 01299 (1974).
18. Council Directive 73/183/Eec abolishing restrictions on freedom of establishment and freedom to provide services for banks and other financial institutions [*Council Directive 73/183/Eec.*]. Council Directive 77/780/EEC on prohibition of legal restrictions for banking activities, which focused on authorization, capital ratios, and cooperation between public supervisors on the oversight of credit institutions with branches in other Member States [*First Council Directive 77/780/Eec.*] Council Directive 83/350/Eec on supervision of credit institutions on a consolidated basis [*Council Directive 83/350/Eec.*] On these Directives: Julien Ernoult et al., *European Banking and Financial Services Law: Third Edition* (Brussels: Larcier, 2008).
19. *First Council Directive 77/780/Eec.*
20. *Commission Recommendation 77/534/Eec of 25 July 1977 Concerning a European Code of Conduct Relating to Transactions in Transferable Securities.*

21. Head of Research at the EEC Commission Directorate-General for Economic and Financial Affairs at the time.
22. Group of Experts Appointed by the EEC Commission, "The Segré Report - the Development of a European Capital Market" (1966).
23. Ibid.
24. Council Directive 79/279/EEC coordinating the conditions for the admission of securities to official stock exchange listings [*Council Directive 79/279/Eec.*]; Council Directive 80/390/EEC on requirements for the drawing up, scrutiny and distribution of the listing particulars [*Council Directive 80/390/Eec.*]; Council Directive 82/121/EEC (so-called Interim Reports Directive) on disclosure of information to be published on a regular basis by companies whose shares had been admitted to official stock exchanges [*Council Directive 82/121/Eec.*]
25. Article 4, *Council Directive 80/390/Eec.*
26. On the different focuses of banking and securities regulation: Andrew Tuch, "Conduct of Business Regulation," in *The Oxford Handbook of Financial Regulation*, ed. Niamh Moloney, Eilís Ferran, and Jennifer Payne (Oxford: Oxford University Press, 2015). At 540.
27. *Commission Recommendation 77/534/Eec of 25 July 1977 Concerning a European Code of Conduct Relating to Transactions in Transferable Securities.*
28. For instance: "information provided to savers must be complete and accurate, since lack of knowledge is a source of imperfection in any market" and "equality of information to which all investors must be entitled".
29. *Rewe-Zentral Ag V Bundesmonopolverwaltung Für Branntwein (Cassis De Dijon)*, ECR I-649 (1979).
30. In the words of Professor Craig: "The general thrust of the Commission's approach was to move away from the concept of harmonization towards that of mutual recognition and equivalence, by building on the Cassis de Dijon jurisprudence." Paul Craig, "The Evolution of the Single Market," in *The Law of the Single European Market - Unpacking the Premises*, ed. Catherine Barnard and Joanne Scott (Portland: Hart Publishing, 2002). At 12.
31. Commission of the European Communities, "Completing the Internal Market: White Paper from the Commission to the European Council" (Brussels, 1985).
32. These imply "the adequacy of the laws of each of the Member States regarding financial regulation, and [... require] them, subject to minimum harmonized standards being adopted at EU level, to restrict free movement only where explicitly permitted in the EC Treaty or where justified by the general good." Brigitte Haar, "Organizing Regional

Systems: The EU Example," in *The Oxford Handbook of Financial Regulation*, ed. Niamh Moloney, Eilís Ferran, and Jennifer Payne (Oxford: Oxford University Press, 2015). At 160.

33. Concerning financial regulation, in its seminal *Alpine* case, the ECJ clarifies that: "It is a restriction on freedom to provide services for a Member State to prohibit financial intermediaries established there from contacting potential clients in another Member State by telephone without their prior consent to offer them services linked to investment in commodities futures, but the restriction is justified by the imperative reason of public interest consisting in maintaining the good reputation of the national financial sector. The smooth operation of financial markets is largely contingent on the confidence they inspire in investors, which depends in particular on the existence of professional regulations serving to ensure the competence and trustworthiness of financial intermediaries. By protecting investors from a method of canvassing which generally catches them unawares, the prohibition of cold calling on a market as speculative as that in commodities futures seeks to secure the integrity of the national financial sector." *Alpine Investments Bv V Minister Van Financiën* (1995). Summary (http://eur-lex.europa.eu/legal-content/EN/TXT/HTML/?uri=CELEX:61993CJ0384&from=IT).
34. In the words of Professors Micklitz and Patterson: "Regulatory private law, in its negative variant through the impact of the four freedoms on the private law and in its positive variant through the bulk of EU rules that have been adopted in the aftermath of the Single European Act." Hans-Wolfgang Micklitz and Dennis Patterson, "From the Nation State to the Market: The Evolution of EU Private Law," in *EUI Working Paper Law 2012/15*, ed. European University Institute (Florence, 2012). At 12. Also: Hans W. Micklitz and Stephen Weatherill, "The Economic Constitution of the European Community," in *European Economic Law*, ed. Hans W. Micklitz and Stephen Weatherill (Farnham, UK: Ashgate Publishing, 1997).
35. *Directive 88/627/Eec.*
36. *Directive 89/298/Eec.* The Offer Prospectus Directive was much narrower than the legislation promulgated in 2003 and in 2017.
37. *Directive 93/22/Eec.* The so-called Investment Services Directive—ISD. This was the cornerstone of the European investment services legislation for around a decade, until MiFID was adopted in 2004. On ISD: Moloney, *EC Securities Regulation, 2nd Ed.* At 13.
38. *Directive 94/19/Ec.*
39. *Directive 97/9/Ec.*

40. *Directive 85/611/Eec.*
41. *Directive 2001/107/Ec.*
42. *Directive 2001/108/Ec.*
43. *Directive 2009/65/Ec.*
44. *Commission Recommendation 583/2010.*
45. *Commission Recommendation 584/2010.*
46. *Commission Directive 2010/42/Eu.*
47. *Commission Directive 2010/43/Eu.*
48. Directive 2014/91/Eu.
49. *How to Protect Investors: Lessons from the EC and the UK.* At 135.
50. *Directive 2001/107/Ec.*
51. *Commission Recommendation 2004/384/Ec.*
52. Ibid. Recital 2.
53. Ibid. Recital 1.
54. Ibid. Recital 1.
55. European Commission—Internal Market and Services Directorate General, "Workshop on Simplified Prospectus - Annotated Agenda of 1st Meeting" (2006). At 1.
56. As it was officially stated in the Internal Market and Services Directorate General web site: European Commission, "Internal Market and Services Directorate General Webpage," http://ec.europa.eu/internal_market/investment/investor_information/index_en.htm.
57. European Commission—Internal Market and Services Directorate General. At 1.
58. Committee of European Securities Regulators - CESR, "A Guide to Clear Language and Layout for the Key Investor Information Document (Kii) - Cesr/10-532" (2010). At 3.
59. Ibid. At 3.
60. Ibid. At 8. In the United States, the Securities and Exchange Commission too considers a document design as a very important element to protect investor and it claims that "the right design choices make a document easier to read and its information easier to understand." Securities and Exchange Commission—SEC, "A Plain English Handbook" (Washington, DC, 1998).
61. CESR. At 9–13.
62. Ibid. At 5.
63. Ibid. At 6.
64. European Securities and Markets Authority—ESMA (2015) "Questions and Answers - Key Investor Information Document (KIID) for

UCITS" 2015/ESMA/631, Paris. Available at: https://www.esma.europa.eu/file/4632/download?token=r1gxfsJP.
65. European Securities and Markets Authority—ESMA (2015) "Questions and Answers - Key Investor Information Document (KIID) for UCITS" 2015/ESMA/631, Paris. Available at: https://www.esma.europa.eu/file/4632/download?token=r1gxfsJP. At 4.
66. *Regulation 1095/2010.*
67. European Securities and Markets Authority—ESMA, "Questions and Answers - Key Investor Information Document for Ucits (Ref. 2012/592)" (Paris, 2012). At 3.
68. On European supervision private law: Olha O. Cherednychenko, "Public Supervision over Private Relationships: Towards European Supervision Private Law?," *European Review of Private Law* 22 no. 1 (2014).
69. Recast available at the following link: http://eur-lex.europa.eu/legal-content/EN/TXT/PDF/?uri=CELEX:02009L0065-20140917&from=EN.
70. *Directive 2014/91/Eu.*
71. *Directive 94/19/Ec.*
72. Directive 2014/49/Eu.
73. *Directive 85/611/Eec.* As amended by Council Directive 88/220/EEC, OJ L 100/31, 19.04.1988.
74. Danilo Galletti, "Le Crisi Bancarie E La Tutela Dei Depositanti," in *Banche E Mercati Finanziari*, ed. Francesco Vella (Torino: Giappichelli, 2009). At 196.
75. *Peter Paul and Others V Bundesrepublik Deutschland*, ECR I-09425 (2004).
76. On this case: Michel Tison, "Do Not Attack the Watchdog! Banking Supervisor's Liability after Peter Paul," *Common Market Law Review* 42, no. 3 (2005). Andrea Biondi and Martin Farley, *The Right to Damages in European Law* (Alphen aan den Rijn: Kluwer Law International, 2009). At 37.
77. *Directive 97/9/Ec.*
78. *Proposal for a Directive of the European Parliament and of the Council Amending Directive 97/9/Ec.*
79. "Withdrawal of Commission Proposals - Oj L 80/17, 7.3.2015."
80. European Commission, "Financial Services: Implementing the Framework for Financial Markets: Action Plan" (Brussels, 1999).
81. Niamh Moloney, "Regulating the Retail Markets," in *The Oxford Handbook of Financial Regulation*, ed. Niamh Moloney, Eilís Ferran, and Jennifer Payne (Oxford: Oxford University Press, 2015). At 742.

82. European Commission, "Financial Services: Commission Outlines Action Plan for Single Financial Market" (Brussels, 1999).
83. Haar. At 167.
84. European Commission, "Financial Services Action Plan (Fsap)," http://europa.eu/legislation_summaries/internal_market/single_market_services/financial_services_general_framework/l24210_en.htm.
85. Moloney, *EC Securities Regulation, 2nd Ed.* At 15.
86. On the relationship between full harmonization measures and national private legal orders: Olha O. Cherednychenko, "Financial Consumer Protection in the EU: Towards a Self-Sufficient European Contract Law for Consumer Financial Services?," *European Review of Contract Law* 10, no. 4 (2014).
87. Council of the European Union, "2283rd Council Meeting - Ecofin 17 July 2000" (Brussels, 2000).
88. Ibid.
89. Ibid.
90. Ibid.
91. Professor Ferran carries out an excellent explanation and assessment of the Lamfalussy Process: Eilís Ferran, *Building an EU Securities Market* (Cambridge: Cambridge University Press, 2004). At 61–119.
92. As stated by the 2010 Omnibus Directive, "[the] European Council endorsed the four-level 'Lamfalussy' approach to make the regulatory process for Union financial legislation more efficient and transparent." Recital 13, *Directive 2010/78/Eu*. The 2010 Omnibus Directive was adopted to "reflect the establishment of ESMA and the Lisbon Treaty settlement relating to administrative rule-making. [It] aligned the major FSAP-era legislative measures to Articles 290 and 291 TFEU." Moloney, *EC Securities Regulation, 2nd Ed.* At 201; 902.
93. As explained by: Hans-Wolfgang Micklitz, "The Regulatory Strategies on Services Contracts in EC Law," ed. European University Institute (Florence, 2008). At 11.
94. Again: ibid. At 11.
95. Boris Bartels et al., *European Banking and Financial Services Law - Fourth Edition* (Brussels: Larcier, 2010). At 351.
96. As depicted in: ibid. At 351.
97. European Commission, "European Banking Committee," https://ec.europa.eu/info/business-economy-euro/banking-and-finance/financial-reforms-and-their-progress/regulatory-process-financial-services/expert-groups-comitology-and-other-committees/european-banking-committee_en.

98. "European Securities Committee," https://ec.europa.eu/info/business-economy-euro/banking-and-finance/financial-reforms-and-their-progress/regulatory-process-financial-services/expert-groups-comitology-and-other-committees/european-securities-committee_en.
99. "European Insurance and Occupational Pensions Committee," https://ec.europa.eu/info/business-economy-euro/banking-and-finance/financial-reforms-and-their-progress/regulatory-process-financial-services/expert-groups-comitology-and-other-committees/european-insurance-and-occupational-pensions-committee_en.
100. "The Commission is empowered to adopt level-2 measures in many areas, and a large number of level-2 Commission regulations and directives are in force. In cases where the regulatory technical standards are designed to further develop, specify or determine the conditions of application of such level-2 measures, they should be adopted only once the relevant level-2 measures have been adopted and should be compatible with that level-2 measure," Recital 13, *Directive 2010/78/Eu*.
101. The three authorities replaced the old "Level 3 Committees" at the beginning of 2011. These "Level 3 Committees" were the Committee of European of Banking Supervisors (CEBS), the Committee of European Securities Regulators (CESR), and the Committee of European Insurance and Occupational Pensions Supervisors (CEIOPS), and they were made up of national regulators and supervisors. See Chap. 5.
102. Micklitz. At 2.
103. Looking at the composition of the ESMA Securities and Markets Stakeholder Group, one realizes that it is predominantly made up of consumers and representatives of the financial industry. *See*: European Securities and Markets Authority—ESMA, "The Securities and Markets Stakeholders Group - Smsg," https://www.esma.europa.eu/about-esma/governance/smsg.
104. Professor Brummer argues that this centralization has "made possible a shift in the transatlantic balance of regulatory power". Chris Brummer, *Soft Law and the Global Financial System: Rule Making in the 21st Century* (Cambridge; New York: Cambridge University Press, 2012).
105. Hans-Wolfgang Micklitz, "The Visible Hand of European Regulatory Private Law—the Transformation of European Private Law from Autonomy to Functionalism in Competition and Regulation," *Yearbook of European Law* 28, no. 1 (2009). At 12.
106. European Commission, "Fsap Evaluation" (Brussels, 2007). At 6.
107. *Directive 2001/24/Ec*.
108. Bartels et al. At 9.

109. *Directive 2001/34/Ec.*
110. The Listing Admission Directive [*Council Directive 79/279/Eec.*]; the Listing Particular Directive [*Council Directive 89/390/Eec.*]; the Interim Reports Directive [*Council Directive 82/121/Eec.*]; and the Major Holdings Directive [*Council Directive 88/627/Eec.*].
111. Bartels et al. At 76.
112. Ibid. At 76.
113. *Directive 2003/6/Ec.*
114. *Directive 2003/71/Ec.*
115. *Directive 2004/109/Ec.*
116. *Directive 2002/87/Ec.*
117. Bartels et al. At 12.
118. Ibid. At 12.
119. Ibid. At 13.
120. As highlighted by the G30 in 2008: "Many large financial firms are involved in a cross-section of products and services rather than in the monoline activities of the past. Indeed, they tend to operate along business lines without regard to legal status of the entities in which the activity is technically situated or recorded for regulatory purposes." G30, "The Structure of Financial Supervision: Approaches and Challenges in a Global Marketplace - Working Group on Financial Supervision" (2008). At 34.
121. On this topic: Annemarie VanDerZwet, "The Blurring of Distinctions between Financial Sectors: Fact or Fiction?," in *De Nederlandsche Bank Occasional Studies*, ed. De Nederlandsche Bank (Amsterdam, 2003). Richard K. Abrams and Michael Taylor, "Issues in the Unification of Financial Sector Supervision," in *IMF Working Papers No 00/213*, ed. International Monetary Fund (Washington, DC, 2000). Richard K. Abrams and Michael W. Taylor, *Assessing the Case for Unified Financial Sector Supervision* (Financial Markets Group, London School of Economics and Political Science, 2002); Martin Čihák and Richard Podpiera, "Is One Watchdog Better Than Three? International Experience with Integrated Financial Sector Supervision," in *IMF Working Papers No 06/57*, ed. International Monetary Fund (Washington, DC, 2006). Martin Čihák and Richard Podpiera, "Integrated Financial Supervision: Which Model?," *The North American Journal of Economics and Finance* 19, no. 2 (2008). Barry Eichengreen and Nergiz Dincer, "Who Should Supervise? The Structure of Bank Supervision and the Performance of the Financial System…," in *NBER Working Paper 17401*, ed. National

Bureau of Economic Research (Cambridge, 2011). Jeroen J. M. Kremers, Dirk Schoenmaker, and Peter J. Wierts, "Cross-Sector Supervision: Which Model?," in *Brookings-Wharton Papers on Financial Services 2003*, ed. Brookings Institution and the Financial Institutions Center at the Wharton School (Philadelphia, 2003).

122. *Directive 2003/6/Ec.*
123. Bartels et al. At 85.
124. Luca Enriques and Matteo Gatti, "Is There a Uniform EU Securities Law after the Financial Services Action Plan?," *Stanford Journal of Law, Business and Finance* 14, no. 43 (2008). At 71
125. The notion of the "reasonable investor" springs from the European Court of Justice (ECJ) consumer case law and it is all in all grounded on the average consumer definition. Importantly, in the *Lloyd/Klijsen* case, the ECJ holds that the reasonable investor is a natural person "deemed to be reasonably well-informed and reasonably observant and circumspect" [ECJ 22 June 1999, Lloyd/Klijsen, ECR 1999, 3819, para.26]. See also this Chapter's Conclusions.
126. Art. 1(2), *Directive 2003/124/Ec.*
127. *Directive 2004/109/Ec.*
128. *Directive 2013/50/Eu.*
129. Bartels et al. At 91.
130. Ibid. At 91.
131. *Directive 2003/71/Ec.*
132. *Directive 2010/73/Eu.*
133. In 2007 the ESME complained that "[i]n practice, the intended maximum harmonization has not been achieved" European Securities Markets Expert Group—ESME, "Report on Directive 2003/71/Ec" (2007). At 5.
134. *Commission Regulation 809/2004.*
135. *Commission Regulation (EC) No 211/2007* of 27 February 2007 amending Regulation (EC) No 809/2004 implementing Directive 2003/71/EC of the European Parliament and of the Council as regards financial information in prospectuses where the issuer has a complex financial history or has made a significant financial commitment; *Commission Delegated Regulation (EU) No 486/2012* of 30 March 2012 amending Regulation (EC) No 809/2004 as regards the format and the content of the prospectus, the base prospectus, the summary and the final terms

and as regards the disclosure requirements; *Commission Delegated Regulation (EU) No 862/2012* of 4 June 2012 amending Regulation (EC) No 809/2004 as regards information on the consent to use of the prospectus, information on underlying indexes and the requirement for a report prepared by independent accountants or auditors; *Commission Delegated Regulation (EU) No 759/2013* of 30 April 2013 amending Regulation (EC) No 809/2004 as regards the disclosure requirements for convertible and exchangeable debt securities; *Commission Delegated Regulation (EU) 2016/301* of 30 November 2015 supplementing Directive 2003/71/EC of the European Parliament and of the Council with regard to regulatory technical standards for approval and publication of the prospectus and dissemination of advertisements and amending Commission Regulation (EC) No 809/2004.

136. Commission Delegated Regulation 382/2014.
137. Jorde deBrito and Sònia Teixeira daMota, "The Pros and Cons of the Prospectus Directive," *International Financial Law Review* (2005), http://www.iflr.com/Article/1984744/The-pros-and-cons-of-the-Prospectus-Directive.html.
138. Commission Regulation 211/2007. Recital 1.
139. Recital 2. Also Article 28.5 and Recital 30 of Commission Regulation 809/2004. Van Dyck carries out an interestingly analysis: Tom Van Dyck, "(Opt-out) Intermediation as an Alternative for Ensuring a True Protection for European Retail Investors?," *Catholic University of Leuven (KUL) Working Paper* (2009).
140. *Commission Delegated Regulation 486/2012.* Recital 14.
141. *Directive 2010/73/Eu.*
142. "This change was made to reduce the burden on financial intermediaries of checking investor status. In practice this means that investment firms can rely on their register of qualified investors under MiFID. The MiFID definition is broadly equivalent to the previous definition in the Prospectus Directive." *See* Dorothee Fischer-Appelt, "Prospectus Directive Amendments – Discussion of Key Changes," *Law and Financial Markets Review* 4, no. 5 (2010). At 495.
143. Recital 15, *Directive 2010/73/Eu.*
144. Article 1.5, ibid.
145. Article 1.5, ibid.
146. *Commission Delegated Regulation 486/2012.*
147. Article 2.1, let. q, *Directive 2003/71/Ec.*
148. Article 6.2, ibid.

149. Article 25.1, ibid.
150. "Civil liability attaches to those persons who have tabled the summary including any translation thereof, and applied for its notification, but only if the summary is misleading, inaccurate or inconsistent when read together with the other parts of the prospectus" Art. 5.2. let. d, ibid.
151. *Directive 2004/39/Ec*. First amendment in 2008: *Directive 2008/10/Ec*.
152. European Commission, "Financial Services: Implementing the Framework for Financial Markets: Action Plan."
153. *Directive 93/22/Eec*.
154. "Initially, the EU pursued only 'minimum' harmonization of the contract-related rules for the provision of investment services in Europe; under the Investment Services Directive (ISD) 1993 Member States were allowed to exceed the level of investor protection envisaged therein." Olha O. Cherednychenko, "Full Harmonisation of Retail Financial Services Contract Law in Europe: A Success or a Failure?," in *Financial Services, Financial Crisis and General European Contract Law: Failure and Challenges of Contracting*, ed. Stefan Grundmann and Yeşim M. Atamer (Alphen aan den Rijn: Kluwer Law International, 2011). At 243.
155. Article 4 of II Level Directive 2006/73/EC implementing the MiFID clearly states that: "Member States may retain or impose requirements additional to those in this Directive only in those exceptional cases where such requirements are objectively justified and proportionate so as to address specific risks to investor protection or to market integrity that are not adequately addressed by this Directive." *Commission Directive 2006/73/Ec*. The reason of this provision lies in the fact that domestic rules very often have the effect of protecting the traditional rent positions of national/local "champions" and hinder competition both domestically and within the Single Market. On full harmonization in MiFID I, see "Full Harmonisation of Retail Financial Services Contract Law in Europe: A Success or a Failure?." At 243. However, the extent of MiFID I harmonization approach is debated; see: Michel Tison, "Financial Market Integration in the Post Fsap Era. In Search of Overall Conceptual Consistency in the Regulatory Framework," in *Investor Protection in Europe: Corporate Law Making, the Mifid and Beyond*, ed. Guido Ferrarini and Eddy Wymeersch (Oxford: Oxford University Press, 2006). In the words of Professor Moloney: "While not formally expressed as a 'maximum harmonization' measure, it was

widely regarded as such." Moloney, *EU Securities and Financial Markets Regulation*. At 334. The author would like to thank Federico Della Negra for raising this point.

156. On MiFID I and its impact on the British regulatory landscape and, in particular, on the then Financial Services Authority's policies and regulations: Paul Nelson, *Capital Markets Law and Compliance* (New York: Cambridge University Press, 2008).
157. "Gold-plating" happens when Member States excessively adopt norms, guidelines, and procedures "at national, regional and local levels, which interfere with the expected policy goals" and they do so with the hidden aim to protect national firms. Matteo Bocci, Jan Maarten De Vet, and Andreas Pauer, "'Gold-Plating' in the Eafrd. To What Extent Do National Rules Unnecessarily Add to Complexity and, as a Result, Increase the Risk of Errors?," in *Ref.: IP/D/AL/FWC/209-056*, ed. European Parliament - Directorate-General for Internal Policies (Brussels, 2014).
158. On the importance of the single passport in the EU Law of Financial Markets: Moloney, *EU Securities and Financial Markets Regulation*.
159. Kwangwook Lee, "Investor Protection in European Union: Post Fsap Directives and Mifid," in *Available at SSRN:* https://ssrn.com/abstract=1339305 *or* https://doi.org/10.2139/ssrn.1339305 (2009). At 20. In the words of Ryan J. Davies: "MiFID is the most significant European Union legislation for investment intermediaries and financial markets *ever* introduced. In general terms, MiFID is designed to provide a common, harmonized set of rules for the provision of investment services in each of the EU member states". Ryan J. Davies, "Mifid and a Changing Competitive Landscape," in *Available at SSRN:* https://ssrn.com/abstract=1117232 *or* https://doi.org/10.2139/ssrn.1117232 (2008).
160. On the civil law effects of MiFID and its interpretative use, Professor Tison: "The wide consensus on the existence of civil law effects of MiFID, and in particular the body of conduct of business rules as further detailed in level 2 measures, will undoubtedly foster the creation of a European investor culture. The convergence to be achieved between supervisors at level 3 in the CESR architecture is likely to spill over to the interpretation of the conduct of business rules in the courts as well." Michel Tison, "The Civil Law Effects of Mifid in a Comparative Law Perspective," in *Financial Law Institute Working Paper 2010-05*, ed. Universiteit Gent - Financial Law Institute (Gent, 2010). At 17.
161. Olha O. Cherednychenko, "European Securities Regulation, Private Law and the Investment Firm-Client Relationship," *European Review of*

Private Law 17, no. 5 (2009); "Full Harmonisation of Retail Financial Services Contract Law in Europe: A Success or a Failure?."; Vanessa Mak, "Review of the Consumer Acquis: Towards Maximum Harmonization?," *European Review of Private Law* 17, no. 1 (2009); "Financial Services and Consumer Protection," in *Research Handbook on EU Consumer and Contract Law*, ed. Christian Twigg-Flesner (Northampton: Edward Elgar, 2016). In the words of Professor Cherednychenko: "It is not excluded that in some cases, private law courts will review the behaviour of investment firms ex post on the basis of the general private law duties of care, which offer more protection to the investor than the maximum harmonization conduct of business rules contained in the MiFID. In fact, denying private law and private law courts a certain degree of autonomy from supervision standards and supervisory authorities involves risks considering that the effectiveness of the EC securities regulation still needs to be proved." Cherednychenko, "European Securities Regulation, Private Law and the Investment Firm-Client Relationship." At 945.

162. In the words of Professor Busch: "The view that the European civil courts should not subject [... *MiFID conduct of business rules*] to private law duties that are stricter than the MiFID duties is the better one. [...] MiFID qualifies as a sophisticated system with a high level of investor protection [... which] provide[s] a well-developed regulatory system." Danny Busch, "Why Mifid Matters to Private Law—the Example of Mifid's Impact on an Asset Manager's Civil Liability," *Capital Markets Law Journal* 7, no. 4 (2012). At 395–396.
163. Matthias Casper and Christian Altgen, "Chapter 4 – Germany," in *Liability of Asset Managers*, ed. Danny Busch and Deborah DeMott (Oxford: Oxford University Press, 2012); Paolo Giudici and Matteo Bet, "Chapter 5 – Italy," ibid.
164. This is particularly true for Italy, where the Court of Cassation held that the regulatory rules adopted by the Italian Securities Regulator (*Commissione Nazionale per le Società e la Borsa*—CONSOB) are mandatory private law rules. *See*: Cassazione Civile, SS.UU., *sentenza 19/12/2007 no 26724*, *Foro italiano*, 2008, I, p 784ff; Cassazione Civile, SS.UU., *sentenza 19/12/2007 no 26724* Giurisprudenza italiana, 2008, I, p 350ff, as reported by Busch, p. 400.
165. Professor Mülbert makes the case for a public-law binding effect on private-law rules when financial services are being provided on a cross-bor-

der basis (Article 31, freedom to provide investment services and activities) or through the establishment of a branch in a host Member State (Article 32, establishment of a branch): "Articles 31 and 32 bar German courts from imposing an obligation on investment firms from other Member States—regardless of whether the firm acts cross-border or through a German branch—to furnish clients with information on specific risks associated with an individual product. German courts are only free to uphold such an obligation with respect to German investment firms if the client specifically asks for this kind of information. One may doubt, however, whether the courts really should establish different levels of investor protection depending on the home country of the investment firm." Peter O. Mülbert, "The Eclipse of Contract Law in the Investment Firm-Client Relationship: The Impact of the Mifid on the Law of Contract from a German Perspective," in *Investor Protection in Europe: Corporate Law Making, the Mifid and Beyond*, ed. Guido Ferrarini and Eddy Wymeersch (Oxford: Oxford University Press, 2006). At 319.

166. Further references on the academic debate: on public and private in finance law, *see*: Alastair Hudson, "The Synthesis of Public and Private in Finance Law," in *Private Law: Key Encounters with Public Law*, ed. Kit Barker and Darryn Jensen (Cambridge: Cambridge University Press, 2013); on the different approach to investor protection between MiFID and the principles of general private law, *see*: Marc Kruithof, "A Differentiated Approach to Client Protection: The Example of Mifid," in *Financial Services, Financial Crisis and General European Contract Law: Failure and Challenges of Contracting*, ed. Stefan Grundmann and Yesim M Atamer (New York: Kluwer Law International, 2011).
167. Olha O. Cherednychenko, "Public and Private Enforcement of European Private Law in the Financial Services Sector," *European Review of Private Law* 24, no. 4 (2015). At 624.
168. *Commission Directive 2006/73/Ec.*
169. François Haas, "The Markets in Financial Instruments Directive: Banking on Market and Supervisory Efficiency," in *International Monetary Fund Working Paper No. 07/250* (2007). At 5.
170. Michael Chlistalla, Uwe Schweickert, and Roland Wittner, "Markets in Financial Instruments Directive - the Way Forward in European Securities Market Integration?," in *E-Finance Lab, Johann Wolfgang Goethe-University - Working Paper* (2006). At 2.

171. Article 14(3) of the ISD provided that: "A Member State may require that transactions relating to the services referred to in paragraph 1 must, where they satisfy all the following criteria, be carried out on a regulated market:

- the investor must be habitually resident or established in that Member State,
- the investment firm must carry out such transactions through a main establishment, through a branch situated in that Member State or under the freedom to provide services in that Member State,
- the transaction must involve a instrument dealt in on a regulated market in that Member State." *Council Directive 93/22/Eec.*

172. Zdenek Kudrna, "Financial Market Regulation: A 'Lamfalussy Exit' from the Joint-Decision Trap," in *The EU's Decision Traps: Comparing Policies*, ed. Gerda Falkner (Oxford: Oxford University Press, 2011). At 82.
173. Article 4 of MiFID I sets forth that an investment firm is "any legal person whose regular occupation or business is the provision of one or more investment services to third parties and/or the performance of one or more investment activities on a professional basis".
174. The author would like to like to thank Mr. Martiniello for exchanges of opinions in this regard.
175. Examples are based on the author's professional experience.
176. Jonathan R. Macey and Maureen O'Hara, "The Law and Economics of Best Execution," *Journal of Financial Intermediation* 6 (1997). At 188.
177. Catherine D'Hondt and Jean-René Giraud, "Mifid: The (in)Famous European Directive?," *EDHEC Position Paper* (2007). At 18.
178. Article 24(1) MiFID I and Article 30(1) MiFID II. Chapter 4 analyzes MiFID client classification.
179. However, collective management of a bunch of individual portfolios can be done if such a cluster is crafted coherently with the content of the discretionary mandates.
180. Commissione Nazionale per le Società e la Borsa—CONSOB, "I Singoli Servizi Di Investimento," http://www.consob.it/web/investor-education/i-singoli-servizi-di-investimento#5.
181. Danny Busch, "Agency and Principal Dealing under the Market in Financial Instruments Directive," in *Agency Law in Commercial Practice*, ed. Danny Busch, Laura Macgregor, and Peter Watts (Oxford: Oxford University Press, 2016). At 151. In the words of Professor Busch: "If an

investment firm deals wholly or partly on behalf of the investor (as intermediary or representative), it has all kinds of duties of care to the investor. If, on the other hand, an investment firm enters into a transaction with an investor solely as a contractual counterparty, it has few if any duties of care. Once it has been established that the firm is acting on behalf of the client, the level of protection depends next on the classification of the client and the exact framework in which the transactions are carried out (i.e. whether the transactions involve execution-only, investment advice, or portfolio management services)." At 142. Professor Busch also takes a critical stance against this solution by stating that "the question of whether allowing the extent of the protection afforded to an investor under MiFID to be largely dependent on the distinction between dealing on own account on the one hand and trading on behalf of the client (and other forms of investment service) on the other is justified [...] must be answered in the negative. An investor may reasonably expect the investment firm used by him or her to look after his or her interests adequately and thus to observe certain duties of care towards him or her." At 175.

182. Article 4.1(13) states that: "'Market operator' means a person or persons who manages and/or operates the business of a regulated market. The market operator may be the regulated market itself".
183. Hans-Wolfgang Micklitz, "The Targeted Full Harmonisation Approach: Looking Behind the Curtain," in *Modernising and Harmonising Consumer Contract Law*, ed. and Reiner Schulze Geraint Howells (Paperback, 2009).
184. Now Article 24(1) MiFID II.
185. Literature on MiFID conduct-of-business rules is vast but the analysis carried out by Cherednychenko is excellent: Cherednychenko, "Financial Consumer Protection in the EU: Towards a Self-Sufficient European Contract Law for Consumer Financial Services?"
186. Jean-Pierre Casey and Karel Lannoo, eds., *The Mifid Revolution* (Cambridge University Press, 2009). At 53.
187. Ibid. At 55.
188. See the point above on the public/private nature of MiFID.
189. Professor Moloney speaks of "the role of law in promoting a cult of retail investment": Niamh Moloney, "Building a Retail Investment Culture through Law: The 2004 Markets in Financial Instruments Directive," *European Business Organization Law Review* 6, no. 3 (2005). At 363.
190. Cherednychenko, "Public and Private Enforcement of European Private Law in the Financial Services Sector." At 632.

191. European Commission, "Background Note on the Draft Commission Directive Implementing Mifid" (2006).
192. Fabrizio Cafaggi and Hans-Wolfgang Micklitz, "Administrative and Judicial Collective Enforcement of Consumer Law in the US and the European Community," in ed. European University Institute - Law Working Paper 2007/22 (2007). At 37. In the words of Marjosola: "The MiFID's private law effects, especially in civil liability context, remain its biggest blind spots." Heikki Marjosola, "What Role for Courts in Protecting Investors in Europe: A View from Finland," *European Review of Contract Law* 10, no. 4 (2014). At 547.
193. *Directive 2004/39/Ec.*
194. Ibid.
195. The Turner Review offers important insights on the regulatory strategies as a response to the global financial crisis. Adair Turner, "Turner Review" (London: Financial Services Authority - FSA, 2009).
196. *Commission Directive 2007/14/Ec.*
197. Luca Enriques and Sergio Gilotta, "Disclosure and Financial Market Regulation," in *The Oxford Handbook of Financial Regulation*, ed. Niamh Moloney, Eilís Ferran, and Jennifer Payne (Oxford: Oxford University Press, 2015). At 527.
198. *Directive 2009/65/Ec.*
199. *Directive 2010/73/Eu.*
200. The "three new European Supervisory Authorities [...] should be aimed at [...] establishing a European single rule book applicable to all financial market participants in the internal market." Recital 5 of Regulation 1095/2010. "The term Single Rulebook was coined in 2009 by the European Council in order to refer to the aim of a unified regulatory framework for the EU financial sector that would complete the single market in financial services." European Banking Authority—EBA, "The Single Rulebook," http://www.eba.europa.eu/regulation-and-policy/single-rulebook. On the Single Rulebook: Moloney, *EU Securities and Financial Markets Regulation*. At 39–41.
201. *Regulation 596/2014/Eu.*
202. *Spector Photo Group Nv and Chris Van Raemdonck V Commissie Voor Het Bank-, Financie- En Assurantiewezen (Cbfa)*, ECR I-12073 (2009). In this case the Court holds that a person who possesses inside information and performs operations related to that information is presumed to have used it. It would be, thus, unnecessary for competent enforcement authorities to provide evidence that that person has "used" inside information "with full knowledge".

203. *Regulation 1060/2009/Ec*. Amended in 2011: *Regulation 513/2011/Eu*.
204. European Market Infrastructure Regulation (EMIR), Regulation 648/2012/Eu.
205. *Regulation 2016/1011/Eu*.
206. A good explanation is provided by the BBC at the following website: BBC, "Libor: What Is It and Why Does It Matter?," http://www.bbc.com/news/business-19199683.
207. *Regulation Eu/236/2012*.
208. European Commission, "Action Plan on Building a Capital Markets Union - Com/2015/0468 Final" (2015).
209. Antonio Marcacci, "What Is Still Missing to Achieve an Optimum Currency Area under EU Law?," *Italian Journal of Public Law* 1-2017 (2017).
210. Indeed, the outcome of the establishment of the Banking Union is "prudential supervision centralised for the systemically important banks in the eurozone, and conduct-of-business supervision decentralised at state level." Karel Lannoo, "Ecb Banking Supervision and Beyond - Ceps Task Force Reports" (Centre for European Policy Studies - CEPS, 2014). At 4. Professor Moloney explains that: "The ECB's competence to engage in specific operational prudential supervision tasks is relatively secure under Article 127(6) TFEU. Technically, this competence might have also sustained ECB supervision of "financial institutions" other than insurance companies (e.g. investment firms and systemically significant actors such as central clearing counterparties), and so supported the holistic, cross-sectoral, functional approach to supervision which the crisis exposed as being necessary. But the vast population of different types of non-bank financial institutions, their weaker connection to the euro-area crisis, and the political and regulatory design difficulties which their inclusion would have generated (not least with respect to subsequent resolution) meant that their exclusion was always a practical reality." Niamh Moloney, "European Banking Union: Assessing Its Risks and Resilience," *Common Market Law Review* 51, no. 6 (2014). At 1659.
211. "Differences regarding the sectoral extent of EU supervision. Some EU countries have an extended definition of credit institutions (i.e. "établissements de crédit"), while other members have much more limited definitions. This is a source of problematic divergences between members that can lead to laxer supervision and regulatory arbitrage." The de Larosière Group, "Report of the High Level Group on Financial Supervision in the EU" (2009). At 28.

212. Commission, "Action Plan on Building a Capital Markets Union - Com/2015/0468 Final." at 19.
213. On FinTech and EU Law: Antonio Marcacci, "Digitally-Provided Financial Services under EU Law: Overcoming the Current Patchwork of Europeanized Private International Law and Sectorially-Harmonized National Private Laws," *Studi sull'integrazione europea* 12, no. 3 (2017).
214. European Commission, "Consumer Financial Services Action Plan: Better Products, More Choice - Com(2017) 139 Final" (2017). At 3.
215. Ibid.
216. "Consultation on Legislative Steps for the Packaged Retail Investment Products Initiative - Objective of the Consultation" (2010).
217. "Optem Report - Study on Pre-Contractual Information for Financial Services" (2008).
218. The Optem Report, in particular, marks the difference between savers and gamblers, thus proving that the same disclosure cannot equally fit anyone's needs. Ibid. At 89–90.
219. Ibid. At 8.
220. Based on studies such as: Synovate, "Consumer Market Study on Advice within the Area of Retail Investment Services - Final Report (2011 Synovate Report)" (2011).
221. European Commission, "Commission Proposes Legislation to Improve Consumer Protection in Financial Services" (Brussels, 2012).
222. Regulation 1286/2014/Eu. Recital 1.
223. Ibid. Recital 3.
224. Ibid.
225. Ibid. Recital 5.
226. In this regard, the 2008 Optem Report had found that many investors "were enthusiastic about the idea of a standardised sheet. Besides the fact that it would facilitate comparisons (as most people expected), for many people it would also help them to get to grips with the sector and gain back some autonomy from banks, financial institutions and other professionals". Commission, "Optem Report - Study on Pre-Contractual Information for Financial Services." At 113.
227. Article 8.2 reads: "An explanatory statement shall appear directly underneath the title of the key information document. It shall read:'This document provides you with key information about this investment product. It is not marketing material. The information is required by law to help you understand the nature, risks, costs, potential gains and

losses of this product and to help you compare it with other products.' "Article 8.3b provides for the following alert when applicable: "You are about to purchase a product that is not simple and may be difficult to understand."

228. European Banking Authority—EBA, "Joint Associations Committee on Retail Structured Products," http://www.eba.europa.eu/regulation-and-policy/consumer-protection-and-financial-innovation/regulatory-technical-standards-on-the-content-and-presentation-of-the-kids-for-priips?p_p_auth=gR5dgLnl&p_p_id=169&p_p_lifecycle=0&p_p_state=maximized&p_p_col_id=column-2&p_p_col_pos=1&p_p_col_count=2&_169_struts_action=%2Fdynamic_data_list_display%2Fview_record&_169_recordId=983669.
229. *Commission Delegated Regulation 2017/653.*
230. Private international law has been "Europeanized" through the adoption of the following Regulations: Rome I [Regulation 593/2008] on the determination of which national law is to applied to contractual obligations in civil and commercial cross-border situations; Rome II [Regulation 864/2007] on tort, non-contractual obligations; Rome III [Council Regulation 1259/2010] on divorce and legal separation; Brussels Regulation I [Council Regulation 44/2001] on Jurisdiction, recognition and enforcement of judgments in civil and commercial matters; and Brussels Regulation II bis [Council Regulation 2201/2003] on conflict of law matters in family law.
231. The words of Professor Svetiev shed light on the nature of Private International Law: "The traditional private international law focus is on functionally equivalent legal rules of different jurisdictions and the legitimate selection of a rule from the perspective of both the sovereigns and the parties involved." Yane Svetiev, "European Regulatory Private Law: From Conflicts to Platforms," in *Varieties of European Economic Law and Regulation: Liber Amicorum for Hans Micklitz*, ed. Kai Peter Purnhagen and Peter Rott (New York: Springer, 2014). At 165.
232. Recital 31: "In accordance with national law, Member States are not obliged to impose both administrative and criminal penalties for the same offence, but they should be able to do so if their national law so permits."
233. Article 40, Regulation 600/2014. ESMA also enjoys coordination powers in relation to product-intervention actions taken by competent authorities (Article 43 MiFIR).

234. Hans-Wolfgang Micklitz, "The Transformation of Enforcement in European Private Law: Preliminary Considerations," *European Review of Private Law* 4 (2015). At 503.
235. The label "MiFID II package" includes both Directive 2014/65/EU and Regulation 600/2014/EU. The label "MiFID II" only refers to Directive 2014/65/EU, whereas the label "MiFIR" on refers to Regulation 600/2014/EU.
236. Directive 2014/65/Eu.
237. Regulation 600/2014/Eu.
238. Despite the wording of Article 24 MiFID II, Professor Moloney rightly points out that MiFID II is de facto a full harmonization Directive in that it allows "[a] Member State [… to] impose additional requirements on investment firms […] only in 'exceptional cases' and where the rules in question are objectively justified and proportionate so as to address specific risks to investor protection or to market integrity which are of particular importance in the circumstances of the market structure of the Member State in question; these rules must not restrict or otherwise affect investment firms' passporting rights (Article 24(12))" Moloney, *EU Securities and Financial Markets Regulation*. At 791.
239. The list of the delegated acts and related RTSs is provided in Chap. 5.
240. The words of CONSOB, the Italian financial authority, implicitly reveal such a shift in regulatory powers: "Inoltre, come criterio generale seguito nell'attribuzione di potestà regolamentare alla Consob, al Regolamento Mercati è stata riservata la concreta declinazione nel sistema domestico delle modalità operative e dei connessi termini relativi all'adempimento di alcuni obblighi previsti dalle norme tecniche di regolamentazione e di attuazione di MiFID II e di MiFIR che, in quanto direttamente applicabili non necessitano di recepimento nell'ordinamento nazionale". [Author's own translation: "Furthermore, as a general criterion based on the attribution of regulatory powers to Consob, the *Regolamento Mercati* incorporates in the domestic system the operating procedures and related terms relating to the fulfillment of certain obligations provided for by the regulatory and implementing technical standards originated from MiFID II and MiFIR which, as directly applicable, do not need to be transposed into national law."] Commissione Nazionale per le Società e la Borsa - CONSOB, "Modifiche Al Regolamento Mercati - Documento Per La Consultazione" (2017).

241. On the two extremes of business values: Christopher Hodges, *Law and Corporate Behaviour: Integrating Theories of Regulation, Enforcement, Compliance and Ethics* (Oxford: Hart Publishing, 2015). At 669.
242. Carmine DiNoia, "Atto Del Governo N. 143 (Mercati Degli Strumenti Finanziari) – Audizione Informale, Commissione Finanze, Camera Dei Deputati" (2017). At 10.
243. European Supervisory Authorities—ESAs, "Placement of Financial Instruments with Depositors, Retail Investors and Policy Holders ('Self Placement')" (2014).
244. *Directive 2014/59/Eu*. The BRRD "stipulates that banks will need to build up sufficient loss-absorbing capacities to enable a failing bank to be stabilised without the need for a bail-out using public funds. This includes a mechanism for writing down (or bailing in) shareholders followed by unsecured creditors." ESAs, "Placement of Financial Instruments with Depositors, Retail Investors and Policy Holders ('Self Placement'),"
245. Article 4(1,23) states that "'organised trading facility' or 'OTF' means a multilateral system which is not a regulated market or an MTF and in which multiple third-party buying and selling interests in bonds, structured finance products, emission allowances or derivatives are able to interact in the system in a way that results in a contract in accordance with Title II of this Directive".
246. Article 32(2b), MiFIR.
247. *Regulation 648/2012/Eu*.
248. Emilio Avgouleas, "Regulating Financial Innovation," in *The Oxford Handbook of Financial Regulation*, ed. Eilís Ferran, Niamh Moloney, and Jennifer Payne (Oxford: Oxford University Press, 2015). At 679.
249. In the words of Dr. Carmine di Noia: "Inefficienza della sola "filosofia della trasparenza" a correggere le asimmetrie informative e mis-selling". [Author's own translation: "*Inefficiency of the only "philosophy of transparency" to correct information asymmetries and mis-selling*"] DiNoia.
250. Ibid.
251. *Commission Delegated Directive 2017/593/Eu*.
252. *Directive 2014/65/Eu*.
253. In 2011 the UK Financial Services Authority pointed out a strong connection between mis-selling and lack of understanding of the merchandise: "In recent mis-selling cases [...] for example Lehman-backed structured investment products where firms sold investments in high

concentrations because they misunderstood the associated and underlying risks." Financial Services Authority—FSA, "Guidance Consultation: Assessing Suitability" (2011). At 22.

254. On the "know the security" principle in the American context: Thomas Lee-Hazen, *Broker-Dealer Regulation in a Nutshell* (Thomson/West, 2003). At 160.
255. Professor Cherednychenko rightly points out that the EU lawmaker has come to a conclusion that "intervention through consumer empowerment at the point-of-sale alone is insufficient to stop products which may cause significant detriment to individual consumers and the financial market as a whole from reaching consumers. The idea behind the new product-oriented approach, therefore, is to deter the creation of investment products which are likely to cause such problems through product development oversight." Olha O. Cherednychenko, "Freedom of Contract in the Post-Crisis Era: Quo Vadis?," *European Review of Contract Law* 10, no. 3 (2014). At 401. For a transnational analysis of the phenomenon: Marcacci, "European Regulatory Private Law Going Global? The Case of Product Governance."
256. Arts. 9(6) and 10(8) of the *Commission Delegated Directive 2017/593/ Eu.*
257. On the link between PG and mis-selling: DiNoia.
258. Marcacci, "European Regulatory Private Law Going Global? The Case of Product Governance."
259. This effect is magnified by Product Intervention which "creates uncertainty for firms and shifts on them the responsibility for assessing the likely consumer detriment". Yane Svetiev and Annetje Ottow, "Financial Supervision in the Interstices between Private and Public Law," *European Review of Contract Law* 10, no. 4 (2014). At 508.
260. Professor Cherednychenko speaks of "hard paternalism in post-crisis financial services regulation". Olha O. Cherednychenko, "Freedom of Contract in the Post-Crisis Era: Quo Vadis?," ibid., no. 3. At 418. Similarly: Moloney, "Regulating the Retail Markets." At 763. On regulatory paternalism: Anthony Ogus, "Regulatory Paternalism: When Is It Justified?," in *Corporate Governance in Context: Corporations, States, and Markets in Europe, Japan, and the US*, ed. Klaus J. Hopt et al. (Oxford: Oxford University Press, 2005). Colin Camerer et al., "Regulation for Conservatives: Behavioral Economics and the Case for Asymmetric Paternalism," *University of Pennsylvania Law Review* 151 (2003). Professor

Guido Comparato too identifies a "new regulatory approach impacting on contractual relations can be viewed as a new wave of limitations to private autonomy, bringing new informative requirements, and even heading towards a more 'paternalistic' direction." Guido Comparato, "Factors Behind the Transformations of Private Law," in *European Regulatory Private Law – Autonomy, Competition and Regulation in European Private Law - Eui Working Paper Law 2016/06*, ed. Hans-Wolfgang Micklitz, Yane Svetiev, and Guido Comparato (Florence: European University Institute, 2016). At 19.

261. The "less-rational investor" label does not imply that investors are irrational but that they need or want to put their trust in someone else's hands in order to make their investment decisions. This is close to what Professor Stout defines as "trusting investors": "trusting investors do not behave as if they had what an economist would call 'rational expectations.' Rational expectations analysis assumes that people not only behave in a purely self-interested fashion, but also expect others always to behave in a purely self-interested fashion. [...] A trusting investor, in contrast, is willing to believe that at least some people [...] might for some reason be more trustworthy. Trusting investors accordingly look to the past: if someone has behaved in a particular fashion before, they assume that person will continue to behave similarly in the future, even if they don't fully understand what drives the behavior. (Economists sometimes describe this sort of backward-looking analysis as 'adaptive expectations,' to distinguish it from rational expectations.)" Lynn A. Stout, "The Investor Confidence Game," *Brooklyn Law Review* 68, no. 2 (2002). At 14–15.
262. The term is borrowed from book the Cass R. Sunstein and Richard H. Thaler, *Nudge: Improving Decisions About Health, Wealth and Happiness* (New York: Penguin, 2008).
263. See Chap. 7 for the definition of Litigation Risk.
264. Similarly, on the combination between private-law relationships and systemic risk, Professors Svetiev and Ottow rightly point out that: "failures in private law relationships have tended to combine with supervisory rules and regulatory requirements so as to exacerbate systemic risks in financial markets." Svetiev and Ottow. At 499.
265. Professors Svetiev and Ottow correctly point out that MiFID II steers "towards an emphasis on punitive administrative remedies for infringements of the rules." Ibid. At 501.

266. This is because, as correctly pointed out by Professor Maclain, "[t]he capacity of regulators to undertake enforcement is linked with their powers to investigate regulatory contraventions." Iain MacNeil, "Enforcement and Sanctioning," in *The Oxford Handbook of Financial Regulation*, ed. Niamh Moloney, Eilís Ferran, and Jennifer Payne (Oxford: Oxford University Press, 2015). At 287.
267. The same intervention powers are granted to the EBA as regards structured deposits by Article 41 MiFIR.
268. And the NCAs in charge of supervising structured deposits.
269. Unlike EIOPA, before making an intervention action ESMA must also ensure that public bodies competent for the oversight, administration, and regulation of physical agricultural markets under Regulation (EC) No 1234/2007 are consulted, where the measure relates to agricultural commodities derivatives (Article 40.3c).
270. Articles 19, 20 and 21. *Commission Delegated Regulation (EU) 2017/567*
271. Grounded on emergency powers under Article 9.5 of ESMA Regulation. See Chap. 5.
272. Heikki Marjosola, "Case C-270/12 (UK V Parliament and Council) – Stress Testing Constitutional Resilience of the Powers of EU Financial Supervisory Authorities – a Critical Assessment of the Advocate General's Opinion," in *EUI Working Paper Law 2014/02*, ed. European University Institute (2014). At 1.
273. Ibid. At 1.
274. Olha O. Cherednychenko, "The Regulation of Retail Investment Services in the EU: Towards the Improvement of Investor Rights?," *Journal of Consumer Policy* 33, no. 4 (2010). At 410. The US fiduciary duty, instead, is historically embedded into the common-law contract tradition and the US suitability rule has been directly developed by SROs and it operates, through private enforcement mechanisms, within the federal-state-SROs institutional framework. *See* Roberta S. Karmel, "Reconciling Federal and State Interests in Securities Regulation in the United States and Europe," *Brooklyn Journal of International Law* 28 (2003).
275. Hans-Wolfgang Micklitz, "Administrative Enforcement of European Private Law," in *The Foundations of European Private Law*, ed. Roger Brownsword et al. (Oxford-Portland: Hart Publishing, 2011). At 563.
276. On a similar wavelength, Marc Lenglet, "Ambivalence and Ambiguity: The Interpretive Role of Compliance Officers," in *Finance: The Discreet Regulator*, ed. Isabelle Huault and Chrystelle Richard (London: Palgrave Macmillan, 2012). At 61.

277. *Regulation 2017/1129/Eu.*
278. As officially stated in Recital 1 of the Prospectus Regulation.
279. Recital 7, *Regulation 2017/1129/Eu.*
280. European Commission, "Securities Prospectus," https://ec.europa.eu/info/business-economy-euro/banking-and-finance/financial-markets/securities-markets/securities-prospectus_en.
281. Article 1(3), *Regulation 2017/1129/Eu.*
282. "Securities Prospectus". Last visited: July 2017.
283. "Infographic: The New Prospectus Regulation" (2017). Last visited: July 2017.
284. "Securities Prospectus". Last visited: July 2017.
285. The summary is, anyhow, quite long as Article 7(3) provides it to be of a maximum length of seven (!) sides of A4-sized paper.
286. The language employed must be clear, non-technical, concise, and comprehensible (Article 7(3)) and cannot contain cross-references to other parts of the prospectus or incorporate information by reference (Article 7(11)).
287. Article 7(4 to 10).
288. In the words of the ESMA Chair, Steven Maijoor: "The crisis has shown that the absence of what we today call the single rulebook and supervisory convergence formed a dangerous cocktail whereby some Member States adopted a less strict approach to financial regulation and less stringent supervision to attract business." Steven Maijoor, "Keynote Speech - the Reform of Financial Markets: Halfway There - Afme European Post-Trade Conference, London - Esma/2014/478" (2014). At 12.
289. Based on the "rational expectations investor" model. Stout. At 7.
290. The EU law "has long been struggling to embed market finance in the single market by deploying a range of mechanisms, including regulatory tools". Niamh Moloney, Eilís Ferran, and Jennifer Payne, "Introduction," in *The Oxford Handbook of Financial Regulation*, ed. Niamh Moloney, Eilís Ferran, and Jennifer Payne (Oxford: Oxford University Press, 2015). At 6.
291. Filippo Zatti, "La Dimensione Costituzionale Della Tutela Del Risparmio. Dalla Tutela Del Risparmio Alla Protezione Dei Risparmiatori/Investitori E Ritorno?," in *Studi in Onore Di Vincenzo Atripaldi*, ed. Marco Benvenuti et al. (Naples: Jovene, 2010).
292. *Estée Lauder Cosmetics Gmbh & Co. Ohg V Lancaster Group Gmbh*, ECR I–117 (2000).
293. Hans-Wolfgang Micklitz, "Jack Is out of the Box – the Efficient Consumer-Shopper," *Juridiska Föreningen i Finland* 3, no. 4 (2009).

294. On the disclosure paradigm as regulatory technique: Emilios Avgouleas, "Emilios Avgouleas, "What Future for Disclosure as a Regulatory Technique? Lessons from Behavioural Decision Theory and the Global Financial Crisis," in *The Future of Financial Regulation*, ed. Justin O'Brien Iain G MacNeil (London: Bloomsbury Publishing, 2010). In the words of Professor Moloney: "Originally deployed as a means for addressing information asymmetries, the natural affiliation between disclosure, empowerment, and the construction of the investor as 'informed and empowered', as well as its support of firm and investor autonomy, led to disclosure becoming a key tool of the pre-crisis movement to promote investor engagement." Moloney, "Regulating the Retail Markets." At 754.
295. In the words of Professor Cherednychenko: "The dominance of the information paradigm pre-crisis." Cherednychenko, "Freedom of Contract in the Post-Crisis Era: Quo Vadis?." At 395.
296. In the words of Professor Moloney: "Disclosure, with its 'self-help' connotations, is strongly associated with the empowerment model." Moloney, *How to Protect Investors: Lessons from the EC and the UK*. At 288.
297. Again, Moloney: "Investor empowerment is [a]llied to this pro-market and instrumental approach […] typically in terms of informed and active investor decision-making, investor autonomy, wider investor choice and deeper investor engagement." Ibid. At 53.
298. Peter Cartwright, "Optimal Consumer Protection in Financial Services," in *ECRI/CEPS SEMINAR at the European Credit Research Institute and Centre for European Policy Studies* (Brussels, 2001). At 7.
299. On such a legislative approach, it has been argued that consumer law cannot be just a tool to filling up the gaps of a market system: "At stake are elements of the correction of market failure and, additionally, the achievement of fairness to consumers (inter alia) as the economically weaker parties. Consumer protection law has a wide range of forms and objectives." Geraint Howells and Stephen Weatherill, eds., *Consumer Protection Law, 2nd Ed.* (Hants Ashgate, 2005).
300. Professors Enriques and Gilotta highlight that many, "especially policymakers, contend that protecting investors is instrumental to the well-functioning—if not to the very existence—of the market and has thus an efficiency justification. Providing investors with adequate protection increases their confidence in the market." Enriques and Gilotta. At 515.
301. Micklitz, "Jack Is out of the Box – the Efficient Consumer-Shopper." At 422. Professor Moloney connects "the nature of the 'financial citizen', the extent to which individuals can be 'financialized' and regarded

as agents of government withdrawal from welfare provision, and the related implications for regulatory design". Moloney, "Regulating the Retail Markets." At 746.

302. In the words of Professor Micklitz: "It is therefore fair to speak of the "rise" of European law following the adoption of the Single European Act. This trend is so obvious that there is no need to discuss it." Micklitz, "The Visible Hand of European Regulatory Private Law—the Transformation of European Private Law from Autonomy to Functionalism in Competition and Regulation." At 18.
303. Again Micklitz: "The starting point is the famous 1985 White Paper on the Completion of the Internal Market, developed under the presidency of Jacques Delors, which paved the way for the adoption of the Single European Act." In: "Judicial Activism of the European Court of Justice and the Development of the European Social Model in Anti-Discrimination and Consumer Law," in *EUI Working Papers LAW 2009/19*, ed. European University Institute (Florence, 2009). At 7.
304. Eddy Wymeersch, "The Reforms of the European Financial Supervisory System," *European Company and Financial Law Review* 7, no. 2 (2010). At 242.
305. "Rational investors, so goes the idea, will read the prospectus and on that basis decide whether or not to invest in the securities that are offered to them." Van Dyck. At 3.
306. On the evolution of disclosure design for the retail markets: Moloney, "Regulating the Retail Markets." At 756.
307. As MiFID I was entering into force, in the 2007 Green Paper on Retail Financial Services the Commission formally recognized that information disclosure "is often inadequate or too complex, making it difficult to compare prices, products and providers and to take an informed financial decision." European Commission, "Green Paper on Retail Financial Services in the Single Market" (Brussels, 2007). At 16.
308. Professor Cherednychenko rightly points out that: "These rules largely reflect the regulatory philosophy of promoting rather than restricting investor autonomy and choice in the retail investment market. Building upon the information paradigm, the pre-crisis EU regulatory regime for investment services embodied in the MiFID I does not intervene closely in the substance of investment decisions or the products distributed to retail investors. Instead, it heavily relies on information- and suitability rules in order to produce well-informed and empowered retail investors who would be able to make good investment decisions

for themselves." Cherednychenko, "Freedom of Contract in the Post-Crisis Era: Quo Vadis?." At 395–396.

309. On the empowered investor: Moloney, *How to Protect Investors: Lessons from the EC and the UK*. At 53–67.
310. On this point: European Securities and Markets Authorities—ESMA, "Final Report - Guidelines on Complex Debt Instruments and Structured Deposits - Esma/2015/1783" (2015); European Securities and Markets Authorities—ESMA, "Guidelines on Complex Debt Instruments and Structured Deposits - Esma/2015/1787" (2016).
311. In Latin: "Let the buyer beware."
312. Moloney, "Regulating the Retail Markets." At 741.
313. Cherednychenko, "Public and Private Enforcement of European Private Law in the Financial Services Sector." at 632. As Cherednychenko writes: "From a legal-technical point of view, European supervision private law rules [...] concern the relationship between a particular business and an administrative agency entrusted with the supervisory and enforcement tasks and, hence, they do not belong to the realm of traditional private law, in particular contract law. At the same time, such rules set standards of behaviour in the relationship between a business and its (potential) client and also aim to protect the latter. In essence, therefore, European supervision private law rules affect the relationships between private parties and can thus be considered as quasi-private." At 632.
314. Professor Chiu speaks of "gatekeepers". Iris H-Y Chiu, *Regulating (from) the Inside: The Legal Framework for Internal Control in Banks and Financial Institutions* (London: Bloomsbury Publishing, 2015). At 271.
315. Cafaggi and Micklitz. At 37.
316. As it is the case under Article 35a of the Credit Rating Agency Regulation: "Where a credit rating agency has committed, intentionally or with gross negligence, any of the infringements listed in Annex III having an impact on a credit rating, an investor or issuer may claim damages from that credit rating agency for damage caused to it due to that infringement. [...] Terms such as "damage", "intention", "gross negligence", "reasonably relied", "due care", "impact", "reasonable" and "proportionate" which are referred to in this Article but are not defined, shall be interpreted and applied in accordance with the applicable national law as determined by the relevant rules of private international law". *Regulation Eu/462/2013*.
317. MiFIR Recital 29 and PRIIPs Recital 25.

318. Moloney, "Regulating the Retail Markets." At 762. Professor MacNeil views an ex post approach as less intrusive in terms of financial innovation than the ex ante approval of products: "Product intervention, on the other hand, is a less intrusive technique which attempts to adjust the balance towards innovation by permitting new products without prior approval but subject to the risk of subsequent intervention. That approach inevitably creates some uncertainty for financial firms in that they are exposed to the risk of subsequent intervention to restrict or limit the sale of new products." Iain MacNeil, "Product Regulation and Governance," *Law and Financial Markets Review* 7, no. 3 (2015). At 135. On product approval, Professors Svetiev and Ottow rightly point out that: "the more that regulatory agencies intrude in the substance of contractual relationships between providers and customers, such as by vetting or approving products or having the responsibility to prevent the marketing of certain types of products, the more customers can legitimately turn to them for facilitating or even providing redress if such products turn sour." Svetiev and Ottow. At 511.The term "moral hazard" has been defined by Professor Paul Krugman as "any situation in which one person makes the decision about how much risk to take, while someone else bears the cost if things go badly". Paul R. Krugman, *The Return of Depression Economics* (London: Penguin UK, 2008). At 165. An interesting legal analysis is given by Tom Baker, "On the Genealogy of Moral Hazard," *Texas Law Review* 75, no. 2 (1996).
319. For Italian readers, on administrative discretion: Bernardo Mattarella, "Il Procedimento," in *Istituzioni Di Diritto Amministrativo*, ed. Sabino Cassese (Milan: Giuffrè Editore, 2012). At 256–270. Interestingly, Professor MacNiel rightly points out that: "The level of discretion granted to the regulator with respect to enforcement is a significant factor for the choice of enforcement strategy." MacNeil, "Enforcement and Sanctioning." At 284.
320. Art. 19, 20 and 21 *Commission Delegated Regulation Eu/2017/567.*
321. Article 19, 20 and 21, ibid.
322. In the words of Joseph Ackermann, then chief executive of Deutsche Bank: "I no longer believe in the market's self-healing power", as reported by Martin Wolf, "The Rescue of Bear Stearns Marks Liberalisation's Limit," *Financial Times* 2008.
323. Already in 2013, the ESAs highlighted how "product intervention should be seen in the round, as part of product design, product governance, and product distribution in order to address consumer protection issues

before and up to point of sale, rather than playing catch-up after products hit the market." Joint Committee of the European Supervisory Authorities—ESAs, "Joint Esas Consumer Protection Day," https://eiopa.europa.eu/Pages/Events/Event-2.aspx.

324. Moloney, *How to Protect Investors: Lessons from the EC and the UK.* At 80. On this subject: Cass R. Sunstein, *Why Nudge?: The Politics of Libertarian Paternalism* (New Haven: Yale University Press, 2015).
325. Professor Cherednychenko speaks of "hard paternalism in post-crisis financial services regulation". Cherednychenko, "Freedom of Contract in the Post-Crisis Era: Quo Vadis?." At 418. Similarly: Moloney, "Regulating the Retail Markets." At 763. On regulatory paternalism: Ogus. Camerer et al.
326. Cherednychenko, "Freedom of Contract in the Post-Crisis Era: Quo Vadis?." At 400.
327. See Chap. 5.
328. For instance, a firm may be fined if it has not put in place controls to monitor the correctness of switching.
329. "What could only be found in a rudimentary form in the 2004 Directive (MIFID I)—the shift from prudential supervision to post market control—is gaining impetus with MIFID II." Hans-Wolfgang Micklitz, "The Public and the Private – European Regulatory Private Law and Financial Services," *European Review of Contract Law* 10, no. 4 (2014). At 473.
330. In these terms: Cherednychenko, "Public Supervision over Private Relationships: Towards European Supervision Private Law?" At 45.

Bibliography

Abrams, Richard K., and Michael Taylor. "Issues in the Unification of Financial Sector Supervision." In *IMF Working Papers No. 00/213*, edited by International Monetary Fund. Washington, DC, 2000.

Abrams, Richard K., and Michael W. Taylor. *Assessing the Case for Unified Financial Sector Supervision.* Financial Markets Group, London School of Economics and Political Science, 2002.

Alpine Investments Bv V Minister Van Financiën, 1995.

Avgouleas, Emilios. "What Future for Disclosure as a Regulatory Technique? Lessons from Behavioural Decision Theory and the Global Financial Crisis."

In *The Future of Financial Regulation*, edited by Iain G. MacNeil and Justin O'Brien, 205–26. London: Bloomsbury Publishing, 2010.

Avgouleas, Emilio. "Regulating Financial Innovation." In *The Oxford Handbook of Financial Regulation*, edited by Eilís Ferran, Niamh Moloney, and Jennifer Payne. Oxford: Oxford University Press, 2015.

Baker, Tom. "On the Genealogy of Moral Hazard." *Texas Law Review* 75, no. 2 (1996): 237–92.

Bank of England. "Bank of England Quarterly Bulletin." 1977.

Bartels, Boris, Julien Ernoult, Sandra Hafner, and Inci Metin. *European Banking and Financial Services Law - Fourth Edition*. Brussels: Larcier, 2010.

BBC. "Libor: What Is It and Why Does It Matter?". http://www.bbc.com/news/business-19199683.

Biondi, Andrea, and Martin Farley. *The Right to Damages in European Law*. Alphen aan den Rijn: Kluwer Law International, 2009.

Bocci, Matteo, Jan Maarten De Vet, and Andreas Pauer. "'Gold-Plating' in the Eafrd. To What Extent Do National Rules Unnecessarily Add to Complexity and, as a Result, Increase the Risk of Errors?" In *Ref.: IP/D/AL/FWC/209-056*, edited by European Parliament - Directorate-General for Internal Policies. Brussels, 2014.

deBrito, Jorde, and Sònia Teixeira daMota. "The Pros and Cons of the Prospectus Directive." *International Financial Law Review*, 2005. http://www.iflr.com/Article/1984744/The-pros-and-cons-of-the-Prospectus-Directive.html.

Brummer, Chris. *Soft Law and the Global Financial System: Rule Making in the 21st Century*. Cambridge; New York: Cambridge University Press, 2012.

Busch, Danny. "Why Mifid Matters to Private Law—the Example of Mifid's Impact on an Asset Manager's Civil Liability." *Capital Markets Law Journal* 7, no. 4 (2012): 386–413.

———. "Agency and Principal Dealing under the Market in Financial Instruments Directive." In *Agency Law in Commercial Practice*, edited by Danny Busch, Laura Macgregor, and Peter Watts. Oxford: Oxford University Press, 2016.

Cafaggi, Fabrizio, and Hans-Wolfgang Micklitz. "Administrative and Judicial Collective Enforcement of Consumer Law in the US and the European Community." In *European University Institute - Law Working Paper 2007/22*, 2007.

Camerer, Colin, Samuel Issacharoff, George Loewenstein, and Ted O'Donoghue. "Regulation for Conservatives: Behavioral Economics and the Case for Asymmetric Paternalism." *University of Pennsylvania Law Review* 151 (2003): 1211–54.

Cartwright, Peter. "Optimal Consumer Protection in Financial Services." In *ECRI/CEPS SEMINAR at the European Credit Research Institute and Centre for European Policy Studies*. Brussels, 2001.

Casey, Jean-Pierre, and Karel Lannoo, eds. *The Mifid Revolution*. Cambridge: Cambridge University Press, 2009.

Casper, Matthias, and Christian Altgen. "Chapter 4 – Germany." In *Liability of Asset Managers*, edited by Danny Busch and Deborah DeMott. Oxford: Oxford University Press, 2012.

CESR, Committee of European Securities Regulators -. "A Guide to Clear Language and Layout for the Key Investor Information Document (Kii) - Cesr/10-532." 2010.

Cherednychenko, Olha O. "European Securities Regulation, Private Law and the Investment Firm-Client Relationship." *European Review of Private Law* 17, no. 5 (2009): 925–52.

———. "The Regulation of Retail Investment Services in the EU: Towards the Improvement of Investor Rights?". *Journal of Consumer Policy* 33, no. 4 (2010): 403–24.

———. "Full Harmonisation of Retail Financial Services Contract Law in Europe: A Success or a Failure?". In *Financial Services, Financial Crisis and General European Contract Law: Failure and Challenges of Contracting*, edited by Stefan Grundmann and Yeşim M. Atamer, 221–58. Alphen aan den Rijn: Kluwer Law International, 2011.

———. "Financial Consumer Protection in the EU: Towards a Self-Sufficient European Contract Law for Consumer Financial Services?". *European Review of Contract Law* 10, no. 4 (2014a): 476–95.

———. "Freedom of Contract in the Post-Crisis Era: Quo Vadis?". *European Review of Contract Law* 10, no. 3 (2014b): 390–421.

———. "Public Supervision over Private Relationships: Towards European Supervision Private Law?". *European Review of Private Law* 22 no. 1 (2014c): 37–68.

———. "Public and Private Enforcement of European Private Law in the Financial Services Sector." *European Review of Private Law* 24, no. 4 (2015): 621–47.

Chiu, Iris H.-Y. *Regulating (from) the Inside: The Legal Framework for Internal Control in Banks and Financial Institutions*. London: Bloomsbury Publishing, 2015.

Chlistalla, Michael, Uwe Schweickert, and Roland Wittner. "Markets in Financial Instruments Directive - the Way Forward in European Securities

Market Integration?." In *E-Finance Lab, Johann Wolfgang Goethe-University - Working Paper*, 2006.
Čihák, Martin, and Richard Podpiera. "Is One Watchdog Better Than Three? International Experience with Integrated Financial Sector Supervision." In *IMF Working Papers No. 06/57*, edited by International Monetary Fund. Washington, DC, 2006.
———. "Integrated Financial Supervision: Which Model?". *The North American Journal of Economics and Finance* 19, no. 2 (2008): 135–52.
Commission Delegated Directive 2017/593/Eu.
Commission Delegated Regulation (Eu) 2016/301.
Commission Delegated Regulation (Eu) 2017/567.
Commission Delegated Regulation 2017/653.
Commission Delegated Regulation 382/2014.
Commission Delegated Regulation 486/2012.
Commission Delegated Regulation 759/2013.
Commission Delegated Regulation 862/2012.
Commission Delegated Regulation Eu/2017/567.
Commission Directive 2006/73/Ec.
Commission Directive 2007/14/Ec.
Commission Directive 2010/42/Eu.
Commission Directive 2010/43/Eu.
Commission of the European Communities. "Completing the Internal Market: White Paper from the Commission to the European Council." Brussels, 1985.
Commission Recommendation 2004/384/Ec.
Commission Recommendation 583/2010.
Commission Recommendation 584/2010.
Commission Recommendation 77/534/Eec of 25 July 1977 Concerning a European Code of Conduct Relating to Transactions in Transferable Securities.
Commission Regulation 211/2007.
Commission Regulation 809/2004.
Comparato, Guido. "Factors Behind the Transformations of Private Law." In *European Regulatory Private Law – Autonomy, Competition and Regulation in European Private Law - Eui Working Paper Law 2016/06*, edited by Hans-Wolfgang Micklitz, Yane Svetiev, and Guido Comparato. Florence: European University Institute, 2016.
CONSOB, Commissione Nazionale per le Società e la Borsa -. "I Singoli Servizi Di Investimento." http://www.consob.it/web/investor-education/i-singoli-servizi-di-investimento#5.

———. "Modifiche Al Regolamento Mercati - Documento Per La Consultazione." 2017.
Council Directive 73/183/Eec.
Council Directive 79/279/Eec.
———.
Council Directive 80/390/Eec.
Council Directive 82/121/Eec.
———.
Council Directive 83/350/Eec.
Council Directive 88/627/Eec.
Council Directive 89/390/Eec.
Council Directive 93/22/Eec.
Council of the European Union. "2283rd Council Meeting - Ecofin 17 July 2000." Brussels, 2000.
Council Regulation 1259/2010.
Council Regulation 2201/2003.
Council Regulation 44/2001.
Craig, Paul. "The Evolution of the Single Market." In *The Law of the Single European Market - Unpacking the Premises*, edited by Catherine Barnard and Joanne Scott. Portland: Hart Publishing, 2002.
D'Hondt, Catherine, and Jean-René Giraud. "Mifid: The (in)Famous European Directive?" *EDHEC Position Paper*, 2007.
Davies, Ryan J. "Mifid and a Changing Competitive Landscape." In SSRN. https://ssrn.com/abstract=1117232 or https://doi.org/10.2139/ssrn.1117232, 2008.
DiNoia, Carmine. "Atto Del Governo N. 143 (Mercati Degli Strumenti Finanziari) – Audizione Informale, Commissione Finanze, Camera Dei Deputati." 2017.
Directive 2001/107/Ec.
Directive 2001/108/Ec.
Directive 2001/24/Ec.
Directive 2001/34/Ec.
Directive 2002/87/Ec.
Directive 2003/124/Ec.
Directive 2003/6/Ec.
Directive 2003/71/Ec.
Directive 2004/109/Ec.
Directive 2004/39/Ec.
Directive 2008/10/Ec.

Directive 2009/65/Ec.
Directive 2010/73/Eu.
Directive 2010/78/Eu.
Directive 2013/50/Eu.
Directive 2014/49/Eu.
Directive 2014/59/Eu.
Directive 2014/65/Eu.
Directive 2014/91/Eu.
Directive 85/611/Eec.
Directive 88/627/Eec.
Directive 89/298/Eec.
Directive 93/22/Eec.

———.

Directive 94/19/Ec.
Directive 97/9/Ec.

EBA, European Banking Authority -. "Joint Associations Committee on Retail Structured Products." http://www.eba.europa.eu/regulation-and-policy/consumer-protection-and-financial-innovation/regulatory-technical-standards-on-the-content-and-presentation-of-the-kids-for-priips?p_p_auth=gR5dgLnl&p_p_id=169&p_p_lifecycle=0&-p_p_state=maximized&p_p_col_id=column-2&p_p_col_pos=1&p_p_col_count=2&_169_struts_action=%2Fdynamic_data_list_display%2Fview_record&_169_recordId=983669.

———. "The Single Rulebook." http://www.eba.europa.eu/regulation-and-policy/single-rulebook.

Eichengreen, Barry, and Nergiz Dincer. "Who Should Supervise? The Structure of Bank Supervision and the Performance of the Financial System…" In *NBER Working Paper 17401*, edited by National Bureau of Economic Research. Cambridge, 2011.

Enriques, Luca, and Matteo Gatti. "Is There a Uniform EU Securities Law after the Financial Services Action Plan?". *Stanford Journal of Law, Business and Finance* 14, no. 43 (2008).

Enriques, Luca, and Sergio Gilotta. "Disclosure and Financial Market Regulation." In *The Oxford Handbook of Financial Regulation*, edited by Niamh Moloney, Eilís Ferran, and Jennifer Payne. Oxford: Oxford University Press, 2015.

Ernoult, Julien, Walburga Hemetsberger, Henning Schoppmann, and Christoph Wengler. *European Banking and Financial Services Law: Third Edition.* Brussels: Larcier, 2008.

ESAs, Joint Committee of the European Supervisory Authorities -. "Joint Esas Consumer Protection Day." https://eiopa.europa.eu/Pages/Events/Event-2.aspx.

ESMA, European Securities and Markets Authorities -. "Final Report - Guidelines on Complex Debt Instruments and Structured Deposits - Esma/2015/1783." 2015.

———, European Securities and Markets Authorities -. "Guidelines on Complex Debt Instruments and Structured Deposits - Esma/2015/1787." 2016.

ESMA, European Securities and Markets Authority -. "The Securities and Markets Stakeholders Group - Smsg.". https://www.esma.europa.eu/about-esma/governance/smsg.

Estée Lauder Cosmetics Gmbh & Co. Ohg V Lancaster Group Gmbh, ECR I–117 (2000).

European Commission. "European Banking Committee." https://ec.europa.eu/info/business-economy-euro/banking-and-finance/financial-reforms-and-their-progress/regulatory-process-financial-services/expert-groups-comitology-and-other-committees/european-banking-committee_en.

———. "European Insurance and Occupational Pensions Committee." https://ec.europa.eu/info/business-economy-euro/banking-and-finance/financial-reforms-and-their-progress/regulatory-process-financial-services/expert-groups-comitology-and-other-committees/european-insurance-and-occupational-pensions-committee_en.

———. "European Securities Committee." https://ec.europa.eu/info/business-economy-euro/banking-and-finance/financial-reforms-and-their-progress/regulatory-process-financial-services/expert-groups-comitology-and-other-committees/european-securities-committee_en.

———. "Financial Services Action Plan (Fsap)." http://europa.eu/legislation_summaries/internal_market/single_market_services/financial_services_general_framework/l24210_en.htm.

———. "Infographic: The New Prospectus Regulation." 2017.

———. "Internal Market and Services Directorate General Webpage." http://ec.europa.eu/internal_market/investment/investor_information/index_en.htm.

———. "Optem Report - Study on Pre-Contractual Information for Financial Services." 2008.

———. "Securities Prospectus." https://ec.europa.eu/info/business-economy-euro/banking-and-finance/financial-markets/securities-markets/securities-prospectus_en.

———. "Withdrawal of Commission Proposals - Oj L 80/17, 7.3.2015." 2015.

———. "Financial Services: Commission Outlines Action Plan for Single Financial Market." Brussels, 1999a.

———. "Financial Services: Implementing the Framework for Financial Markets: Action Plan." Brussels, 1999b.

———. "Background Note on the Draft Commission Directive Implementing Mifid." 2006a.

——— - Internal Market and Services Directorate General. "Workshop on Simplified Prospectus - Annotated Agenda of 1st Meeting." 2006b.

———. "Fsap Evaluation." Brussels, 2007a.

———. "Green Paper on Retail Financial Services in the Single Market." Brussels, 2007b.

———. "Consultation on Legislative Steps for the Packaged Retail Investment Products Initiative - Objective of the Consultation." 2010.

———. "Commission Proposes Legislation to Improve Consumer Protection in Financial Services." Brussels, 2012.

———. "Action Plan on Building a Capital Markets Union - Com/2015/0468 Final." 2015.

———. "Consumer Financial Services Action Plan: Better Products, More Choice - Com (2017) 139 Final." 2017.

European Securities and Markets Authority - ESMA. "Questions and Answers - Key Investor Information Document for Ucits (Ref. 2012/592)." Paris, 2012.

European Securities Markets Expert Group – ESME. "Report on Directive 2003/71/Ec." 2007.

European Supervisory Authorities - ESAs. "Placement of Financial Instruments with Depositors, Retail Investors and Policy Holders ('Self Placement')." 2014.

Ferran, Eilís. *Building an EU Securities Market.* Cambridge: Cambridge University Press, 2004.

Financial Services Authority - FSA. "Guidance Consultation: Assessing Suitability." 2011.

First Council Directive 77/780/Eec.

Fischer-Appelt, Dorothee. "Prospectus Directive Amendments – Discussion of Key Changes." *Law and Financial Markets Review* 4, no. 5 (2010).

G30. "The Structure of Financial Supervision: Approaches and Challenges in a Global Marketplace - Working Group on Financial Supervision." 2008.

Galletti, Danilo. "Le Crisi Bancarie E La Tutela Dei Depositanti." In *Banche E Mercati Finanziari*, edited by Francesco Vella. Torino: Giappichelli, 2009.

Giudici, Paolo, and Matteo Bet. "Chapter 5 – Italy." In *Liability of Asset Managers*, edited by Danny Busch and Deborah DeMott. Oxford: Oxford University Press, 2012.

Group of Experts Appointed by the EEC Commission. "The Segré Report - the Development of a European Capital Market." 1966.

Haar, Brigitte. "Organizing Regional Systems: The EU Example." In *The Oxford Handbook of Financial Regulation*, edited by Niamh Moloney, Eilís Ferran, and Jennifer Payne. Oxford: Oxford University Press, 2015.

Haas, François. "The Markets in Financial Instruments Directive: Banking on Market and Supervisory Efficiency." In *International Monetary Fund Working Paper No. 07/250*, 2007.

Hodges, Christopher. *Law and Corporate Behaviour: Integrating Theories of Regulation, Enforcement, Compliance and Ethics*. Oxford: Hart Publishing, 2015.

Howells, Geraint, and Stephen Weatherill, eds. *Consumer Protection Law*, 2nd ed. Hants: Ashgate, 2005.

Hudson, Alastair. "The Synthesis of Public and Private in Finance Law." In *Private Law: Key Encounters with Public Law*, edited by Kit Barker and Darryn Jensen, 231–64. Cambridge: Cambridge University Press, 2013.

Karmel, Roberta S. "Reconciling Federal and State Interests in Securities Regulation in the United States and Europe." *Brooklyn Journal of International Law* 28 (2003).

Kremers, Jeroen J. M., Dirk Schoenmaker, and Peter J. Wierts. "Cross-Sector Supervision: Which Model?" In *Brookings-Wharton Papers on Financial Services 2003*, edited by Brookings Institution and the Financial Institutions Center at the Wharton School, 225–43. Philadelphia, 2003.

Krugman, Paul R. *The Return of Depression Economics*. London: Penguin UK, 2008.

Kruithof, Marc. "A Differentiated Approach to Client Protection: The Example of Mifid." In *Financial Services, Financial Crisis and General European Contract Law: Failure and Challenges of Contracting*, edited by Stefan Grundmann and Yesim M Atamer, 105–62. New York: Kluwer Law International, 2011.

Kudrna, Zdenek. "Financial Market Regulation: A 'Lamfalussy Exit' from the Joint-Decision Trap." In *The EU's Decision Traps: Comparing Policies*, edited by Gerda Falkner. Oxford: Oxford University Press, 2011.

Lannoo, Karel. "Ecb Banking Supervision and Beyond - Ceps Task Force Reports." Centre for European Policy Studies - CEPS, 2014.

Lee, Kwangwook. "Investor Protection in European Union: Post Fsap Directives and Mifid." In *SSRN*. https://ssrn.com/abstract=1339305 or https://doi.org/10.2139/ssrn.1339305, 2009.

Lee-Hazen, Thomas. *Broker-Dealer Regulation in a Nutshell*. Eagan: Thomson/West, 2003.

Lenglet, Marc. "Ambivalence and Ambiguity: The Interpretive Role of Compliance Officers." In *Finance: The Discreet Regulator*, edited by Isabelle Huault and Chrystelle Richard. London: Palgrave Macmillan, 2012.

Macey, Jonathan R., and Maureen O'Hara. "The Law and Economics of Best Execution." *Journal of Financial Intermediation* 6 (1997): 188–223.

MacNeil, Iain. "Enforcement and Sanctioning." In *The Oxford Handbook of Financial Regulation*, edited by Niamh Moloney, Eilís Ferran, and Jennifer Payne. Oxford: Oxford University Press, 2015a.

———. "Product Regulation and Governance." *Law and Financial Markets Review* 7, no. 3 (2015b): 135–37.

Maijoor, Steven. "Keynote Speech - the Reform of Financial Markets: Halfway There - Afme European Post-Trade Conference, London - Esma/2014/478." 2014.

Mak, Vanessa. "Review of the Consumer Acquis: Towards Maximum Harmonization?". *European Review of Private Law* 17, no. 1 (2009): 55–73.

———. "Financial Services and Consumer Protection." In *Research Handbook on EU Consumer and Contract Law*, edited by Christian Twigg-Flesner. Northampton: Edward Elgar, 2016.

Marcacci, Antonio. "What Is Still Missing to Achieve an Optimum Currency Area under EU Law?". *Italian Journal of Public Law* 1-2017 (2017).

———. "Digitally-Provided Financial Services under EU Law: Overcoming the Current Patchwork of Europeanized Private International Law and Sectorially-Harmonized National Private Laws." *Studi sull'integrazione europea* 12, no. 3 (2017a).

———. "European Regulatory Private Law Going Global? The Case of Product Governance." *European Business Organization Law Review* 18, no. 2 (2017b): 305–32.

Marjosola, Heikki. "Case C-270/12 (UK V Parliament and Council) – Stress Testing Constitutional Resilience of the Powers of EU Financial Supervisory Authorities – a Critical Assessment of the Advocate General's Opinion." In *EUI Working Paper Law 2014/02*, edited by European University Institute, 2014a.

———. "What Role for Courts in Protecting Investors in Europe: A View from Finland." *European Review of Contract Law* 10, no. 4 (2014b): 545–70.

Mattarella, Bernardo. "Il Procedimento." In *Istituzioni Di Diritto Amministrativo*, edited by Sabino Cassese. Milan: Giuffrè Editore, 2012.

Micklitz, Hans-Wolfgang. "The Regulatory Strategies on Services Contracts in EC Law," edited by European University Institute. Florence, 2008.

———. "Jack Is out of the Box – the Efficient Consumer-Shopper." *Juridiska Föreningen i Finland* 3, no. 4 (2009a): 417–36.

———. "Judicial Activism of the European Court of Justice and the Development of the European Social Model in Anti-Discrimination and Consumer Law." In *EUI Working Papers LAW 2009/19*, edited by European University Institute. Florence, 2009b.

———. "The Targeted Full Harmonisation Approach: Looking Behind the Curtain." In *Modernising and Harmonising Consumer Contract Law*, edited by Reiner Schulze Geraint Howells, pp. 47–86: Paperback, 2009c.

———. "The Visible Hand of European Regulatory Private Law—the Transformation of European Private Law from Autonomy to Functionalism in Competition and Regulation." *Yearbook of European Law* 28, no. 1 (2009d): 3–59.

———. "Administrative Enforcement of European Private Law." In *The Foundations of European Private Law*, edited by Roger Brownsword, Hans-Wolfgang Micklitz, Leone Niglia, and Stephen Weatherill, 563–92. Oxford-Portland: Hart Publishing, 2011.

———. "The Public and the Private – European Regulatory Private Law and Financial Services." *European Review of Contract Law* 10, no. 4 (2014).

———. "The Transformation of Enforcement in European Private Law: Preliminary Considerations." *European Review of Private Law* 4 (2015): 491–524.

Micklitz, Hans-Wolfgang, and Dennis Patterson. "From the Nation State to the Market: The Evolution of EU Private Law." In *EUI Working Paper Law 2012/15*, edited by European University Institute. Florence, 2012.

Micklitz, Hans W., and Stephen Weatherill. "The Economic Constitution of the European Community." In *European Economic Law*, edited by Hans W. Micklitz and Stephen Weatherill. Farnham, UK: Ashgate Publishing, 1997.

Moloney, Niamh. "Building a Retail Investment Culture through Law: The 2004 Markets in Financial Instruments Directive." *European Business Organization Law Review* 6, no. 3 (2005): 341–421.

———. *EC Securities Regulation*, 2nd ed. Oxford EC Law Library. Oxford: Oxford University Press, 2008.

———. *How to Protect Investors: Lessons from the EC and the UK*. Cambridge: Cambridge University Press, 2010.

———. *EU Securities and Financial Markets Regulation*. Oxford: Oxford University Press, 2014a.

———. "European Banking Union: Assessing Its Risks and Resilience." *Common Market Law Review* 51, no. 6 (2014b): 1609–70.

———. "Regulating the Retail Markets." In *The Oxford Handbook of Financial Regulation*, edited by Niamh Moloney, Eilís Ferran, and Jennifer Payne. Oxford: Oxford University Press, 2015.

Moloney, Niamh, Eilís Ferran, and Jennifer Payne. "Introduction." In *The Oxford Handbook of Financial Regulation*, edited by Niamh Moloney, Eilís Ferran, and Jennifer Payne. Oxford: Oxford University Press, 2015.

Mülbert, Peter O. "The Eclipse of Contract Law in the Investment Firm-Client Relationship: The Impact of the Mifid on the Law of Contract from a German Perspective." In *Investor Protection in Europe: Corporate Law Making, the Mifid and Beyond*, edited by Guido Ferrarini and Eddy Wymeersch, 299–320. Oxford: Oxford University Press, 2006.

Nelson, Paul. *Capital Markets Law and Compliance*. New York: Cambridge University Press, 2008.

Ogus, Anthony. "Regulatory Paternalism: When Is It Justified?". In *Corporate Governance in Context: Corporations, States, and Markets in Europe, Japan, and the US*, edited by Klaus J. Hopt, Eddy Wymeersch, Hideka Kanda, and Harald Baum. Oxford: Oxford University Press, 2005.

Peter Paul and Others V Bundesrepublik Deutschland, ECR I-09425 (2004).

Proposal for a Directive of the European Parliament and of the Council Amending Directive 97/9/Ec.

Regulation 1060/2009/Ec.

Regulation 1095/2010.

Regulation 1286/2014/Eu.

Regulation 2016/1011/Eu.

Regulation 2017/1129/Eu.

Regulation 513/2011/Eu.

Regulation 593/2008.

Regulation 596/2014/Eu.

Regulation 600/2014.

Regulation 600/2014/Eu.

Regulation 648/2012/Eu.

Regulation 864/2007.

Regulation Eu/236/2012.

Regulation Eu/462/2013.

Rewe-Zentral Ag V Bundesmonopolverwaltung Für Branntwein (Cassis De Dijon), ECR I-649 (1979).

Reyners V Belgium, ECR 00631 (1974).

SEC, Securities and Exchange Commission. "A Plain English Handbook." Washington, DC, 1998.

Spector Photo Group Nv and Chris Van Raemdonck V Commissie Voor Het Bank-, Financie- En Assurantiewezen (Cbfa), ECR I-12073, 2009.

Stout, Lynn A. "The Investor Confidence Game." *Brooklyn Law Review* 68, no. 2 (2002a): 407–37.

———. "The Investor Confidence Game." *Brooklyn Law Review* 68, no. 2 (2002b).

Sunstein, Cass R. *Why Nudge?: The Politics of Libertarian Paternalism*. New Haven: Yale University Press, 2015.

Sunstein, Cass R., and Richard H. Thaler. *Nudge: Improving Decisions About Health, Wealth and Happiness*. New York: Penguin, 2008.

Supervision, Basel Committee on Banking. "Basel Committee Organisation and Governance." https://www.bis.org/bcbs/organ_and_gov.htm.

Svetiev, Yane. "European Regulatory Private Law: From Conflicts to Platforms." In *Varieties of European Economic Law and Regulation: Liber Amicorum for Hans Micklitz*, edited by Kai Peter Purnhagen and Peter Rott, 153–78. New York: Springer, 2014.

Svetiev, Yane, and Annetje Ottow. "Financial Supervision in the Interstices between Private and Public Law." *European Review of Contract Law* 10, no. 4 (2014): 496–544.

Synovate. "Consumer Market Study on Advice within the Area of Retail Investment Services - Final Report (2011 Synovate Report)." 2011.

The de Larosière Group. "Report of the High Level Group on Financial Supervision in the EU." 2009.

Tison, Michel. "Do Not Attack the Watchdog! Banking Supervisor's Liability after Peter Paul." *Common Market Law Review* 42, no. 3 (2005): 639–75.

———. "Financial Market Integration in the Post Fsap Era. In Search of Overall Conceptual Consistency in the Regulatory Framework." In *Investor Protection in Europe: Corporate Law Making, the Mifid and Beyond*, edited by Guido Ferrarini and Eddy Wymeersch. Oxford: Oxford University Press, 2006.

———. "The Civil Law Effects of Mifid in a Comparative Law Perspective." In *Financial Law Institute Working Paper 2010–05*, edited by Universiteit Gent - Financial Law Institute. Gent, 2010.

Tuch, Andrew. "Conduct of Business Regulation." In *The Oxford Handbook of Financial Regulation*, edited by Niamh Moloney, Eilís Ferran, and Jennifer Payne. Oxford: Oxford University Press, 2015.

Turner, Adair. "Turner Review." London: Financial Services Authority - FSA, 2009.

Van Binsbergen V Bedrijfsvereniging Metaalnijverheid, ECR 01299, 1974.

Van Dyck, Tom. "(Opt-out) Intermediation as an Alternative for Ensuring a True Protection for European Retail Investors?". *Catholic University of Leuven (KUL) Working Paper*, 2009.

Van Empel, Martijn. "Financial Services in the EU: Harmonization and Liberalization." In *Financial Services in Europe: An Introductory Overview*, edited by Martijn van Empel. Boston Kluwer, 2008.

VanDerZwet, Annemarie. "The Blurring of Distinctions between Financial Sectors: Fact or Fiction?" In *De Nederlandsche Bank Occasional Studies*, edited by De Nederlandsche Bank. Amsterdam, 2003.

Wolf, Martin. "The Rescue of Bear Stearns Marks Liberalisation's Limit." *Financial Times*, 2008.

Wymeersch, Eddy. "The Reforms of the European Financial Supervisory System." *European Company and Financial Law Review* 7, no. 2 (2010): 240–65.

Zatti, Filippo. "La Dimensione Costituzionale Della Tutela Del Risparmio. Dalla Tutela Del Risparmio Alla Protezione Dei Risparmiatori/Investitori E Ritorno?". In *Studi in Onore Di Vincenzo Atripaldi*, edited by Marco Benvenuti et al., 1469–94. Naples: Jovene, 2010.

4

The Relationship Between an Investment Service Provider and a Retail Investor: EU and the United States Compared

The following pages examine the legal relationships between a retail investor and an investment services provider in the EU and in the United States in order to ascertain the existing gaps and verify whether Europe can learn anything from the American experience. Before starting, it must be borne in mind that the United States is a common-law system and securities laws can leverage on the contract as it has been evolving in the American common-law tradition. Nothing like that exists in Europe, where the EU law of financial markets is mainly addressed to Member States and their national public enforcers, and the contract plays a different role, as examined in the previous chapter.

Moreover, only recently the legal relationship between an investment service provider and a retail investor has become a matter subject to EU law, as the very first piece of legislation directly handling this topic in a more coherent fashion was the 2004 MiFID I. In the United States, instead, the first federal securities legislation affecting retail investors was enacted in the 1930s, when the intervention of the federal government was prompted by the financial meltdown that started on 29 October 1929—also known as "Black Tuesday".[1] During the decade known as the "Great Depression", several national legislative reforms for financial markets were adopted, changing the US securities law and establishing the

© The Author(s) 2018
A. Marcacci, *Regulating Investor Protection under EU Law*,
https://doi.org/10.1007/978-3-319-90297-5_4

structure for a federal system of investor protection. The Acts of the Great Depression decade (1930s–1940s), such as the 1933 Securities Act,[2] the 1934 Securities Exchange Act (SEA),[3] and the 1940 Investment Advisers Act (IAA),[4] were designed to both protect investors and prevent market crashes by means of transparency between security issuers and investors, and prevention of frauds.[5] At the time they were enacted, these Acts represented an innovative solution.[6]

Significantly, the very general skeleton of the investor protection structure laid down during the 1930s–1940s has remained substantially stable for all these years, even if it has passed through different regulatory époques, like the deregulation era[7] which deeply affected the US financial services markets and intermediaries infrastructure.

4.1 The Relationship Between Investment Firms and Investors in the EU: Public-Law Customer Categorization and Conduct-of-Business Rules

4.1.1 Categorization of Clients

MiFID I introduced the "retail investor" in the EU law for the first time in 2004. One of the most important aspects envisaged by MiFID I was the new categorization of clients on the basis of their financial knowledge, needs, and experience. Article 11(1) of the Investment Services Directive (ISD) already envisaged that Member States should draw up rules of conduct that must "take account of the professional nature of the person for whom the service is provided".[8] However, ISD did not mention any harmonizing rationale and Member States were free to implement it in many ways.[9] On the contrary, not only does MiFID explicitly set forth clear-cut categories but it also requires firms—usually their internal Compliance Function—to adopt "appropriate written internal policies and procedures to"[10] categorize their own clients.

Under MiFID I/II a client is defined as "any natural or legal person to whom an investment firm provides investment or ancillary services"[11] (thus excluding investment activities).[12] Subsequently, MiFID I provided for three categories of clients, which MiFID II has left unchanged[13]:

Retail clients:	MiFID I/II avoid strictly defining what a retail client is, and it just gives a residual account: "Retail client means a client who is not a professional client."[14] However, it is clear that retail clients are those who need greater protection and MiFID I/II compel investment firms to pay particular attention when providing services and products to this category.
Professional clients:	A professional client is a "client who possesses the experience, knowledge and expertise to make its own investment decisions and properly assess the risks that it incurs".[15] To be considered *professional* a client needs to meet the criteria listed in Annex II of MiFID II. The rationale of this category is to reduce the costs borne by investment firms and generated by the higher level of protection granted to retail investors. In order to do so, MiFID I/II lower the level of protection for those customers who already possess the experience and knowledge necessary to understand the risk involved in products or services.
Eligible counterparties:	Eligible counterparties are institutions or firms having such wide knowledge as to exempt an investment firm from the obligations set forth to protect retail clients. Eligible counterparties can be considered to be a species of the professional client genus[16] and can be a credit institution, central bank, investment fund, pension fund, national public authority (government), international organization, and so on. Significantly, MiFID I did not require the general obligation of fair dealing to be applicable to eligible counterparties, but MiFID II has

upturned this element and now the general obligation also applies to them.[17] In order to avoid abuses in terms of classification of such a highly professional group, the eligible counterparties category is not relevant for advisory services (portfolio management and investment advice) and for the underwriting or placing of financial instruments service, where an investment firm has only two options to classify a client: either retail or professional.[18]

As the 2010 Directive amending the Prospectus Directive shows, the categorization of customers delineated by MiFID can be used as the starting point for a legal evolution that differentiates legal solutions on the basis of clients' characteristics. Directive 94/19/EC on deposit-guarantee schemes and the Bank Recovery and Resolution (BRR) Directive[19] on the recovery and resolution of credit institutions and investment firms, even if they do not use MiFID classification, anyhow provide for the differential treatment of retail depositors due to their level of sophistication. The rationale is to focus on the need to avoid a typical *moral hazard* situation—namely, when someone does not (entirely) pay the consequences of the risks undertaken and, thus, abuses the protections provided either by the system or by someone else.[20] However, it should be flagged that, despite the more investor-friendly approach of UCITS V, the UCITS framework still has a uniform level of investor protection for all opened investment undertakings raising capital from the public, without considering the level of sophistication of the unit holders and without differentiating between types of investors.[21] Nevertheless, Units in collective investment undertakings are financial instruments and investors buying them are protected under MiFID.

Article 45.3 of the Commission Delegated Regulation supplementing MiFID II[22] clarifies that an investment firm has the power to change a client categorization either on its own initiative or at the request of the client but only if complying with the following conditions:

1. When a client is classified as an eligible counterparty, it can elect to be classified as a professional or retail client.

2. When a client is classified as a professional client, it can elect to be classified as a retail client.

The category shift allowed by MiFID II Delegated Regulation is, thus, only *in melius*. This is coherent with the strong investor protection leitmotiv of the MiFID legislative package and the fact that a professional client may ask to be treated as a retail customer does not release the investment firm from its responsibility to ensure that a client is accurately categorized according to the internal categorization procedures monitored by the Compliance Function.

4.1.2 Conflicts of Interest and Remuneration

Conflicts of interest are a very complex phenomenon[23] that MiFID I/II try to address mostly through internal organizational measures, with the aim to prevent that actual or potential conflicts of interests adversely affect the interests of a firm's clients and, eventually, result in a decline of investors' confidence.[24] In this regard, MiFID II follows the framework originally established by MiFID I.

Article 18 of MiFID I already envisaged that investment firms adopt internal policies and procedures in order to identify, prevent, resolve, keep track, and disclose actual and potential conflicts of interest generated in different situations. These situations can be internal to the firm (e.g., between investment advisers [IAs] belonging to different branches but competing with each other in terms of revenues gained); between a firm and its clients (due to remuneration schemes); and between a firm's clients when investment services are being provided (when clients of the same firm have conflicting interests).

However, under Article 18.1 MiFID I firms had to "take all *reasonable* steps to identify conflicts of interest", now under Article 23.1 MiFID II firms shall "take all *appropriate* steps" [our emphasis]. This implies that investment firms must adopt an higher, more objective standard[25] when laying down written policies that delineate internal procedures, tasks, and responsibilities to follow when providing services, such as, for instance, resolving the actual problem of internal business managers exercising inappropriate influence over the way retail advisers recommend investment products to their customers. The Compliance Function is (usually) in charge of drafting such internal procedures and must do that by using its risk-based approach when evaluating such higher, more objective standard of "*appropriate* steps" in order to be able to properly detect where conflicts actually lie.

In this regard, MiFID II finally recognizes the open issue of remuneration and incentive structures[26] in that they ultimately affect the handling of conflicts of interest, particularly in the distribution of products at retail level and related mis-selling cases.[27] A firm's management body (i.e., often the Board), supported by the internal Compliance Function and the Human Resources department, is responsible for defining, adopting, and overseeing the firm's Remuneration Policy. Such Remuneration Policy must be coherent with the Conflicts of Interests Policy, govern the business conduct of the firm's selling staff,[28] and ensure that the staff performance is not remunerated or assessed "in a way that conflicts with its duty to act in the best interests of its clients".[29]

In particular, the selling staff cannot be incentivized to recommend a financial instrument when the firm's instruments inventory "could offer a different financial instrument which would better meet that client's needs".[30] The Compliance Function—in executing its tasks as second-level control function—must monitor the observance of such standards of behavior to ensure that the integrity of the market and the interest of clients are granted at single firm level.

Article 27 of the Commission Delegated Regulation supplementing MiFID II[31] follows the path already opened by the 2013 ESMA Guidelines on Remuneration Policies[32] and clarifies that:

- Remuneration criteria should be spelled out and implemented through appropriate internal procedures taking into account the interests of the firm's clients.
- Remuneration policies and practices apply to all relevant persons with a direct or indirect impact on the firm's corporate behavior, thus contributing to the spreading of a culture of compliance at firm level.
- Appropriate qualitative criteria should be considered, including compliance with the applicable regulations and non-financial rewards like career advancements (Recital 40).

- While the management body approves the Remuneration Policy, it is for the senior managers to supervise its implementation. The Compliance Function is to be involved (1) for advice, before the Policy is adopted; and (2) on a daily basis in order to execute the necessary monitoring.
- Fixed and variable remunerations must be balanced so as to avoid that variable remunerations based on sales targets disproportionately outweigh the fixed part and may adversely affect the interests of clients.

Concerning disclosure of conflicts of interest, MiFID provides that if a conflict of interest arises when a service is being sold, the provider has to communicate the existence of the conflict in detail—also mentioning the steps taken to handle and mitigate the conflict—and on a durable medium.[33] Such a communication overcomes the "disclose or abstain"[34] method.

Importantly, Article 34 of the Commission Delegated Regulation supplementing MiFID II[35] handles the thorny issue of the overreliance on disclosure. The Article affirms that disclosure should be treated as a "last resort", that is, an option to use when all other organizational measures fail to ensure that a risk to damage a client's interests cannot be entirely prevented. Furthermore, the Regulation provides for disclosure to be far less generic and be designed on the client's actual profile and category: general references to conflicts of interests should be replaced with description of the conflicts of interest that arise in the provision of investment and/or ancillary services. This is viewed as a support for less-sophisticated investors to make more informed investment decisions.

4.1.3 Inducements and Investment Advice

A topic strictly related to conflicts of interest is the so-called inducements. This term refers to indirect compensations, funds, goods, services, and even non-monetary benefits (other than fees and commissions due for the executed service) that an investment firm or any of its employees receive from (or pay to) a third party in connection to the service provided to a client (Article 26, Commission MiFID I implementing

Directive 2006/73/EC). Inducements are a sort of "side payments"[36] from a third party that may indicate that an investment firm might not be acting "honestly, fairly and professionally in accordance with the best interests of its clients" when providing investment or ancillary services (Article 24.1 of MiFID II).

Professor Jackson labels this phenomenon as the "trilateral dilemma".[37] This dilemma occurs when advisers recommending an investment receive inducements connected to that investment. Such inducements may lead investment firms to give biased advice and increase the final cost of recommended products as well. However, inducements may also be an efficient—or even innocuous—way to finance the distribution of financial products and services,[38] a very important element for retail markets. To overcome the trilateral dilemma, Article 24.9 of MiFID II[39] clarifies that such payments or benefits are allowed when they:

(a) Are designed to improve the quality of the service provided
(b) Do not impair compliance with the firm's duty to act in the best interest of its clients

Article 11 of the Commission Delegated Directive supplementing MiFID II[40] gives guidance on the conditions to follow in order to meet these two requirements. In more detail, an inducement is allowed when it is justified by the provision of an additional or higher-level service to the relevant client, proportional to the level of the received inducement itself; does not directly benefit the firm—included its shareholders or employees—without giving benefits to the relevant client; and is justified by the provision of an ongoing benefit to the relevant client in relation to an ongoing inducement.

Importantly, investment firms must disclose both ex ante and on an ongoing basis the existence, nature, and amount of such payments and/or benefits (or—when this is not possible—the method of calculating such an amount), in a comprehensive, accurate, and understandable manner before service is provided (Article 24.9 MiFID II). An investment firm must disclose ongoing inducements at least once a year by individually informing its clients on the actual amount of benefits and/or payments received or paid.[41]

MiFID II makes no changes to the definition of "investment advice" but it anyhow changes the framework set forth by MiFID I by modifying the relationship between inducements and the advice service and introducing the new "Independent Advice" notion. To label its advice service as "independent", an investment firm must now prove that it provides such a service (Article 24.7) by assessing a sufficient range of sufficiently different[42] financial instruments available on the market in order to ensure that the client's investment objectives are suitably met. Article 53 of the Commission Delegated Regulation supplementing MiFID[43] provides the investment firm to define and implement an internal selection process—usually crafted with the support of the Compliance Function—in order to assess and compare such a sufficient range of financial instruments.

Moreover, in order to provide an investment advice service on an independent basis, the financial instruments assessed must not be limited to those issued or provided by:

- "the investment firm itself or by entities having close links with the investment firm; or,
- other entities with which the investment firm has such close legal or economic relationships, such as contractual relationships, as to pose a risk of impairing the independent basis of the advice provided."[44]

Significantly, minor non-monetary benefits[45] that can enhance the quality of service and that are of a scale and nature not capable of impairing compliance with the investment firm's duty to act in the best interest of its clients are acceptable but must be openly disclosed (article 24.7 MiFID II). Furthermore, if a firm offers an investment advice service on both an independent and non-independent basis, appropriate disclosure—in a durable medium—on the nature of the advice must be given alongside the duty to present itself as independent advisory firm only with respect to the services actually provided on an independent basis.[46]

Finally, Article 12.1 of the Commission Delegated Directive[47] integrates MiFID II provisions on independent advice by compelling investment firms that provide an independent advice service to set up an internal policy to ensure that "all fees, commissions or monetary benefits received from third parties in relation to the provision of independent investment advice and portfolio management shall be transferred in full to the client". The responsibility for drafting and monitoring of the implementation of the internal policy is usually on the shoulders of the Compliance Function, which should ensure that this internal policy is coherent with the Remuneration Policy and the Conflict-of-Interest Policy, due to the obvious links crossing these matters.

4.1.4 Suitability and Appropriateness

The suitability and appropriateness tests (carried out as interviews) were introduced by Article 19.4-5 of MiFID I. They stem from the *know your customer*[48] principle which implies that firms must learn and take into account their clients' needs and risk profiles when advising an investment or making an investment choice on the behalf of their clients. Importantly, Article 25.1 MiFID II now clearly affirms the *know the security* principle, by stating that "natural persons giving investment advice or information about financial instruments [... and] services [... must] possess the necessary knowledge and competence to fulfil their obligations".

The suitability test, in particular, applies to both retail and professional clients in case of discretionary portfolio management and investment advice, so-called advisory services. This test has been conceived as a tool for service providers to obtain all the information necessary in order to assess the clients' financial knowledge and expertise, alongside their financial situation and goals, so as to recommend investments that are suitable for their needs. If a customer does not want to reveal specific information or the product is "inadequate" according to the client's financial picture, then the investment firm cannot execute the operation: the suitability test can prevent financial instruments from being advised or being inserted into a client's portfolio.[49] Alike other features of MiFID I/II, investment firms are required to have in place and be able to demonstrate adequate policies and internal procedures regarding the suitability and appropriateness, which are typically drafted and monitored by the internal Compliance Function.[50] Interestingly, some firms have recently introduced "psychological questions" in their suitability interview in order to better define a client's inclination to risk.

MiFID II does not make substantial changes to the MiFID I suitability rule but, nevertheless, it digs further into its features and the related disclosure obligations. Very importantly, Article 25.2 MiFID II requires investment firms performing advisory services to explicitly consider a client's ability to bear losses, and to ensure that when a package of services or products is concerned, an assessment of the overall bundled package—and not just the single components—is carried out. Furthermore, when providing investment advice, a firm has to deliver a report to its retail clients including an outline of the advice provided and how the recommendation is suitable according to the retail client profile.[51]

The ability to bear losses is particularly significant because it seems to establish an EU public-law (proto)version of the "hardship" feature which resembles—even if without overlapping—the excessive onerousness features already provided by several national civil codes such as Article 1467 of Italian Civil Code (*Sezione III: Dell'eccessiva onerosità*), Article 1195 of the French Civil Code (*Sous-section 1: Force obligatoire*), or § 313 of the German Civil Code (*Störung der Geschäftsgrundlage*). However, unlike the national civil codes which provide the "hardship/excessive onerousness" feature with a remedy to be enforced before a court (usually, the renegotiation or the contract rescission), MiFID II enshrines the "client's ability to bear losses" into the suitability framework and, thus, redirects it toward public enforcement (administrative sanctions).

Furthermore, Article 24.4 MiFID II sets forth that when an investment advice service is provided, the investment firm must, well before the service is executed, inform the client whether s/he will be given a *periodic suitability assessment* of the recommended financial instruments. This statement must be on a durable medium, specifying the advice and how the recommendation meets the preferences, objectives, and other characteristics of the client.[52]

Article 54 of the Commission Delegated Regulation[53] clarifies that investment firms are responsible for determining the extent of the information to be collected from their clients[54] in light of all the features of the provided advisory services, and are responsible for taking reasonable steps to ensure that such collected information is reliable. Such information is necessary for the service provider to understand, under its responsibility, the essential facts about the client and to have a reasonable basis for determining whether the recommended product is suitable or not.

The suitability requirement may raise a twofold responsibility on the part of the firm: a contractual liability toward the client (depending on the domestic private-law regimes)[55] and administrative sanctions (should the domestic supervisor certify that the firm has not promptly complied).[56] The trend is clear: proceduralizing the suitability requirement—a key aspect of the trust-based client-service provider relationship—through public regulation rather than leaving the issue only at contractual level.

The appropriateness test applies to non-advisory services and has been conceived as a tool whereby providers request the necessary information about clients' financial knowledge and experience in the field related to a transaction requested by or proposed to the customers, in order to evaluate whether the investment is appropriate or not.[57] A key difference with the suitability test is that the appropriateness test does not require a firm to obtain information concerning the financial objectives and situation of the client.[58] Furthermore, unlike what happens with the suitability test, the appropriateness test cannot stop investment from executing their clients' orders,[59] thus the burden of the risk rests on the customer's shoulders who chooses to invest in an inappropriate financial solution.

The appropriateness test can be skipped for those instruments deemed to be "non-complex"[60] and whose operations are executed through "execution-only" services (such as execution and/or the reception and transmission of client orders). Article 19.6 of MiFID I listed several large categories of "non-complex" financial instruments—such as money market instruments and shares admitted to trading on a regulated market. Article 38 of the 2006 Commission implementing Directive,[61] instead, envisaged the criteria—like instrument's liquidity, its likelihood to be readily understood by the average retail investor, and the public availability of information—to assess whether an instrument left out of by the Article 19.6 could be categorized as "non-complex".

MiFID II has severely decreased the amount of financial instruments that can be assessed as "non-complex", due to the concerns raised by a post-crisis industry behavior. Indeed, due to a combination of several market factors and in search of higher returns,[62] investment firms had increasingly approached more sophisticated investment strategies and products for retail clients. To avoid negative fallouts hammering retail investors' confidence in the market, Article 25 has thus introduced a *psychological element*, which provides that those instruments "that embed a derivative or incorporate a structure which makes it difficult for the client to understand the risk involved" are automatically excluded by the "non-complex" category.

In addition to this, Article 57 of the Commission Delegated Regulation supplementing MiFID II[63] specifies that an instrument can be assessed as non-complex when there are frequent opportunities to realize that instrument at publicly available prices, validated in an independent way from the issuer; and when that instrument does not incorporate a clause, a condition or a trigger that could fundamentally alter the nature of the risk or the pay-out profile,[64] or it does not include explicit or implicit exit charges which makes the instrument illiquid. If it is quite straightforward to single out which financial instruments contain a clause like that, it is not easy for a financial firm to detect the scope of the frequency at which a financial instrument can be redeemed in order to evaluate its complexity.

4.1.5 Information Disclosure

As showed in Chap. 2, all kinds of information disclosure have always played a key role in the EU law.[65] Although MiFID I introduced contract-based tools such as the suitability and appropriateness tests and MiFID II introduced PG meant to overcome the sole reliance on disclosure, MiFID I/II do not abandon information disclosure (as it was just showed in case of conflicts of interest). The objective of information disclosure is that to empower investors.[66]

Under MiFID I, Article 19(2) stated that "all information, including marketing communications, addressed by the investment firm to clients or potential clients shall be fair, clear and not misleading. Marketing communications shall be clearly identifiable as such." Article 24(3) of MiFID II has equally reproduced the content.

Article 19(3) of MiFID I gave details on mandatory information. Current Article 24(4) substantially replaces old Article 19(3) by stating that appropriate information concerning the "firm and its services, the financial instruments and proposed investment strategies, execution venues and all costs and related charges" must be given "in good time" to actual and prospective clients, and that "information on financial instruments and proposed investment strategies must include appropriate guidance on and warnings of the risks associated with investments". However, current Article 24(4) is broader and gives further details, for instance, on the investment advice (inter alia, it is now mandatory to state whether this is provided on an independent basis or not) and portfolio management (concerning the disclosure of inducements) services.

Compared to MiFID I, MiFID II delegated acts strongly increase the details of ex ante and ex post information disclosure. Article 44 of the Commission Delegated Regulation supplementing MiFID II[67] sets the general scene for information disclosure by reaffirming the firms' duty to provide their actual or potential retail and professional customers with "fair, clear and not misleading information". In particular, Art. 44(2) (re) highlights the role of the "average consumer" as it indicates that information must be "presented in a way that it is likely to be understood by [...] the average member of the group to whom it is directed".

Interestingly, with the aim to improve the consistency of the information investors receive, firms are required to present information "in the same language throughout all forms of information and marketing materials that are provided to each client, unless the client has accepted to receive information in more than one language".[68] This implies that a French-speaking investor can accept to receive an information material, for instance, in Spanish without having it translated into French. However, in case the same investor refuses to accept to receive that information in Spanish, then a firm must be ready to provide all information in French (which would very likely lead to translation costs for the firm).

On comparative information, Art. 44(3) makes it clear that information comparing services and products is to be "meaningful and presented in a fair and balanced way", that the sources of that information are specified, and that "the key facts and assumptions used to make the comparison are included." Similar, but more stringent, requirements apply to information containing an indication of past or future performance of an instrument, a financial index, or a service.

Further to Article 44, the Commission Delegated Regulation 2017/565[69] provides for a set of Articles—45–50—that give further details on specific disclosure topics. This set of articles lays down the form (a durable medium or a website) and the timing (good time before the provision of a service)[70] of the contract; the mandatory information about the investment firm itself, its services (e.g., the timing, frequency, and nature of the explanatory reports concerning the performance of the services provided),[71] and the marketed financial instruments; information concerning safeguarding of client financial instruments or client funds; and information on costs and associated charges.

Information on financial instruments is particularly important. It requires firms to communicate to their customers the nature of the specific type of instrument provided, its functioning and performance in different market conditions (both positive and negative), alongside risks particularly related to that specific type of instrument in order "to enable the client to take investment decisions on an informed basis" (Article 48). The internal Compliance Function may consider either producing a stand-alone document or amending an existing one (by incorporating the new mandatory information) which specifies the characteristics of the specific type of financial instrument concerned. Particular attention must be paid to the so-called composed instruments, namely those contracts composed of two or more different financial instruments or services (Article 48.4). In this case, the firm must adequately describe the legal nature of the contract, its single components, the way the components interact with each other, and how this affects the investment risks. Given the wording of the Delegated Regulation, the internal Compliance Function may decide that a general, fixed description of what a composed instrument is not enough: the description should be bespoke and tailored on the features of the specific instrument being marketed with the aim of making the investor aware of its characteristics.

Composed financial instruments should not be confused with packages meant as "cross-selling practices". These occur when a firm offers an investment service alongside "another service or product as part of a package or as a condition for the same agreement or package".[72] Within this context, ESMA even distinguishes between bundled (if the products/services offered are available separately and the customer can choose to buy them separately) and tied (if at least one of the products/services offered are not available separately) packages.[73] However, the internal Compliance Function should bear in mind that a bundled/tied package is not financial instrument but it represents a selling practice turned into a contract incorporating financial instruments, products, and services.

Finally, the internal Compliance Function must pay particular care to ex ante and ex post disclosure on costs and associated charges (Article 50).[74] First of all, professional clients and eligible counterparties may agree to receive a limited amount of the information on costs and charges. However, investment firms cannot limit disclosure in case advisory services (for professional clients) or when, irrespective of the investment service provided, the financial instruments concerned embed a derivative (for both professional clients and eligible counterparties).[75] Retail customers, instead, must always receive such information in a complete and accurate manner. Firms may provide their retail clients with a "customized" disclosure: a standard document reproducing mandatory information and a bespoke document with more detail information to be delivered upon request.

Looking at the substance, firms must aggregate all costs and associated charges charged by the investment firm/other parties and those costs/charges associated with the manufacturing and managing of financial instruments.[76] Annex II of the Delegated Regulation provides for a very detailed list of costs to be disclosed, alongside examples: for instance, the cost item "One-off charges related to the provision of an investment service" is exemplified through deposit fees, termination fees, and switching costs.[77] This implies that the internal Compliance Function must carry out a due analysis of all of the costs and charges of its own services and marketed products, dissect them according to the guidance provided by the Delegated Regulation, and, finally, make them visibly readable and understandable by the average investor through, for instance, illustrations depicting the cumulative effect of costs on return, including any anticipated spikes or fluctuations in the costs (!).[78]

The European lawmaker makes full ex ante disclosure on aggregated costs and charges for financial instruments and investment services mandatory. Firms shall disclose such information about the aggregated costs and charges when they recommend (e.g., under the advice service) or market (in case of distribution or placement agreements with a product manufacturer or issuer)[79] a specific financial instrument or when a UCITS KIID or PRIIPs KID is to be provided.[80] This is so for the reasonable fact that a firm can only know the details of the financial instruments it recommends through advisory services or it places/distributes or when it is in a position to retrieve such information through KIID/KID. It would be, instead, excessively and unproportionally burdensome for a firm to collect information on instruments a client is requesting to invest via a service of reception and transmission of orders but of which the firm has not information.

Significantly, the Delegated Regulation imposes to use the actual costs incurred as a proxy for the expected costs and charges. Should these not be available, then reasonable estimations of costs must be produced. Whereas the word "actual" clarifies what a firm is required to do, the word "reasonable" leaves the door open to different interpretations, which may diverge not only from Member State to Member State but also between public and private enforcers in the very same Member State. In this case, a firm's Compliance Function may be induced to follow a more conservative approach.

Ex post information (Article 50.9) on all costs and charges related to both the financial instrument(s) and investment service(s) supplied must be provided on an annual basis in case an ongoing relationship with a client during the year has taken place. However, it is not clear when such ex post information should be delivered in case the relationship is ended before the end of the year. Importantly, such information must be based on costs actually incurred and be provided on a personalized basis: it is, thus, quite important that investment firms distributing financial instruments have solid "information on costs and charges" agreements with instrument issuers and manufacturers in order to be able to provide their customers with such ex post information. The internal Compliance Function usually reviews such agreements on information on costs and charges.

It is clear that information disclosure still plays an important role in MiFID II investor protection regime. Delegated Regulation 2017/565 profoundly digs into firms' disclosure duties up to the point it sets forth very detailed requirements on the information on costs and charges to be unveiled to the customer and that the customer should acknowledge (which would make her/him responsible for, at least, reading the information provided). Obviously, the Delegated Regulation does not lay down any EU-wide private enforcement remedy and national courts still apply national civil remedial rules, thus making the case for a strong coordination at EU level of public enforcement of potential violations.

4.1.6 Best Execution and Order Handling

The previous chapter describes the "best execution" duty as the obligation for investment service firms to grant their clients the most favorable terms available for their trades[81] and, contractually speaking, it can be defined as "an obligation of means"[82] that an investment firm holds toward its clients. MiFID I already required firms to adopt and implement internal measures and procedures to provide a fair and efficient execution of clients' orders. In this regard, MiFID II further clarifies that investment firms must unfold internal processes and arrangements in order to promptly, fairly, and expeditiously provide the execution of their client orders, in relation to other client orders or the trading interests of the firm itself—so to reduce and, when possible, avoid conflicts of interests (Article 28.1). The Compliance Function is generally in charge of drafting the internal execution policy shaped by the "best execution" duty and of monitoring its correct application.

Article 21 MiFID I already stated that "Member States shall require that investment firms take all *reasonable* [our emphasis] steps to obtain, when executing orders, the best possible result for their clients taking into account price, costs, speed, likelihood of execution and settlement, size, nature or any other consideration relevant to the execution of the order. Nevertheless, whenever there is a specific instruction from the client the investment firm shall execute the order following the specific instruction. [...] Member States shall require investment firms to establish and implement an order execution policy to allow them to obtain, for their client orders, the best possible result." Furthermore, Recital 66, of the second-level Commission Directive 2006/73/EC specified that "An investment firm should apply its execution policy to each client order that it executes with a view to obtaining the best possible result for the client in accordance with that policy."

Even if the general structure has remained substantially unchanged, MiFID II has made some important improvements. First of all, Article 27 MiFID II has replaced "reasonable" with "sufficient".[83] This implies that the execution would not be considered "best" when all reasonable steps have been taken but these are not sufficient. The requirement looks more burdensome than before, in terms of both contractual liability and prospective administrative sanctions.

MiFID I Article 21.2-3 already required investment firms to "establish and implement an order execution policy to allow them to obtain, for their client orders, the best possible result [.... This policy] shall include, in respect of each class of instruments, information on the different venues where the investment firm executes its client orders and the factors affecting the choice of execution venue. It shall at least include those venues that enable the investment firm to obtain on a consistent basis the best possible result for the execution of client orders". MiFID II Article 27(5) now requires that, alongside disclosure of the order execution policy and after obtaining the client's consent on it, firms explain "clearly, in sufficient detail and in a way that can be easily understood by clients", how orders are executed. This implies that firms are not only required to inform about the execution policy but they are supposed to try to *educate* their own customers on the way their orders are routed. Furthermore, an investment firm must notify their clients of any *material* changes to its order execution policy and arrangements.

Still in terms of transparency, MiFID II now requires investment firms to summarize and publish on an yearly basis, and "for each class of financial instruments, the top five execution venues in terms of trading volumes where they executed client orders in the preceding year and information on the quality of execution obtained" (Article 27.6). This might reveal to be quite a heavy burden on the shoulders of investment firms and a strong competition feeder for execution venues.

On a more operative side, Article 27.1 specifies that when an investment firm executes a client's order for a financial instrument through an order routing system which can enter more than one execution venue (so-called *smart routing*[84]), then a firm must consider the commissions and costs for executing the order on each of the eligible venues when assessing best execution. On the other hand, a firm can ex ante choose one single execution venue to carry out a particular set of clients' orders but, in this case, the firm must still ensure the best possible result compared to market conditions (dynamic versus static best execution).[85] In either case, in order to detect and address actual and potential deficiencies, an investment firm (often, the internal Compliance Function) shall monitor the correct functioning of its best execution systems—for instance through random sample-based controls of deal data and the oversight of significant market events which may lead to amendments in the execution policy—and be able to prove before both their customers and public enforcers that the orders have been executed in accordance with the firm's execution policy.

When dealing with retail and professional clients, firms must adopt internal policies, procedures, and arrangements—usually drafted and monitored by the Compliance Function—in order to "provide for the prompt, fair and expeditious execution of client orders, relative to other client orders or the trading interests of the investment firm" (Article 22 MiFID I and Article 28 MiFID II). The difference between best execution and client order handling is that while the former concerns the execution of orders in the market, the latter concerns the safeguard of the position of the client within the firm.[86]

The 2017 Commission Delegated Regulation supplementing MiFID[87] provides for a set of articles[88] that give further details on how firms must execute orders. On client order handling, Article 67 of the Delegated Regulation spells out the three basic conditions firms must comply with:

1. Orders executed on behalf of clients must be promptly and accurately recorded and allocated.
2. Otherwise comparable client orders must be executed sequentially and promptly unless the order features or prevailing market conditions make it impracticable, or the client interests require otherwise.
3. As soon as a firm becomes aware of any material difficulties about the proper execution of orders, it must promptly inform the retail client concerned.

The EU lawmaker tries, on the one hand, to guarantee an equal and fair execution of "otherwise comparable client orders" by imposing the proceduralization of client order handling at firm level. On the other hand, a firm is made responsible for directly taking care of the interests of their clients and—when it comes to retail—duly informing them of any difficult circumstances.

Concerning the investment firm-retail client relationship, Article 44 of MiFID I 2006 Commission Directive had already introduced the "total consideration" as an important feature when dealing with retail clients: "the price of the financial instrument and the costs related to execution, which shall include all expenses incurred by the client which are directly related to the execution of the order, including execution venue fees, clearing and settlement fees and any other fees paid to third parties involved in the execution of the order." As a corollary, the predecessor of ESMA, the CESR, had also reaffirmed the importance of the total consideration for retail clients.[89] MiFID II has "upgraded" the total consideration feature for retail customers directly into the Article 27.1 of the first-level Directive.

Significantly, Article 27.2 confirms the importance given to inducements by clarifying their relationship with the best execution rule in that a firm is now not allowed to "receive any remuneration, discount or non-monetary benefit for routing client orders to a particular trading venue or execution venue which would infringe the requirements on conflicts of interest or inducements".

Finally, an investment Firm A can choose to offer its clients only the service of Reception and Transmission of Orders and hire another Firm B to execute its client's orders (thus, the firm B providing the service of Execution of Orders). In this case, the Execution Policy of Firm A must identify the executing Firm(s) "with which the orders are placed or to which [... Firm A] transmits orders for execution" (Article 65.5, Delegated Regulation).[90] This Execution Policy is to be disclosed to the Firm A's customers and becomes part of the contractual arrangement between the investment firm and its clients. This is important from a contractual liability viewpoint due to the fact that the Firm A shall regularly "monitor the execution quality of the [... executing Firm(s)] identified in [... its] policy and, where appropriate, correct any deficiencies", even by assessing "whether a material change has occurred" (Article 65.7, Delegated Regulation).[91]

4.1.7 Product Governance

Product Governance was firstly conceived by the Financial Services Authority (FSA)—the then British Regulator—with a view to identifying "potential consumer detriment at a far earlier stage",[92] thus pushing service providers' duties at a much upper step of the value-chain ladder. For the FSA the term "governance" meant "systems and controls in relation to product design, product management and distribution strategy".[93] After carrying out ad hoc analysis, indeed, the FSA had come to realize that a lack of firms' internal product development and marketing processes was likely to lead to poorly designed products and mis-selling cases.[94] For this reason, a soft-law document in the version of a Guidance was issued in 2012 by the FSA.[95]

MiFID II incorporates the British idea of PG and turns it into hard law through Recital 71, Articles 9, 16.3, and 24 of the first-level Directive and through Articles 9 and 10 of the second-level Directive.[96] PG covers all MiFID-regulated services and all products falling within the scope of MiFID II—that is, financial instruments and structured deposits[97]—and it directly applies to all MiFID firms. Using the categories already introduced by the PRIIPs Regulation,[98] PG delineates duties and responsibilities for manufacturers and distributors: the former create, develop, issue, and/or design a financial instrument, while the latter offer/sell investment services and products crafted by third parties.[99]

The distinction between manufacturers and distributors is not formalistic but, instead, substantial due to the fact that they are subject to specific, different duties, on the basis of the diverse roles they play:

Manufacturers: Firms must carry out identification of a target client market for each product and each service created. Client targeting must be both positive (which client is compatible with which product) and negative (which client is not compatible with which product)[100] and determined on the risk profile and the charging structure of a product. Importantly, the product design cannot be based on "a business model that relies on poor client outcomes to be profitable"[101] but on clients' benefits. Scenario analyses[102] and product stress tests are to be performed in order to assess risks of poor outcomes and evaluate whether the product may represent a threat to the financial markets' orderly functioning. Those involved in crafting a product and developing its related scenario analyses and stress tests must have the necessary knowledge to understand the product, its risk and features; and run a periodic review. Finally, manufacturing activity is to be coherent with the proper management of actual and potential conflicts of interests[103] (which includes remuneration policies).

Distributors: Identification of a target client market for each product and each service delivered, in both a positive and negative way.[104] To do so, distributors can tap into the available results of the existing suitability tests. In addition, distributors must also receive consistent and adequate information from manufacturers concerning a product or service so as to be able to fully understand it and, consequently, identify the compatible target market.[105] Communication of product information is established to ad hoc information agreements between distributors and manufacturers.[106] Very importantly, such agreements should contractualize the reciprocal "compliance risk", that is, the risk that either the manufacturer or the distributor does not receive the necessary information to fulfill with the PG duties. For instance, in case a manufacturer omits to communicate a product's important feature and a distributor is fined for inadequate PG arrangements, then the distributor should claim for contract-based damages whose calculation method or percentage could be already foreseen by the standing information agreement. For this reason, it is very important that the Compliance Function internally review such information agreements (even if the Legal department remains in charge of drafting the

> contracts). Finally, periodic review and, when necessary, update of the PG processes and procedures alongside the distributed products and the provided services must take place.[107] In case of malfunctions, remedial actions are to be taken. The periodic review, as well, should be run by the Compliance Function, alongside the second-level controls aimed at detecting mis-selling on a transaction-by-transaction basis.

The information agreements between distributors and manufacturers on distributed products are legally mandatory when the distributor is not the manufacturer. Within this agreement context, complementary duties apply: distributors must take all reasonable steps to obtain all the necessary information from manufacturers and disclose them the results of sales and periodic product reviews, whereas manufacturers must communicate a product's characteristics, provide the most precise information,[108] and use the sales and review information received by a distributor for their internal reviews.

Importantly, a distributor's duties apply even when it distributes products manufactured by non-MiFID firms.[109] In this case, the non-MiFID firms must give the distributor the necessary information—when not publicly available[110]—to fully understand the product, the potential outcome, and risk profile, in order for the distributor to define a target market client. This means that PG rules indirectly affect non-MIFID firms, like UCITS management companies whose UCITS quotes are distributed via the retail networks of MiFID firms, such as banks authorized to perform investment services.

The investor protection nature of the PG regime is confirmed by paragraph 10 of Article 10 which deals with the distribution chain issue and states that the firm with the direct relationship with a client carries the ultimately responsibility for complying with the PG requirements. This, anyhow, does not imply that the other firms involved in the chain are not responsible, as they must "ensure that relevant product information is passed from the manufacturer to the final distributor in the chain".[111]

4.2 The Relationship Between Broker-Dealers/Investment Advisers and Investors in the United States: Suitability and Fiduciary Duty

4.2.1 The Evolution of the US Financial Legislation and the Protection of Investors

As said above, until the 1930s, regulation of financial markets was entirely handled at state level and there was no federal securities law as we mean it today. However, during the Great Depression decade the three following key pieces of legislation affecting either directly or indirectly investor protection were enacted: the 1933 Securities Act,[112] the 1934 SEA,[113] and the 1940 IAA.[114]

The 1933 Securities Act was adopted in order to pursue two main goals: (a) making markets more transparent so as to give investors more and better information through a "full, accurate and complete statement of all pertinent facts concerning issues of the securities"[115]; (b) avoiding deceptive and fraudulent behaviors.[116] Furthermore, Section 2(a)(1) provided quite a wide definition of security,[117] which was later on clarified by the Supreme Court (US SC).[118]

Whereas the 1933 Act deals with the securities' issuance and admission to registration,[119] that is, *primary markets*, the 1934 SEA focuses on the trading of securities and the regulation of the financial industry more generally,[120] that is, *secondary markets*. The SEA is very important because it regulates brokers and dealers and provides the general scheme for their registration with the public authorities.

The Act gives a definition of "broker", who is a "person engaged in the business of effecting transactions in securities for the account of others" [SEA Section 3(4)], and a "dealer", who is a "person engaged in the business of buying and selling securities for such person's account" [SEA Section 3(a)(5)]. It then creates the Securities and Exchange Commission (SEC), the US federal securities supervisor, and establishes the agency's administrative structure and enforcement powers.[121] Legally speaking—at least on paper—brokerage services are *agency* services, whereas dealing services are *principal* activities.[122] It may be difficult to carve *dealing* out of *brokerage* (and the other way around) when both services/activities are being carried out by the same firm. This conundrum occurs in both the United States and Europe, as the new attempted balance for the so-called self-placement[123] between "dealing on own account" and "execution of orders on behalf of clients" under MiFID II openly proves (see Chap. 3).

The rationale which led the Congress to enact the 1934 Act was the idea that broker-dealers (BDs) managing clients' funds had to comply with professional duties[124] linked to the information disclosure: indeed, the US Legislator wanted the new securities statutes to "substitute a philosophy of full disclosure for the philosophy of *caveat emptor*".[125] Disclosure was the queen tool employed by the 1933 and 1934 Acts to protect investors, in terms of transparency on securities issuance, on the quantity and quality of information provided, on the prevention of fraud, and on liabilities for companies issuing securities.

The 1934 Act was amended in 1938 by the Maloney Act[126] which allowed the establishment of associations of brokers and dealers, and gave them the power to oversee the conduct of their members and to self-regulate over-the-counter transactions.[127] It, furthermore, gave the SEC the authority to supervise such Self-Regulatory Organizations (SROs), particularly through a registration procedure.[128]

The role of the SROs is very important for BDs because these associations can adopt conduct-of-business rules based on the principles set forth by the SEA, such as fairness and transparency,[129] which deeply affect the relationship between broker-dealers and retail investors. Their statutorily provided regulatory powers are a mark of how far the US legal system places "great faith and reliance upon the principle of industry self-regulation."[130] Since the 1930s, the SROs have been seen as providing an essential support to the SEC, as the words of the then SEC Chairperson William Douglas prove: "Government would keep the shotgun, so to speak, behind the door, loaded, well oiled, cleaned, ready for use but with the hope it would never have to be used."[131]

As of July 2017,[132] the only national securities association registered with the SEC under Section 15A of the SEA is the Financial Industry Regulatory Authority (FINRA) and all broker-dealers that trade with the public are required to become its members by successfully passing qualification exams.[133] FINRA is the result of the 2007 merger, approved by the SEC[134] in Release No. 34-56145,[135] between the enforcement arms of the New York Stock Exchange and the National Association of Securities Dealers—NASD.[136] It is funded by its self-regulated members and it publicly states that its official object is to "protect America's investors by making sure the broker-dealer industry operates fairly and honestly"[137] and it is fully "dedicated to investor protection and market integrity through effective and efficient regulation of broker-dealers".[138]

The areas where FINRA operates are the following[139]: registration of BD firms; routine examination of members' activities; enforcement of both its own rules and federal securities laws; education programs for investors; issuance of trade reports with information on a wide range of financial instruments; and the management of the largest US securities arbitration system[140] for the resolution of disputes between investors and registered brokerage firms. Over time, the SEC has actively reviewed NASD/FINRA's regulatory actions.[141]

The IAA of 1940,[142] as amended in 1960, deals with a figure other than the broker-dealer, the IA, and takes a different approach. Though somehow similar to BDs, section 202(a)(11) of the 1940 Advisers Act defines an "IA" as a "person who, for compensation, engages in the business of advising others, either directly or through publications or writings, with respect to the value of securities or to the advisability of investing in, purchasing, or selling securities or a person who, for compensation and as part of a regular business, issues or adopts analyses or a report concerning securities". Mutatis mutandis, if viewed from a European perspective, the core business of an IA would be to provide the MiFID "investment advice" service. Indeed, the 1940 Act was adopted to regulate the business of providing investment advice against compensation in a time when such business was a largely unregulated.[143]

The definition given by the IAA marks three elements that define a person, legal or natural, an IA: (a) the provision of advice, reports, or analyses to others concerning securities; (b) the provision of these services are organized as a business; (c) and for compensation. Importantly, the Section 202(a)(11)(C) of the Advisers Act lists those firms excludes[144] from the definition of IA, such as certain BDs that provide advisory services solely incidentally[145] "to the conduct of his business as a broker or dealer and who receives no special compensation therefor"; alongside banks and banking holding companies, even when the service provider formally meets the three elements above.[146]

However, the great leap forward in terms of investor protection was added by the US SC in 1963 when it held that the IAA "reflects a congressional recognition of the delicate fiduciary nature of an investment advisory relationship." [And it reflects] "a congressional intent to eliminate, or at least expose, all conflicts of interest which might incline an investment adviser—consciously or unconsciously—to render advice which was not disinterested."[147] This was already heralded by scholars such as Professor Wilsey, who already in 1949 pointed out the actual nature of IAs: "As a consequence of the need for trained assistance and for unbiased aid there came into existence firms and individuals who specialize in advising investors as to their investment policies."[148]

The fiduciary duty introduced for IAs by the US SC is a general principle related to contracts, that stems from the laws of agency and trusts[149] and imposes "special duties upon those who occupy a relationship of trust and confidence with their clients".[150] The fiduciary duty is very important, and the following sections will show that the key difference in terms of investor protection between BDs and IAs mainly concerns this territory.[151]

From the end of the 1960s through the end of the 1970s, no major legislative reforms took place.[152] At the beginning of the 1980s, the Regan presidency kicks off the so-called age of deregulation and in 1982 Congress passed the Garn–St. Germain Depository Institutions Act.[153] This piece of legislation deregulated the activities of Savings and Loans,[154] expanding their investment and lending possibilities in order to promote competition in the sector. This Act was defined as the "granddaddy"[155] of the 1980s' deregulation-friendly legislation, and it was harshly criticized for being one of the main causes of the Savings and Loans crisis.[156]

Another key piece of legislation adopted in the deregulation era was the 1999 Financial Services Modernization Act—the so-called Gramm-Leach-Bliley Act (GLB Act).[157] The main change brought about by the Act was the ending of the division between commercial and investment banks as designed by the 1933 Banking Act. Under the GLB Act, big investment or commercial banks could turn into financial holding companies owning commercial banks and thrift institutions.[158] In the words of the Federal Reserve: "The Gramm-Leach-Bliley Act of 1999 ("Act") will significantly impact the financial services industry. By repealing provisions of the Glass-Steagall Act, the Act facilitates affiliations between banks, securities firms, and insurance companies."[159] The ambition was to boost a more efficient market.

Importantly, the GLB Act was so centered on the idea of liberalizing market forces that it left a "significant regulatory gap by failing to give to the SEC or any agency the authority to regulate large investment bank holding companies."[160] The gap created by the GLB Act concerned the fact that big entities were substantially exonerated from some important reporting concerning their capital, the maintenance of liquidity, or the submission of leverage requirements.

The GLB Act was followed by the Sarbanes-Oxley Act[161] (SOA) of 2002, enacted in the aftermath of a series of bankruptcies and accounting scandals,[162] and concerns the regulations and standards of financial practice, accounting, and corporate governance.[163] It is important to mention the SOA because it introduced provisions aimed at improving the financial disclosure of public companies and gives the SEC new powers. Moreover, SOA created a new section 15D in the SAE that provided that the SEC or a "registered securities association or national securities exchange" adopt "rules reasonably designed to address conflicts of interest that can arise when securities analysts recommend equity securities in research reports and public appearances, in order to improve the objectivity of research and provide investors with more useful and reliable information". Finally, the SEC was endowed with powers to censure, exclude, and even ban securities professionals from practicing.

The goal of law was to reestablish investors' confidence in securities markets through tougher disclosure provisions and strengthened corporate accounting controls.[164] Importantly, the SOA follows the "disclosure philosophy" which perceives the provision of accurate information as the best method to improve public confidence in capital markets.

As the crisis burst in 2008, Congress responded with the adoption of the 2010 Dodd-Frank Wall Street Reform[165] (DFA) and the 2012 JOBS Act,[166] which alleviates securities requirements for small businesses. The DFA is particularly important since it makes a wide range of changes within the American financial system by directly dealing with investor protection as well. As a first step, Section 913(g) of the DFA gives a statutory definition of the retail investor as "a natural person, or the legal representative of a natural person, who (a) receives personalized investment advice about securities from a broker, dealer, or investment adviser, and (b) uses such advice primarily for personal, family or household purposes".

Subsequently—apart from an increase in point of sales disclosure—Section 913 also required the SEC staff to carry out an in-depth Study on the brokerage-dealing and advisory industry. In particular, the Study focuses on the following: the need to extend the fiduciary duty to brokers when they deal with retail investors, in order to overcome the regulatory gaps, shortcomings, and overlaps of the current regulation; the option of abolishing the broker-dealer exclusion from the definition of "Investment Adviser" under the 1940 Advisers Act; and, the possibility to apply the fiduciary duty and other requirements that already exist under the Advisers Act to BDs as well.[167]

The following pages concern the main duties to which BDs and IAs are subject. Even if the two categories have different regulatory frameworks, they are both subject to anti-fraud rules (under Sections 10/15 SEA and Section 206 IAA), to duties of best execution and duties of loyalty and care (fiduciary duty and suitability).[168] Importantly, the SEC Study (and, above all, the prospective regulation stemming thereof) may in the future affect the current regulatory landscape, at the benefit of the legal protection of retail investors in the United States.

4.2.2 Information Disclosure

Mandatory disclosure has always played a key role in the US legal landscape governing financial markets.[169] As said above, key disclosure requirements were firstly introduced by the Securities Act and the Exchange Act with the aim to spread information during the period when a firm goes public and to make secondary markets more transparent. Such requirements were conceived as the primary tool whereby all investors, both sophisticated and less-sophisticated or unsophisticated investors,[170] can protect their own interests by learning about the actual financial situation of a firm issuing instruments such as equity and debt. Disclosure appeared (and it partially continues to appear today) as *the* tool for opening markets to business while maintaining its efficiency.[171]

For BDs a failure to disclose information to their customers can be punished under Section 10b of the SEA and related SEA Rule 10b-5 on securities frauds. In particular, under SEA Rule 10b-10 concerning transaction confirmation, a BD must simply disclose, in writing, specific information to customers either at or before the completion of a transaction. For instance, the BD must notify its customer "the date and time of the transaction (or the fact that the time of the transaction will be furnished upon written request to such customer) and the identity, price, and number of shares or units (or principal amount) of such security purchased or sold by such customer".[172] Importantly, the BD must also disclose whether it is acting as agent or as principal. In the former case, the BD must reveal the "amount of any remuneration received or to be received by the broker"[173] from its customer in connection with a specific transaction.

The situation is more complex when a BD recommends a security. In this case, the BD "is obliged to give honest and complete information when recommending a purchase or sale"[174] of a security and "must disclose material adverse facts of which it is aware [. … including] disclosure of 'adverse interests' such as 'economic self-interest' that could have influenced its recommendation".[175]

Disclosure duties for IAs are directly connected with their fiduciary duty toward their customers.[176] In the seminal *Capital Gains* case, the US SC states that IAs are required to "eliminate, or at least to expose, all conflicts of interest which might incline an investment adviser—consciously or unconsciously—to render advice which was not disinterested".[177] The Court also specified that such federal[178] fiduciary duty is "an affirmative duty of 'utmost good faith, and full and fair disclosure of all material facts,' as well as an affirmative obligation 'to employ reasonable care to avoid misleading'"[179] customers. On the basis of this, the

SEC has carried out important enforcement activity against IAs' fraudulent behavior.[180]

Alongside the principle of disclosure of all material information in connection with an IA's fiduciary duty, key disclosure rules for IAs are the Advisers Act Rule 204-3—the so-called brochure rule—and Advisers Act Rule 206(4)-4. On the one hand, the "brochure rule" provides that IAs deliver annually to clients (and initially to prospective clients) their brochure, on a written form. This brochure must include, inter alia, the adviser's background financial information and disciplinary history; its methods of analysis, business practices and services; the risks of losses; the adviser's brokerage agreements (the use of soft dollars); and the range of fees applied.[181]

On the other hand, Advisers Act Rule 206(4)-4 provides that IAs must disclose (a) all material facts concerning a financial condition "that is reasonably likely to impair the ability of the adviser to meet contractual commitments to clients"[182]; and (b) "a legal or disciplinary event that is material to an evaluation of the adviser's integrity or ability to meet contractual commitments to clients".[183]

4.2.3 Conflicts of Interest and Prohibited Remuneration-Linked Practices

The more developed the market, the more complex the conflicts of interest that can arise between investors and their investment services providers. Over time, the SEC has identified several malpractices that stem from a conflict-of-interest situation and very likely result in detriments for retail investors. Some of them are the following: soft-dollar arrangements, scalping, and churning.

The so-called soft-dollar practices[184] arise out of a situation when an IA is affiliated to a BD and has the incentive to send customers' orders to the latter even if it does not supply the best execution services.[185] The SEC has defined such practices as those arrangements under which products or services, namely, brokerage and research, "other than execution of securities transactions [...] are obtained by an adviser from or through a broker in exchange for the direction by the adviser of client brokerage transactions to the broker."[186]

The SEC has introduced a "safe harbor" clause envisaging that:

> an individual or firm must exercise 'investment discretion' over an account, as defined in Section 3(a)(35) of the Exchange Act,[187] in order to use client commissions to obtain research under Section 28(e) of the Exchange Act ("Section 28(e)") [..., and] that a person who exercises investment discretion with respect to an account shall not be deemed to have acted unlawfully or to have breached a fiduciary duty solely by reason of his having caused the account to pay more than the lowest available commission if such person determines in good faith that the amount of the commission is reasonable in relation to the value of the brokerage and research services provided.[188]

Thus, an IA neither acts unlawfully nor breaches their fiduciary duty, as long as they meet the condition of good faith[189] when determining the reasonable amount of the commission. This implies that the extent of the shield provided by the safe harbor must be seen in concrete situations and it cannot be theoretically drawn beforehand. Importantly, IAs have the burden of proof.

Scalping is a fraudulent practice which happens when an IA purchases (or already owns) a security before recommending his/her clients to buy it, knowing in advance that the recommendation will raise the price of the security in question; afterward, the IA sells the stock at the higher post-recommendation price.[190] The negative aspect of scalping is that it "is based on the making recommendations without disclosing the conflict of interest arising out of the shares owned by the person making the recommendation".[191]

In the *Capital Gains* case, the US SC holds that this practice constitutes a fraud: "the high standard of business morality exacted by our laws regulating the securities industry do not permit an investment adviser to trade on the market effect of his own recommendations without fully and fairly revealing his personal interest(s) in these recommendations to his clients".[192] Indeed, in the very same case, the US SC held that the Adviser Act Section 206 not only covers frauds when the adviser has the intention to deceive but also covers conflict-of-interest situations when "nondisclosure of material facts" would make the IA benefit from its advisory recommendations.[193] Through this case, the US SC introduced the "fiduciary duty" for IAs (see below).

Churning is a practice that occurs when a BD, "acting in his own interests and against those of his customer, induces transactions in the customer's account which are excessive in size and frequency in light of the character of the account".[194] Churning is classified by Rule 15c1-7 as a "manipulative, deceptive, or other fraudulent device or contrivance".[195]

The key aspect of churning lies in the fact that the broker abuses the customer's confidence when handling her/his account and this happens "whenever the broker or dealer is in a position to determine the volume and frequency of transactions by reason of the customer's willingness to follow the suggestions of the broker or dealer and he abuses the customer's confidence by overtrading".[196] To demonstrate that her/his account has been "churned", the plaintiff must show (1) that the broker could exercise control over the trading of the account in question, (2) that the trading operated by the broker oversized the customer's investment objectives, and (3) that the broker acted with the requisite scienter.[197]

4.2.4 Best Execution

The way in which a BD executes a client's orders may affect the outcome of the transaction. To avoid abusive behavior on the part of BDs, the SEC has developed the so-called best execution that has become a key feature of the US system of investor protection, long before it entered the European legal landscape.

Broker-dealers, when acting either as an agent or as a principal,[198] are subject to the obligation to "execute customers' trades at the most favorable terms reasonably available under the circumstances, i.e., at the best reasonably available price".[199] The SEC clarified that is not the lowest possible commission cost but it is the best qualitative execution, in that the service provide must "execute securities transactions for clients in such a manner that the client's total cost or proceeds in each transaction is the most favorable under the circumstances".[200] Thus, there can be many examples to specify what best execution is, but the "best reasonably available price"[201] is the ultimate paradigm to assess an execution as "best".

Alongside the price, the SEC has given the following six additional parameters to gauge an execution as best: "(1) the size of the order; (2) the speed of execution available on competing markets; (3) the trading characteristics of the security; (4) the availability of accurate information comparing markets and the technology to process the data; (5) the availability of access to competing markets; and (6) the cost of such access."[202]

Also IAs have a duty to "seek best execution of client securities transactions",[203] which implies that IAs have to "'periodically and systematically' evaluate the execution they are receiving for their clients".[204] As seen above, this is connected to the "soft-dollar" practice and occurs when an IA has the responsibility to choose the BD through which a client's order is executed. The SEC has clarified that an IA "should consider the full range and quality of a broker's services in placing brokerage including, among other things, the value of research provided as well as execution capability, commission rate, financial responsibility, and responsiveness".[205]

The European and American best execution provisions are substantially similar: the main difference is the importance of the price element in order to assess whether the service provided was the best possible result. In Europe, the result "can be judged in terms of price, speed, likelihood of execution and settlement, size, nature of the order. In the United States, the concept covers also a number of factors, but with the price being typically the most important".[206]

4.2.5 Fiduciary Duty and Suitability

The title of this section is fiduciary duty *and* suitability because, while the first one is usually applied to IAs, the second mostly refers to broker-dealers. The rationale for having two different regimes—also defined as a "bifurcated structure"[207]—comes from the difference in the tasks theoretically assigned to IAs and BDs.[208] From the 1930s onward, brokers and dealers have been considered as arm's-length salesmen that effect "transactions in securities for the accounts of others" (brokers), and directly buy and sell securities on their own account (dealers).[209] IAs, instead, provide investment advice and are prohibited from dealing financial instruments out of their own accounts, unless strict conditions are met.[210]

Thus, the relationship with clients should be *less* burdensome for BDs than for IAs[211]: "A broker-dealer is more likely to have a duty to make full disclosure when recommending a security, but is less likely to have an unqualified duty to provide the client with useful market information concerning the client's present portfolio even when the broker-dealer is aware of such information."[212] Although this is true in many cases, BDs do not only deal with their customers at arm's length.[213] Indeed, when a "firm exercises actual or de facto control over a customer's account because of a customer's trust and confidence, [then] the broker may owe a fiduciary obligation to the customer."[214] Thus, the line bordering the two categories is not clear-cut.

From all this it can be said that there are some circumstances,[215] in particular under state law,[216] in which BDs are deemed to have a fiduciary duty toward their customers, while they do not have such a duty under other circumstances. On top of this, the "SEC too has been inconsistent in articulating brokers' duties".[217] Nevertheless, good faith and honesty always represent basic duties for brokers and dealers.[218] The situation is, however, different for IAs who are subject to a federal fiduciary duty.[219]

4.2.5.1 Broker-Dealers: Shingle Theory and Suitability

During the 1930s, the SEC developed the so-called shingle theory,[220] endorsed by case law,[221] which is characterized by a tacit nature of representation[222] and implies that a broker who puts out a "shingle" is capable of representing their customers fairly, responsibly, and professionally.[223] The shingle theory was necessary because, from an investor's viewpoint, the agent-principal transaction can be similar to some brokerage transactions between BDs and their customers.[224] Professor Madison perfectly explains that this similarity happens when BDs sell an investor certain securities that they do not already own, thus generating an agency-like brokerage transaction that might imply a fiduciary duty from the BDs toward the investor:

> Such a fiduciary relationship does not exist when stock or bond salesperson sells securities that it already owns to an investor, also known as a “dealer” transaction, because there is no agency relationship. Rather, the relationship is between two principals to a transaction similar to buying goods in a retail store. In a retail store setting, the storeowner generally owns the goods he sells to the customer rather than taking the customer’s order and purchasing the goods on a market to provide to the customer. Indeed, taking an order in a store and tracking down to fulfill the order may not provide for expedient commerce. If a retail storeowner did business by purchasing the goods for each customer order on an open market, an agency relationship would exist.[225]

However, despite the agency-like qualities, Professor Karmel specifies that the “shingle theory is not based upon the law of agency because a broker-dealer may act as either agent or principal”.[226] Karmel also clarifies that the shingle theory is based on the industry (i.e., SROs’) standards of fair dealing, namely, the industry principles of custom and usage that are the grounds for common-law duties,[227] “although over the year the SEC has encapsulated certain fair dealing obligations into its rules”.[228] Similarly, Professor Lee-Hazen considers the shingle theory as a “corollary to fiduciary duty”,[229] which the SEC has applied in its enforcement actions.[230]

The “know the security obligation”[231] means that BDs must know the object of their recommendation, namely, the security in question: they need to know the features of the securities sold and facts need to support the recommendation.[232] The rationale behind the “know the security obligation” is similar to that of the shingle theory: BDs recommending a security give their customers the idea that they know what they are recommending, by implying that they are informed and their recommendation has a factual basis[233]; that is, the broker “has made a thorough investigation on which it based its recommendation.”[234]

Within this framework, SRO rules also require BDs to fairly deal with their customers and to “observe high standards of commercial honor and just and equitable principles of trade".[235] Coherently to that, brokers are also subject to the so-called suitability rule,[236] an obligation of fair dealing[237] that implies that brokers should know whether a recommended security suits their customer's investment profile.[238] The New York Stock Exchange Rule 405—also known as the "Know Your Customer" rule—requires that "every member organization is required to: [...] Use due diligence to learn the essential facts relevant to every customer, every order, every cash or margin account accepted or carried by such organization". Then, the NASD rule 2310 (now FINRA Rule 2111) clearly specifies what is meant by suitability:

> In recommending to a customer the purchase, sale or exchange of any security, a member shall have reasonable grounds for believing that the recommendation is suitable for such customer upon the basis of the facts, if any, disclosed by such customer as to his other security holdings and as to his financial situation and needs. [...] Prior to the execution of a transaction recommended to a non-institutional customer ... a member shall make reasonable efforts to obtain information concerning: (1) the customer's financial status, (2) the customer's tax status; (3) the customer's investment objectives; and (4) such other information used or considered to be reasonable by such member or registered representative in making recommendations to the customer.[239]

A key stone of the suitability rule is that brokers must have "reasonable grounds for believing"[240] that the recommendation is suitable for a customer. Brokers do not have the obligation of being right every time they make an investment recommendation, but they, instead, have the duty to act reasonably on the basis of the information provided by their customer.[241] In that vein, brokers must "make a customer-specific determination of suitability and [...] tailor [their] recommendations to the customer's financial profile and investment objectives".[242]

Importantly, the standards of conduct of a BD cannot be waived or negotiated away by customers through disclosure.[243] However, even though the suitability rule is important for customers, it has not been established by the SEC, but by SROs[244]: the consequence of this is that the mere violation of this rule does "not provide an independent basis for private relief".[245] However, Professor Lee-Hazen clarifies that a violation of the suitability rule may be relevant in SEA Rule 10b-5 actions, whose essence is fraud and deception.[246]

Finally, in case of institutional accounts, FINRA Rule 2111(b) provides an exemption to the customer-specific suitability duty.[247] This applies when a broker: "has a reasonable basis to believe that the institutional customer is capable of evaluating investment risks independently, [... and] the institutional customer affirmatively indicates that it is exercising independent judgment in evaluating the [...] recommendations".[248]

4.2.5.2 Investment Adviser: Fiduciary Duty

IAs are subject to a fiduciary duty toward their customers, which requires "'undivided' or 'single-minded' loyalty, thus limiting the financial intermediary's pursuit of self-interest".[249] In *Capital Gains*,[250] the US SC wanted to protect the IAs' customers by stating that the Advisers Act was intended to cover both "nondisclosure of material facts" and "technical fraud".[251]

Professors Haas and Howard explain that, according to the Court, a conflict of interests arises when an IA can directly benefit from investment recommendations.[252] Thus, to protect investors in this kind of situation, they need to be in a position to understand whether an IA "is serving 'two masters' or only one, 'especially if one of the masters happens to be [personal] economic interest'".[253] Given the impossibility to prohibit any possible conflict of interest, the US SC requires IAs to disclose such conflicts when they happen.[254]

Haas and Howard further explain that a fiduciary duty englobes disclosure, a duty of loyalty, and a duty of care.[255] Acting with loyalty toward customers means that an IA has to behave "in a manner consistent with the best interest of its client and must not subrogate client interests to its own".[256] The duty of care, instead, applies when an IA makes investment recommendations.[257] In this circumstance, an IA is required to conduct its business professionally,[258] and to "make a reasonable investigation to determine that it is not basing its recommendations on materially inaccurate or incomplete information".[259]

Finally, IAs can be held liable if they do not disclose their conflicts of interests[260] and "all material[261] facts regarding the conflict so that the client can make an informed decision whether to enter into or continue an advisory relationship with the adviser".[262] Importantly, Item 8 of Form ADV Part 2A (Uniform Application for Investment Adviser Registration)[263] requires IAs to disclose the methods of analysis they employ, the investment strategies, and risk of loss,[264] so that customers can examine such methods.

4.2.5.3 The Watershed Between Investment Advisers and Broker-Dealers

The "bifurcated regulatory regime"[265] which distinguishes IAs from BDs is a core characteristic of the US system. The main distinction between the two concerns the application of fiduciary standards: whereas it is clear that IAs owe fiduciary duties toward their customers, such a fiduciary obligation does not always apply to brokers and dealers who are mostly perceived as salespersons.[266] In order to protect investors, BDs need to comply with other rules, such as the suitability rule or "standards of commercial honor and just and equitable principles of trade".[267] As a result, rules on disclosures of conflicts for BDs are weaker than those applied to advisers,[268] and whereas IAs are mostly regulated by more flexible principle-based[269] rules, BDs follow a more rigid rule-based regulatory approach.[270]

However, retail, less-sophisticated investors are largely unaware of the differences of such a double regulatory regime.[271] Despite the definition of retail investors by the DFA, all types of investors are de facto viewed through the same eyes, and retail investors just *happen* to consult and invest their money a broker rather than an IA.

The fiduciary duty has developed over time through the law of trust[272] and, as it is not a strict canon, is easily adaptable to different circumstances, business models, and commission structures.[273] Owing a fiduciary duty to a customer implies behaving in the costumer's best interest by complying with the duties of loyalty and care,[274] so that even the disclosure of conflicts of interests becomes a core element of the fiduciary duty.[275] The Study on Investment Advisers and Broker-Dealers states that the content of the fiduciary duty, as developed by the SEC and the courts over time, has addressed problems on "disclosure of conflicts of interest, suitability and reasonable basis for investment advice, and principal trading and cross trading".[276]

Broker-dealers and IAs have always had different tasks. Expressed in a European (MiFID) language, the former are usually receptors/executors of clients' orders, whereas the latter provide advisory services. Thus, investors with deeper knowledge of the financial markets could directly trade through BDs (e.g., RTO service under MiFID), while those with less expertise could seek out the services of an IA (e.g., portfolio management under MiFID). The idea lying behind this system is that all investors are deemed to be sufficiently rational to be able to choose the kind of service they think they need.

The distinction is clear on paper. However, the two roles have blurred[277] over the past thirty years, and this has seriously undermined the original scaffolding. Moreover, frequent crises have deteriorated the confidence of retail investors, who are not usually able to distinguish the different legal implications of the two regimes: "the investors have a reasonable expectation that the advice that they are receiving is in their best interest",[278] no matter whether they using services provided by a BD or an IA. This phenomenon has been delved into and "[e]xisting studies suggest that investors do not have a clear understanding about the distinction between broker-dealers and investment advisers and their different levels of fiduciary responsibility".[279]

The need to avoid requiring retail investors to be "proactive" in studying both how finance works and how financial regulations are designed is one of the main reasons behind the next probable regulatory steps in the United States. The January 2011 study[280] of the SEC staff recommends that the SEC change the current regulation on fiduciary duty, thus extending the IAs' fiduciary duty standards to brokers[281] when they make investment suggestions to retail investors. Other proposals for reforms are, instead, dismissed (such as maintaining the existing regulatory framework, enhancing disclosure requirements, and, finally, developing a best-interests standard-of-conduct for BDs).[282]

In March 2013 the SEC has taken a first step toward a possible uniform fiduciary standard for BDs and IAs. The US Authority has issued

Release No. 34-69013[283] whereby it officially seeks "data and other information, in particular quantitative data and economic analysis, relating to the benefits and costs that could result from various alternative approaches regarding the standards of conduct and other obligations of broker-dealers and investment advisers".[284] The aim is to adopt a regulation that applies a uniform fiduciary standard to BDs and IAs.

As of July 2017, in the aftermath of the 2016 decision of the Department of Labor to treat persons providing remunerated investment advice on retirement plans as fiduciaries,[285] the SEC seems to be willing to move forward on the issue of a fiduciary duty for BDs offering personalized investment.[286] However, the adoption of a uniform fiduciary standard is a complex exercise and Professor Laby rightly points out that even if a fiduciary standard should be imposed on brokers, this should be done cautiously on brokers providing advice.[287] This choicc would follow the logic underpinning the difference between suitability and appropriateness under MiFID in Europe: whereas the former applies to advisory services, the latter applies to non-advisory services (with the exclusion of non-complex instruments). Similarly, when a broker is not providing advice, it should not be subject to a fiduciary duty.[288]

4.3 Emulating the US Approach

This chapter has shown that the US system for investor protection is grounded on an encounter between market regulation through securities laws, regulations and SROs' rules, and principles of contract law.[289] The former set concerns the market infrastructure and it regulates how market players must behave in order to achieve an efficient financial market, with particular attention historically paid to market transparency through disclosure. The latter regards common-law principles, as developed over the time, aimed at counterbalancing the power asymmetry between a weaker and a stronger counterparty. Traditionally speaking, given their role in the financial markets, broker-dealers have been regulated statutorily and by SROs' rules focused on their efficient and non-misleading business conduct. Quite the opposite, IAs, given the agency-like services they provide and their proximity toward less-sophisticated market players like retail investors, have been bound to the common-law principle of fiduciary duty (which more rarely applies to BDs, in particular when they make investment recommendations). This is, by and large, a short summary of the US part of this chapter.

Against this backdrop, mandatory disclosure plays a key role in US securities laws.[290] This is so for the following reasons: (1) mandatory disclosure permits different sources of information to be compared; (2) it reduces agency costs; (3) it overcomes externalities; (4) it reduces duplicative research and, thus, research costs of investors.[291] Furthermore, information disclosure is also meant to level "the playing field between sophisticated and ordinary investors",[292] in what is defined as "market egalitarianism", that has so much influenced securities laws in both the United States and Europe.[293]

Nevertheless, disclosure for broker-dealers stems from statutory anti-fraud norms and SROs' conduct-of-business rules, whereas disclosure for IAs hinges upon their fiduciary duty toward their customers.[294] Notably, the border between the two categories of service providers is now hard to grasp,[295] in particular for retail investors. The 2011 Study of the SEC highlights the fact that the same firm can be registered as both a BD and an IA and, thus, offer both brokerage-dealing and investment advisory services, and this can be confusing for retail investors. Such investors may, in fact, have investment accounts subject to IA or BD regulation and receive advisory services from "dual-hatted"[296] personnel that are also subject to BD and IA regulation.[297]

The 2011 Study of the SEC does not completely overcome the problem of how retail investors perceive the two categories of service providers. Indeed, on the one hand, the Study maintains the current distinction between BDs and IAs, but on the other hand, it overcomes one of the core elements of this distinction by recommending a uniform fiduciary standard,[298] without giving any clear implementation directive on how to do so.[299] Importantly, in line with the Prospectus, UCITS, and PRIIPs legislative reforms in Europe, the Study reaffirms the importance of disclosure by recommending that the SEC adopt a disclosure summary containing key information on the broker/IA's services and products.[300] Coherently, the Study stresses the need to facilitate a "uniform, simple and clear"[301] disclosure of conflicts of interests to retail customers.

EU law of financial markets is only apparently similar and the US model (and its theoretic approach) cannot be copied-and-pasted in Europe. First, in Europe MiFID regulates investment services without dealing with the distinction between IAs and BDs, and the "investment firm" category is supposed to cover both of the US service providers.[302] MiFID draws, indeed, a distinction between services: dealing own account/reception and transmission of orders/execution of orders are closer to what in the United States would be the activity of a BD; whereas portfolio management and advice are closer to what in the United States would be the activity of an IA. Coherently, under MiFID the advisory services are covered by the suitability test, which might be viewed as a European public-law surrogate of the US fiduciary duty. Importantly, there is no equivalent "appropriateness test" in the United States,[303] and BDs' duties must be interpreted according to the specific circumstances of the services supplied.

Second, there is no single European contract law embedded in a European Civil Code. The EU law of investment services—above all, MiFID I/II—introduces public-law rules on business of conduct *without* substituting them with a single EU body of private law. As Professor Micklitz rightly points out: "what is missing at the EU level is, in continental language, a European civil code or, in common law language, a European law on contract and tort. [...] Therefore, trans-border conflicts within the EU have to be solved through private international law means."[304] Indeed, contracts concerning investment services concluded by two counterparties—such as an investment firm and a retail investor—residing in two different Member States are channeled through rules of "Europeanized private international law"[305] (in particular, Rome I[306] and Brussels Regulation I-bis[307]) but the contract itself is still governed by national private-law norms. As a consequence, there is no pan-European contract-based fiduciary duty, and even if a piece of EU financial market legislation would mention it, it would have to be construed according to national private-law traditions.

Notably, the term "fiduciary duty" is typical of the law of trust as fleshed out of the common-law tradition and it is difficult to find perfect equivalences in Mainland Europe.[308] European national private-law systems obviously cover and regulate situations where one of the counterparties of a contractual relationship is required to behave in the best interests of the other counterparty. Nevertheless, the Anglo-American term *fiduciary duty* is not directly and unequivocally translatable, nor is there any *federal*, European contract law on which such a principle could blossom from scratch.

Third, even if it can be perceived as a surrogate of the fiduciary duty due to the fact that it is entrenched in contracts, the MiFID suitability (and appropriateness) was introduced as a public enforcement tool.[309] Such tool is used (1) by public enforcers when executing enforcement procedures aimed at assessing providers' conduct of services[310]; (2) to add a degree of uniformity to service providers' behavior throughout the Union (and create a level playing field)[311]; and, (3) to boost customers' confidence in their investment providers.[312] Against this backdrop, the *fully* rational investors (execution-only business not covered by the appropriateness test), the *average* rational investors (for services covered by the appropriateness test), and the *less* rational investors (for advice and portfolio management) are used as yardsticks to gauge the public enforcement of financial supervisors. The MiFID suitability and appropriateness tests, indeed, do not provide for private-law remedies, which rest on the shoulders of the national legal systems, but they have been conceived as tools directly harmonizing supervisory standards[313] and indirectly harmonizing diverging national private laws (civil or horizontal effect of the financial regulatory provisions).[314]

Fourth, European norms follow a market-building model and are conceived as instruments to build and reinforce the single market, by overstepping the "boundaries between contract law and unfair commercial practices law".[315] European public-law rules on investment services tend to merge advertising, pre-contractual information, and contract conclusion[316] to increase market transparency and ease private relationships: this is clearly shown in bundled/tied packages of products under MiFID II, which are selling practices regulated by hard- and soft-law measures in order to provide information with the purpose of entering into financial instrument contracts.

Fifth, the disclosure paradigm is in Europe canalized through public, rather than private, law and SROs' standards. The regulatory approach to retail investor protection followed at the European level is strongly inspired by the information disclosure paradigm already used in the United States (and softened by the fiduciary duty). At first glance, the EU appears to be attracted to the US "gravitational pull",[317] and the increasing harmonization approach[318] employed during the 2000s is also justified by the need to catch up to the United States.[319] However, unlike the US one, the European disclosure paradigm is practically only based on public law (or Regulatory Private Law).

To conclude, the underpinning values of the EU law of investor protection are mirrored in the pattern of justice it conveys. The US-inspired, disclosure-led protection has been meant to empower all the potential investors and grant access to "those who are excluded from the market or to those who face difficulties in making use of the market freedoms".[320] Within such an *ökonomischer* dimension of the function of law,[321] the recent intra-firm proceduralization of contract-law-based principles of investor protection under the MiFID II Product Governance is designed to make the market work efficiently at *macro* level by avoiding/reducing mis-selling cases at *micro* level.[322] The rebalancing connection between the *macro* and the *micro* level is leading to reshape the contour of justice under the EU law: from *pure access justice* inspired by the US model of fairness of market access[323] to *paternalistic access justice* where investors are guided to make rational investment decisions, with their autonomy being limited for their own protection.[324]

The key takeaway of this comparative exercise is that the Americanization of the EU law of investor protection is only partial. Even if the US-inspired driving value of market access permeates the structure of the EU investor protection system, the US legal protection of investors is—as said at the outset—grounded on an encounter between the common law, statutes and standards produced by the SROs. The EU law, instead, is inherently regulatory[325] and detached from the contract itself, and so are its enforcement procedures, as the following chapters on public and private enforcement mechanisms will try to show.

Notes

1. *See:* Robin S. Doak, *Black Tuesday: Prelude to the Great Depression* (Compass Point Books, 2008). At 13.
2. *The Truth in Securities Act* (May 27, 1933).
3. *The Securities Exchange Act.*
4. *Investment Advisers Act.*
5. Francesco D'Alessandro, *Regolatori Del Mercato, Enforcement E Sistema Penale* (Torino: Giappichelli, 2014). At 406.
6. In the words of Professor D'Alessandro: "riforme da cui 'tutto ebbe inizio'" [Author's own translation from Italian: "reforms from which it all began"] ibid. At 406.
7. Greta R. Krippner, *Capitalizing on Crisis: The Political Origins of the Rise of Finance* (Cambridge, MA: Harvard University Press, 2011). At 83–84.
8. *Directive 93/22/Eec.*
9. Marc Kruithof and Walter VanGerven, "A Differentiated Approach to Client Protection: The Example of Mifid," ed. Financial Law Institute - Universiteit Gent (2010). At 7.
10. Section II.2. in Annex II to MiFID I.
11. Article 4 (1,9) MiFID II and Article 4 (1,10) MiFID I.
12. Professor Busch points out that "if an investment firm acts solely as an investor's contractual counterparty (dealing on own account), this constitutes an investment activity and the investor is not a 'client' within the meaning of MiFID. Nor, therefore, is there a client classification obligation." Danny Busch, "Agency and Principal Dealing under the Market in Financial Instruments Directive," in *Agency Law in Commercial Practice*, ed. Danny Busch, Laura Macgregor, and Peter Watts (Oxford: Oxford University Press, 2016). At 151.
13. *Directive 2014/65/Eu.*
14. Article 4.1(11) MiFID II.
15. Annex II, MiFID II.
16. Danny Busch, Busch. At 152.
17. Article 30(1): "Member States shall ensure that, in their relationship with eligible counterparties, investment firms act honestly, fairly and professionally and communicate in a way which is fair, clear and not misleading, taking into account the nature of the eligible counterparty and of its business." Interestingly, in July 2017 the Italian Court of Cassation already endorsed the application of the general obligation of

fair dealing to eligible counterparties and declared void a derivative contract on the grounds that the investment service provider should have acted in the best interests of the clients [*Cassazione Civile, Sez. I, 31 Luglio 2017, N. 19013, 2017* (2017).].

18. At 152.
19. *Directive 2014/59/Eu.*
20. On "moral hazard": Paul R. Krugman, *The Return of Depression Economics* (London: Penguin UK, 2008). At 165. Tom Baker, "On the Genealogy of Moral Hazard," *Texas Law Review* 75, no. 2 (1996).
21. See: Marc Kruithof, "A Differentiated Approach to Client Protection: The Example of Mifid," in *Financial Services, Financial Crisis and General European Contract Law: Failure and Challenges of Contracting*, ed. Stefan Grundmann and Yesim M. Atamer (New York: Kluwer Law International, 2011). At 9.
22. *Commission Delegated Regulation 2017/565/Eu.*
23. *See* Christoph Kumpan and Patrick C. Leyens, "Conflicts of Interest of Financial Intermediaries - Towards a Global Common Core in Conflicts of Interest Regulation," *European Company and Financial Law Review* 4, no. 1 (2008).
24. Conflicts of interest are particularly insidious when an investment firm provides a combination of the execution of orders on behalf of clients service and dealing on own account, that is, when in order to execute a client's order the firm is the direct counterparty of its own client (by either creating a financial instrument or using an instrument in its own inventory). In such a business model, the internal advisory service provided by the Compliance Function is as delicate as necessary.
25. Niamh Moloney, *Eu Securities and Financial Markets Regulation* (Oxford: Oxford University Press, 2014). At 373.
26. Article 23.1, MiFID II.
27. In the words of Professor Moloney: "Remuneration structures have very considerable potential to misalign incentives in the distribution process. The well-documented detriment which can follow includes biased advice, failure to provide debt reduction advice, poor product selection, inappropriate advice to switch products, and ultimately mis-selling." Niamh Moloney, "Regulating the Retail Markets," in *The Oxford Handbook of Financial Regulation*, ed. Niamh Moloney, Eilís Ferran, and Jennifer Payne (Oxford: Oxford University Press, 2015). At 757. Also the ESAs already in 2013 highlighted how, "[o]n the topic of sales incentives, it was felt that in order to avoid mis-selling of financial

products, several changes in sales culture are urgently required." Joint Committee of the European Supervisory Authorities—ESAs, "Joint Esas Consumer Protection Day," https://eiopa.europa.eu/Pages/Events/Event-2.aspx, *Joint ESAs Consumer Protection Day*.

28. Article 9.3(c), MiFID II.
29. Article 24.10, MiFID II. Professor Enriques carries out the perfect example of "an investment bank [...] assisting a company in an IPO; and no matter how independent the people in the brokerage arm can be 'on paper', they may be tempted to stuff their clients' portfolios with those shares, if they think that this will be appreciated by the firm's top management." Luca Enriques, "Conflicts of Interest in Investment Services: The Price and Uncertain Impact of Mifid's Regulatory Framework," in *Investor Protection in Europe*, ed. Guido Ferrarini and Eddy Wymeersch (New York: Oxford University Press, 2006). At 332. This example heralded the reasoning under the MiFID II upgrade of the independence level of the Compliance Function: from the top management to the firm's management body (see Chap. 7).
30. Article 24.10, MiFID II.
31. Article 27, *Commission Delegated Regulation 2017/565/Eu*.
32. European Securities and Markets Authority—ESMA, "Remuneration Policies and Practices (Mifid) - Esma/2013/606," https://www.esma.europa.eu/sites/default/files/library/2015/11/2013-606_en.pdf.
33. Article 23.2–3.
34. Antonella Antonucci, "Regole Di Condotta E Conflitto Di Interesse," *Banca, borsa e titoli di credito* 2009, no. 1 (2009). At 10.
35. *Commission Delegated Regulation 2017/565/Eu*.
36. Howell Jackson, "The Trilateral Dilemma in Financial Regulation," in *Overcoming the Saving Slump: How to Increase the Effectiveness of Financial Education and Saving Programs*, ed. Anna Maria Lusardi (Chicago: University of Chicago Press, 2009).
37. Ibid.
38. Ibid.
39. On the trilateral dilemma and MiFID: Andrew Tuch, "Conduct of Business Regulation," in *The Oxford Handbook of Financial Regulation*, ed. Niamh Moloney, Eilís Ferran, and Jennifer Payne (Oxford: Oxford University Press, 2015). At 561.
40. *Commission Delegated Directive 2017/593/Eu*.
41. Article 11.5(c), Commission Delegated Directive 2017/593/Eu.
42. In terms of type of instrument and issuers or product providers.

43. *Commission Delegated Regulation 2017/565/Eu.*
44. Article 24.10, MiFID II.
45. Article 12.3 Commission Delegated Directive 2017/593/Eu provides a list of criteria to qualify benefits as acceptable minor non-monetary benefits.
46. Article 53, *Commission Delegated Regulation 2017/565/Eu.*
47. *Commission Delegated Directive 2017/593/Eu.*
48. Jean-Pierre Casey and Karel Lannoo, eds., *The Mifid Revolution* (Cambridge University Press, 2009). At 55.
49. Ibid. At 55.
50. Article 54.9 *Commission Delegated Regulation 2017/565/Eu.*
51. Article 54.12 Commission Delegated Regulation 2017/565/Eu.
52. "Where an investment firm provides a service that involves periodic suitability assessments and reports, the subsequent reports after the initial service is established may only cover changes in the services or instruments involved and/or the circumstances of the client and may not need to repeat all the details of the first report." Article 54.12 *Commission Delegated Regulation 2017/565/Eu.*
53. Commission Delegated Regulation 2017/565/Eu.
54. Such as "information regarding the financial situation of the client or potential client shall include, where relevant, information on the source and extent of his regular income, his assets, including liquid assets, investments and real property, and his regular financial commitments." Article 54.4 Commission Delegated Regulation 2017/565/Eu.
55. On the resistance of national laws against the intrusion of European regulatory contract law: Olha O. Cherednychenko, "Financial Consumer Protection in the Eu: Towards a Self-Sufficient European Contract Law for Consumer Financial Services?," *European Review of Contract Law* 10, no. 4 (2014). At 486–491. Also: Federico DellaNegra, "The Private Enforcement of the Mifid Conduct of Business Rules. An Overview of the Italian and Spanish Experiences," ibid.
56. Even if stated in a pre-MiFID legislative landscape, the words of Professor Avgouleas on ISD conduct-of-business rules already forecast the phenomenon consolidated by MiFID I and MiFID II: "Conduct of business rules usually create both regulatory (public law) and contractual-tortious (private law) obligations." Emilios Avgouleas, "The Harmonisation of Rules of Conduct in Eu Financial Markets: Economic Analysis, Subsidiarity and Investor Protection," *European Law Journal* 6, no. 1 (2000). At 74.

57. Article 25.3.
58. Article 25.3.
59. Casey and Lannoo. At 55.
60. On this point: European Securities and Markets Authorities—ESMA, "Final Report - Guidelines on Complex Debt Instruments and Structured Deposits - Esma/2015/1783" (2015). *Final Report - Guidelines on complex debt instruments and structured deposits - ESMA/2015/1783.*
61. *Commission Directive 2006/73/Ec.*
62. ESMA specifies that such market factors are: (1) low returns from the traditional forms of investments or ordinary deposits, and (2) market volatility. European Securities and Markets Authority—ESMA, "Mifid Practices for Firms Selling Complex Products - Esma/2014/146" (Paris, FR, 2014). At 1.
63. *Commission Delegated Regulation 2017/565/Eu.*
64. Such as the right to convert the instrument into a different kind of investment (Article 57d).
65. "As is clear from the 2002 DMD, marketing disclosure is a core concern for EU retail policy, given potential investor vulnerability." Niamh Moloney, "Building a Retail Investment Culture through Law: The 2004 Markets in Financial Instruments Directive," *European Business Organization Law Review* 6, no. 3 (2005). At 384.
66. "The objective [...] appears to be to build an informed and empowered investor base, using relevant and comprehensible information." Ibid. At 386.
67. *Commission Delegated Regulation 2017/565/Eu.*
68. Article 44(2f), ibid.
69. Ibid.
70. Regarding the disclosure of information in "good time before the provision of investment services" (Article 46), the Compliance Function should find operative solutions in case of reception of orders via online means or over the phone. The first case looks easier and may be resolved by providing the client with an information sheet before s/he can actually enter the order. The second case is more delicate and a more conservative approach might be an automatic message reading the information sheet for the customer. However, this could very much delay the operation and the customer should be free to choose the information sheet via email in order to quickly proceed with the order.
71. Article 47(1f).
72. Article 4(42), MiFID II.

73. European Securities and Markets Authority—ESMA, "Guidelines on Cross-Selling Practices" (2016).
74. Article 50 Commission Delegated Regulation 2017/565/Eu.
75. Article 50(1).
76. Article 50(2).
77. Annex II, *Commission Delegated Regulation 2017/565/Eu.*
78. Article 50(10).
79. Recital 75, *Commission Delegated Regulation 2017/565/Eu.*
80. Article 50 (5), ibid.
81. Jonathan R. Macey and Maureen O'Hara, "The Law and Economics of Best Execution," *Journal of Financial Intermediation* 6 (1997). At 188.
82. Catherine D'Hondt and Jean-René Giraud, "Mifid: The (in)Famous European Directive?," *EDHEC Position Paper* (2007). At 18.
83. Moloney, *Eu Securities and Financial Markets Regulation.* At 521.
84. On smart order routing: Tobias Conte and Matthias Burghardt, "A Process Model for Best Execution," in *Enterprise applications and services in the finance industry: 3rd international workshop* (Montreal: FinanceCom 2007, 2007).
85. On the industry evolution toward an order-by-order Best Execution: ibid.
86. Busch. At 159.
87. *Commission Delegated Regulation 2017/565/Eu.*
88. Article 64 on the Best Execution criteria; Article 65 on the duty of investment firms carrying out portfolio management and reception and transmission of orders to act in the best interests of the client; Article 66 on the Execution Policy; Article 67 on general principles (for client order handling); Article 68 on aggregation and allocation of orders; Article 69 on aggregation and allocation of transactions for own account [importantly, a firm must pay particular attention, by complying with specified conditions, in case of aggregated transactions for own account, since it may generate conflicts of interests between the firm and its clients]; Article 70 on prompt fair and expeditious execution of client orders and publication of unexecuted client limit orders for shares traded on a trading venue.
89. Committee of European Securities Regulators—CESR, "Best Execution under Mifid. Public Consultation - Cesr/07-050b" (2007). At 8.
90. *Commission Delegated Regulation 2017/565/Eu.*
91. Ibid.

92. Financial Services Authority—FSA, "Fg12/09, Retail Product Development and Governance – Structured Product Review" (2012). At 3.
93. Ibid. At 4.
94. Ibid. At 5.
95. Ibid.
96. *Commission Delegated Directive 2017/593/Eu.*
97. Insurance Policies, even if widely distributed through commercial banks' retail networks, fall under the remit of the Insurance Distribution Directive (*Directive 2016/97/Eu.*) which provides for product oversight and governance requirements for insurance undertakings and insurance distributors.
98. Regulation 1286/2014/Eu.
99. Articles 9 and 10 of the *Commission Delegated Directive 2017/593/Eu.*
100. Article 9.
101. Article 9.
102. The Delegated Directive provides for a list of non-exhaustive list negative conditions to be taken into account: "(a) the market environment deteriorated; (b) the manufacturer or a third party involved in manufacturing and or functioning of the financial instrument experiences financial difficulties or other counterparty risk materializes; (c) the financial instrument fails to become commercially viable; or (d) demand for the financial instrument is much higher than anticipated, putting a strain on the firm's resources and/or on the market of the underlying instrument." Article 9.10, *Commission Delegated Directive 2017/593/Eu.*
103. Article 9 of the ibid. requires that the firm assess whether a financial product creates a situation where clients may be adversely affected if they take "(a) an exposure opposite to the one previously held by the firm itself; or (b) an exposure opposite to the one that the firm wants to hold after the sale of the product".
104. Article 10.2.
105. Article 10.2.
106. In early August 2017, the European Fund and Asset Management Association (EFAMA) endorsed and published the European MiFID Template (EMT). The EMT is a template for information exchange that can be used by both product manufacturers and distributors, and it provides for a minimum set of data, such as a product's target market

and costs and charges disclosure. European Fund and Asset Management Association—EFAMA, "European Mifid Template (Emt)" (2017).

107. Article 10.2.
108. Article 10.2.
109. Article 10.1.
110. Article 10.2.
111. Article 10.10.
112. *The Truth in Securities Act.*
113. *The Securities Exchange Act.*
114. *Investment Advisers Act.*
115. *Laylin K. James, "The Securities Act of 1933," Michigan Law Review* 32, no. 5 (1934). At 630.
116. Ibid. At 630.
117. Section 2(a)(1) states that: "The term "security" means any note, stock, treasury stock, security future, bond, debenture, evidence of indebtedness, certificate of interest or participation in any profit-sharing agreement, collateral-trust certificate, preorganization certificate or subscription, transferable share, investment contract, voting-trust certificate, certificate of deposit for a security, fractional undivided interest in oil, gas, or other mineral rights, any put, call, straddle, option, or privilege on any security, certificate of deposit, or group or index of securities (including any interest therein or based on the value thereof), or any put, call, straddle, option, or privilege entered into on a national securities exchange relating to foreign currency, or, in general, any interest or instrument commonly known as a "security", or any certificate of interest or participation in, temporary or interim certificate for, receipt for, guarantee of, or warrant or right to subscribe to or purchase, any of the foregoing." The Truth in Securities Act, ch. 38, title I, Sec. 1, 48 Stat. 74. [1933b].
118. *Securities and Exchange Commission V. W. J. Howey Co.*, 328 U.S. 293 (1946). In this case the Court held that when a contract "involves an investment of money in a common enterprise with profits to come solely from the efforts of others", then the contract at issue is to be considered as an "investment contract", capable of triggering the investor protection rules conveyed by the Securities Act of 1933.
119. Department of the Treasury, "Blueprint for a Modernized Financial Regulatory Structure" (Washington, DC, 2008). At 56.
120. Ibid. At 56.

121. "The 1934 created the Securities and Exchange Commission (SEC), and is the organic statute governing the wide panoply of the SEC's administrative authority." Thomas Lee-Hazen, *Principles of Securities Regulation, Revised* (St. Paul: West Academic, 2017). At 201.
122. "Unlike a broker who acts as agent, a dealer acts as principal." Securities and Exchange Commission—SEC, "Broker Dealer Registration," https://www.sec.gov/fast-answers/answersbdregishtm.html.
123. Dealing self-issued instruments directly with customers.
124. Matthew P. Allen, "A Lesson from History, Roosevelt to Obama — the Evolution of Broker-Dealer Regulation: From Self-Regulation, Arbitration, and Suitability to Federal Regulation, Litigation, and Fiduciary Duty," *Entrepreneurial Business Law Journal* 5, no. 1 (2009). At 20. Steven A. Ramirez, "The Professional Obligations of Securities Brokers under Federal Law: An Antidote for Bubbles?," *University of Cincinnati Law Review* 70, no. 2 (2002). At 534.
125. *Sec V. Capital Gains Research Bureau, Inc.*, 375 U.S. 180, 191 (1963).
126. *Over-the-Counter Market Act.*
127. "The object of this amendment, the Maloney Act, was to encourage over-the-counter dealers to organize and regulate their activities under governmental supervision." Tamar Hed-Hofmann, "The Maloney Act Experiment," *Boston College Law Review* 6, no. 2 (1965). At 187.
128. Francis A. Bonner, at the 1938 yearly convention of the Investment Bankers' Association of America, remarked that: "We have an opportunity here to set up our rules of business conduct under a system of business penalties". Francis A. Bonner, "The over-the-Counter Market and the Maloney Act," in *Annual Convention of the Investment Bankers' Association of America*, ed. Investment Bankers' Association of America (White Sulphur Springs, 1938).
129. Securities and Exchange Commission—SEC, "Study on Investment Advisers and Broker-Dealers" (Washington, DC, 2011). At iii.
130. Richard W. Jennings, "Self-Regulation in the Securities Industry: The Role of the Securities and Exchange Commission," *Law and Contemporary Problems* 29 (1964). At 663.
131. Reported by Joel Seligman, "Cautious Evolution or Perennial Irresolution: Stock Market Self-Regulation During the First Seventy Years of the Securities Exchange Commission," *Business Lawyer* 59, no. 4 (2004). At 1361.
132. See the SEC official website: Securities and Exchange Commission—SEC, "Self-Regulatory Organization Rulemaking," https://www.sec.

gov/rules/sro.shtml. See also: Financial Industry Regulatory Authority—FINRA, "Sec Approval of Finra Funding Portal Rules and Related Forms. January 2016," https://www.finra.org/sites/default/files/Regulatory-Notice-16-06.pdf. At 6; As specified in 2015 by the SEC: "While FINRA is the only registered national securities association at present, we recognize that a new national securities association or associations could register with us in the future." Securities and Exchange Commission—SEC, "Exchange Act Release No 76324 (October 20, 2015)" (2015). At 157.

133. "Study on Investment Advisers and Broker-Dealers." At 47.
134. Carrie Johnson, "Sec Approves One Watchdog for Brokers Big and Small," *The Washington Post* July 27, 2007.
135. Securities and Exchange Commission—SEC, "Release No. 34-56145" (Washington, DC, 2007).
136. The NASD was established in 1939 and formally registered with the SEC under the auspices of the Maloney Act on 7 August 1939. The *NASD Uniform Practice Code* was adopted in 1941 and it is now the *FINRA Uniform Practice Code* (UPC) [*see*: Financial Industry Regulatory Authority—FINRA, "Finra Website - Uniform Practice Code (Upc)," http://www.finra.org/Industry/Compliance/MarketTransparency/UPC/.]
137. "About Finra," http://www.finra.org/aboutfinra/.
138. Ibid.
139. "What We Do," http://www.finra.org/about/what-we-do.
140. "Arbitration and Mediation," http://www.finra.org/arbitration-and-mediation. All contracts between investors and FINRA-registered broker-dealers provide a clause which waives both of the parties' right to trial in a court. This system was also backed by the US SC in 1987 in the *Shearson/American Express v. McMahon* case. The important Study carried out by the SEC staff does not make any recommendation as regards the arbitration system. *See*: SEC, "Study on Investment Advisers and Broker-Dealers."
141. Eric Pan, "Organizing Regional Systems: The Us Example," in *The Oxford Handbook of Financial Regulation*, ed. Niamh Moloney, Eilís Ferran, and Jennifer Payne (Oxford: Oxford University Press, 2015). At 199.
142. *Investment Advisers Act*.

143. Securities and Exchange Commission—SEC, "Certain Broker-Dealers Deemed Not to Be Investment Advisers - Release Nos. 34-51523; Ia-2376; File No. S7-25-99" (2005). At 22.
144. On genesis and evolution of the Broker-Dealer exclusion: Arthur B. Laby, "Reforming the Regulation of Broker-Dealers and Investment Advisers," *The Business Lawyer* 65, no. 2 (2010).
145. As clearly explained by Professor Laby: "Although brokers also give advice, they have shielded themselves from adviser regulation by taking advantage of an exclusion in the Advisers Act. 4 Under this exclusion, as long as a broker's advice is "solely incidental" to brokerage services and the broker charges only commissions and not asset-based fees, the broker is excluded from Advisers Act regulation." "Fiduciary Obligations of Broker-Dealers and Investment Advisers," *Villanova Law Review* 55 (2010). At 702.
146. SEC, "Study on Investment Advisers and Broker-Dealers." At 15–16. If the investment advisory services are performed by a separately identifiable department or division of a bank, then that department or division, but not the entire bank, is considered as an "investment adviser" and must register. Ibid. At 89. As it was difficult to figure out whether a recommendation was purely incidental or not, the SEC adopted the "Certain Broker-Dealers Deemed Not to Be Investment Advisers" Rule ["Certain Broker-Dealers Deemed Not to Be Investment Advisers - Release Nos. 34-51523; Ia-2376; File No. S7-25-99."].
147. *Sec. V. Capital Gains Research Bureau, Inc.*, 375 U.S. 180, 191 (1963). On this: Charles G. Nickson, "The Regulation of Investment Advice: Subscription Advisers and Fiduciary Duties," *Michigan Law Review* 63, no. 7 (1965).
148. H. Lawrence Wilsey, "The Investment Advisers Act of 1940," *The Journal of Finance* 4, no. 4 (1949). At 286. Very interestingly, Wilsey also added: "Prior to the passage of the Act some members of the profession expected it not only to restrict their activities, but also to tend to break down the fiduciary relationship between the adviser and his client by requiring disclosure of their moves and the details of their transactions. However, no attempt has been made by the Securities and Exchange Commission, nor under the present act could any be made, to infringe upon this client-adviser relationship." At 296–297.
149. Jeffrey J. Haas and Steven Howard, *Investment Adviser Regulation in a Nutshell* (Eagan, MN: Thomson West, 2008). At 218.

150. Ibid. At 218. On the features of fiduciary obligations, see the seminal contribution of Professor DeMott: Deborah DeMott, "Beyond Metaphor: An Analysis of Fiduciary Obligation," *Duke Law Journal* 1988, no. 37 (1988).
151. SEC, "Study on Investment Advisers and Broker-Dealers."
152. It is worth mentioning the 1970 Securities Investor Protection Act, which established the Securities Investor Protection Corporation (SIPC) and was promulgated in the aftermath of the so-called "back office crisis" [see: Joel Seligman, *The Transformation of Wall Street: A History of the Securities and Exchange Commission and Modern Corporate Finance, 3rd Ed.* (New York: Aspen Publishers, 2003).] The SIPC "oversees the liquidation of member broker-dealers that close when the broker-dealer is bankrupt or in financial trouble, and customer assets are missing". Securities Investor Protection Corporation—SIPC, "Sipc Mission," https://www.sipc.org/about-sipc/sipc-mission.
153. *Garn–St. Germain Depository Institutions Act.*
154. By and large, it is possible to find a translation of "Savings & Loans" for Continental European banks: in France these institutions are named "caisses d'épargne", in Italy "casse di risparmio", in Spain "cajas de ahorros", in Germany "Sparkassen". On savings banks in Europe: Ignazio Angeloni, "Savings Banks in the European Banking Landscape," in *Financial Meeting of the Confederación Española de Cajas de Ahorros*, ed. European Central Bank - Banking Supervision (Madrid, 2014).
155. Ralph Nader, "Opening the Door to New Taxpayer Bailouts," http://nader.org/1998/02/01/opening-the-door-to-new-taxpayer-bailouts/.
156. Paul Krugman, "Reagan Did It," *The New York Times* May 31, 2009.
157. *Gramm-Leach-Bliley Act.*
158. "[T]he Act allows existing bank holding companies to acquire full-service securities firms and insurance companies, and it allows securities firms and insurance companies to acquire a bank (and thereby become a bank holding company)." Board of Governors of the Federal Reserve System - U.S. Department of the Treasury, "Report to the Congress on Financial Holding Companies under the Gramm–Leach–Bliley Act" (Washington, DC, 2003). At 1.
159. Federal Reserve Bank of San Francisco, "Banking Information: Overview of the Gramm-Leach-Bliley Act" (San Francisco, CA, 2000). As mentioned in: Securities and Exchange Commission—SEC, "Sec's

Oversight of Bear Stearns and Related Entities: The Consolidated Supervised Entity Program" (2008). At 47.

160. Christopher Cox, "Chairman Cox Announces End of Consolidated Supervised Entities Program," http://www.sec.gov/news/press/2008/2008-230.htm.
161. *Sarbanes-Oxley Act.*
162. Allison Fass, "One Year Later, the Impact of Sarbanes-Oxley," *Forbes* 2003.
163. Treccani—Dizionario di Economia e Finanza, "Sarbanes-Oxley Act" (2012).
164. Ibid.
165. *Dodd-Frank Wall Street Reform and Consumer Protection Act.*
166. *Jumpstart Our Business Startups Act.* For a critical appraisal of the outcomes of this piece of legislation: Donald C. Langevoort and Robert B. Thompson, "'Publicness' in Contemporary Securities Regulation after the Jobs Act," *Georgetown Law Journal* 101 (2013).
167. SEC, "Study on Investment Advisers and Broker-Dealers." At i–ii.
168. Tuch. At 549–550.
169. In the words of Professor Avgouleas: "In an attempt to clean up US markets from abuse in the post-1929 crash era, the Roosevelt administration created widespread disclosure regimes for securities issuers and traders by means of the so-called New Deal Statutes: mainly the Securities Act 1933 and the Securities Exchange Act 1934." Emilios Avgouleas, "What Future for Disclosure as a Regulatory Technique? Lessons from Behavioural Decision Theory and the Global Financial Crisis," in *The Future of Financial Regulation*, ed. Iain G MacNeil and Justin O'Brien (Oxford: Hart Publishing, 2010). At 206. In her seminal article Professor Romano makes the case for a different approach on US securities regulations—labeled "competitive federalism"—also reforming mandatory disclosure through an opt-out option for legal systems with a lesser level of investor protection (that rational investors will likely reject by not buying securities issued thereunder): Roberta Romano, "Empowering Investors: A Market Approach to Securities Regulation," *The Yale Law Journal* 107, no. 5 (1998). Apart from investor protection, information disclosure is crucial for insider trading, as was held by the United States Court of Appeals Second Circuit in the seminal case *Sec V. Texas Gulf Sulphur Co.*, 401 F.2d 833 (2d Cir. 1968).

170. A critical assessment of whether disclosure is useful for US unsophisticated investors is given by Easterbrook and Fischel: "Some say that uninformed investors are exploited investors; whoever knows less will get a raw deal. Others maintain that fear of such exploitation erodes confidence whether or not these investors lose out. Disclosure rules equalizing access and simplifying the presentation of information, so all can understand it, overcome the problem, whichever way it is put. This argument is as unsophisticated as the investors it is supposed to protect. It disregards the role of markets in impounding information in prices. So long as informed traders engage in a sufficient amount of searching for information and bargains, market prices will reflect all publicly available information." Frank H. Easterbrook and Daniel R. Fischel, "Mandatory Disclosure and the Protection of Investors," *Virginia Law Review* 70, no. 4 (1984). At 693–694.
171. On the importance of disclosure in the efficient allocation of financial resources: Luca Enriques and Sergio Gilotta, "Disclosure and Financial Market Regulation," in *The Oxford Handbook of Financial Regulation*, ed. Niamh Moloney, Eilís Ferran, and Jennifer Payne (Oxford: Oxford University Press, 2015).
172. Rule 10b-10.
173. Rule 10b-10.
174. *Henryk De Kwiatkowski, Plaintiff-Appellee, V. Bear, Stearns & Co., Inc., Bear, Stearns Securities Corporation, and Bear Stearns Forex Inc., Defendants-Appellants, Andalbert J. Sabini, Defendant, 306 F.3d 1293 (2d Cir. 2002)*, 306 F.3d 1293 (2d Cir. 2002). As reported by the SEC, "Study on Investment Advisers and Broker-Dealers." At 54.
175. "Failure to Disclose Material Facts - Securities Act Rel. No. 8333/ Securities Exchange Act Rel. No. 48758" (2003). At 5.
176. Kristina A. Fausti, "A Fiduciary Duty for All," *Duquesne Business Law Journal* 2009–2010, no. 2 (2010). At 187–189.
177. *Sec V. Capital Gains Research Bureau, Inc.*
178. Professor Laby points out that whereas "federal fiduciary standards" apply to Investment Advisers [at 717], "brokers' fiduciary obligations arises because the duties emanate from both federal and state law" [at 712]. Laby, "Fiduciary Obligations of Broker-Dealers and Investment Advisers."
179. *Sec V. Capital Gains Research Bureau, Inc.*
180. SEC, "Study on Investment Advisers and Broker-Dealers." At 22.
181. Haas and Howard. At 111–117, 172–173.
182. Advisers Act Rule 206(4)-4.

183. Advisers Act Rule 206(4)-4.
184. D. Bruce Johnsen, "The Sec's 2006 Soft Dollar Guidance: Law and Economics", ed. George Mason Law & Economics Research Paper No. 08-25 (2008).
185. Haas and Howard. At 236.
186. Securities and Exchange Commission—SEC, "Disclosure by Investment Advisers Regarding Soft Dollar Practices - Release No. 34-35375; Ia-1469; S7-5-95" (1995).
187. "A person exercises "investment discretion" with respect to an account if, directly or indirectly, such person (a) is authorized to determine what securities or other property shall be purchased or sold by or for the account, (b) makes decisions as to what securities or other property shall be purchased or sold by or for the account even though some other person may have responsibility for such investment decisions, or (c) otherwise exercises such influence with respect to the purchase and sale of securities or other property by or for the account as the Commission, by rule, determines, in the public interest or for the protection of investors, should be subject to the operation of the provisions of this title and the rules and regulations thereunder." Section 3(a)(35) of the Securities Exchange Act of 1934.
188. Securities and Exchange Commission—SEC, "Inspection Report on the Soft Dollar Practices of Broker-Dealers, Investment Advisers and Mutual Funds," ed. SEC Office of Compliance Inspections and Examinations (1998).
189. The term "good faith" differs between and within civil and common-law legal systems. It is suffice here to mention that in Continental Europe *good faith* has different meanings according to the national legal traditions (in Italy, for example, it is possible to divide good faith into *buona fede soggettiva*—namely when one of the contractual parties does not know s/he harms the other party's rights; and *buona fede oggettiva*—namely the fact that contractual parties must behave loyally with one another). Differently, in the US legal tradition the term "good faith"—imported from Mainland Europe—changes its boundaries depending on whether it is applied to the performance of a contract or to the enforcement of a contract. *See*: Allan Farnsworth, "The Concept of Good Faith in American Law," in *Good Faith and Fault in Contract Law*, ed. Jack Beatson and Daniel Friedmann (Clarendon Press, 1997).
190. Thomas Lee-Hazen, *Broker-Dealer Regulation in a Nutshell* (Thomson/West, 2003). At 171. Also Professor Laby explains that "Scalping occurs

when an adviser purchases a security for its own account and then recommends the same security to its clients without disclosing the firm's ownership. The adviser then sells its shares at a profit. This practice may injure a client for at least two reasons. First, the adviser's trading may diminish the investors' profits. The client's purchase price may have been lower or the sale price higher had the adviser not bought or sold in advance of the client. Second, scalping presents an egregious conflict of interest because of the risk that the adviser is recommending the security not on the merits, but only to prop up the price." Laby, "Fiduciary Obligations of Broker-Dealers and Investment Advisers." At 716.

191. Lee-Hazen, *Broker-Dealer Regulation in a Nutshell.* At 171.
192. *Sec V. Capital Gains Research Bureau, Inc.*
193. Haas and Howard. At 219.
194. Harvard Law Review Note, "Churning by Securities Dealers," *Harvard Law Review* 80, no. 4 (1967). Also: Securities and Exchange Commission—SEC, "Admin. Proc. File No. 3-8370 - in the Matter of Donald A. Roche - Rel. No. 38742" (1997).
195. Lee-Hazen, *Broker-Dealer Regulation in a Nutshell.* At 180.
196. *Norris & Hirshberg, Inc. V. Sec, 21 S.E.C. 865, 890 (1946), Afd Norris & Hirshberg, Inc., V. Sec,* 177 F.2d 228 (D.D.C. 1949). As reported by Barbara Black, "Application of Respondeat Superior Principles to Securities Fraud Claims under the Racketeer Influenced and Corrupt Organizations Act (Rico)," ed. Pace Law Faculty Publications - Paper 9 (1984).
197. Louis Loss and Joel Seligman, *Fundamentals of Securities Regulation* (Aspen, 2004). At 1097. Scienter means that the person is "acting with a mental state embracing intent to deceive, manipulate or defraud". SEC, "Study on Investment Advisers and Broker-Dealers." At 45.
198. "Study on Investment Advisers and Broker-Dealers." At 70.
199. "17 Cfr Parts 200, 201, et al. - Regulation Nms; Final Rule" (2005). At 44.
200. "Interpretive Release Concerning the Scope of Section 28(E) of the Securities Exchange Act of 1934 and Related Matters - Exchange Act Release No. 23170 (April 23, 1986)" (1986). At 15.
201. "17 Cfr Parts 200, 201, et al. - Regulation Nms; Final Rule." At 44.
202. "Study on Investment Advisers and Broker-Dealers." At 69.

203. "Administrative Proceeding Advisers Act Rel. No. 232" (Washington, DC, 2002), referring to *Kidder Peabody & Co., Inc., Edward B. Goodnow*, Advisers Act Rel. No. 232 (October 16, 1968).
204. Lee-Hazen, *Broker-Dealer Regulation in a Nutshell.* At 134.
205. SEC, "Interpretive Release Concerning the Scope of Section 28(E) of the Securities Exchange Act of 1934 and Related Matters - Exchange Act Release No. 23170 (April 23, 1986)." At 15.
206. Tanja Bošković, Caroline Cerruti, and Michel Noël, "Comparing European and U.S. Securities Regulations: Mifid Versus Corresponding U.S. Regulations," in *World Bank Publications*, ed. The World Bank (Washington, DC, 2010). 23.
207. Tuch. At 548.
208. In the words of Professor Laby: "Brokers and advisers, however, are subject to different laws and regulations that bear greatly on their duties and responsibilities to clients. Brokerage firms, which historically charge commissions, are regulated under the Securities Exchange Act of 1934 and rules imposed by the Financial Industry Regulatory Authority (FINRA), the self-regulatory organization (SRO) for broker-dealers. Advisory firms, which typically charge asset-based fees, are regulated under the Investment Advisers Act of 1940." Laby, "Fiduciary Obligations of Broker-Dealers and Investment Advisers." At 701–702.
209. Allen. At 21.
210. Laby, "Fiduciary Obligations of Broker-Dealers and Investment Advisers." At 731.
211. "Although the differences may be exaggerated, the fiduciary obligation imposed by the Advisers Act appears broader than the duties imposed on brokers through application of the Exchange Act's antifraud rules and FINRA requirements." Ibid. At 727.
212. Lee-Hazen, *Broker-Dealer Regulation in a Nutshell.* At 156.
213. As rightly pointed out in the Rand Report: "Unlike the case of investment advisers [...], broker-dealers are not categorically bound—by statute, regulation, or precedent—to a per se rule imposing fiduciary obligations toward clients. Instead, the existence of fiduciary obligations within a broker-client relationship has historically been significantly more contingent, turning ultimately on the factual nature of the relationship (usually as interpreted by courts and arbitrators)." Angela Hung et al., "Investor and Industry Perspectives on Investment Advisers and Broker-Dealers," ed. RAND Institute for Civil Justice (2008). At 10.

214. Roberta S. Karmel, "Is the Shingle Theory Dead," *Washington and Lee Law Review* 52, no. 4 (1995). At 1273. Also Lee-Hazen: "When a broker has discretion with respect to executing transactions, the broker is a fiduciary. Similarly, when a broker recommends securities or transactions, heightened duties apply." Thomas Lee-Hazen, "Are Existing Stock Broker Standards Sufficient? Principles, Rules and Fiduciary Duties," *Columbia Business Law Review* 2010, no. 3 (2010). At 737.
215. Lee-Hazen offers an overview of the situations when a court may or may not recognize a fiduciary duty: *Broker-Dealer Regulation in a Nutshell.* At 154–158.
216. Laby, "Fiduciary Obligations of Broker-Dealers and Investment Advisers." At 712–714.
217. Ibid. At 705.
218. *Messer V. E.F. Hutton & Co., 833 F.2d 909 (11th Cir. 1987)*, mentioned by Lee-Hazen, *Broker-Dealer Regulation in a Nutshell.* At 157.
219. Laby, "Fiduciary Obligations of Broker-Dealers and Investment Advisers." At 713–714.
220. Allen D. Madison, "Derivatives Regulation in the Context of the Shingle Theory." *Columbia Business Law Review* 1999 (1999). At 278.
221. *Charles Hughes & Co. V. Sec*, 139 F.2d 434 (2d Cir. 1943), cert. denied, 321 U.S. 786. Mentioned in Laby, "Fiduciary Obligations of Broker-Dealers and Investment Advisers." At 722.
222. Tuch. At 553.
223. Lee-Hazen, *Broker-Dealer Regulation in a Nutshell.* Lee-Hazen clarifies that a broker is liable—through the shingle theory—under Rule 10b-5 only when the plaintiff is in a position to prove a causal link between an alleged breach of this professional representation and an injury to the plaintiff herself. At 158–159.
224. Madison. At 279.
225. Ibid. At 279. Similarly, professor Laby explains that "[t]he differences between brokers and advisers are palpable. When a broker-dealer recommends a security, for example, the firm, acting as a dealer, is permitted to sell the security to a customer from the firm's own account—much like an automobile dealer sells its inventory off the lot. By contrast, to guard against conflicts of interest, an investment adviser is severely restricted from selling its own inventory to an advisory client". Laby, "Fiduciary Obligations of Broker-Dealers and Investment Advisers." At 702.
226. Karmel. At 1275.
227. Ibid. At 1275.

228. Ibid. At 1275.
229. Lee-Hazen, *Broker-Dealer Regulation in a Nutshell.* At 158.
230. Ibid. At 159.
231. Ibid. At 160.
232. Ibid. At 160.
233. Ibid. At 161.
234. *Alton Box Board Co. V. Goldman Sachs & Co., 560 F.2d 916, 922 (8th Cir. 1977).* Also mentioned by *Broker-Dealer Regulation in a Nutshell.* At 161.
235. Financial Industry Regulatory Authority—FINRA, "2010. Standards of Commercial Honor and Principles of Trade" (2008).
236. Lee-Hazen, *Broker-Dealer Regulation in a Nutshell.* At 161–166.
237. SEC, "Study on Investment Advisers and Broker-Dealers." At 59.
238. Financial Industry Regulatory Authority—FINRA, "Finra Rule 2111 (Suitability) Faq" (2008).
239. "2310. Recommendations to Customers (Suitability)" (1996).
240. "Im-2310-3. Suitability Obligations to Institutional Customers" (1996).
241. Indeed, a broker "cannot recommend a security unless there is an adequate and reasonable basis for such recommendation". *Hanly V. Sec*, 415 F.2d 589, 596 (2d Cir. 1969).
242. Securities and Exchange Commission—SEC, "F.J. Kaufman and Co., Exchange Act Release No. 27535, 50 Sec164 - December 13, 1989" (Washington, DC, 1989). As mentioned by "Exchange Act Release No. 34-37835, October 17, 1996" (Washington, DC, 1996).
243. "Study on Investment Advisers and Broker-Dealers." At 50.
244. Lee-Hazen, *Broker-Dealer Regulation in a Nutshell.* At 161.
245. Ibid. At 161.
246. Ibid. At 161.
247. Financial Industry Regulatory Authority—FINRA, "2110. Recommendations - 2111. Suitability" (2002).
248. Ibid.
249. Tuch. At 541.
250. *Sec V. Capital Gains Research Bureau, Inc.*
251. Haas and Howard. At 219.
252. Ibid. At 219.
253. Ibid. At 219.
254. Ibid. At 219.
255. Ibid. At 220–223.

256. Securities and Exchange Commission—SEC, "Final Rule: Proxy Voting by Investment Advisers - Release No. Ia-2106; File No. S7-38-02" (2003).
257. Haas and Howard. At 222.
258. Professional qualification of investment advisers has always been an important issue, as Owens already pointed it out in 1973: Hugh F. Owens, "Investment Adviser Regulation: A Subject Too Long Neglected," *Financial Analysts Journal* 29, no. 1 (1973). At 13.
259. Securities and Exchange Commission—SEC, "Concept Release on the U.S. Proxy System - Release Nos. 34-62495; Ia-3052; Ic-29340; File No. S7-14-10" (2010). At 119.
260. "Study on Investment Advisers and Broker-Dealers." At 22.
261. Haas and Howard specify that information is material when "there is a substantial likelihood that a reasonable client would attach importance to it". Haas and Howard. At 221.
262. SEC, "Study on Investment Advisers and Broker-Dealers." At 23.
263. Item 8 of Form ADV Part 2A of Uniform Application for Investment Adviser Registration ["Form Adv" (2013).]: "Methods of Analysis, Investment Strategies and Risk of Loss:

    A. Describe the methods of analysis and investment strategies you use in formulating investment advice or managing assets. Explain that investing in securities involves risk of loss that *clients* should be prepared to bear.
    B. For each significant investment strategy or method of analysis you use, explain the material risks involved. If the method of analysis or strategy involves significant or unusual risks, discuss these risks in detail. If your primary strategy involves frequent trading of securities, explain how frequent trading can affect investment performance, particularly through increased brokerage and other transaction costs and taxes.
    C. If you recommend primarily a particular type of security, explain the material risks involved. If the type of security involves significant or unusual risks, discuss these risks in detail.

264. "Study on Investment Advisers and Broker-Dealers." At 28.
265. Tuch. At 547.
266. SEC, "Study on Investment Advisers and Broker-Dealers." At 106.
267. Ibid. At 106.
268. Ibid. At 106.

269. Ibid. At 104.
270. Ibid. At 102.
271. Ibid. At i. In the words of Professor Laby: "The [...] SEC [...] has recognized for over ten years that the two groups are erasing the outward differences between them, and retail customers today see little difference between a broker and an adviser." Laby, "Fiduciary Obligations of Broker-Dealers and Investment Advisers." At 702.
272. David J. Seipp, "Trust and Fiduciary Duty in the Early Common Law," *Boston University Law Review* 91 (2011). At 1011–1012.
273. SEC, "Study on Investment Advisers and Broker-Dealers." At viii.
274. Ibid. At 21.
275. Ibid. At 21.
276. Ibid. At 22.
277. Allen. At 30.
278. SEC, "Study on Investment Advisers and Broker-Dealers." At 101.
279. Hung et al. At 33.
280. SEC, "Study on Investment Advisers and Broker-Dealers."
281. On the issue of application of fiduciary-like duties to brokers: Donald C. Langevoort, "Brokers as Fiduciaries," *University of Pittsburgh Law Review* 71, no. 3 (2010).
282. SEC, "Study on Investment Advisers and Broker-Dealers."
283. "Duties of Brokers, Dealers, and Investment Advisers (Release No. 34-69013; Ia-3558; File No. 4-606)" (Washington, DC, 2013).
284. Ibid.
285. Employee Benefits Security Administration—Department of Labor, "Definition of the Term "Fiduciary"; Conflict of Interest Rule-Retirement Investment Advice," https://www.federalregister.gov/documents/2016/04/08/2016-07924/definition-of-the-term-fiduciary-conflict-of-interest-rule-retirement-investment-advice.
286. A new consultation "Public Comments from Retail Investors and Other Interested Parties on Standards of Conduct for Investment Advisers and Broker-Dealers" was issued in order to gather information and data and, on these grounds, assess the range of potential regulatory actions. As of the time of writing, comments are still being received and collected.Securities and Exchange Commission—SEC, "Public Comments from Retail Investors and Other Interested Parties on Standards of Conduct for Investment Advisers and Broker-Dealers - Submitted Comments," https://www.sec.gov/comments/ia-bd-conduct-standards/iabdconductstandards.htm.

287. Laby, "Fiduciary Obligations of Broker-Dealers and Investment Advisers." At 704. Professor Lee-Hazen, however, points out that "there are many examples of particular broker-dealer fiduciary obligations in the existing law. In fact, any time a securities broker acts as something more than a mere order taker, heightened obligations attach. There is no doubt that expressly stating that broker-dealers are fiduciaries will provide further emphasis on their obligations. However, even in the absence of a legislative or regulatory declaration to that effect, heightened standards for broker-dealers are already well established." Lee-Hazen, "Are Existing Stock Broker Standards Sufficient? Principles, Rules and Fiduciary Duties." At 761–762.
288. On this wavelength, Professor Laby argues that "[a] fiduciary duty should be imposed on a broker providing advice regardless of the method of compensation employed". Laby, "Fiduciary Obligations of Broker-Dealers and Investment Advisers." At 740.
289. "The US approach involves multiple layers of rules, sources of law, and regulators. The product is a complex and often esoteric amalgam of laws" Tuch. At 546.
290. On mandatory disclosure and investor protection, the seminal article of Professors Easterbrook and Fischel gives a critical appraisal on the US federal disclosure laws: Easterbrook and Fischel.
291. Stephen J. Choi and A. C. Pritchard, *Securities Regulations: The Essentials* (New York, NY: Aspen Publishers, 2008). At 23–24.
292. Iris H-Y Chiu, "Examining the Justifications for Mandatory Ongoing Disclosure in Securities Regulation," *The Company Lawyer* 26, no. 3 (2007). At 67.
293. In the words of Professors Enriques and Gilotta: " 'market egalitarianism', has received strong support in the past and has profoundly influenced the evolution of securities regulation on both sides of the Atlantic (for example, it gave rise to the ban on insider trading in the US and has long shaped much of the SEC policy as regards MD)" [MD: mandatory disclosure]. Enriques and Gilotta. At 515.
294. Fausti. At 187–189.
295. In the words of Professor Laby: "Over the past twenty-five years, changes in the financial services industry have blurred the line between brokers and advisers, defying the logic of the bifurcated regulatory scheme". Laby, "Reforming the Regulation of Broker-Dealers and Investment Advisers." At 398.
296. SEC, "Study on Investment Advisers and Broker-Dealers." At 13.

297. Ibid. At 13.
298. Ibid. At 112.
299. On 21 January 2011, commissioners Kathleen L. Casey and Troy A. Paredes released a joint statement regarding the Study stating that the Study lacks "adequate articulation or substantiation of the problems that would purportedly be addressed via" new SEC regulation; it does not "adequately recognize the risk that its recommendations could adversely impact investors"; it "does not identify whether retail investors are systematically being harmed or disadvantaged under one regulatory regime as compared to the other and, therefore, the Study lacks a basis to reasonably conclude that a uniform standard or harmonization would enhance investor protection". "Statement by Sec Commissioners Kathleen L. Casey and Troy A. Paredes: Statement Regarding Study on Investment Advisers and Broker-Dealers" (Washington, DC, 2011). The Securities Industry and Financial Markets Association (SIFMA), a leading financial business association, also criticized the Study by stating that simply imposing the Investment Advisers Act of 1940 (Advisers Act) fiduciary standard on the broker-dealer business model is "ill-advised because the Advisers Act was not designed to regulate brokerage activity". SIFMA suggests the "implementation of a new harmonized fiduciary standard holds the most promise for overall better protection for retail customers, while preserving their access to, and choice among, financial products and services". Securities Industry and Financial Markets Association—SIFMA, "Sifma Submits Comments to the Sec on the Sec Study to Comply with Section 913 of Dodd-Frank Act" (2011).
300. SEC, "Study on Investment Advisers and Broker-Dealers." At 117.
301. Ibid. At 117.
302. With a focus on brokers/dealers, also highlighted by Bošković, Cerruti, and Noël.
303. Tuch. At 558.
304. Hans-Wolfgang Micklitz, "The Internal Vs. The External Dimension of European Private Law—a Conceptual Design and a Research Agenda," in *EUI Working Paper Law 2015/35*, ed. European University Institute (Florence, 2015). At 1–2.
305. Ibid. At 4.
306. *Regulation 593/2008.*
307. *Council Regulation 1215/2012.*

308. On this point: Antonio Marcacci, "European Regulatory Private Law Going Global? The Case of Product Governance," *European Business Organization Law Review* 18, no. 2 (2017).
309. What Professor Cherednychenko defines "European Supervision Private Law": Olha O. Cherednychenko, "Public Supervision over Private Relationships: Towards European Supervision Private Law?," *European Review of Private Law* 22, no. 1 (2014).
310. Ibid.
311. In the words of Pervenche Berès, Chair of the Economic and Monetary Affairs Committee in 2007: "To further integrate the European financial markets, thus creating a real level playing field for all European stakeholders." As reported by Alessandra Chirico, "Suitability and Appropriateness under Mifid: 'Faithful Watchdogs' or 'Terrible Twins'?," in *ECMI Policy Brief - No. 9/September 2007* (Centre for European Policy Studies - CEPS, 2007). At 1.
312. On thc link between MiFID conduct-of-business rules and customers' confidence: ibid. At 2.
313. On the issue of the conduct-of-business rules as supervision standards in MiFID, see Olha O. Cherednychenko, "The Regulation of Retail Investment Services in the Eu: Towards the Improvement of Investor Rights?," *Journal of Consumer Policy* 33, no. 4 (2010).
314. In the words of Della Negra: "The civil or horizontal effect of the financial regulatory provisions entails that the investor can invoke EU regulatory law in the absence of a national remedy or that he can claim for a 'conform' interpretation of national contract law." DellaNegra.
315. Hans-Wolfgang Micklitz, "The Visible Hand of European Regulatory Private Law—the Transformation of European Private Law from Autonomy to Functionalism in Competition and Regulation," *Yearbook of European Law* 28, no. 1 (2009). At 33.
316. Ibid. At 33.
317. Eric J. Pan, "Harmonization of Us–Eu Securities Regulation: The Case for a Single European Securities Regulator," *Law & Policy of International Business* 34, no. 2 (2003). At 525.
318. Hans-Wolfgang Micklitz, "Jack Is out of the Box – the Efficient Consumer-Shopper," *Juridiska Föreningen i Finland* 3, no. 4 (2009). At 424–425.
319. As it is evident from the parallels drawn in the Lamfalussy Committee's Final Report. The Committee of Wise Men—Lamfalussy Committee, "Final Report of the Committee of Wise Men on the Regulation of European Securities Markets" (2001).

320. Hans-Wolfgang Micklitz, "Social Justice and Access Justice in Private Law," in *EUI Working Paper Law 2011/2*, ed. European University Institute (Florence, 2011). At 2.
321. Ibid. At 6.
322. In a similar context, Professors Svetiev and Ottow highlight in their seminal article how: "'contamination' from poor business conduct and product design as well as misselling of products is regarded as a source of prudential stability problems." Yane Svetiev and Annetje Ottow, "Financial Supervision in the Interstices between Private and Public Law," *European Review of Contract Law* 10, no. 4 (2014). At 513.
323. I am referring to "the idea of fairness of market access [... that] may be found in the Anglo-American legal system". Micklitz, "The Visible Hand of European Regulatory Private Law—the Transformation of European Private Law from Autonomy to Functionalism in Competition and Regulation." At 13.
324. Professor Cherednychenko: "The range of investment products available on financial markets, and hence consumer choice and autonomy in the investment product market, can thus be limited for the sake of consumer protection against the risks involved in many such products." Olha O. Cherednychenko, "Freedom of Contract in the Post-Crisis Era: Quo Vadis?," *European Review of Contract Law* 10, no. 3 (2014). At 401.
325. As Professor Cherednychenko states: "It has been widely noted that the acquis communautaire in the field of contract law aims to create the internal market and is therefore regulatory in nature." "Financial Consumer Protection in the Eu: Towards a Self-Sufficient European Contract Law for Consumer Financial Services?." At 478.

Bibliography

Allen, Matthew P. "A Lesson from History, Roosevelt to Obama—the Evolution of Broker-Dealer Regulation: From Self-Regulation, Arbitration, and Suitability to Federal Regulation, Litigation, and Fiduciary Duty." *Entrepreneurial Business Law Journal* 5, no. 1 (2009): 1–96.

Alton Box Board Co. V. Goldman Sachs & Co., 560 F.2d 916, 922 (8th Cir. 1977).

Angeloni, Ignazio. "Savings Banks in the European Banking Landscape." In *Financial Meeting of the Confederación Española de Cajas de Ahorros*, edited by European Central Bank - Banking Supervision. Madrid, 2014.

Antonucci, Antonella. "Regole Di Condotta E Conflitto Di Interesse." *Banca, borsa e titoli di credito* 2009, no. 1 (2009): 9–20.

Avgouleas, Emilios. "The Harmonisation of Rules of Conduct in EU Financial Markets: Economic Analysis, Subsidiarity and Investor Protection." *European Law Journal* 6, no. 1 (2000): 72–92.

———. "What Future for Disclosure as a Regulatory Technique? Lessons from Behavioural Decision Theory and the Global Financial Crisis." In *The Future of Financial Regulation*, edited by Iain G MacNeil and Justin O'Brien. Oxford: Hart Publishing, 2010.

Baker, Tom. "On the Genealogy of Moral Hazard." *Texas Law Review* 75, no. 2 (1996): 237–92.

Black, Barbara. "Application of Respondeat Superior Principles to Securities Fraud Claims under the Racketeer Influenced and Corrupt Organizations Act (Rico)," edited by Pace Law Faculty Publications - Paper 9, 1984.

Board of Governors of the Federal Reserve System - U.S. Department of the Treasury. "Report to the Congress on Financial Holding Companies under the Gramm–Leach–Bliley Act." Washington, DC, 2003.

Bonner, Francis A. "The over-the-Counter Market and the Maloney Act." In *Annual Convention of the Investment Bankers' Association of America*, edited by Investment Bankers' Association of America. White Sulphur Springs, 1938.

Bošković, Tanja, Caroline Cerruti, and Michel Noël. "Comparing European and U.S. Securities Regulations: Mifid Versus Corresponding U.S. Regulations." In *World Bank Publications*, edited by The World Bank. Washington, DC, 2010.

Busch, Danny. "Agency and Principal Dealing under the Market in Financial Instruments Directive." In *Agency Law in Commercial Practice*, edited by Danny Busch, Laura Macgregor, and Peter Watts. Oxford: Oxford University Press, 2016.

Casey, Jean-Pierre, and Karel Lannoo, eds. *The Mifid Revolution*: Cambridge University Press, 2009.

Cassazione Civile, Sez. I, 31 Luglio 2017, N. 19013, 2017 (2017).

CESR, Committee of European Securities Regulators. "Best Execution under Mifid. Public Consultation - Cesr/07-050b." 2007.

Charles Hughes & Co. V. Sec, 139 F.2d 434 (2d Cir. 1943), cert. denied, 321 U.S. 786.

Cherednychenko, Olha O. "Financial Consumer Protection in the EU: Towards a Self-Sufficient European Contract Law for Consumer Financial Services?". *European Review of Contract Law* 10, no. 4 (2014a): 476–95.

———. "Freedom of Contract in the Post-Crisis Era: Quo Vadis?". *European Review of Contract Law* 10, no. 3 (2014b): 390–421.

———. "Public Supervision over Private Relationships: Towards European Supervision Private Law?". *European Review of Private Law* 22, no. 1 (2014c): 37–68.

———. "The Regulation of Retail Investment Services in the EU: Towards the Improvement of Investor Rights?". *Journal of Consumer Policy* 33, no. 4 (2010): 403–24.

Chirico, Alessandra. "Suitability and Appropriateness under Mifid: 'Faithful Watchdogs' or 'Terrible Twins'?" In *ECMI Policy Brief - No. 9/September 2007*: Centre for European Policy Studies - CEPS, 2007.

Chiu, Iris H.-Y. "Examining the Justifications for Mandatory Ongoing Disclosure in Securities Regulation." *The Company Lawyer* 26, no. 3 (2007): 67–74.

Choi, Stephen J., and A. C. Pritchard. *Securities Regulations: The Essentials*. New York, NY: Aspen Publishers, 2008.

Commission Delegated Directive 2017/593/Eu.

Commission Delegated Regulation 2017/565/Eu.

Commission Directive 2006/73/Ec.

Conte, Tobias, and Matthias Burghardt. "A Process Model for Best Execution." In *Enterprise applications and services in the finance industry: 3rd international workshop*. Montreal: FinanceCom 2007, 2007.

Council Regulation 1215/2012.

Cox, Christopher. "Chairman Cox Announces End of Consolidated Supervised Entities Program.". http://www.sec.gov/news/press/2008/2008-230.htm.

D'Alessandro, Francesco. *Regolatori Del Mercato, Enforcement E Sistema Penale*. Torino: Giappichelli, 2014.

D'Hondt, Catherine, and Jean-René Giraud. "Mifid: The (in)Famous European Directive?" *EDHEC Position Paper*, 2007.

DellaNegra, Federico. "The Private Enforcement of the Mifid Conduct of Business Rules. An Overview of the Italian and Spanish Experiences." *European Review of Contract Law* 10, no. 4 (2014): 571–95.

DeMott, Deborah. "Beyond Metaphor: An Analysis of Fiduciary Obligation." *Duke Law Journal* 1988, no. 37 (1988): 879–924.

Directive 93/22/Eec.

Directive 2014/59/Eu.

Directive 2014/65/Eu.

Directive 2016/97/Eu.

Doak, Robin S. *Black Tuesday: Prelude to the Great Depression*. Compass Point Books, 2008.

Dodd-Frank Wall Street Reform and Consumer Protection Act.

Easterbrook, Frank H., and Daniel R. Fischel. "Mandatory Disclosure and the Protection of Investors." *Virginia Law Review* 70, no. 4 (1984): 669–715.

EFAMA, European Fund and Asset Management Association. "European Mifid Template (Emt)." 2017.

Enriques, Luca. "Conflicts of Interest in Investment Services: The Price and Uncertain Impact of Mifid's Regulatory Framework." In *Investor Protection in Europe*, edited by Guido Ferrarini and Eddy Wymeersch. New York: Oxford University Press, 2006.

Enriques, Luca, and Sergio Gilotta. "Disclosure and Financial Market Regulation." In *The Oxford Handbook of Financial Regulation*, edited by Niamh Moloney, Eilís Ferran, and Jennifer Payne. Oxford: Oxford University Press, 2015.

ESAs, Joint Committee of the European Supervisory Authorities. "Joint Esas Consumer Protection Day.". https://eiopa.europa.eu/Pages/Events/Event-2.aspx.

ESMA, European Securities and Markets Authorities. "Final Report - Guidelines on Complex Debt Instruments and Structured Deposits - Esma/2015/1783." 2015.

ESMA, European Securities and Markets Authority. "Guidelines on Cross-Selling Practices." 2016.

———. "Remuneration Policies and Practices (Mifid) - Esma/2013/606." https://www.esma.europa.eu/sites/default/files/library/2015/11/2013-606_en.pdf.

European Securities and Markets Authority - ESMA. "Mifid Practices for Firms Selling Complex Products - Esma/2014/146." Paris, FR, 2014.

Farnsworth, Allan. "The Concept of Good Faith in American Law." In *Good Faith and Fault in Contract Law*, edited by Jack Beatson and Daniel Friedmann, 153–70. Clarendon Press, 1997.

Fass, Allison. "One Year Later, the Impact of Sarbanes-Oxley." *Forbes*, 2003.

Fausti, Kristina A. "A Fiduciary Duty for All." *Duquesne Business Law Journal* 2009–2010, no. 2 (2010).

Federal Reserve Bank of San Francisco. "Banking Information: Overview of the Gramm-Leach-Bliley Act." San Francisco, CA, 2000.

Financial Industry Regulatory Authority - FINRA. "2110. Recommendations - 2111. Suitability." 2002.

FINRA, Financial Industry Regulatory Authority. "2010. Standards of Commercial Honor and Principles of Trade." 2008a.

———. "2310. Recommendations to Customers (Suitability)." 1996a.

FINRA, Financial Industry Regulatory Authority. "About Finra.". http://www.finra.org/aboutfinra/.
FINRA, Financial Industry Regulatory Authority. "Arbitration and Mediation.". http://www.finra.org/arbitration-and-mediation.
FINRA, Financial Industry Regulatory Authority. "Finra Rule 2111 (Suitability) Faq." 2008b.
FINRA, Financial Industry Regulatory Authority. "Finra Website - Uniform Practice Code (Upc).". http://www.finra.org/Industry/Compliance/MarketTransparency/UPC/.
FINRA, Financial Industry Regulatory Authority. "Im-2310-3. Suitability Obligations to Institutional Customers." 1996b.
———. "Sec Approval of Finra Funding Portal Rules and Related Forms. January 2016." https://www.finra.org/sites/default/files/Regulatory-Notice-16-06.pdf.
FINRA, Financial Industry Regulatory Authority. "What We Do.". http://www.finra.org/about/what-we-do.
FSA, Financial Services Authority. "Fg12/09, Retail Product Development and Governance – Structured Product Review." 2012.
Garn–St. Germain Depository Institutions Act.
Gramm-Leach-Bliley Act.
Haas, Jeffrey J., and Steven Howard. *Investment Adviser Regulation in a Nutshell.* Eagan, MN: Thomson West, 2008.
Hanly V. Sec, 415 F.2d 589, 596 (2d Cir. 1969).
Harvard Law Review Note. "Churning by Securities Dealers." *Harvard Law Review* 80, no. 4 (1967): 869–86.
Hed-Hofmann, Tamar. "The Maloney Act Experiment." *Boston College Law Review* 6, no. 2 (1965): 187–218.
Henryk De Kwiatkowski, Plaintiff-Appellee, V. Bear, Stearns & Co., Inc., Bear, Stearns Securities Corporation, and Bear Stearns Forex Inc., Defendants-Appellants, Andalbert J. Sabini, Defendant, 306 F.3d 1293 (2d Cir. 2002), 306 F.3d 1293 (2d Cir. 2002).
Hung, Angela, Noreen Clancy, Jeff Dominitz, Eric Talley, Claude Berrebi, and Farrukh Suvankulov. "Investor and Industry Perspectives on Investment Advisers and Broker-Dealers." edited by RAND Institute for Civil Justice, 2008.
Investment Advisers Act.
Jackson, Howell. "The Trilateral Dilemma in Financial Regulation." In *Overcoming the Saving Slump: How to Increase the Effectiveness of Financial Education and Saving Programs*, edited by Anna Maria Lusardi, 82–118. Chicago: University of Chicago Press, 2009.

James, Laylin K. "The Securities Act of 1933." *Michigan Law Review* 32, no. 5 (1934).

Jennings, Richard W. "Self-Regulation in the Securities Industry: The Role of the Securities and Exchange Commission." *Law and Contemporary Problems* 29 (1964): 663–90.

Johnsen, D. Bruce. "The Sec's 2006 Soft Dollar Guidance: Law and Economics", edited by George Mason Law & Economics Research Paper No. 08-25, 2008.

Johnson, Carrie. "Sec Approves One Watchdog for Brokers Big and Small." *The Washington Post* July 27, 2007.

Jumpstart Our Business Startups Act.

Karmel, Roberta S. "Is the Shingle Theory Dead." *Washington and Lee Law Review* 52, no. 4 (1995): 1271.

Krippner, Greta R. *Capitalizing on Crisis: The Political Origins of the Rise of Finance*. Cambridge, MA: Harvard University Press, 2011.

Krugman, Paul. "Reagan Did It." *The New York Times*, May 31, 2009.

Krugman, Paul R. *The Return of Depression Economics*. London: Penguin UK, 2008.

Kruithof, Marc. "A Differentiated Approach to Client Protection: The Example of Mifid." In *Financial Services, Financial Crisis and General European Contract Law: Failure and Challenges of Contracting*, edited by Stefan Grundmann and Yesim M Atamer, 105–62. New York: Kluwer Law International, 2011.

Kruithof, Marc, and Walter VanGerven. "A Differentiated Approach to Client Protection: The Example of Mifid." edited by Financial Law Institute - Universiteit Gent, 2010.

Kumpan, Christoph, and Patrick C. Leyens. "Conflicts of Interest of Financial Intermediaries - Towards a Global Common Core in Conflicts of Interest Regulation." *European Company and Financial Law Review* 4, no. 1 (2008): 72–100.

Labor, Employee Benefits Security Administration - Department of. "Definition of the Term "Fiduciary"; Conflict of Interest Rule-Retirement Investment Advice.". https://www.federalregister.gov/documents/2016/04/08/2016-07924/definition-of-the-term-fiduciary-conflict-of-interest-rule-retirement-investment-advice.

Laby, Arthur B. "Fiduciary Obligations of Broker-Dealers and Investment Advisers." *Villanova Law Review* 55 (2010a): 701–42.

———. "Reforming the Regulation of Broker-Dealers and Investment Advisers." *The Business Lawyer* 65, no. 2 (2010b): 395–440.

Langevoort, Donald C. "Brokers as Fiduciaries." *University of Pittsburgh Law Review* 71, no. 3 (2010).

Langevoort, Donald C., and Robert B. Thompson. "'Publicness' in Contemporary Securities Regulation after the Jobs Act." *Georgetown Law Journal* 101 (2013): 337–86.

Lee-Hazen, Thomas. "Are Existing Stock Broker Standards Sufficient? Principles, Rules and Fiduciary Duties." *Columbia Business Law Review* 2010, no. 3 (2010): 709–62.

———. *Broker-Dealer Regulation in a Nutshell.* Thomson/West, 2003.

———. *Principles of Securities Regulation, Revised.* St. Paul: West Academic, 2017.

Loss, Louis, and Joel Seligman. *Fundamentals of Securities Regulation.* Aspen, 2004.

Macey, Jonathan R., and Maureen O'Hara. "The Law and Economics of Best Execution." *Journal of Financial Intermediation* 6 (1997): 188–223.

Madison, Allen D. "Derivatives Regulation in the Context of the Shingle Theory". *Columbia Business Law Review* 1999 (1999): 271–328.

Marcacci, Antonio. "European Regulatory Private Law Going Global? The Case of Product Governance." *European Business Organization Law Review* 18, no. 2 (2017): 305–32.

———. "Public Supervision of Securities Markets in Europe: Still Running Behind the US?". *Federalismi* 2015, no. 15 (2015).

Messer V. E.F. Hutton & Co., 833 F.2d 909 (11th Cir. 1987).

Micklitz, Hans-Wolfgang. "The Internal Vs. The External Dimension of European Private Law—a Conceptual Design and a Research Agenda." In *EUI Working Paper Law 2015/35*, edited by European University Institute. Florence, 2015.

———. "Jack Is out of the Box – the Efficient Consumer-Shopper." *Juridiska Föreningen i Finland* 3, no. 4 (2009a): 417–36.

———. "Social Justice and Access Justice in Private Law." In *EUI Working Paper Law 2011/2*, edited by European University Institute. Florence, 2011.

———. "The Visible Hand of European Regulatory Private Law—the Transformation of European Private Law from Autonomy to Functionalism in Competition and Regulation." *Yearbook of European Law* 28, no. 1 (2009b): 3–59.

Moloney, Niamh. "Building a Retail Investment Culture through Law: The 2004 Markets in Financial Instruments Directive." *European Business Organization Law Review* 6, no. 3 (2005): 341–421.

———. *EU Securities and Financial Markets Regulation.* Oxford: Oxford University Press, 2014.

———. "Regulating the Retail Markets." In *The Oxford Handbook of Financial Regulation*, edited by Niamh Moloney, Eilís Ferran, and Jennifer Payne. Oxford: Oxford University Press, 2015.

Nader, Ralph. "Opening the Door to New Taxpayer Bailouts.". http://nader.org/1998/02/01/opening-the-door-to-new-taxpayer-bailouts/.

Nickson, Charles G. "The Regulation of Investment Advice: Subscription Advisers and Fiduciary Duties." *Michigan Law Review* 63, no. 7 (1965): 1220–39.

Norris & Hirshberg, Inc. V. Sec, 21 S.E.C. 865, 890 (1946), Afd Norris & Hirshberg, Inc, V. Sec, 177 F.2d 228 (D.D.C. 1949).

Over-the-Counter Market Act.

Owens, Hugh F. "Investment Adviser Regulation: A Subject Too Long Neglected." *Financial Analysts Journal* 29, no. 1 (1973): 12–14, 18, 86–87.

Pan, Eric. "Organizing Regional Systems: The US Example." In *The Oxford Handbook of Financial Regulation*, edited by Niamh Moloney, Eilís Ferran, and Jennifer Payne. Oxford: Oxford University Press, 2015.

Pan, Eric J. "Harmonization of US–EU Securities Regulation: The Case for a Single European Securities Regulator." *Law & Policy of International Business* 34, no. 2 (2003): 499–536.

Ramirez, Steven A. "The Professional Obligations of Securities Brokers under Federal Law: An Antidote for Bubbles?". *University of Cincinnati Law Review* 70, no. 2 (2002).

Regulation 593/2008.

Regulation 1286/2014/Eu.

Romano, Roberta. "Empowering Investors: A Market Approach to Securities Regulation." *The Yale Law Journal* 107, no. 5 (1998): 2359–430.

Sarbanes-Oxley Act.

SEC, Securities and Exchange Commission. "17 Cfr Parts 200, 201, Et al. - Regulation Nms; Final Rule." 2005a.

———. "Admin. Proc. File No. 3-8370 - in the Matter of Donald A. Roche - Rel. No. 38742." 1997.

———. "Administrative Proceeding Advisers Act Rel. No. 232." Washington, DC, 2002.

———. "Broker Dealer Registration." https://www.sec.gov/fast-answers/answersbdregishtm.html.

———. "Certain Broker-Dealers Deemed Not to Be Investment Advisers - Release Nos. 34-51523; Ia-2376; File No. S7-25-99." 2005b.

———. "Concept Release on the U.S. Proxy System - Release Nos. 34-62495; Ia-3052; Ic-29340; File No. S7-14-10." 2010.

———. "Disclosure by Investment Advisers Regarding Soft Dollar Practices - Release No. 34-35375; Ia-1469; S7-5-95." 1995.
———. "Duties of Brokers, Dealers, and Investment Advisers (Release No. 34-69013; Ia-3558; File No. 4-606)." Washington, DC, 2013a.
———. "Exchange Act Release No. 76324 (October 20, 2015)." 2015.
———. "Exchange Act Release No. 34-37835, October 17, 1996." Washington, DC, 1996.
———. "F.J. Kaufman and Co., Exchange Act Release No. 27535, 50 Sec164 - December 13, 1989." Washington, DC, 1989.
———. "Failure to Disclose Material Facts - Securities Act Rel. No. 8333 / Securities Exchange Act Rel. No. 48758." 2003a.
———. "Final Rule: Proxy Voting by Investment Advisers - Release No. Ia-2106; File No. S7-38-02." 2003b.
———. "Form Adv." 2013b.
———. "Inspection Report on the Soft Dollar Practices of Broker-Dealers, Investment Advisers and Mutual Funds." edited by SEC Office of Compliance Inspections and Examinations, 1998.
———. "Interpretive Release Concerning the Scope of Section 28(E) of the Securities Exchange Act of 1934 and Related Matters - Exchange Act Release No. 23170 (April 23, 1986)." 1986.
SEC, Securities and Exchange Commission. "Public Comments from Retail Investors and Other Interested Parties on Standards of Conduct for Investment Advisers and Broker-Dealers - Submitted Comments.". https://www.sec.gov/comments/ia-bd-conduct-standards/iabdconductstandards.htm.
SEC, Securities and Exchange Commission. "Release No. 34-56145." Washington, DC, 2007.
SEC, Securities and Exchange Commission. "Self-Regulatory Organization Rulemaking.". https://www.sec.gov/rules/sro.shtml.
SEC, Securities and Exchange Commission. "Statement by Sec Commissioners Kathleen L. Casey and Troy A. Paredes: Statement Regarding Study on Investment Advisers and Broker-Dealers." Washington, DC, 2011a.
———. "Study on Investment Advisers and Broker-Dealers." Washington, DC, 2011b.
Sec V. Capital Gains Research Bureau, Inc., 375 U.S. 180, 191 (1963).
Sec V. Texas Gulf Sulphur Co., 401 F.2d 833 (2d Cir. 1968).
Sec. V. Capital Gains Research Bureau, Inc, 375 U.S. 180, 191 (1963).
Securities and Exchange Commission - SEC. "Sec's Oversight of Bear Stearns and Related Entities: The Consolidated Supervised Entity Program." 2008.

Securities and Exchange Commission V. W. J. Howey Co., 328 U.S. 293 (1946).
The Securities Exchange Act.
Securities Industry and Financial Markets Association - SIFMA. "Sifma Submits Comments to the Sec on the Sec Study to Comply with Section 913 of Dodd-Frank Act." 2011.
Securities Investor Protection Act.
Securities Investor Protection Corporation - SIPC. "Sipc Mission.". https://www.sipc.org/about-sipc/sipc-mission.
Seipp, David J. "Trust and Fiduciary Duty in the Early Common Law." *Boston University Law Review* 91 (2011): 1011–37.
Seligman, Joel. "Cautious Evolution or Perennial Irresolution: Stock Market Self-Regulation During the First Seventy Years of the Securities Exchange Commission." *Business Lawyer* 59, no. 4 (2004): 1347–87.
———. *The Transformation of Wall Street: A History of the Securities and Exchange Commission and Modern Corporate Finance*, 3rd ed. New York: Aspen Publishers, 2003.
Svetiev, Yane, and Annetje Ottow. "Financial Supervision in the Interstices between Private and Public Law." *European Review of Contract Law* 10, no. 4 (2014): 496–544.
The Committee of Wise Men - Lamfalussy Committee. "Final Report of the Committee of Wise Men on the Regulation of European Securities Markets." 2001.
Treasury, Department of the. "Blueprint for a Modernized Financial Regulatory Structure." Washington, DC, 2008.
Treccani - Dizionario di Economia e Finanza. "Sarbanes-Oxley Act." 2012.
The Truth in Securities Act. May 27, 1933.
Tuch, Andrew. "Conduct of Business Regulation." In *The Oxford Handbook of Financial Regulation*, edited by Niamh Moloney, Eilís Ferran, and Jennifer Payne. Oxford: Oxford University Press, 2015.
Wilsey, H. Lawrence. "The Investment Advisers Act of 1940." *The Journal of Finance* 4, no. 4 (1949): 286–97.

Part II

The Law-in-Action

5

Public Enforcement

5.1 Public Enforcement in the EU: The European Securities Markets Authority[1]

As shown in Chap. 3, the EU law of financial markets started blossoming in the 1980s and the 1990s. A need for coordination was being perceived throughout Europe, and on 8 December 1997, the Securities Commissions of the Member States of the European Economic Area (EEA) gathered in Paris and, through the adoption of a Charter, established the Forum of European Securities Commissions (FESCO).[2] FESCO was designed as a forum where national regulators could cooperate with each other and share their experience to facilitate the fair and efficient realization of the rising European single financial market.[3] Furthermore, the Forum was meant to be the place where national authorities could develop common regulatory standards on financial market supervision—particularly on those aspects still not harmonized under the European law at that time—and offer the broadest possible mutual assistance and cross-border cooperation.[4]

With the introduction of the single European currency, on 1 January 1999[5] the European financial markets' integration quickly accelerated.

© The Author(s) 2018

A. Marcacci, *Regulating Investor Protection under EU Law*,
https://doi.org/10.1007/978-3-319-90297-5_5

A few months earlier, in June 1998, the European Council in Cardiff had asked the Commission to put forward an action plan for financial services in order to maximize the benefits of the euro.[6] On October 1998, the Commission had already presented the Communication titled "Financial Services: Building a framework for action".[7] This framework focused on actions dealing with five fields: wholesale markets, retail financial markets, supervisory cooperation, taxation, and policy group. The Vienna European Council, held in December 1998, asked the Commission to adopt a detailed plan, and on 11 May 1999, the Commission issued the Communication titled "Financial Services: Implementing the framework for financial markets: Action Plan".[8]

On 17 July 2000, the Council of Economic and Finance Ministers made the decision to establish the Committee of Wise Men on the Regulation of European Securities Markets, the so-called Lamfalussy Committee.[9] As highlighted above, it was created in order to "respond effectively to the challenges of integrating the financial markets".[10] Importantly, the Lamfalussy Committee's mission to develop a more effective approach as regards transposition and implementation was much more detailed than that of the FESCO, which remained a coordination lieu.

In February 2001, the Lamfalussy Committee adopted its Final Report[11] and developed the so-called Lamfalussy Procedure, a four-level law-making process aimed at speeding up the adoption of European legislation dealing with financial markets (Chap. 3). Soon after, in June 2001, FESCO was effectively replaced by the Committee of European Securities Regulators (CESR).[12] CESR was made up of national public authorities competent in the field of securities, and it was conceived as an independent advisory group whose main task was to assist the Commission in preparing level 2 draft implementing measures.[13] Moreover, CESR was also tasked with coordinating its members by adopting soft-law instruments[14] (level 3 of the Lamfalussy procedure), although all supervision powers and functions rested on the national authorities' hands until 2011, with voices making the case for a single European Authority.[15]

In the aftermath of the world financial crisis of 2008–2009, the President of the European Commission set up an independent High

Level Group on financial supervision.[16] Its aim was to make recommendations about the strengthening of the European supervisory architecture covering all financial sectors through the establishment of a more efficient, integrated, and sustainable European system of supervision in "light of the failures of financial supervision exposed by the financial crisis".[17] The group was chaired by Jacques De Larosiere. On 25 February 2009, the group released the so-called Larosiere Report,[18] which recommended a general reorganization of the European system of financial supervision in such a way that it ensured there would be not only micro-prudential supervision (individual firms' stability) but also macro-prudential oversight (the stability of the financial system as a whole).

In September 2009 the European Commission, following the suggestions put forward by the Larosiere Report, proposed[19] to replace the existing second-level committees with agencies endowed with certain powers and functions, all gathered under the umbrella of the Joint Committee of ESAs. The aim was to build a working European System of Financial Supervision (ESFS),[20] made up of the three new authorities[21]: a European Systemic Risk Board (ESRB),[22] the ESAs' Joint Committee, and the domestic competent authorities. The ESRB is tasked with a soft, very-high-level macro-prudential supervision,[23] whereas the three authorities[24] are in charge of sectorial regulation (banking, insurance, and securities). The one concerning capital markets is the ESMA, which replaced the CESR. The Joint Committee[25] coordinates cross-sectorial regulation, which is particularly important in the case of financial conglomerates and self-placement[26] of securities on the part of banks licensed to carry out investment services under MiFID. Coordination is at the heart of the ESFS. Indeed, Article 8.1(d) of the ESMA establishing Regulation states that the Authority must "cooperate closely with the ESRB, in particular by providing the ESRB with the necessary information for the achievement of its tasks and by ensuring a proper follow up to the warnings and recommendations of the ESRB". In the 2014 Report to the European Parliament and the Council,[27] the European Commission declared that the ESAs were already successfully built and running.

5.1.1 ESMA Objectives, Legal Basis, and Powers as "EU Authority"

Article 1.5 of Regulation 1095/2010 establishing ESMA states that the primary task of the Authority is "to protect the public interest by contributing to the short, medium and long-term stability and effectiveness of the financial system". It should do so by improving and ensuring the "integrity, transparency, efficiency and orderly functioning of financial markets"; contributing to a sound, "effective and consistent level of regulation and supervision"; "strengthening international supervisory coordination"; "preventing regulatory arbitrage and promoting equal conditions of competition"; "ensuring the taking of investment and other risks are appropriately regulated and supervised"; and "enhancing customer protection".[28] Investor protection is, thus, an administrative responsibility that is ancillary to the key task of ensuring the correct functioning of the market.

Coherently with these very-high-profile aims, Regulation 1095/2010 is based on Article 114 TFEU, which confirms that ESMA's grounding objective is to "improve the conditions for the establishment and functioning of the internal market".[29] Indeed, Article 114 TFEU has been largely used as the cornerstone for building the internal market, and the market's "establishment and functioning"[30] is a factor to be considered by all legislative measures taken under this article. Such use of Art. 114 TFEU as legal basis to solve the EU's institutional shortcomings has been criticized, particularly because there was no precedence for such a large-scale institutional structure to be built on this "slender legal base".[31] Possible alternative legal bases for ESMA-like agencies were proposed but they are yet to come to fruition.[32]

A crucial point to note here is the nature of ESMA as an EU agency. Traditionally speaking, European agencies[33] cannot enjoy full decision-making and rulemaking powers, even if they are bodies of secondary Union law, have legal personality, and are permanent and relatively independent actors.[34] ESMA has legal personality[35] as well as administrative and financial autonomy from other European institutions[36]; it enjoys a certain degree of organizational autonomy[37] from the Commission and, importantly, its headquarters are not in Brussels but in Paris. Moreover,

ESMA appears to have a larger autonomy, in terms of governance and independence, than traditional European agencies.[38]

However, all these aspects cannot hide the existence of some serious hurdles. This is because some restrictions to the EU agencies' powers were firmly established by the ECJ in 1957,[39] at the outset of the European integration process. In the *Meroni* case, Professors Griller and Orator[40] give an account of the four important principles stated by the ECJ. First, coherently with the idea that *nemo plus iuris transferre potest quam ipse habet*, the ECJ excluded the possibility for a delegating authority to delegate on other bodies powers different from those already possessed by the delegator under the Treaty.[41] Second, a delegation of powers cannot be presumed, but the delegating authority must make an express delegation.[42] Third, a delegation of "discretionary powers" is unlawful because it can "make possible the execution of actual economic policy",[43] thus replacing "the choices of the delegator by the choices of the delegate",[44] and causing "an actual transfer of responsibility".[45] Finally, a delegation of discretionary powers is unlawful because it would jeopardize the balance of powers between the European institutions.[46]

For around fifty years, the ECJ case law has not authorized the creation of European agencies endowed with "discretionary power to translate broad legislation guidelines into concrete instruments".[47] This approach has for long been "a constitutional limit to delegation"[48] and it has substantially impeded the establishment of regulatory agencies[49] with functions and powers like those belonging to US federal regulatory agencies, such as the SEC.[50]

Only very recently the ECJ has partially overcome the *Meroni* doctrine and updated its old approach. In the Case C-270/12,[51] so-called SSR Case, the ECJ dismissed an appeal brought by the United Kingdom against Article 28 of the Short Selling Regulation (SSR).[52] On the basis of the Article 9.5 of ESMA establishing Regulation, indeed, Article 28 of the SSR gives ESMA important emergency powers, in particular the power to adopt legally binding measures on EU Member States should particular circumstances be likely to occur. The ECJ held that "the exercise of the powers under Article 28 of Regulation No 236/2012 is circumscribed by various conditions and criteria which limit ESMA's discretion [... and such powers] are precisely delineated and amenable to judicial review".[53]

As defined by Marjosola, these special ESMA's powers are *parallel* and *secondary*[54] to those wielded by national authorities, since ESMA can jump in only in case of a "threat to the orderly functioning and integrity of financial markets or to the stability of the whole or part of the financial system in the Union and there are cross-border implications"[55] and if "no competent authority has taken measures to address the threat or one or more of the competent authorities have taken measures that do not adequately address the threat".[56] However, more importantly, ESMA's emergency powers are also *hierarchically superior*[57] as the measures adopted under Article 28's remit "prevail over any previous measure taken by a competent authority".[58]

However, the update[59] of the *Meroni* doctrine does not automatically imply that ESMA has now been endowed with direct regulatory and supervisory powers. Concerning the former, ESMA may draft technical standards that must be submitted to the EU Commission, which has the ultimate power to endorse them. Concerning the latter, specific legislation leveraging on Article 9.5 powers have been granted not only under the SSR but also under AIFMD (Article 47) and under MiFIR (Product Intervention—Article 40—and Position Management Powers—Article 45). However, Case C-270/12 clarified and stabilized ESMA's remit and opened the (political) door to wider and deeper regulatory delegations, as the ESMA normative production under MiFID II and the important product intervention powers under MiFIR seem to prove.

The ESMA is, thus, not a *pure* regulatory agency, as it is a kind of a mélange between a regulator and a coordinator of national regulators.[60] The transfer of the decision-making powers from the Commission is not only toward ESMA but, de facto, also toward national regulators, which, however, can exercise such powers only together (at the ESMA Board) and not individually, thus making ESMA's coordination role between competent authorities crucial.[61] This implies a constant flux of decision-making powers moving throughout the EU multilevel system—which is also evident in the intervention powers recently granted by MiFIR in case of major infringements. Eventually, a problem arises as to where to stop this flux, so that Europe is able to protect itself from hidden dangers likely to jeopardize the correct functioning of its financial system.

5.1.2 Governance Structure

ESMA is made up of a Board of Supervisors, a Management Board, a Chairperson, Executive Director, and a Board of Appeal.[62] The Board of Supervisors is the core element of ESMA and has been described as a "hub-and-spoke system", where the rulemaking at EU level is the hub and the implementation at domestic level is the spokes.[63] It is in charge of making the decisions referred to in Chap. 2 of the establishing Regulation and, more specifically, it has to deal with the primary tasks and powers set out in Article 8. The Board is made up of the Chairperson (chosen by the Board and with non-voting power), the head of the Member States' national public financial authorities (with voting powers), one representative of the Commission (with non-voting power), one representative of the ESRB (with non-voting power), and one representative of each of the other two ESAs (with non-voting power).[64] The decisions of the Board of Supervisors are usually taken by a simple majority of its members,[65] although in some cases a qualified majority of its members is required.[66]

The Management Board is the watchdog of ESMA. It has to ensure that ESMA carries out its mission and performs its tasks, as laid down in the establishing Regulation.[67] This Board is made up of the Chairperson and six other members of the Board of Supervisors, and is elected by and from the voting members of the Board of Supervisors.[68]

The Chairperson is the figure who represents the Authority. S/he is a full-time independent professional, appointed for five years "by the Board of Supervisors on the basis of merit, skills, knowledge of financial market participants and markets, and of experience relevant to financial supervision and regulation, following an open selection procedure".[69] S/he is responsible for preparing the work of the Board of Supervisors and chairs the meetings of the Board of Supervisors and the Management Board.[70] Article 49 clearly states the level of independence enjoyed by the Chairperson: "[T]he Chairperson shall neither seek nor take instructions from the Union institutions or bodies, from any government of a Member State or from any other public or private body."[71] This independence should be guaranteed by the fact that Chairperson may be removed from office only by the European Parliament following a decision of the Board of Supervisors.[72]

The Executive Director is a full-time independent professional, appointed for five years by the Board of Supervisors, subject to being confirmed by the European Parliament.[73] Like the Chairperson, the Executive Director should be elected "on the basis of merit, skills, knowledge of financial market participants and markets, and experience relevant to financial supervision and regulation and managerial experience, following an open selection procedure".[74] Article 53 provides for the list of tasks of the Executive Director: management of the Authority; preparation of the work of the Management Board; implementation of the ESMA annual work program under the guidance of the Board of Supervisors and under the control of the Management Board. Moreover, the Executive Director is also in charge of preparing a multiannual work program and of drafting a report with a section on ESMA's regulatory and supervisory activities and a section on financial and administrative matters.[75] Finally, s/he is responsible for drafting ESMA's preliminary budget.[76]

Standing Committees already existed under the CESR regime and their task is to develop proposals for approval by the Board of Supervisor.[77] These Committees are chaired by senior national representatives, usually a Member of the Board of Supervisors, and they gather national experts who are supported by the ESMA staff, acting as *rapporteurs* for the Committees.[78] Hence, most of the Committees' work takes place at Level 3 of the Lamfalussy procedure. The Committees also have Consultative Working Groups that provide technical advice during the normative drafting process.[79] Such Groups are made up of market participants such as practitioners, consumers, and end-users.

The Board of Appeal is a joint body of all the ESAs. It is composed of six members and six alternates, "individuals of a high repute with a proven record of relevant knowledge and professional experience, including supervisory, experience to a sufficiently high level in the fields of banking, insurance, occupational pensions, securities markets or other financial services".[80] Given the nature of this body, legal expertise seems to be particularly relevant for its correct functioning. Parties affected by decisions adopted by ESMA have the right to appeal to this ESA joint body.[81] Appeals against certain individual decisions of the ESAs and the decisions themselves can be appealed before the ECJ.[82] Appeals can be brought to the ESMA against decisions that are addressed to the appealing legal or natural person or decisions which, even though they are addressed to another person, are of direct and individual concern to the appealing person.[83]

The composition of the Board of Supervisors, the procedures whereby its financial guidelines are enacted, and the close cooperation between the ESAs contribute to reinforcing the idea that ESMA is at the top of the rulemaking flux for the securities regulations in Europe. Significantly, ESMA's formal political responsibility is crystallized by its accountability before the European Parliament and the Council (Article 3), whereas its de facto regulatory responsibility emerges as the degree of detail of its own made rules deepens.

The way ESMA is funded reflects its key feature of being a hybrid of national and supranational nature: it receives 40% of the necessary resources from the EU and 60% from the national authorities' funds.[84] ESMA is internally organized through the following seven departments: Markets; Investors and Issuers; Supervision; Corporate Affairs; Risk Analysis and Economics; Legal, Convergence and Enforcement; Resources.[85] Finally, it is interesting to highlight the number of staff employed by ESMA: it was only 221 full-time equivalents in 2017.[86] The US SEC with its 4200 employees[87] embarrassingly dwarfs ESMA.

Very recently, the European Commission—via the "ESA Consultation Paper"[88]—asked for stakeholders' opinion on how to reform the ESAs, including ESMA, in four broad areas: (1) tasks and powers, (2) governance, (3) supervisory architecture, and (4) funding. Concerning the governance topic, the Commission proposed a rebalancing of tasks between the Board of Supervisors and the Management Board, which would let the former "focus more on policy and substance"[89]; furthermore, the role and mandate of the Chairperson should be strengthened. Concerning the funding topic, the Commission proposes to shift to an (either fully or partially) industry-based funding.[90]

5.1.3 The ESMA's Rulemaking Powers

5.1.3.1 Regulatory Powers

Article 8.1 generally describes the tasks entrusted to ESMA: working in order to establish high-quality common regulatory and supervisory standards and practices; contributing to the consistent application of legally binding Union acts; monitoring and assessing market developments;

organizing and conducting peer review analyses of competent authorities; contributing to the consistent and coherent functioning of colleges of supervisors; stimulating and facilitating the delegation of tasks and responsibilities among competent authorities; and, interestingly, promoting investor protection. All this may look quite vague, so the following passages are devoted to examining what ESMA does in detail.

First and foremost, ESMA's most important task is the development of regulatory and implementing technical standards (RTSs and ITSs) within the framework of the Single Rulebook.[91] When legislative powers are conferred under Articles 290 and 291 TFEU, ESMA adopts regulatory and implementing drafts which will later be endorsed by the Commission. These standards must be purely technical and avoid implying any strategic decisions or policy choices. Moreover, their content must be within the limits of the legislative acts of delegation on which they are based.

Besides the limits in terms of content and leeway, as of July 2017 ESMA Single Rulebook has flourished though the adoption of a great deal of Technical Standards[92] under MiFID II. Compared to the MiFID I implementing measures, the following list clearly proves the de facto increased rulemaking power of ESMA:

- RTS Article 7(4) Authorisation of investment firms
- RTS Article 27(10) Best Execution
- RTS Article 34(8) Passporting of investment services
- RTS Article 35(11) Passporting of investment services
- RTS Article 80(3) Cooperation and exchange of information between NCA
- RTS Article 46(7) Registration of third country firms
- ITS Article 7(5) Authorisation of investment firms
- ITS Article 34(9) Passporting of investment services
- ITS Article 35(12) Passporting of investment services
- ITS Article 71(7) Sanctions
- ITS Article 80(4) Cooperation and exchange of information between NCA
- ITS Article 81(4) Cooperation and exchange of information between NCA
- ITS Article 84(4) Consultation prior to authorisation

These standards are very meticulous, much more than MiFID I 2006 Implementing Directive. RTS Article 27.10[93], which was poured into the Commission Delegated Regulation (EU) 2017/575,[94] for example, sets forth very detailed obligations for execution venues to publish the data concerning the execution quality of their transactions. For instance, Article 3 lists the specific information (like "*nature, number and average duration of any outage, within the venue's normal trading period, that interrupted trading across all instruments available to trade at the venue on the date of the trading day*") to be published and Table 1 of the Annex provides the industry with a standardized format to fill. Similarly, Article 4 on *Price* clearly mandates that trading venues must publish intra-day information as "the simple average price of all transactions that were executed in the two minutes starting at each of the reference times 9.30.00, 11.30.00, 13.30.00 and 15.30.00 UTC on that date and for each size range as set out in Article 9". It is no wonder that with such a detailed level of regulation, the regulatory leeway of domestic regulators is almost zero.

ESMA RTSs are "binding" to a certain degree. The "binding" feature is given by the fact that the Commission must explain to ESMA why it does not want to endorse ESMA's drafts, or what and where it wants to amend.[95] When a "collision" between the Commission and ESMA happens, a six-week period of talks between ESMA and the Commission starts and, at the expiration of that period, the Commission still retains the power to reject the proposed standards. However, Article 10 clearly states that the Commission cannot "change the content of a draft regulatory technical standard prepared by the Authority without prior coordination with the Authority". Finally, Article 10.4 states that RTSs must be adopted as either Commission's regulations or decisions and published in the *Official Journal of the European Union*.

As regards the implementation of financial regulations by Member States, ESMA has the power to issue ITSs. Article 15 specifies that these ITSs must be "technical", without implying strategic decisions or policy choices. The content of these implementing standards must determine the conditions of application of EU financial regulations. As already shown in the case of RTSs, ESMA's draft ITSs must be submitted to the Commission in order to be endorsed. The issuance system is rather the same as that applicable to the draft RTSs, and the ITSs are adopted as regulations or decisions as well.

When a national regulator fails to comply with EU financial regulations, in particular when it does not guarantee that a financial market participant satisfies the requirements provided by EU law, ESMA can be called upon to ferret out an alleged breach or non-application of Union law. ESMA can act upon a request from one or more competent authorities, the European Parliament, the Council, the Commission or the Securities and Markets Stakeholder Group, or on its own initiative. This is a fast-track procedure provided by Article 17 and aims at ensuring the concrete application of Union law, so as to overcome the hurdles posed by the lengthy procedure for a breach of EU law taken by the Commission before the ECJ.

ESMA has a two-month window to issue a recommendation to the national regulator in which actions to comply with EU law are suggested. If the national regulator does not comply within one month, the Commission, taking into account ESMA's recommendations, can issue a formal opinion requiring the competent authority to take the action necessary to comply with Union law. In case of non-compliance and where it is necessary "to remedy in a timely manner such non compliance in order to maintain or restore neutral conditions of competition in the market or ensure the orderly functioning and integrity of the financial system",[96] ESMA can "adopt an individual decision addressed to a financial market participant requiring the necessary action to comply with its obligations under Union law including the cessation of any practice".[97] This ESMA decision has the power to prevail over previous decisions adopted by the national regulation on the same issue.

In this vein, Article 18 already provides that when the ESRB or ESMA considers that an emergency situation may arise, it must send a confidential recommendation with an assessment of the situation to the Council. The Council determines whether an emergency situation exists or not and, if so, it must inform the European Parliament and the Commission. When the Council determines that a situation is so serious that its developments are likely to jeopardize the "the orderly functioning and integrity of financial markets or the stability of the whole or part of the financial system in"[98] the European Union, ESMA may adopt individual decisions requiring national regulators to take the necessary action. If a national regulator does not comply with an ESMA decision, ESMA can intervene and adopt an individual decision directly addressed to financial market participants, in which the European Authority lays down the necessary actions and/or the cessation of any practice.

Article 19 provides ESMA with the power to settle disagreements between competent authorities in cross-border situations, replacing the CESR mediation mechanism. ESMA can issue binding legal decisions in order to compel national regulators to either take or refrain from specific actions necessary to settle the issue. Article 82 of MiFID II also recalls such power on "binding mediation" in case of disagreements between NCAs.

Article 21 provides that when a college of supervisors is established in order to monitor European cross-border banks, ESMA staff can participate in the activities of the college, including on-site examinations. Moreover, ESMA should ensure a "consistent and coherent functioning of colleges of supervisors for cross-border institutions across the Union, taking account of the systemic risk posed by financial market participants".[99] Within colleges of supervisors ESMA can: collect information in order to facilitate the work of the college; initiate and coordinate EU-wide stress tests in order to assess the resilience of financial market players; promote effective and efficient supervisory activities; oversee the tasks carried out by national regulators; and "request further deliberations of a college in any cases where it considers that the decision would result in an incorrect application of Union law or would not contribute to the objective of convergence of supervisory practices".[100]

5.1.3.2 ESMA in the Lamfalussy Process

ESMA plays an important role in the Lamfalussy procedure. In the second phase of this process, ESMA adopts technical standards and helps the Commission draft a more detailed legislation, such as the Commission Delegated Acts. When supporting the Commission, ESMA is wearing its "advisor" hat, channeling the opinions of the national regulators on the ESMA Board and conveying these views directly to the Commission, which will enact also on the basis of such opinions.[101]

At level 3, ESMA develops its own soft-law instruments, such as guidelines, reviews, and recommendations, which contribute to the development of the "Single Rulebook".[102] This is the phase where ESMA enjoys significant "regulatory" leeway due to the fact that it can adopt (apparently soft) normative texts not only addressed to national authorities, but also directly to market participants. On the one hand, these norms are formally soft, in that they are not binding; however, the recipients' behavior is assessed also on how far they have been spontaneously compliant with such guidelines and recommendations.[103]

Moreover, during the third phase of the Lamfalussy process, ESMA carries out an important supervisory convergence task aimed at "building a common supervisory culture among national competent authorities".[104] This is particularly important in a system based on the home country principle where the quality of the implementation of the rules depends on the domestic level[105] and supervisory convergence is necessary for a well-functioning financial market.[106] ESMA works on supervisory convergence through, for example, peer review analysis[107] to test the quality of the nationally implemented regulation. Needless to say that the developing of the Single Rulebook and the effort to foster supervisory convergence go hand in hand.[108]

Finally, in the fourth phase ESMA may choose to leverage on the above-mentioned fast-track procedure to address issues of non-proper application of the EU legislation.[109] This procedure grants the ESMA the power to investigate an alleged breach or non-application of Union law, thus giving ESMA the important role of stabilizer of EU law.

5.1.3.3 ESMA and Investor Protection

In the words of the European Commission, in order to "ensure investor and consumer protection, [...ESMA is] promoting "*transparency, fairness and simplicity*" for consumer financial products or services, notably by collecting, analysing and reporting on consumer trends, developing training standards and contributing to the development of disclosure rule".[110] As shown above, investor protection is an essential tool in making the single market function efficiently, and this is particularly so in a post-crisis situation where investors' confidence in the market must be restored. Thus, it was inevitable that ESMA would have gained a role in promoting the protection of retail investors through "transparency, simplicity and fairness".[111] Article 8.2(i) clearly states that ESMA must have the powers to "develop common methodologies for assessing the effect of product characteristics and distribution processes on the financial position of financial market participants and on consumer protection".

Interestingly, the establishing regulation[112] designs ESMA as a "data analyzer" (by collecting, analyzing, and reporting data on consumer trends); a coordinator of national financial education projects; a "trainer" for the industry (by developing uniform training standards for the industry); and, most importantly, the coordinator for more harmonized disclosure rules. Both "supervisory" and "regulatory" powers are granted in order to carry out these tasks: the monitoring of new and existing financial activities and the adoption of guidelines and recommendations, with the official aim being the promotion of "the safety and soundness of markets and convergence of regulatory practice".[113]

Thus, the *raison d'être* of ESMA investor protection function is to guarantee the correct functioning of the European financial market. Indeed, it could not be any different: ESMA is based on Article 114 TFEU. This characteristic is confirmed by several facts: Article 9 groups together consumer protection, financial activities, and financial innovation, as if consumer protection were the justification for ESMA intervening in "regulating" financial activities[114] and, above all, financial innovation. Moreover, the possibility to issue "warnings" is envisaged for situations in which a financial activity poses a serious threat to ESMA basic objectives, such as the protection of the public interest through "the short, medium and long-term stability and effectiveness of the financial system".[115] However, the instrumental role of investor protection is even more evident in Article 9.5 which endows ESMA with the power of prohibiting or restricting financial activities that are highly likely to threaten the orderly functioning and integrity of financial markets or the stability of the whole or a part of the EU financial system (to be activated under Article 18 of ESMA Regulation or on the grounds of sectoral legislation).

Finally as regards ESMA's investor protection task, it is interesting to notice that Article 10.1 provides that ESMA must conduct open public consultations on draft RTSs and analyze the potential related costs and benefits. These two elements may look promising when it comes to dealing with the protection of retail investor: apparently, investors can now have their say in the decision-making process and the costs they bear may be included in the cost-benefit analysis.

Interestingly, the ESMA website has developed an "investor corner" where a retail investor can be guided on two relevant issues. The first section is the "check if a firm is regulated" page, which helps an investor find out whether the firm s/he wants to invest her/his money with is actually regulated. The second section is the "Get Ready To Invest—Dos and Don'ts" page, which lists what a retail investor is supposed to do and, on the contrary, what should be avoided. In addition, the "File A Complaint" and "Frauds and Scams" sections offer retail investors quite detailed information about how to file a complaint against financial market participants (which makes reference to the FIN-NET schemes, see Chap. 6) and inform the public about the fraudulent use of ESMA's name and logo to promote frauds and scams.

Finally, the page "Warning And Publications For Investors" lists information warnings addressed to investors such as the one on "CFDs, binary options and other speculative products",[116] issued in July 2016. This warning alerts investors that such financial products are "inherently risky, complex and speculative" and, thus, unfit for a retail investor, and it warns on the fact that they are usually marketed and sold in an aggressive way.

The Standing Committee on investor protection and intermediaries[117] is one of the ESMA standing committees. It contributes to elaborating standards and to providing advice on topics such as conduct of business and distribution of investment products.[118] These activities are partnered with the effort to foster supervisory convergence among national authorities.[119] The link between investor protection and supervisory convergence (Article 29 of the ESMA Regulation) reaffirms the public-based approach of the EU law of investor protection.

A first example of the drive toward a deeper convergence of national policies in the area of investor protection comes in the form of a 2008 document entitled "A Consumer's Guide to MiFID—Investing in Financial Products".[120] This was mainly directed at retail consumers but it should also be used by national supervisors as a tool to implement investor protection rules uniformly throughout Europe, thus providing firms with a more certain and uniform legal landscape.

In April 2011, another important document was released, the "MiFID Q&A in the area of investor protection and intermediaries".[121] The purpose of this document was to foster regulatory convergence throughout

Europe and to "promote common supervisory approaches and practices in the application of MiFID and its implementing measures".[122] It was thus addressed to national authorities, which must ensure that "in their supervisory activities their actions are converging along the lines of the responses adopted by"[123] ESMA.

With the adoption of the MiFID II package and PRIIPs, the guidance activity on investor protection has strongly increased, similarly to the above-shown increase of technical standards in qualitative and quantitative terms. The section of the ESMA's website "MiFID—Investor Protection" lists Q&As, Opinions, and Guideline documents dealing with the investor protection issue:

- Guidelines on certain aspects of the MiFID suitability requirements;
- Guidelines on remuneration policies and practices (MiFID);
- Guidelines on certain aspects of the MiFID compliance function requirements;
- Guidelines for the assessment of knowledge and competence;
- Guidelines on complex debt instruments and structured deposits;
- Guidelines on cross-selling practices;
- Q&As on MiFID: Common positions agreed by CESR Members of the Investor Protection and Intermediaries Standing Committee;
- Q&As on Understanding the definition of advice under MiFID;
- Q&As on MiFID in the area of investor protection and intermediaries;
- Q&As on MiFID complex and non-complex financial instruments for the purposes of the Directive's appropriateness requirements;
- Q&As on Best Execution under MiFID;
- Q&As on MiFID II and MiFIR Investor protection topics.

Particularly important is the constantly updated "Q&As on MiFID II and MiFIR investor protection topic"[124] which provide detailed clarifications on several topics such as best execution; suitability and appropriateness tests; client categorization, and investment advice. Similarly, the recently launched "Consultation on Guidelines on certain aspects of the MiFID II suitability requirements"[125] is meant to help the Compliance Function of investment firms and credit institutions which provide investment advice and discretionary portfolio management services to navigate through the uncertain waters of MiFID II requirements and turning them into intra-firm processes and procedures. As a matter of practice, in the current uncertain re-regulation époque, even soft-law documents such as Q&As are often used by investment firms' internal Compliance Functions as quasi-hard law.

5.1.4 The Direct Supervisory and Enforcement Activity of ESMA

The need to centralize supervisory and enforcement powers at EU level had already been forecast by CESR in 2004 in the so-called Himalaya Report.[126] Six years later, Article 9.5 endows ESMA with the power to prohibit or restrict financial *activities* that are highly likely to threaten the orderly functioning and integrity of financial markets or the stability of the whole or a part of the EU financial system. Such power to prohibit and restrict this kind of financial activity must be specified by the legislative acts[127] conferring powers on ESMA, or can be wielded in case of the emergency situations (Article 18). The key characteristic of the Article 9.5 prohibition/restriction power is not the fact that an activity may be unsuitable for the average retail investor, but the fact that such an activity may be a possible threat to the financial market.

MiFIR product intervention powers[128] (Chap. 3) are granted under Article 9.5, and they concretize ESMA's[129] actual enforcement responsibilities by linking emergency powers to financial *products*. For this reason, these powers are likely to tighten ESMA's grip on investor protection, even if they can be wielded only for very major infringements. MiFIR is pushing toward a direction already discreetly paved by the ESMA establishing Regulation.

Indeed, since its inception, ESMA has seen its enforcement powers growing, in a path leading toward a slow but constant centralization of public enforcement at European level in the field of investor protection. Alongside product intervention powers under Article 40 MiFIR, also Article 45 MiFIR on position management, Article 28 Short Selling

Regulation, and Article 47 AIFMD[130] leverage on Article 9.5 of the ESMA Regulation.

Alongside Article 9.5 emergency powers, ESMA is entrusted with exclusive, direct supervisory, and enforcement powers in (only) three cases: the supervision of Credit Rating Agencies (CRAs) under the CRA Regulation 118,[131] the supervision of Trade Repositories under the European Market Infrastructure Regulation—EMIR,[132] and supervision of non-EU investment firms providing services without the establishment of a branch under Article 46–49 MiFIR.

The CRA Regulation grants ESMA the powers to register CRAs, request information, launch investigations, and carry out on-site inspections. Likewise, the supervision of Trade Repositories is substantially based on the supervision of CRAs.[133] Finally, the supervision of non-EU investment firms under MiFIR goes hand in hand with the power of the European Commission to adopt an "Equivalence decision" stating that "the legal and supervisory arrangements of that third country ensure that firms authorised in that third country comply with legally binding prudential and business conduct requirements" (Article 47). Importantly, ESMA can withdraw the registration of a non-EU firm in case it "is acting in a manner which is clearly prejudicial to the interests of investors" or if the non-EU firm's competent authority "has not taken the appropriate measures needed to protect investors" (Article 49).

For the time being, ESMA's enforcement actions have been restricted to two single, limited areas that only very indirectly affect retail investors' welfare—CRAs and Trade Repository.[134] It is yet to be seen whether and the extent to which ESMA will exercise its new product intervention powers for very major infringements under MiFIR: this is going to be an important yardstick to measure ESMA's impact on retail investor protection. However, even if ESMA will not use its secondary and emergency product intervention powers in the near future, the very existence of these powers is likely to give ESMA a stronger leverage in terms of supervisory convergence. This is because domestic enforcers might be stimulated to avoid being replaced by ESMA and wield their powers by meeting the European Authority's expectations.

In its ESA Consultation Paper,[135] with regard to "tasks and powers" and "supervisory architecture", the European Commission is considering "optimising existing tasks and powers"[136] and endowing ESMA with new direct supervisory powers.[137] Furthermore, the current model of sector-related supervision (banking, insurance, securities) is also put into question with regard to consumer protection.[138] Aware of the weaknesses of ESMA and the complexities of the market, the European Commission seems to be trying to improve the current situation within the legal framework of the existing Treaties and against the backdrop of the current political landscape.

5.2 Public Enforcement in the United States: The Role of the Securities and Exchange Commission

5.2.1 The Architecture of Financial Supervision in the United States

The US public supervisory framework for financial markets is remarkably complex. The current US regulatory architecture can be defined as "activity based"[139] and can be briefly sketched as following:

1. Four federal depository and banking regulators (Federal Reserve System[140]—FED; Office of the Comptroller of the Currency[141]—OCC; Federal Deposit Insurance Corporation[142]—FDIC; and National Credit Union Administration[143]—NCUA).[144] In addition, each state has its own banking supervisor.
2. One federal securities regulator (Securities and Exchange Commission—SEC). In addition, each state has its own securities supervisor. Plus SROs, in particular the Financial Industry Regulatory Authority—FINRA, which enjoys broad regulatory powers.
3. One federal derivatives regulator (Commodity Futures Trading Commission—CFTC).[145]
4. One federal specialized Consumer Financial Protection office (Bureau of Consumer Financial Protection—CFPB). The CFPB was estab-

lished by the Dodd-Frank Wall Street Reform and Consumer Protection Act of 2010[146] as an independent bureau within the Federal Reserve System. The Bureau has centralized the powers to regulate consumer protection previously belonging to seven different federal regulators,[147] like the Fed, the FDIC and the OCC. However, some important retail products are excluded from the Bureau's scope—such as products and services provided by insurance companies and real estate brokers. Moreover, another important exemption is specified in Title X concerning the persons regulated by the SEC, the CFTC, state securities commissions: all these products, services, and their providers will continue to be regulated by their current regulators. This is why the SEC is still the key figure for retail investor protection in the United States.

5. More than wholly state-based fifty regulators for the insurance sector. Significantly, the 2010 Dodd-Frank Act established the Treasury's Federal Insurance Office (FIO). This is responsible for monitoring and gathering information on the insurance sector, and for representing the United States in international fora on insurance matters.[148]

In addition, the Federal Financial Institutions Examination Council (FFIEC) was established in 1979 as formal interagency body tasked with adopting principles and standards and making recommendations to foster consistency in the supervision of financial institutions. It gathers the FED, the FDIC, the NCUA, the OCC, and the CFPB.[149] Finally, the 2010 Dodd-Frank Act established the Financial Stability Oversight Council (FSOC) to monitor macro stability of the US financial system.[150]

The US securities sector looks like a tripartite system,[151] based on the interaction between federal, states', and SROs' regulations (the latter operating under SEC's supervision).[152] The SEC competes with other federal financial regulators, like the CFTC for derivatives,[153] the Federal Reserve Board, and the Department of the Treasury, concerning the powers to regulate products, instruments, and the financial industry.[154] Quite often, federal agencies work together and issue joint final rules, as it is the case for the Volcker Rule,[155] meant to avoid commercial banks taking up too risky activities and, thus, to indirectly protect (retail) investors through market stability.

The overall picture is not easy to understand. In order to make it clearer, it is useful to apply the explanation scheme proposed by Chatzimanoli[156] in which she clearly depicts the relationships between (1) the federal securities regulator and state securities regulators; (2) the federal securities regulator and other financial regulators; (3) the federal securities regulator and SROs.

The SEC and state regulators[157]: Regarding policy development, the SEC has always had an approach inclined to "cooperation, coordination and sharing of information"[158] with state authorities.[159] Enforcement too is characterized by a fruitful "cooperation between the two levels of government".[160] This is particularly true for smaller enforcement cases, whereas "the bigger and most important ones will be enforced by the SEC",[161] as they have a federal and/or interstate effect[162] and state regulators might not be able to address the situation.[163]

The SEC and other financial regulators[164]: Due to an increasingly complex financial market, in 1974 Congress established the CFTC "with the mandate to regulate commodity futures and option markets in the United States".[165] The derivative business is very complex and the SEC and the CFTC need to cooperate and work together, especially in information sharing.[166] An example of this coordination can be the 2008 *Agreement to Enhance Coordination, Facilitate Review of New Derivative Products.*

Additionally, the SEC assists the Department of Justice in carrying out its exclusive authority in bringing criminal prosecutions concerning violations of securities laws.[167] Further, the SEC also cooperates with the US postal authorities (which have investigation powers over mail frauds connected to securities offerings)[168]; and with the US Department of Treasury, which has the power to regulate the offerings of its sovereign securities.[169]

The SEC and SROs[170]: As already said, the SEC has the power to watch over the self-regulatory organizations, such as FINRA. Indeed, the SEC examines and approves both new rules emanated by SROs and changes made to existing rules, and over time it has actively reviewed NASD/FINRA's regulatory actions.[171] Moreover, the SEC is the appeal body for the determinations by self-regulatory organizations.[172]

5.2.2 The Securities and Exchange Commission

5.2.2.1 Official Mission and Functions

The SEC was established in 1934 by the Securities Exchange Act "to serve investors".[173] Indeed, its vision is the promotion of "a market environment that is worthy of the public's trust and characterized by transparency and integrity"[174] and its key mission is "to protect investors, maintain fair, orderly, and efficient markets, and facilitate capital formation".[175] The SEC has the responsibility to:

1. "interpret and enforce federal securities laws;
2. issue new rules and amend existing rules;
3. oversee the inspection of securities firms, brokers, investment advisers, and ratings agencies;
4. oversee private regulatory organizations in the securities, accounting, and auditing fields; and,
5. coordinate U.S. securities regulation with federal, state, and foreign authorities."[176]

The SEC carries out regulatory, supervisory, and adjudicative functions.[177] Regulatory powers are used to create *erga omnes* rules; supervisory powers are used in order to monitor domestic financial markets and to enforce statutes and regulations, even via investigations, when firms do not comply with the law; while, finally, adjudicative powers are used to take administrative actions and issue decisions.[178]

5.2.2.2 Organization

The SEC, based in Washington DC, has five Commissioners, appointed for five years by the President of the United States.[179] The President also designates the Chairman, the agency's chief executive.[180] As of 2017, the Commission has approximately 4600[181] staff employed working full time, and it is funded by the US federal government: "[A]ll fees go to the U.S. Treasury, and the entire budget of the Commission comes via the appropriations[182] process."[183]

The SEC is divided into five Divisions: Division of Corporation Finance; Division of Trading and Markets; Division of Investment Management; Division of Enforcement; and the recently created Division of Economic and Risk Analysis. Due to the federal nature of the Commission, the SEC has eleven regional offices all around the country.[184]

Division of Corporation Finance: The Division of Corporation Finance is at the very first stage of investor protection since it ensures that important "information about the companies' financial condition and business practices"[185] is provided in order to enable investors to make informed investment decisions. Indeed, the work of the Division is aimed at improving the quality of the information disclosure likely to affect an investor's decision concerning whether to buy, sell, or hold a security: the "Division's staff routinely reviews the disclosure documents filed by companies".[186]

The Division of Corporation Finance "assists the Commission in executing its responsibility to oversee corporate disclosure of important information to the investing public [… and it] documents[187] that publicly held companies are required to file with the Commission."[188] Importantly, the "Division's staff provides companies with assistance interpreting the Commission's rules and recommends to the Commission new rules for adoption."[189]

Furthermore, this Division also gives interpretive assistance[190] to companies about how to comply with the SEC rules and forms, and it "uses no-action letters to issue guidance in a more formal manner".[191] Indeed, a company asks for a no-action letter when it wants to market in a product an "uncharted legal territory in the securities industry"[192] or is using a peculiar financial technique.[193] In such an instance, the Division responds by explaining whether it would or would not advice the Commission to take action.[194] Finally, the Division also gives "administrative interpretations"[195] of key legislation such as the 1933 Act and the 1934 Act and suggests implementing regulations thereof.[196]

Interestingly, the federal Division of Corporation Finance examines the so-called registration statements for newly-offered securities.[197] On the contrary, in Europe prospectuses for newly offered financial instruments are not reviewed by ESMA but by the domestic competent authorities and, on the basis of that review, securities can then freely move throughout the Union thanks to the "single passport for issuers".

Division of Trading and Markets: The Division of Trading and Markets officially "assists the Commission in executing its responsibility for maintaining fair, orderly, and efficient markets"[198] by supervising the markets. In order to do so, the Division monitors, on a daily basis, the major securities market actors, such as the securities exchanges, securities firms, self-regulatory organizations (SROs), clearing agencies, and CRAs.[199] FINRA is under the oversight of the Division of Trading and Markets.[200] Importantly, the Division is responsible for implementing the SEC's financial integrity program for broker-dealers,[201] which is aimed at boosting investors' confidence in the financial industry by imposing rules such as those on sufficient liquid assets, on the orderly maintenance of books, and on record-keeping.[202]

Division of Investment Management: The Division of Investment Management regulates investment companies—like mutual funds, closed-end funds, exchange-traded funds, and unit investment trusts[203]—as well as federally registered investment advisers[204] and securities research analysts.[205] It does so in order to ensure "that disclosures about [...] investments [sold by financial intermediaries] are useful to retail customers, and that the regulatory costs which consumers must bear are not excessive".[206] As regards investment advisers, that is, those operators who have a direct contact with retail investors, these individuals/firms must register with the SEC if they manage $100 million or more in clients' assets.[207] Those investment advisers who, instead, manage less than $100 million in clients' assets, must register in the state where they have their principal place of business.[208]

Moreover, as officially stated by the SEC,[209] the Division assists "the Commission in interpreting laws and regulations for the public and SEC inspection and enforcement staff"[210]; it responds "to no-action requests and requests for exemptive relief"[211]; it reviews "investment company and investment adviser filings"[212]; it assists "the Commission in enforcement matters involving investment companies and advisers"[213]; and advises "the Commission on adapting SEC rules to new circumstances".[214]

This Division is at the front line of retail investor protection because it deals with information disclosure concerning key actors of the US retail financial system. Coherently, the Division's webpage[215] has very useful information for investors aimed at improving their knowledge and understanding of financial markets.

Division of Enforcement: The SEC brings "hundreds of civil enforcement actions against individuals and companies"[216] on a yearly basis. Its enforcement activity is so important that its role "can be seen as mainly that of an enforcer rather than of a regulator".[217] For this reason, the Division of Enforcement is vital for the functioning of the Commission.

The Division of Enforcement was established in 1972 in order to rationalize the work previously undertaken by other divisions.[218] It investigates possible violations of securities laws, and recommends the Commission to start investigations of possible breaches of securities laws and bring civil actions before federal courts or ALJs[219] (with the Division directly "prosecuting these cases on behalf of the Commission"[220]). Importantly, the SEC is not authorized to act on behalf of individual investors on a general basis, even if in some cases the ill-gotten gains can be refunded to defrauded customers.[221]

Division of Economic and Risk Analysis: The Division of Risk, Strategy, and Financial Innovation was established in the aftermath of the 2007–2009 financial crisis as the SEC's "think-tank".[222] It was officially established in September 2009 with the aim to "integrate financial economics and rigorous data analytics into the core mission of the"[223] Commission, by relying "on a variety of academic disciplines, quantitative and non-quantitative approaches, and knowledge of market institutions and practices".[224]

The key tasks of the Division are: (a) analysis of the potential economic effects of SEC's rulemaking and actions[225]; (b) performance of quantitative and qualitative research, and execution of risk assessment[226]; (c) support to the Division of Enforcement in enforcement proceedings and settlement negotiations through the provision of economic and quantitative analysis.[227]

Office of Investors' Advocate: This Office was recently established (in 2014) with the purpose of carrying out four core functions: (1) being a voice of investors, by bringing their needs before the SEC, the SROs, and the Congress; (2) assisting retail investors, by appointing an Ombudsman that resolves problems between investors and the SEC or the SROs; (3) executing studies on investor behavior, "to gain insight into investor behavior and provide data regarding policy choices"[228]; (4) supporting the SEC's Investor Advisory Committee. Importantly, even if the Investor Advocate reports to the SEC Chair, its autonomy is granted by the duty to directly submit reports to Congress.[229]

5.2.3 The SEC Rulemaking Procedure

The Securities and Exchange Commission can issue its own *erga omnes* regulations[230] based on the purview granted by federal legislation such as the 1933 Securities Act,[231] the 1934 Securities Exchange Act, the 1940 Investment Advisers Act,[232] and the recent 2010 Dodd-Frank Wall Street Reform and Consumer Protection Act.[233] These significant pieces of legislation do not only contain directly applicable rules but also give the SEC the responsibility for adopting and, then, enforcing those implementing rules necessary for the correct functioning of the US financial markets, such as the Rule 10b-5.

The SEC adopts its own rules through a three-step process: Concept Release, Rule Proposal, Rule Adoption.[234] The Concept Release step is not taken every time the SEC must issue a new rule or change an old one, but only when an "issue is so unique or complicated that the SEC seeks public input before issuing a proposed rule".[235] With a Concept Release the SEC depicts the issue at hand, describes the hurdles encountered, and gives a picture of the different potential regulatory paths that can be followed.[236] The public, including both financial firms and associations and private citizens, can submit their opinions using an online form or via e-mail, which requires very little personal information (first name, last name, and e-mail address).[237] Commentators can send their comments even via paper and, since all comments are made publicly available on the SEC web site, those paper-based are converted into PDF and posted on the website.[238]

Rules are discussed and provisionally drafted by the Commission staff, and this is the second step of the SEC's rulemaking procedure. Indeed, when a Rule Proposal is adopted, it is subsequently published on the Commission's official website in order to make it publicly available: "[P]ublic's input on the proposal is considered as a final rule is drafted."[239] The aim of this transparency practice is, again, to let the industry and the US citizens voice their views on the proposed norm. The system for the submission of comments used for Concept Releases is also used for Rule Proposals.[240]

The third and last step concerns the adoption of the rule. The Commission is officially committed to taking into account all comments sent by both financial firms and associations and private citizens when adopting a new rule or an amendment to an existing one.[241] The entry into force can be delayed or immediate; in either case, a compliance date is mentioned.[242]

5.2.4 The SEC Enforcement Activity

The enforcement activity is, de facto, the main way through which the Commission operates, thus making the SEC more of an "enforcer" than a simple "regulator".[243] This is important for the investor protection matter, even if the SEC does not operate by taking into account the interest of single investors,[244] but it views the public general interest and it operates accordingly—by trying to preserve and boost the efficient functioning of securities markets.[245]

Before a formal investigation: In this phase, the SEC's Office of Compliance Inspections and Examinations (OCIE) is devoted to analyzing registered entities' activity. The OCIE's official mission is "to protect investors, ensure market integrity and support responsible capital formation through risk-focused strategies that: (1) improve compliance; (2) prevent fraud; (3) monitor risk; and (4) inform policy".[246] If, after an examination, compliance deficiencies and/or internal control weaknesses are identified, then a deficiency letter is sent requesting the firm under examination to take the necessary steps to address the situation.[247] However, when the identified issues cannot be handled through a deficiency letter, then the OCIE refers the matter directly to the Enforcement Division,[248] which examines the situation and evaluates whether to commence an investigation.[249]

The investigation: When the SEC staff believes that some wrongdoing has occurred, then they will inform the potential defendant by sending a "Wells Notice".[250] This is a communication that "(1) informs the person the staff has made a preliminary determination to recommend that the Commission file an action or institute a proceeding against them; (2) identifies the securities law violations that the staff has preliminarily determined to include in the recommendation; and (3) provides notice that the person may make a submission to the Division and the Commission concerning the proposed recommendation."[251]

The potential defendant can reply to a Wells Notice by sending a "Wells submission", explaining why the SEC should not bring actions or why the proposed recommendation should not be adopted.[252] It is for the Commission to decide whether an enforcement action is necessary. If so, then the Commissioners have two options: filing a complaint either with a US District Court or within the Commission before an ALJ, depending on the type of measure the SEC thinks would best fit the case.[253]

Remedies available through an administrative procedure: Through an administrative proceeding process, run by ALJs, the SEC can impose quite a wide range of sanctions upon the defendants.[254] ALJs are independent of the SEC but they play a "prominent role in SEC enforcement".[255] They must consider both the evidence submitted by the Enforcement Division staff and the evidence presented by the defendant.[256] At the end of this proceeding, an ALJ issues an initial decision[257] that includes relevant facts, legal conclusions, and recommended sanctions.[258] The initial decision can be appealed by both the Division and the SEC supervisee to the Commission, which has the power to confirm it, reverse it, or request additional hearings.[259]

As explained by Stella,[260] the following are the most common remedies available through an administrative proceeding. (1) *Civil monetary penalty*, which "is defined in relevant part as any penalty, fine, or other sanction that: (a) is for a specific amount, or has a maximum amount, as provided by federal law; and (b) is assessed or enforced by an agency in an administrative proceeding or by a federal court pursuant to federal law".[261] (2) *Disgorgements*, that is, the repayment of illegally obtained gains,[262] whose amount "need[s] only be a reasonable approximation of profits causally connected to the violation".[263] (3) *Cease and desist order*: this is an order issued by the SEC under Section 8A of the 1933 Act aimed at prohibiting or desisting parties from committing actions that the SEC finds illegal.[264] The SEC is required to notify the order and grant the opportunity for hearing.[265] (4) *Associational sanctions*: this applies to a person associated to a financial firm (or that is seeking to become associated with it) that the SEC finds in violation of federal securities laws.[266] Through such sanctions, the SEC can impede or limit the person's activity.[267] This kind of sanction is sometimes corollary to a cease and desist order.[268]

Remedies available in a civil suit: As explained by Stella,[269] these are the most common remedies available to the SEC in a civil suit: (1) *Injunctions*, through which a court restrains a party from doing certain acts in the future.[270] (2) *Temporary restraining order*, a short-term injunction through which a court orders a party to cease doing a specific action.[271] (3) *Ancillary relief*, ancillary remedies aimed at avoiding that the defendant perpetuates misconducts, such as *asset freeze*.[272] (4) *Officer and director bars*, when a court prohibits a person from acting as an officer or director of a public company.[273] (5) *Civil monetary penalties*, when a court imposes a monetary penalty if this is so requested by the SEC.[274]

5.3 The Slow Building of a Single Law-Enforcer and Regulator

The chapter shows the three key differences between the European and American authorities: governance; regulatory remit; enforcement powers. Such differences can be historically justified, but are less and less relevant if the current size and level of complexity of the EU and US securities markets are taken into account.[275] The institutional weaknesses of the ESMA strongly emerge when comparing its regulatory and enforcement powers with those of the SEC.

If we look at the SEC, we have the clear picture of an agency behaving like an enforcer rather than a simple regulator.[276] The enforcement powers granted to the SEC let it adopt an approach that—according to the gravity of enforcement case at hand—can be more or less incline toward deterrence.[277] The SEC can choose which remedy is more apt to ensure the correct enforcement of securities regulations, as it can either select a "public law" path and apply administrative remedies, or bring a civil lawsuit before a court and ask for a civil remedy.[278]

Concerning the SEC's public enforcement, it is worth noting that the US administrative law substantially differs from the Continental European tradition and one of the main differences concerns the so-called administrative law courts. In the United States ALJs are not specialized courts as they are in most of the European civil law countries, where administrative courts apply special proceedings that are different from private-law procedures and were specifically designed for these kinds of cases. An example of such a court is the Italian *Tribunale Amministrativo Regionale*, the German *Verwaltungsgerichte*, the French *Tribunal Administratif*, or the Polish *Wojewódzkie Sądy Administracyjne* (WSA).

The US ALJs are "independent adjudicators",[279] working in a government agency, and their task is to make decisions or issue sanctions[280] within the remit of that agency. The US ALJs are not the "special" judges for the government. In carrying out their work, the ALJs handle trial-like "'formal' hearings"[281] relating to a situation concerning their agency and someone, either a natural or a legal person, affected by a decision made by the agency.[282]

When we, instead, look at ESMA's powers and functions, on the one hand, we notice that the adoption of technical standards within the framework of the Single Rulebook is the most important improvement from the CESR situation,[283] but—even if its regulatory powers have been strengthened and stabilized by the SSR Case[284]—they are yet to be formally recognized in full.[285] The investor protection sphere, in particular, is (still) "a shared competence of the EU and Member States and [...] the limits of the subsidiarity principle"[286] must be respected. In this area, at least up to MiFID II, quite a common perception in the industry was that ESMA was basically playing a "moral suasion" role, exercised through guidelines and opinions crafted by the Standing Committee on investor protection.[287]

However, given the extensive width of the regulatory delegation under MiFID II, also ESMA "soft normative power" through guidelines and reports is meant to increase in the mid-run. This is because the European financial industry and, in particular, investment firms' internal Compliance Functions are very interested in learning ESMA's opinions in order to gain key interpretative guidance and navigate the choppy regulatory waters successfully. In addition, due to the impact of ESMA's detailed MiFID II/MiFIR guidelines on the industry, NCAs themselves seem to increasingly rely on ESMA to indicate their home industry what direction is to be followed. So, ESMA soft normative production has de facto gained ground, as the abundance of norms produced by ESMA under the MiFID II package clearly proves.

On the other hand, due to a lack of direct, wide-range enforcement powers, ESMA is still not comparable to its US counterpart. Apart from some specific cases—such as Trade Repositories under EMIR, CRAs—ESMA's new supervisory and enforcement powers under MiFIR are, indeed, activated under the main condition of a compliance failure by a national regulator. This makes it clear that ESMA still does not have a general, independent (from the necessary support of domestic authorities) power to watch over market players[288] and it can step in only when major infringements occur.[289]

However, the new Product Intervention powers provided by MiFIR are likely to change the ESMA-national authorities' relationship on enforcement. Such powers can push toward either an actual centralization of enforcement powers (in case ESMA actually happens to use such powers) or an increase of ESMA's soft influence on domestic authorities about *when* and *how* the intervention powers should be employed against major infringements of the law. The second case is more likely, at least the short run.

Within this context, such major infringements diverge from minor infringements in that the former concern the management of "emergency" type of risks, whereas the latter regard the management of "normal" risks.[290] Does not only this separation reflect the intricate multigovernance structure of the EU but it shows how the distinction between the gravity of the infringements goes hand in hand with the level of intervention.[291] At the lowest level of this ranking, we find the Compliance Function in charge of designing and monitoring the intra-firm complaints-handling procedures conceived as a frontline to address very minor infringements. At the top level of this ranking—the emergency level—we now find ESMA, with domestic authorities turning into "local branches" of ESMA.

The new powers granted to ESMA prove how the original European enforcement architecture—which placed rulemaking at the EU level and law-enforcement at Member States level[292]—has been changing over the last years, at least for the financial sector. The fact that Article 114 TFEU is used as a basis for the MiFIR intervention powers is essentially because enforcement has been construed as an integral part of the substance of the EU law,[293] thus bypassing the *constitutional* constraints provided by the Treaty which does not grant the EU with explicit competences to regulate the enforcement of the EU law.[294]

However, the slogan "quasi-centralized regulation, totally-decentralized supervision and enforcement"[295] is, for the time being, still valid. At least for enforcement, national supervisors still maintain all actual powers concerning the day-to-day supervision and enforcement, with ESMA pushing for a common Union supervisory culture, supported by consistent supervisory practices.[296] However, the extensive normative production under MiFID II has de facto enlarged ESMA's regulatory powers, leaving domestic regulators with reduced leeway (up to the point they by now seem to behave like domestic embedders of ESMA's interpretations of EU rules). Importantly, with ESMA growing in importance, the strong coordination between itself and the European Commission is more than necessary, in order to avoid impasses such as that on the definition of FX contracts.[297]

Thus, for the time being, the ESMA cannot yet be defined as a full-fledged supranational regulator at EU level.[298] This is compounded by the fact that the core functions of ESMA are carried out by its Board which is, at bedrock, a forum of national regulators entitled to take quasi-binding decisions that must be reviewed by the European Commission. As has been correctly noted by Alford: "The success of integrating European financial markets, particularly wholesale markets, facilitated by the common currency, the euro, has highlighted the need for improved supervisory coordination among EU regulators. However, colleges of regulators are not supranational regulators."[299] Even the way ESMA is funded reflects its key feature of being a hybrid of national and supranational nature.[300]

ESMA is not a "pure" regulatory and enforcer agency yet, but a kind of a mélange between a quasi-complete-regulator, an enforcement-practice coordinator of national watchdogs, and an emergency enforcer.[301] Nevertheless, if it is not the same hand running regulation, supervision, and enforcement, these are likely to detach from one another.[302] The EU lawmaker is conscious of this[303] and this is why MiFIR has introduced emergency enforcement powers to be activated when major infringements occur. And since enforcement is what matters the most for the industry (the compliance risk is, ultimately, the risk to be fined), local enforcement practices based on different interpretations of common regulations may lead to confusion and may puzzle the work of pan-European firms' Internal Audit and Compliance Functions. For this reason, the combination within ESMA of (ordinary) regulatory powers, (emergency) enforcement responsibilities, and the effort to build a common supervisory culture among domestic authorities may make the landscape clearer for larger European investment firms in the coming future.

As correctly flagged by the ERPL and showed in the first Part of the book, the EU lawmaker has always paid close attention to public normative production and public enforcement procedures as a tool to establish the single European Financial Market by opening up domestic markets and letting capital freely flow throughout the Union. However, such reliance on public, rather than private, enforcement mechanisms has not yet produced a single European watchdog tasked with regulating and monitoring the single European financial services market, nor does it seem to be possible to establish it without changing the Treaties.

Thus, compared to the United States, Europe is still embroiled in an institutional weakness caused by a lack of a pan-European agency truly endowed with full-fledged regulatory and public enforcement powers.[304] The Americanization of the EU enforcement structures is still far from reality. Although the regulatory leitmotiv has been influenced by the US market-based system—as shown in the first Part—the EU is far from reproducing the complex public enforcement system existing at federal level since the 1930s. The (over)reliance of the EU law on public enforcement mechanism is still an (over)reliance on coordination of NCAs, which sounds inconsistent with the very nature of the market integration objective at EU level and the political "commitment to progress towards an ever closer union".[305] What it is yet to be seen is the effects that the new centralization trend brought about by the MiFIR intervention powers will generate.

Notes

1. Some parts of the following sections have been previously published in Antonio Marcacci, "Public Supervision of Securities Markets in Europe: Still Running Behind the US?," *Federalismi* 2015, no. 15 (2015).
2. Commission des opérations de bourse—COB, "Communiqué Relatif a La Création Du Forum of European Securities Commissions De Fesco," (1997).

3. Ibid.
4. Ibid.
5. The euro was officially established by the 1992 Maastricht Treaty, and it was introduced in non-physical form on 1 January 1999. The physical introduction of the single European currency took place on 1 January 2002.
6. Niamh Moloney, *Eu Securities and Financial Markets Regulation* (Oxford: Oxford University Press, 2014). At 25.
7. European Commission, "Communication of the Commission—Financial Services: Building a Framework for Action," (Brussels: COM (98) 525 final, 1998).
8. "Financial Services: Implementing the Framework for Financial Markets: Action Plan," (Brussels 1999).
9. Council of the European Union, "Regulation of European Securities Markets—the Terms of Reference for the Committee of Wise Men—10491/00," (Brussels 2000).
10. Ibid.
11. The Committee of Wise Men—Lamfalussy Committee, "Final Report of the Committee of Wise Men on the Regulation of European Securities Markets," (2001).
12. European Commission, "Commission Decision Establishing the Committee of European Securities Regulators," (Brussels: C(2001) 1501 final, 2001).
13. Ibid. At 4.
14. It is quite difficult to categorize "soft-law" arrangements because "instruments may be included within this generic term for a number of reasons: (1) they have been articulated in non-binding form according to traditional modes of law-making; (2) they contain vague and imprecise terms; (3) they emanate from bodies lacking international law-making authority; (4) they are directed at non-state actors whose practice cannot constitute customary international law; (5) they lack any corresponding theory of responsibility; (6) they are based solely upon voluntary adherence, or rely upon non-judicial means of enforcement." Christine Chinkin, "Normative Development in the International Legal System," in *Commitment and Compliance: The Role of Non-Binding Norms in the International Legal System*, ed. Dinah Shelton (New York: Oxford University Press, 2000). At 30.
15. Eric J. Pan, "Harmonization of US–Eu Securities Regulation: The Case for a Single European Securities Regulator," *Law & Policy of International*

Business 34, no. 2 (2003); Yannis Avgerinos, "The Need and the Rationale for a European Securities Regulator," in *Financial Markets in Europe: Towards a Single Regulator?*, ed. Mads Andenas and Yannis Avgerinos (London: Kluwer Law International, 2003). Gerard Hertig and Ruben Lee, "Four Predictions About the Future of Eu Securities Regulation," *Journal of Comparative Law Studies* 3, no. 2 (2003). Gilles Thieffry, "The Case for a European Securities Commission," in *Regulation Financial Services in the 21st Century*, ed. Eilís Ferran and Charles A.E. Goodhart (Oxford-Portland: Hart Publishing 2001).

16. European Commission, "Press Release—High Level Expert Group on Eu Financial Supervision to Hold First Meeting on 12 November—Ip/08/1679," (2008).
17. European Commission, "European System of Financial Supervision," https://ec.europa.eu/info/business-economy-euro/banking-and-finance/financial-supervision-and-risk-management/european-system-financial-supervision_en.
18. The de Larosière Group, "Report of the High Level Group on Financial Supervision in the Eu," (2009).
19. European Commission, "Proposal for a Regulation of the European Parliament and of the Council Establishing a European Securities and Markets Authority—Com(2009) 503 Final," (Brussels 2009); "Proposal for a Regulation of the European Parliament and of the Council Establishing a European Insurance and Occupational Pensions Authority—Com(2009) 502 Final," (Brussels 2009); "Proposal for a Regulation of the European Parliament and of the Council Establishing a European Banking Authority—Com(2009) 501 Final," (Brussels 2009).
20. *Regulation 1095/2010*. Art. 2.
21. Professor Moloney raises the critics that "effective retail market governance in the EU is ill-served by the current split of retail market issues across the three sector-specific European Supervisory Authorities (ESMA, the European Banking Authority, and the European Insurance and Occupational Pensions Authority) given the cross-sector nature of retail market risk and the prevalence of substitutable products." Niamh Moloney, "Regulating the Retail Markets," in *The Oxford Handbook of Financial Regulation*, ed. Niamh Moloney, Eilís Ferran, and Jennifer Payne (Oxford: Oxford University Press, 2015). At 754.
22. *Regulation 1092/2010*. Article 6 lists the members of the General Board of the ESRB: (*a*) the President and the Vice-President of the ECB;

(*b*) the Governors of the national central banks; (*c*) a Member of the Commission; (*d*) the Chairperson of the European Supervisory Authority (European Banking Authority); (*e*) the Chairperson of the European Supervisory Authority (European Insurance and Occupational Pensions Authority); (*f*) the Chairperson of the European Supervisory Authority (European Securities and Markets Authority); (*g*) the Chair and the two Vice-Chairs of the Advisory Scientific Committee; (*h*) the Chair of the Advisory Technical Committee.

23. Professor Haar assesses the weakness of the ESRB that appears "as a coordination mechanism among central bankers, rather than a self-standing organization on its own, particularly as it has been set up by a regulation under Article 114 TFEU as a body without legal personality or autonomous intervention power. This rather weak status is also adversely affected by its lack of legal enforcement powers because, without more, the ESRB's warnings and recommendations (through which it operates) are not legally binding, even though it can bring to bear political pressure on the basis of an 'act or explain' mechanism". Brigitte Haar, "Organizing Regional Systems: The Eu Example," in *The Oxford Handbook of Financial Regulation*, ed. Niamh Moloney, Eilís Ferran, and Jennifer Payne (Oxford: Oxford University Press, 2015). At 179.
24. The European Banking Authority, established by *Regulation 1093/2010*; the European Insurance and Occupational Pensions Authority, established by *Regulation 1094/2010*; and the European Securities and Markets Authority (ESMA), established by *Regulation 1095/2010.*
25. As the official ESAs' website states: "Through the Joint Committee, the three ESAs coordinate their supervisory activities in the scope of their respective responsibilities regularly and closely and ensure consistency in their practices." Joint Committee of the European Supervisory Authorities—ESAs, "About Us," https://esas-joint-committee.europa.eu/about-us.
26. On Self-Placement, see: European Supervisory Authorities—ESAs, "Placement of Financial Instruments with Depositors, Retail Investors and Policy Holders ('Self Placement')," (2014).
27. European Commission, "Report on the Operation of the European Supervisory Authorities (Esas) and the European System of Financial Supervision (Esfs), Com(2014) 509 Final," (2014). At 2.
28. Article 1.5, *Regulation 1095/2010.*
29. *United Kingdom V European Commission and Council*, ECR I-3771 (2006). Para. 42.

30. *Germany V. Parliament and Council (Tobacco Advertising)* ECR I-8419 (2000). Para. 84. Literature on the EU Law and the Single Market is vast, for a recent important contribution: Anthony Arnull and Damian Chalmers, *The Oxford Handbook of European Union Law* (Oxford: Oxford University Press, 2015).
31. Elaine Fahey, "Does the Emperor Have Financial Crisis Clothes? Reflections on the Legal Basis of the European Banking Authority," *The Modern Law Review* 74, no. 4 (2011). At 581. As regards critiques about the Commission's approach on the creation of European agencies: Stefan Griller and Andreas Orator, "Everything under Control? The "Way Forward" for European Agencies in the Footsteps of the Meroni Doctrine," *European Law Review* 35, no. 1 (2010). At 5.
32. As reported in Fahey. (At 590) The British House of Commons suggested that the flexibility clause of Article 308 EC (now Article 352 TFEU) could provide a better basis for the European financial reforms package, due to the fact that it implies unanimity. However, it may be easily said that unanimity is a serious functioning issue itself, which de facto does not allow the establishment of a fast, pan-European problem-solving institution. [House of Commons—Treasury Committee, "The Committee's Opinion on Proposals for European Financial Supervision—Sixteenth Report of Session 2008–09," (2009).]
33. Furthermore, it should be pointed out that "no one common definition of an agency may be identified" and an agreed common understanding is yet to come. Michelle Everson, "Independent Agencies: Hierarchy Beaters?," *European Law Journal* 1, no. 2 (1995). As reported by: Griller and Orator. At 5.
34. Griller and Orator. At 5.
35. Regulation 1095/201*0*. Art. 5.
36. Ibid. Recital 14.
37. Griller and Orator.
38. Eddy Wymeersch, "The Reforms of the European Financial Supervisory System—an Overview," *European Company and Financial Law Review* 7, no. 2 (2010). At 253.
39. *Meroni & Co Industrie Metallurgiche Spa V High Authority of the European Coal and Steel Community (Meroni I)*, ECR 133 (1957); and *Meroni & Co Industrie Metallurgiche Spa V High Authority of the European Coal and Steel Community (Meroni Ii)*, ECR 133 (1958).
40. Griller and Orator. At 10.
41. Ibid. At 10.

42. Ibid. At 10.
43. *Meroni & Co Industrie Metallurgiche Spa V High Authority of the European Coal and Steel Community (Meroni I).*
44. Ibid.
45. Ibid.
46. Also: Xenophon A. Yataganas, "Delegation of Regulatory Authority in the European Union—the Relevance of the American Model," ed. Harvard Law School—Jean Monnet Working Paper 03/01 (Cambridge 2001). At 27.
47. Damien Geradin and Nicolas Petit, "The Development of Agencies at Eu and National Levels: Conceptual Analysis and Proposals for Reform," ed. NYU School of Law—Jean Monnet Working Paper 01/04 (New York 2004). At 49.
48. Paul Craig, *Eu Administrative Law—2nd Edition* (Oxford: Oxford University Press, 2012). At 155.
49. For the debate on European regulatory agencies, see: Giandomenico Majone, "Delegation of Regulatory Powers in a Mixed Polity," *European Law Journal* 8, no. 3 (2002).
50. For the categorization of EU agencies, see: Griller and Orator.
51. *United Kingdom of Great Britain and Northern Ireland V European Parliament and Council of the European Union* (2014).
52. *Regulation Eu/236/2012.* This piece of European legislation is aimed at directly harmonizing short selling in Europe. In the C-270/12 press release, the ECJ has circumscribed short selling as the "practice consisting in the sale of shares and securities not owned by the vendor at the time of the sale with a view to benefiting from a fall in the price of the shares and securities". The Court also added that in "the event of disturbance on the financial markets, the regulation seeks, inter alia, to prevent an uncontrolled fall in the price of financial instruments as a result of the effect of short selling". Court of Justice of the European Union—ECJ, "The Power of the European Securities and Markets Authority to Adopt Emergency Measures on the Financial Markets of the Member States in Order to Regulate or Prohibit Short Selling Is Compatible with Eu Law—Press Realise No. 7/14," (2014).
53. *United Kingdom of Great Britain and Northern Ireland V European Parliament and Council of the European Union* Pars 45 and 53.
54. Heikki Marjosola, "Case C-270/12 (Uk V Parliament and Council)—Stress Testing Constitutional Resilience of the Powers of Eu Financial Supervisory Authorities—a Critical Assessment of the Advocate

General's Opinion," in *EUI Working Paper Law 2014/02*, ed. European University Institute (2014). At 1.

55. Article 28.2a, SSR.
56. Article 28.2b, SSR.
57. Marjosola. At 1.
58. Article 28.11, SSR. The United Kingdom based its appeal on several assumptions, in particular the fact that the emergency regulatory powers granted to ESMA violate the above-mentioned *Meroni* doctrine. The United Kingdom also asserted that by granting ESMA the authority to adopt non-legislative acts of general application the SSR had violated the limits imposed by Articles 290 and 291 of the TFEU regarding EU non-legislative acts. Moreover, the United Kingdom also claimed that Article 114 TFEU was an inadequate basis for the SSR because it could not give ESMA the power to issue individual decisions binding on third parties. The Council and the Parliament (with the support of the Commission, Spain, France, and Italy) responded by stating that the emergency powers granted to ESMA were to be judged "in the light of the modernisation of EU agency law that occurred under the Lisbon Treaty, particularly with respect to judicial review of acts of agencies having legal effects" [Niilo Jääskinen, "Opinion of the Advocate General Jääskinen on Case C-270/12," (2013)]. ECJ backed the Council's and the Parliament's position, making Article 28 fully legal.
59. Or the "mellowing" of the *Meroni* doctrine: Jacques Pelkmans and Marta Simoncini, "Mellowing Meroni: How Esma Can Help Build the Single Market," (Centre for European Policy Studies—CEPS, 2014).
60. Even if the Authority under scrutiny is the European Banking Authority, the critical assessment of professors Ferrarini and Chiarella can be adapted to ESMA: "The European supervisory framework [...] substantially belongs to the [...model of] enhanced cooperation [...] [T]he creation of the ESFS and the ESAs did not substantially change the allocation of powers and responsibilities amongst authorities, but enhanced coordination mechanisms." Guido Ferrarini and Luigi Chiarella, "Common Banking Supervision in the Eurozone: Strengths and Weaknesses," (ECGI—Law Working Paper No. 223/2013, 2013). At 38. Professor Moloney states that ESMA "can be regarded as hovering 'above' and 'beside' the NCAs. It might also be regarded as a form of 'supervisor of supervisors' or 'system supervisor', overseeing the quality, consistency, and effectiveness of supervision in the EU financial market". Moloney, *Eu Securities and Financial Markets Regulation.* At 973.

61. "The Authority shall fulfil a general coordination role between competent authorities, in particular in situations where adverse developments could potentially jeopardise the orderly functioning and integrity of financial markets or the stability of the financial system in the Union." Article 31 Regulation 1095/2010.
62. Article 6 Regulation 1095/2010.
63. Haar. At 178. Professor Haar mentions Professor Wymeersch: Eddy Wymeersch, "The European Financial Supervisory Authorities or Esas," in *Financial Regulation and Supervision: A Post-Crisis Analysis*, ed. Guido Ferrarini, Klaus J. Hopt, and Eddy Wymeersch (Oxford: Oxford University Press, 2012).
64. Article 40.1.
65. Article 44.1.
66. Article 44.1.
67. Article 47.1.
68. Article 45.
69. Article 48.2.
70. Article 48.1.
71. Article 49.
72. Article 48.5.
73. Article 51.1.
74. Article 51.2.
75. Article 53.
76. Article 53.
77. European Securities and Markets Authority—ESMA, "Standing Committees," https://www.esma.europa.eu/about-esma/working-methods/standing-committees.
78. Ibid.
79. Ibid.
80. *Regulation 1095/2010*. Article 58.2. Quite a complex designation system is laid down in art. Article 58.3.
81. Article 60.1.
82. Article 61.1.
83. Article 60.1.
84. European Securities and Markets Authority—ESMA, "Frequently Asked Questions—a Guide to Understanding Esma," (2011). At 13. Regulation 1095/2010, Chap. 7—Financial Provisions.
85. "Esma Organigramme," https://www.esma.europa.eu/about-esma/esma-in-short/esma-organigramme. An eighth one has been established for Brexit.

86. European Securities and Markets Authority—ESMA, "2017 Work Programme—Esma/2016/1419," (2016).
87. Securities and Exchange Commission—SEC, "Sec Employees," https://www.sec.gov/spotlight/sec-employees.shtml.
88. European Commission, "Public Consultation on the Operations of the European Supervisory Authorities," (2017).
89. Ibid. At 19.
90. Ibid. At 22–23.
91. Regulatory technical standards, alongside recommendations and guidelines, make up ESMA Single Rulebook. European Securities and Markets Authority—ESMA, "2012 Work Programme," (2011). At 4.
92. "Investor Protection Policy—Mifid Ii Rts & Its," https://www.esma.europa.eu/policy-rules/mifid-ii-and-investor-protection/investor-protection-policy.
93. RTS 27—C(2016) 3333 final. http://ec.europa.eu/finance/securities/docs/isd/mifid/rts/160608-rts-27_en.pdf.
94. *Commission Delegated Regulation (Eu) 2017/575.*
95. Article 10, ESMA Regulation.
96. Article 17.6.
97. Article 17.6.
98. Article 18.
99. Article 21.2.
100. Article 21.2.
101. See ESMA official website: European Securities and Markets Authority—ESMA, "Who We Are," https://www.esma.europa.eu/about-esma/who-we-are.
102. In the words of the ESMA chair: "Since its inception three and a half years ago, ESMA has contributed to the creation of an EU single rulebook by developing technical standards and guidelines, and by assisting the European Institutions, and the European Commission in particular, in providing technical advice." Steven Maijoor, "Statement by Steven Maijoor Chair European Securities and Markets Authority—Econ Committee, European Parliament 23 September 2014—Esma/2014/1164," (2014).
103. In particular, Article 16.3 of ESMA Regulation states that "competent authorities and financial market participants shall make every effort to comply with [...ESMA's] guidelines and recommendations".

104. European Securities and Markets Authority—ESMA, "Supervisory Convergence" https://www.esma.europa.eu/convergence/supervisory-convergence. This phenomenon has already started, as reported by Svetiev and Ottow in their seminal article: "All officials interviewed from the different authorities suggested that the EU legislative framework has had a decisive influence on local supervision, not only at the legislative level, but also in the development of national supervisory capacities in the areas of investor protection." Yane Svetiev and Annetje Ottow, "Financial Supervision in the Interstices between Private and Public Law," *European Review of Contract Law* 10, no. 4 (2014). At 538.
105. In the words of Professor Haar: "Home country control results in Member States' dependence on the quality of each other's regulation and supervision." At 171. Haar.
106. This concept is plainly reaffirmed by Recital 137 of MiFID II which states that: "It is necessary to enhance convergence of powers at the disposal of competent authorities so as to pave the way towards an equivalent intensity of enforcement across the integrated financial market." Convergence also elicits criticism as it is clarified by Svetiev and Ottow: "The adoption of a uniform model of supervision and enforcement, which may additionally reduce variety in private contracting and corporate governance, [is] particularly problematic because any deficiencies in the chosen approach to enforcement would be magnified across the EU and limit the opportunities for learning from divergent supervisory techniques." Svetiev and Ottow. At 501.
107. Peer reviews are conducted under Article 30 of the establishing Regulation. European Securities and Markets Authority—ESMA, "Peer Review Report—Compliance with Ssr as Regards Market Making Activities—Esma/2015/1791," (2016).
108. In the words of the ESMA Chair, Steven Maijoor: "ESMA will focus on the implementation of MiFIDII/MiFIR in 2017, this reflects our shift as a supervisory authority from building the single rulebook to ensuring the application of that rulebook through convergent supervisory practices across the European Union." European Securities and Markets Authority—ESMA, "Press Release—Esma to Focus on Supervisory Convergence Issues in 2017—Esma/2016/1458," (2016). Also the European Commission in its Green Paper on the Capital Market Union: "Although regulatory frameworks for capital markets have largely been harmonised, the success of reforms also depends on the

implementation and consistent enforcement of the rules. The ESAs play a key role in promoting convergence. [...] To the extent that national supervisory regimes may result in differing investor protection levels, barriers to cross-border operations and discouraging companies seeking financing in other Member States, there may be a further role for the ESAs to play in increasing convergence." European Commission, "Green Paper—Building a Capital Markets Union—Com(2015) 63 Final," (2015). At 22.

109. ESMA, "Frequently Asked Questions—a Guide to Understanding Esma." At 5.
110. European Commission, "Public Consultation on the Operations of the European Supervisory Authorities." At 9.
111. *Regulation 1095/2010*. Article 9.
112. Article 9.
113. *Regulation 1095/2010*.Art.9 (2).
114. As George Bentson says: "[the justification for financial regulation is] protection of consumers from the loss of their investments, fraud and misrepresentation, unfair treatment and insufficient information, incompetent employees of financial-services providers, and invidious discrimination." George J. Benston, "Regulating Financial Markets: A Critique and Some Proposals," ed. American Enterprise Institute for Public Policy and Research (Washington, DC, 1999).
115. Article 1.5.
116. European Securities and Markets Authority—ESMA, "Warning About Cfds, Binary Options and Other Speculative Products—Esma/2016/1166," https://www.esma.europa.eu/sites/default/files/library/2016-1166_warning_on_cfds_binary_options_and_other_speculative_products_0.pdf.
117. "Standing Committees".
118. Committee of European Securities Regulators—CESR, "Questions and Answers on Mifid: Common Positions Agreed by Cesr Members of the Investor Protection and Intermediaries Standing Committee—Cesr/10-589," (2010). At 1.
119. Ibid. At 1.
120. Committee of European Securities Regulators—CESR, "A Consumer's Guide to Mifid—Investing in Financial Products," (Paris 2008).
121. European Securities and Markets Authority—ESMA, "Mifid Q&a in the Area of Investor Protection and Intermediaries," (Paris 2011).

122. Ibid. At 3.
123. Ibid. At 3.
124. European Securities and Markets Authority—ESMA, "Q&as on Mifid Ii and Mifir Investor Protection Topic—Esma35-43-349," (2017).
125. "Consultation on Guidelines on Certain Aspects of the Mifid Ii Suitability Requirements—Esma35-43-748," (2017).
126. CESR highlighted five areas in need of supervisory centralization: (1) EU-wide public offerings of highly standardized products, (2) standardized UCITS, (3) accounting standards for listed companies, (4) credit rating agencies, and (5) certain trans-European market infrastructures (e.g., exchanges and related, clearing and settlement services). Committee of European Securities Regulators—CESR, "Preliminary Progress Report: Which Supervisory Tools for the Eu Securities Markets? An Analytical Paper by Cesr—Ref: 04-333f," (2004). At 17. Only points 4 and 5 have been adopted with CRA Regulation and, partially, with EMIR for trade repositories for OTC Derivatives.
127. *Regulation 1095/2010*. Article 1.2.
128. Article 40 MiFIR.
129. And EBA's enforcement responsibilities on structured deposits.
130. *Directive 2011/61/Eu*.
131. *Regulation 1060/2009/Ec*., as amended by *Regulation 513/2011/Eu*.
132. *Regulation 648/2012/Eu*.
133. Moloney, *Eu Securities and Financial Markets Regulation*. At. 670.
134. European Securities and Markets Authority—ESMA, "Enforcement Actions," https://www.esma.europa.eu/supervision/enforcement/enforcement-actions.
135. European Commission, "Public Consultation on the Operations of the European Supervisory Authorities."
136. Eight important points are developed under this section: (1) work on supervisory convergence; (2) non-binding measures; (3) work on consumer and investor protection; (4) enforcement powers; (5) international aspects of the ESAs' work; (6) access to data; (7) powers in relation to reporting; and, (8) financial reporting. Ibid. At 7–15.
137. Ibid. At 16.
138. In particular the Commission asks whether there would "be merit in maximising synergies (both from an efficiency and effectiveness perspective) between the EBA and EIOPA while possibly consolidating certain consumer protection powers within ESMA in addition to the

ESMA's current responsibilities" or whether EBA and EIOPA should "remain as standalone authorities". Ibid. At 22.
139. Eric Pan, "Organizing Regional Systems: The US Example," in *The Oxford Handbook of Financial Regulation*, ed. Niamh Moloney, Eilís Ferran, and Jennifer Payne (Oxford: Oxford University Press, 2015). At 200.
140. The Federal Reserve System is the central banking system of the United States. Federal Reserve System—FED, "About the Fed," https://www.federalreserve.gov/aboutthefed.htm.
141. As officially stated by its website, the OCC's primary mission is to charter, regulate, and supervise all national banks and federal savings associations and to supervise the federal branches and agencies of foreign banks. Office of the Comptroller of the Currency—OCC, "About the Occ," https://www.occ.treas.gov/about/what-we-do/mission/index-about.html.
142. The FDIC is the federal independent agency organized as a corporation which insures deposits against bank failures. Federal Deposit Insurance Corporation—FDIC, "About Fdic," https://www.fdic.gov/about/.
143. As officially stated by its website, the NCUA is an independent federal agency that charters and supervises federal credit unions and insures savings in federal and most state-chartered credit unions across the country through the National Credit Union Share Insurance Fund. National Credit Union Administration—NCUA, "About Ncua," https://www.ncua.gov/.
144. The 2010 Dodd-Frank Act shut down the Office of Thrift Supervision (OTS) and distributed its competences among the FED, the OCC, and the FDCI. Apart from this change, "the reforms instituted by the Dodd–Frank Act did not significantly reduce the number of federal agencies, and it retained the activity-based character of the US financial regulatory system." Pan. At 213.
145. The CFTC website states that its mission "to foster open, transparent, competitive, and financially sound markets. By working to avoid systemic risk, the Commission aims to protect market users and their funds, consumers, and the public from fraud, manipulation, and abusive practices related to derivatives". At Commodity Futures Trading Commission—CFTC, "About the Cftc—Mission Statement," http://www.cftc.gov/About/MissionResponsibilities/index.htm.
146. *Dodd-Frank Wall Street Reform and Consumer Protection Act.*
147. Ibid. Title X: Bureau of Consumer Financial Protection, Sec. 1061: Transfer of Consumer Financial Protection Functions.

148. US Department of the Treasury, "Federal Insurance Office," https://www.treasury.gov/about/organizational-structure/offices/Pages/Federal-Insurance.aspx.
149. Federal Financial Institutions Examination Council—FFIEC, "About the Ffiec," https://www.ffiec.gov/about.htm.
150. US Department of the Treasury, "Financial Stability Oversight Council," https://www.treasury.gov/initiatives/fsoc/Pages/home.aspx.
151. Despina Chatzimanoli, "Law and Governance in the Institutional Organisation of Eu Financial Services: The Lamfalussy Procedure and the Single Supervisor Revisited" (PhD Thesis, European University Institute, 2009). At 230.
152. The SEC oversight of SROs is an indispensable task due to the "inherent conflict of interests involved in self-regulation". Luis A. Aguilar, "The Need for Robust Sec Oversight of Sros," https://www.sec.gov/news/public-statement/2013-spch050813laahtm.
153. For instance, under Title VII of Dodd-Frank Act, the SEC has regulatory authority over "security-based swaps", whereas the CFTC has jurisdiction over all other derivatives. Securities and Exchange Commission—SEC, "Derivatives," https://www.sec.gov/spotlight/dodd-frank/derivatives.shtml.
154. Roberta S. Karmel, "Reconciling Federal and State Interests in Securities Regulation in the United States and Europe," *Brooklyn Journal of International Law* 28 (2003). At 495.
155. *Final Rules—Prohibitions and Restrictions on Proprietary Trading and Certain Interests in, and Relationships with, Hedge Funds and Private Equity Funds*.
156. Chatzimanoli. At 232–233.
157. Ibid. At 232–233.
158. Ibid. At 233.
159. However, difficulties linked to the relationship between federal and states regulators occurred over time, and in order to "resolve decades of inefficiency and conflict in the federal-state regulatory framework", the 1996 National Securities Markets Improvement Act (NSMIA) expanded federal jurisdiction on certain securities—in particular, mutual funds. Linda M. Stevens, "Comments: The National Securities Markets Improvement Act (Nsmia) Savings Clause: A New Challenge to Regulatory Uniformity," *University of Baltimore School of Law* 38, no. 3 (2009). At 445.

160. Chatzimanoli. At 233.
161. Ibid. At 233.
162. Ibid. At 233.
163. Ibid. At 233.
164. Ibid. At 232–233.
165. Commodity Futures Trading Commission—CFTC, "Cftc Mission & Responsibilities," (Washington, DC, 2013).
166. Commodity Futures Trading Commission CFTC and Securities and Exchange Commission SEC, "Cftc, Sec Sign Agreement to Enhance Coordination, Facilitate Review of New Derivative Products," news release, 2008, http://www.cftc.gov/PressRoom/PressReleases/pr5468-08.
167. Chatzimanoli. At 234. Professor MacNeil highlights the importance of settlements level that the SEC and the Department of Justice have agreed with global banks in the wake of the financial crisis. Iain MacNeil, "Enforcement and Sanctioning," in *The Oxford Handbook of Financial Regulation*, ed. Niamh Moloney, Eilís Ferran, and Jennifer Payne (Oxford: Oxford University Press, 2015). At 298.
168. Chatzimanoli. At 234.
169. Ibid. At 234.
170. Ibid. At 234.
171. Pan. At 199.
172. *Appeal of Determinations by Self-Regulatory Organizations*; *Commission Consideration of Determinations by Self-Regulatory Organizations.* In particular, paragraph a) of Rule 420 states: "An application for review by the Commission may be filed by any person who is aggrieved by a determination of a self-regulatory organization with respect to any: (1) final disciplinary sanction; (2) denial or conditioning of membership or participation; (3) prohibition or limitation in respect to access to services offered by that self-regulatory organization or a member thereof; or (4) bar from association as to which a notice is required to be filed with the Commission pursuant to Section 19(d)(1) of the Exchange Act, 15 U.S.C. 78s(d)(1)."
173. Roberta S. Karmel, "Mutual Funds, Pension Funds, Hedge Funds and Stock Market Volatility—What Regulation by the Securities and Exchange Commission Is Appropriate," *Notre Dame Law Review* 80, no. 3 (2003). At 909.
174. Securities and Exchange Commission—SEC, "2012 Agency Financial Report," (2013). At 6.

175. Ibid. At 6.
176. "What We Do," http://www.sec.gov/about/whatwedo.shtml#org.
177. Chatzimanoli. At 226.
178. Ibid. At 226.
179. Securities and Exchange Commission—SEC, "About Commissioners," https://www.sec.gov/Article/about-commissioners.html.
180. Ibid.
181. "What We Do".
182. "An appropriations measure provides budget authority to an agency for specified purposes. Budget authority allows federal agencies to incur obligations and authorizes payments to be made out of the Treasury. Discretionary agencies and programs, and appropriated entitlement programs, are funded each year in appropriations acts." Bill Heniff Jr., "Overview of the Authorization-Appropriations Process," (CRS Report for Congress, 2012).
183. Donald C. Langevoort, "Structuring Securities Regulation in the European Union: Lessons from the U.S. Experience," in *Investor Protection in Europe: Corporate Law Making, the Mifid and Beyond* ed. Guido Ferrarini and Eddy Wymeersch (New York: Oxford University Press, 2006). At 498.
184. Securities and Exchange Commission—SEC, "Sec Regional Offices," (2017).
185. "What We Do".
186. Ibid.
187. The documents include: "registration statements for newly-offered securities; annual and quarterly filings (Forms 10-K and 10-Q); proxy materials sent to shareholders before an annual meeting; annual reports to shareholders; documents concerning tender offers (a tender offer is an offer to buy a large number of shares of a corporation, usually at a premium above the current market price); and filings related to mergers and acquisitions." Ibid.
188. Ibid.
189. Ibid.
190. Ibid.
191. Ibid.
192. Ibid.
193. Ibid.
194. "Division of Corporation Finance," (2013).

195. Ibid.
196. Ibid.
197. Ibid.
198. "What We Do".
199. Ibid.
200. Securities and Exchange Commission—SEC, "Division of Trading and Markets," (2017).
201. SEC, "What We Do". On financial responsibility for Broker-Dealers see also: "Amendments to Financial Responsibility Rules for Broker-Dealers—Release No. 34-55431; File No. S7-08-07," (2007).
202. Schiff Hardin LLP, "Regulatory Update—Sec Proposes Amendments to Its Broker-Dealer Financial Responsibility Rules," https://www.schiffhardin.com/Templates/Media/files/archive/binary/broker-dealer-financial-responsibility-rules.pdf.
203. Securities and Exchange Commission—SEC, "Division of Investment Management," (2013).
204. Ibid.
205. "What We Do".
206. Ibid.
207. SEC—Division of Investment Management, "Regulation of Investment Advisers by the U.S. Securities and Exchange Commission," (2013). At 9.
208. Ibid. At 9.
209. SEC, "What We Do".
210. Ibid.
211. Ibid.
212. Ibid.
213. Ibid.
214. Ibid.
215. "Investment Management," (2017).
216. "What We Do".
217. Chatzimanoli. At 252. And in the words of Professor Coffee: "Although the SEC also uses "ex ante" regulation, it seems more committed than other regulators to a policy of general deterrence through large penalties." In John C. Coffee Jr., "Law and the Market: The Impact of Enforcement," ed. Columbia Law and Economics Working Paper No. 304 (2007). At 80. In the same vein professor Langevoort: "The point, then, is that 'regulation by enforcement' is the norm in the U.S. and should be a focus of any analysis of regulatory strategy" Langevoort. At 491.

218. Securities and Exchange Commission—SEC, "About the Division of Enforcement," https://www.sec.gov/enforce/Article/enforce-about.html.
219. "What We Do".
220. Ibid.
221. "About the Division of Enforcement".
222. "About the Division of Economic and Risk Analysis," https://www.sec.gov/dera/about.
223. Ibid.
224. Ibid.
225. "What We Do".
226. Ibid.
227. Ibid.
228. Securities and Exchange Commission—SEC, "Office of the Investor Advocate," https://www.sec.gov/page/investor-advocate-landing-page.
229. Ibid.
230. The SEC rulemaking process is usually quite active; see: Victor M. Rosenzweig, "Quarterly Survey of Sec Rulemaking and Major Appellate Decisions," *Securities Regulation Law Journal* Spring 2014 (2014).
231. See: SecuRities and Exchange Commission—SEC, "Securities Act Rules," https://www.sec.gov/divisions/corpfin/guidance/securitiesactrules-interps.htm.
232. See: "General Information on the Regulation of Investment Advisers" https://www.sec.gov/divisions/investment/iaregulation/memoia.htm.
233. Such as the Volcker Rule: *Final Rules—Prohibitions and Restrictions on Proprietary Trading and Certain Interests in, and Relationships with, Hedge Funds and Private Equity Funds.*
234. Securities and Exchange Commission—SEC, "Rulemaking, How It Works," https://www.sec.gov/fast-answers/answersrulemakinghtm.html.
235. Ibid.
236. Ibid.
237. See, for example, the page for the submission of Comments on File No. S7-35-11: "Submit Comments on S7-35-11—Submit Comments on S7-35-11," https://www.sec.gov/cgi-bin/ruling-comments?ruling=s7-35-11&rule_path=/comments/s7-35-11&file_num=S7-35-11&action=Show_Form&title=Treatment%20of%20Asset-Backed%20Issuers%20under%20the%20Investment%20Company%20Act.
238. "How to Submit Comments," https://www.sec.gov/rules/submitcomments.htm.

239. "Rulemaking, How It Works".
240. Securities and Exchange Commission—SEC, "How to Submit Comments," https://www.sec.gov/rules/submitcomments.htm.
241. SEC, "Rulemaking, How It Works".
242. Ibid.
243. Chatzimanoli. At 252; Coffee Jr. At 80.
244. SEC, "About the Division of Enforcement".
245. In fields such as "concealed from investors risks, terms, and improper pricing in CDOs and other complex structured products", the SEC enforcement effort has been quite active in post-crisis period: "Sec Enforcement Actions Addressing Misconduct That Led to or Arose from the Financial Crisis," https://www.sec.gov/spotlight/enf-actions-fc.shtml#keyStatistics.
246. "Office of Compliance Inspections and Examinations," https://www.sec.gov/ocie.
247. "Examinations by the Securities and Exchange Commission's Office of Compliance Inspections and Examinations," (Washington, DC 2012). At 29.
248. Ibid. At 30.
249. Ibid. At 30.
250. "Enforcement Manual," ed. Division of Enforcement (2015). At 19.
251. Ibid. At 19.
252. Ibid. At 21.
253. "What We Do".
254. Ibid.
255. MacNeil. At 292–293.
256. SEC, "What We Do".
257. See the official webpage: "Alj Initial Decisions," https://www.sec.gov/litigation/aljdec.shtml.
258. Administrative sanctions include: "cease and desist orders, suspension or revocation of broker-dealer and investment advisor registrations, censures, bars from association with the securities industry, civil monetary penalties, and disgorgement". "What We Do".
259. See: ibid.
260. Paolo Stella, *L'enforcement Nei Mercati Finanziari* (Milano: Giuffré, 2008). At 160–169.
261. Securities and Exchange Commission—SEC, "Adjustments to Civil Monetary Penalty Amounts—Release Nos. 33-8530; 34-51136; Ia-2348; Ic-26748," (2005).

262. "One agency that can bring civil suits directly against violators is the Securities and Exchange Commission (SEC). The SEC routinely files suit in federal district court against parties who are accused of securities fraud under federal law and the Commission's own regulations. The SEC is empowered to seek injunctions, the "disgorgement" of ill-gotten gains, and civil penalties". John M. SchebII and Hemant Sharma, *An Introduction to the American Legal System* (New York: Wolters Kluwer Law & Business, 2015).
263. Sec V. First City Financial Corporation, Ltd., et al., Appellants, 890 F.2d 1215, 1228 (D.C. Cir. 1989).
264. *The Truth in Securities Act*, (May 27, 1933).—Section 8A—Cease-and-Desist Proceedings. Explained by: Stella. At 161.
265. *The Truth in Securities Act*—Section 8A—Cease-and-Desist Proceedings. At 162.
266. At 163.
267. Ibid. At 163.
268. Ibid. At 164.
269. Ibid. At 153–160.
270. Ibid. At 156.
271. Ibid. At 154.
272. Ibid. At 154.
273. Ibid. At 158.
274. Also in administrative proceedings. Ibid. At 169.
275. International Monetary Fund—IMF, "Global Financial Stability Report—Market Developments and Issues," (Washington, DC: IMF Publication Services, 2004). The size of the EU financial markets is given by the sum of the Euro Area (Table 3.3 at page 80) and the UK financial markets (Table 3.7 at page 84).
276. Chatzimanoli. At 252; Coffee Jr. At 80.
277. Professor MacNeil identifies two main enforcement approaches: deterrence based versus compliance based. "A deterrence-based approach to enforcement focuses on certainty and severity of the punishment for contravention and its potential to deter both the individual transgressor and the wider regulated community. Effective deterrence requires in principle that the expected penalty should exceed the social harm caused by the regulatory contravention but that may be difficult to quantify especially when a regulatory contravention is only one of several causes of the social harm. By way of contrast, a compliance-based

approach focuses on the capacity of negotiation and persuasion to promote compliance with regulatory rules." MacNeil. At 282–283.

278. SEC, "What We Do".
279. Securities and Exchange Commission—SEC, "Office of Administrative Law Judges," https://www.sec.gov/alj. Administrative law judges were established under the Administrative Procedure Act of 1946 which "sought to ensure the ALJs' judicial capability and objectivity by precluding agencies from evaluating the ALJs' performance and by assigning responsibility for determining their qualifications, compensation, and tenure to the U.S. Civil Service Commission, later the Office of Personnel Management (OPM)." United States General Accounting Office, "Administrative Law Judges—Comparison of Sec and Cftc Programs," (1995). At 4.
280. "In administrative proceedings, after finding violations of the securities or commodities acts or rules, ALJs are to decide which, if any, sanctions are warranted against the alleged violators." Ibid. At 5.
281. Ibid. At 4.
282. "The parties to the proceedings are typically the SEC or CFTC and each person or firm named as a respondent in the complaint." Ibid. At 4.
283. "In contrast to CESR, ESMA is meant to have 'real teeth'. To exercise its tasks, it was, inter alia, given a greater say in shaping a European single rulebook and allocated powers to take individual decisions." Pierre Schammo, "The European Securities and Markets Authority: Lifting the Veil on the Allocation of Powers," *Common Market Law Review* 48, no. 6 (2011). At 1880.
284. *United Kingdom of Great Britain and Northern Ireland V European Parliament and Council of the European Union*.
285. Professors Van Gestel and Van Golen suggest that "the ESAs should be given a more independent position. Instead of deriving their legitimacy from the EU legislature via the Commission, we suggest to cut-through this 'transmission-belt' but at the same time increase the accountability of the ESAs by codifying procedural rules with regard to stakeholder participation, consultation, and judicial review for those affected by the rules and decisions of regulatory agencies." Rob van Gestel and Thomas van Golen, "Enforcement by the New European Supervisory Agencies: Quis Custodiet Ipsos Custodes ?," in *Varieties of European Economic Law and Regulation: Liber Amicorum for Hans Micklitz*, ed. Kai Peter Purnhagen and Peter Rott (New York: Springer, 2014). At 757.

286. European Commission, "Public Consultation on the Operations of the European Supervisory Authorities." At 10.
287. On the basis of the discussions held and the opinions exchanged by the author with his peers.
288. As also explained in: ESMA, "Frequently Asked Questions—a Guide to Understanding Esma." At 8.
289. "The distinction between minor and major infringements is decisive for the level of intervention in a multigovernance structure." Hans-Wolfgang Micklitz, "The Transformation of Enforcement in European Private Law: Preliminary Considerations," *European Review of Private Law* 4 (2015). At 502.
290. Ibid. At 503.
291. Ibid. At 503.
292. Ibid. At 492.
293. Ibid. At 492.
294. Ibid. At 492.
295. Paraphrases of "Central regulation, Local supervision" by Wymeersch, "The Reforms of the European Financial Supervisory System—an Overview." At 253.
296. Article 29 and Article 8.1(b), *Regulation 1095/2010.*
297. In February 2014 the ESMA (European Securities and Markets Authority—ESMA, "Re: Classification of Financial Instruments as Derivatives—Esma/2014/184" (2014)) recognized how a lack of uniform definition of derivative contracts in the European Union—in particular for foreign exchange forwards and physically settled commodity forwards—would prevent the convergent application of a key anti-crisis piece of legislation like EMIR [*Regulation 648/2012/Eu*]. In his letter to the European Commission, the ESMA's Chairman warned how the divergences in the definitions of what constitutes a derivative contract "result in the inconsistent application of EMIR" and asked the Commission to use the implementing powers granted by Article 4(2) of MiFID I in order to clarify the definitions contained in MiFID I itself. Unfortunately, the Commission responded that due to a sunset clause contained in Article 64a of MiFID I it was not possible to address this issue through a MIFID I implementing tool, but a MiFID II implementing measure had to be awaited European Commission, "Letter to Esma on Classification of Financial Instruments—Markt/G3/Gw/Bh Ares(2014)," (2014). Leaving aside the sunset clause back-

stop legally preventing the Commission from unraveling this complicated situation, it is crystal-clear how in such highly sensitive cases the ESMA is powerless.

298. In the same vein, Fahey claims that the European Banking Authority, ESMA's "sister", "does not appear to establish anything close to a supranational regulator at EU level", Fahey. At 593.
299. Duncan E. Alford, "The Use of Colleges of Regulators under European Union Banking Law," *Journal of International Banking Law and Regulation* 24, no. 355 (2009). At 360. As mentioned by Fahey. At 594.
300. ESMA, "Frequently Asked Questions—a Guide to Understanding Esma." At 13. See: *Regulation 1095/2010*, Chap. 7—Financial Provisions.
301. This seems to confirm the forecast made by Professors Hertig and Lee about the establishment of a European Securities and Exchange Commission which would be able "to investigate possible infringements and make its findings and recommendations public. This "soft enforcement" approach will provide incentives for Member States to undertake corrective action and also foster private litigation." Hertig and Lee.
302. In a similar fashion, Professor Langevoort states how "securities law involves a combination of standard-setting and enforcement. [...] standard setting and enforcement cannot be separated without a severe loss of regulatory quality: enforcement discretion is a key standard setting mechanism. And if enforcement discretion has a local bias, then a fragmented system of enforcement will create a series of gaps." Langevoort. At 488, 501–502.
303. In its "ESA Consultation Paper", with regard to supervisory convergence, the European Commission reaffirms that "In order to fully benefit from the Single Rulebook, legal acts must be interpreted and applied in a convergent and consistent manner and compliance must be supervised in a consistent way. [...] It is therefore necessary to reflect on how the supervisory and enforcement tools currently available could be developed to enable the ESAs to achieve tangible results [...] For example, assessing how the existing supervisory tools could better enable the ESAs to influence a change of behaviour of NCAs, to take action where an NCA refuses to act, or to mitigate potential risks to orderly markets, financial stability or investor protection." Furthermore, the Commission states that "a reflection [should be made] on the use of

the current tools and powers, and on the necessity and ways to potentially extend [...ESMA's] mandate to robustly follow up on supervisory convergence and enforcement". In addition the Commission states that the power to carry out enforcement actions "also complements [... ESMA's] important work on supervisory convergence as it contributes to ensuring high quality financial supervision across the EU." European Commission, "Public Consultation on the Operations of the European Supervisory Authorities." At 7–10.

304. Even if it is framed in a pre-ESAs/Larosière dimension, Professor Langevoort carries out an analysis of the US SEC and raises the question whether Europe should adopt an SEC-like authority. Several hurdles are examined by Langevoort on the transplanting of the SEC in Europe, such as political, economic, cultural, and federal (Member States) issues. Langevoort concludes by stating that "Whether one admires the SEC or not, we should admit that its replication in Europe would not be particularly easy. For better or worse, a European SEC would be a markedly different creature." Langevoort. At 506.
305. European Council—Heads of State or Government, "Solemn Declaration on European Union—Stuttgart 19 June 1983," (Stuttgart Bulletin of the European Communities, No. 6/1983, 1983).

Bibliography

Aguilar, Luis A. "The Need for Robust SEC Oversight of SROS". https://www.sec.gov/news/public-statement/2013-spch050813laahtm.

Alford, Duncan E. "The Use of Colleges of Regulators Under European Union Banking Law." *Journal of International Banking Law and Regulation* 24, no. 7 (2009): 355.

Appeal of Determinations by Self-Regulatory Organizations.

Arnull, Anthony, and Damian Chalmers. *The Oxford Handbook of European Union Law*. Oxford: Oxford University Press, 2015.

Avgerinos, Yannis. "The Need and the Rationale for a European Securities Regulator." In *Financial Markets in Europe: Towards a Single Regulator?*, edited by Mads Andenas and Yannis Avgerinos. London: Kluwer Law International, 2003.

Benston, George J. *Regulating Financial Markets: A Critique and Some Proposals*. Washington, DC: American Enterprise Institute for Public Policy and Research, 1999.

CESR, Committee of European Securities Regulators. "Preliminary Progress Report: Which Supervisory Tools for the EU Securities Markets? An Analytical Paper by CESR – Ref: 04-333f." 2004.

———. "A Consumer's Guide to MiFID – Investing in Financial Products." Paris, 2008.

———. "Questions and Answers on MiFID: Common Positions Agreed by CESR Members of the Investor Protection and Intermediaries Standing Committee – CESR/10-589." 2010.

CFTC, Commodity Futures Trading Commission. "CFTC Mission & Responsibilities." Washington, DC, 2013.

———. "About the CFTC – Mission Statement." http://www.cftc.gov/About/MissionResponsibilities/index.htm.

Chatzimanoli, Despina. "Law and Governance in the Institutional Organisation of EU Financial Services: The Lamfalussy Procedure and the Single Supervisor Revisited" PhD Thesis, European University Institute, 2009.

Chinkin, Christine. "Normative Development in the International Legal System." In *Commitment and Compliance: The Role of Non-Binding Norms in the International Legal System*, edited by Dinah Shelton. New York: Oxford University Press, 2000.

COB, Commission des opérations de bourse. "Communiqué Relatif a La Création Du Forum of European Securities Commissions De Fesco." 1997.

Coffee, John C., Jr. "Law and the Market: The Impact of Enforcement." Columbia Law and Economics Working Paper No. 304, 2007.

Commission Consideration of Determinations by Self-Regulatory Organizations.

Commission Delegated Regulation (EU) 2017/575.

Council of the European Union. "Regulation of European Securities Markets – The Terms of Reference for the Committee of Wise Men – 10491/00." Brussels, 2000.

Craig, Paul. *EU Administrative Law.* 2nd ed. Oxford: Oxford University Press, 2012.

Directive 2011/61/Eu.

Dodd-Frank Wall Street Reform and Consumer Protection Act.

ECJ, Court of Justice of the European Union. "The Power of the European Securities and Markets Authority to Adopt Emergency Measures on the Financial Markets of the Member States in Order to Regulate or Prohibit Short Selling Is Compatible with EU Law – Press Realise No. 7/14." 2014.

ESAs, European Supervisory Authorities. "Placement of Financial Instruments with Depositors, Retail Investors and Policy Holders ('Self Placement')." 2014.

ESAs, Joint Committee of the European Supervisory Authorities. "About US." https://esas-joint-committee.europa.eu/about-us.
ESMA, European Securities and Markets Authority. "2012 Work Programme." 2011a.
———. "Frequently Asked Questions – A Guide to Understanding ESMA." 2011b.
———. "MiFID Q&A in the Area of Investor Protection and Intermediaries." Paris, 2011c.
———. "Re: Classification of Financial Instruments as Derivatives – ESMA/2014/184." 2014.
———. "Peer Review Report – Compliance with SSR as Regards Market Making Activities – ESMA/2015/1791." 2016a.
———. "2017 Work Programme – ESMA/2016/1419." 2016b.
———. "Press Release – ESMA to Focus on Supervisory Convergence Issues in 2017 – ESMA/2016/1458." 2016c.
———. "Consultation on Guidelines on Certain Aspects of the MiFID II Suitability Requirements – ESMA35-43-748." 2017a.
———. "Q&As on MiFID II and MiFIR Investor Protection Topic – ESMA35-43-349." 2017b.
———. "Enforcement Actions". https://www.esma.europa.eu/supervision/enforcement/enforcement-actions.
———. "ESMA Organigramme". https://www.esma.europa.eu/about-esma/esma-in-short/esma-organigramme.
———. "Investor Protection Policy – MiFID II RTS & ITS". https://www.esma.europa.eu/policy-rules/mifid-ii-and-investor-protection/investor-protection-policy.
———. "Standing Committees". https://www.esma.europa.eu/about-esma/working-methods/standing-committees.
———. "Supervisory Convergence". https://www.esma.europa.eu/convergence/supervisory-convergence.
———. "Warning About CFDS, Binary Options and Other Speculative Products – ESMA/2016/1166". https://www.esma.europa.eu/sites/default/files/library/2016-1166_warning_on_cfds_binary_options_and_other_speculative_products_0.pdf.
———. "Who We Are". https://www.esma.europa.eu/about-esma/who-we-are.
European Commission. "Communication of the Commission – Financial Services: Building a Framework for Action." Brussels: COM (98) 525 Final, 1998.

———. "Financial Services: Implementing the Framework for Financial Markets: Action Plan." Brussels, 1999.

———. "Commission Decision Establishing the Committee of European Securities Regulators." Brussels: C(2001) 1501 Final, 2001.

———. "Press Release – High Level Expert Group on EU Financial Supervision to Hold First Meeting on 12 November – Ip/08/1679." 2008.

———. "Proposal for a Regulation of the European Parliament and of the Council Establishing a European Banking Authority – COM(2009) 501 Final." Brussels, 2009a.

———. "Proposal for a Regulation of the European Parliament and of the Council Establishing a European Insurance and Occupational Pensions Authority – COM(2009) 502 Final." Brussels, 2009b.

———. "Proposal for a Regulation of the European Parliament and of the Council Establishing a European Securities and Markets Authority – COM(2009) 503 Final." Brussels, 2009c.

———. "Letter to ESMA on Classification of Financial Instruments – Markt/G3/Gw/Bh ARES(2014)." 2014a.

———. "Report on the Operation of the European Supervisory Authorities (ESAS) and the European System of Financial Supervision (ESFS), COM(2014) 509 Final." 2014b.

———. "Green Paper – Building a Capital Markets Union – COM(2015) 63 Final." 2015.

———. "Public Consultation on the Operations of the European Supervisory Authorities." 2017.

———. "European System of Financial Supervision." https://ec.europa.eu/info/business-economy-euro/banking-and-finance/financial-supervision-and-risk-management/european-system-financial-supervision_en.

European Council – Heads of State Government. "Solemn Declaration on European Union – Stuttgart 19 June 1983." 24–9. Stuttgart Bulletin of the European Communities, No. 6/1983, 1983.

Everson, Michelle. "Independent Agencies: Hierarchy Beaters?". *European Law Journal* 1, no. 2 (1995): 180–204.

Fahey, Elaine. "Does the Emperor Have Financial Crisis Clothes? Reflections on the Legal Basis of the European Banking Authority." *The Modern Law Review* 74, no. 4 (2011): 581–95.

FDIC, Federal Deposit Insurance Corporation. "About FDIC." https://www.fdic.gov/about/.

FED, Federal Reserve System. "About the FED." https://www.federalreserve.gov/aboutthefed.htm.

Ferrarini, Guido, and Luigi Chiarella. "Common Banking Supervision in the Eurozone: Strengths and Weaknesses." ECGI – Law Working Paper No. 223/2013, 2013.

FFIEC, Federal Financial Institutions Examination Council. "About the FFIEC." https://www.ffiec.gov/about.htm.

Final Rules – Prohibitions and Restrictions on Proprietary Trading and Certain Interests in, and Relationships with, Hedge Funds and Private Equity Funds.

Geradin, Damien, and Nicolas Petit. *The Development of Agencies at EU and National Levels: Conceptual Analysis and Proposals for Reform.* Jean Monnet Working Paper 01/04. New York: NYU School of Law, 2004.

Germany V. Parliament and Council (Tobacco Advertising) ECR I-8419, 2000.

Gestel, Rob van, and Thomas van Golen. "Enforcement by the New European Supervisory Agencies: Quis Custodiet IPSOS Custodes ?". In *Varieties of European Economic Law and Regulation : Liber Amicorum for Hans Micklitz,* edited by Kai Peter Purnhagen and Peter Rott, 757–80. New York: Springer, 2014.

Griller, Stefan, and Andreas Orator. "Everything Under Control? The "Way Forward" for European Agencies in the Footsteps of the Meroni Doctrine." *European Law Review* 35, no. 1 (2010): 3–35.

Haar, Brigitte. "Organizing Regional Systems: The EU Example." In *The Oxford Handbook of Financial Regulation,* edited by Niamh Moloney, Eilís Ferran and Jennifer Payne. Oxford: Oxford University Press, 2015.

Heniff, Bill, Jr. "Overview of the Authorization-Appropriations Process." CRS Report for Congress, 2012.

Hertig, Gerard, and Ruben Lee. "Four Predictions About the Future of EU Securities Regulation." *Journal of Comparative Law Studies* 3, no. 2 (2003): 359–77.

House of Commons – Treasury Committee. "The Committee's Opinion on Proposals for European Financial Supervision – Sixteenth Report of Session 2008–09." 2009.

IMF, International Monetary Fund. *Global Financial Stability Report – Market Developments and Issues.* Washington, DC: IMF Publication Services, 2004.

Jääskinen, Niilo. "Opinion of the Advocate General Jääskinen on Case C-270/12." 2013.

Karmel, Roberta S. "Mutual Funds, Pension Funds, Hedge Funds and Stock Market Volatility – What Regulation by the Securities and Exchange Commission Is Appropriate." *Notre Dame Law Review* 80, no. 3 (2003a): 909–50.

———. "Reconciling Federal and State Interests in Securities Regulation in the United States and Europe." *Brooklyn Journal of International Law* 28 (2003b): 495.

Langevoort, Donald C. "Structuring Securities Regulation in the European Union: Lessons from the U.S. Experience." In *Investor Protection in Europe: Corporate Law Making, the MiFID and Beyond*, edited by Guido Ferrarini and Eddy Wymeersch. New York: Oxford University Press, 2006.

MacNeil, Iain. "Enforcement and Sanctioning." In *The Oxford Handbook of Financial Regulation*, edited by Niamh Moloney, Eilís Ferran and Jennifer Payne. Oxford: Oxford University Press, 2015.

Maijoor, Steven. "Statement by Steven Maijoor Chair European Securities and Markets Authority – ECON Committee, European Parliament, 23 September 2014 – ESMA/2014/1164." 2014.

Majone, Giandomenico. "Delegation of Regulatory Powers in a Mixed Polity." *European Law Journal* 8, no. 3 (2002): 319–39.

Marjosola, Heikki. "Case C-270/12 (Uk V Parliament and Council) – Stress Testing Constitutional Resilience of the Powers of EU Financial Supervisory Authorities – A Critical Assessment of the Advocate General's Opinion." *EUI Working Paper Law 2014/02*. European University Institute, 2014.

Meroni & Co. Industrie Metallurgiche Spa V High Authority of the European Coal and Steel Community (Meroni I), ECR 133, 1957.

Meroni & Co. Industrie Metallurgiche Spa V High Authority of the European Coal and Steel Community (Meroni Ii), ECR 133, 1958.

Micklitz, Hans-Wolfgang. "The Transformation of Enforcement in European Private Law: Preliminary Considerations." *European Review of Private Law* 4 (2015): 491–524.

Moloney, Niamh. *EU Securities and Financial Markets Regulation*. Oxford: Oxford University Press, 2014.

———. "Regulating the Retail Markets." In *The Oxford Handbook of Financial Regulation*, edited by Niamh Moloney, Eilís Ferran and Jennifer Payne. Oxford: Oxford University Press, 2015.

NCUA, National Credit Union Administration. "About NCUA." https://www.ncua.gov/.

OCC, Office of the Comptroller of the Currency. "About the OCC." https://www.occ.treas.gov/about/what-we-do/mission/index-about.html.

Pan, Eric J. "Harmonization of US–EU Securities Regulation: The Case for a Single European Securities Regulator." *Law & Policy of International Business* 34, no. 2 (2003): 499–536.

———. "Organizing Regional Systems: The US Example." In *The Oxford Handbook of Financial Regulation*, edited by Niamh Moloney, Eilís Ferran and Jennifer Payne. Oxford: Oxford University Press, 2015.

Pelkmans, Jacques, and Marta Simoncini. "Mellowing Meroni: How ESMA Can Help Build the Single Market." Centre for European Policy Studies – CEPS, 2014.

Regulation 1060/2009/Ec.

Regulation 1092/2010.

Regulation 1093/2010.

Regulation 1094/2010.

Regulation 1095/2010.

Regulation 513/2011/Eu.

Regulation 648/2012/Eu.

Regulation Eu/236/2012.

Rosenzweig, Victor M. "Quarterly Survey of SEC Rulemaking and Major Appellate Decisions." *Securities Regulation Law Journal* 42, no. 1 (Spring 2014): 93–102.

Schammo, Pierre. "The European Securities and Markets Authority: Lifting the Veil on the Allocation of Powers." *Common Market Law Review* 48, no. 6 (2011): 1879–914.

Scheb, John M., II, and Hemant Sharma. *An Introduction to the American Legal System*. New York: Wolters Kluwer Law & Business, 2015.

Schiff Hardin LLP. "Regulatory Update – SEC Proposes Amendments to Its Broker-Dealer Financial Responsibility Rules." https://www.schiffhardin.com/Templates/Media/files/archive/binary/broker-dealer-financial-responsibility-rules.pdf.

SEC, Commodity Futures Trading Commission CFTC and Securities and Exchange Commission. "CFTC, SEC Sign Agreement to Enhance Coordination, Facilitate Review of New Derivative Products." *News Release*, 2008. http://www.cftc.gov/PressRoom/PressReleases/pr5468-08.

SEC, Division of Investment Management. "Regulation of Investment Advisers by the U.S. Securities and Exchange Commission." 2013.

SEC, Securities and Exchange Commission. "Adjustments to Civil Monetary Penalty Amounts – Release Nos. 33-8530; 34-51136; Ia-2348; Ic-26748." 2005.

———. "Amendments to Financial Responsibility Rules for Broker-Dealers – Release No. 34-55431; File No. S7-08-07." 2007.

———. "Examinations by the Securities and Exchange Commission's Office of Compliance Inspections and Examinations." Washington, DC, 2012.

———. "2012 Agency Financial Report." 2013a.

———. "Division of Corporation Finance." 2013b.
———. "Division of Investment Management." 2013c.
———. "Enforcement Manual." Division of Enforcement, 2015.
———. "Investment Management." 2017a.
———. "Sec Regional Offices." 2017b.
———. "Division of Trading and Markets." 2017c.
———. "About Commissioners." https://www.sec.gov/Article/about-commissioners.html.
———. "About the Division of Economic and Risk Analysis." https://www.sec.gov/dera/about.
———. "About the Division of Enforcement." https://www.sec.gov/enforce/Article/enforce-about.html.
———. "Alj Initial Decisions." https://www.sec.gov/litigation/aljdec.shtml.
———. "Derivatives." https://www.sec.gov/spotlight/dodd-frank/derivatives.shtml.
———. "How to Submit Comments." https://www.sec.gov/rules/submitcomments.htm.
———. "Office of Compliance Inspections and Examinations." https://www.sec.gov/ocie.
———. "Rulemaking, How It Works." https://www.sec.gov/fast-answers/answersrulemakinghtm.html.
———. "SEC Enforcement Actions Addressing Misconduct that Led to or Arose from the Financial Crisis." https://www.sec.gov/spotlight/enf-actions-fc.shtml#keyStatistics.
———. "Submit Comments on S7-35-11 – Submit Comments on S7-35-11." https://www.sec.gov/cgi-bin/ruling-comments?ruling=s7-35-11&rule_path=/comments/s7-35-11&file_num=S7-35-11&action=Show_Form&title=Treatment%20of%20Asset-Backed%20Issuers%20under%20the%20Investment%20Company%20Act.
———. "What We Do." http://www.sec.gov/about/whatwedo.shtml#org.
———. "General Information on the Regulation of Investment Advisers." https://www.sec.gov/divisions/investment/iaregulation/memoia.htm.
———. "How to Submit Comments." https://www.sec.gov/rules/submitcomments.htm.
———. "Office of Administrative Law Judges." https://www.sec.gov/alj.
———. "Office of the Investor Advocate." https://www.sec.gov/page/investor-advocate-landing-page.
———. "SEC Employees." https://www.sec.gov/spotlight/sec-employees.shtml.
———. "Securities Act Rules." https://www.sec.gov/divisions/corpfin/guidance/securitiesactrules-interps.htm.

Sec V. First City Financial Corporation, Ltd., et al., Appellants, 890 F.2d 1215, 1228 (D.C. Cir. 1989).

Stella, Paolo. *L'enforcement Nei Mercati Finanziari*. Milano: Giuffré, 2008.

Stevens, Linda M. "Comments: The National Securities Markets Improvement Act (Nsmia) Savings Clause: A New Challenge to Regulatory Uniformity." *University of Baltimore School of Law* 38, no. 3 (2009): 445–83.

Svetiev, Yane, and Annetje Ottow. "Financial Supervision in the Interstices Between Private and Public Law." *European Review of Contract Law* 10, no. 4 (2014): 496–544.

The Committee of Wise Men – Lamfalussy Committee. "Final Report of the Committee of Wise Men on the Regulation of European Securities Markets." 2001.

The de Larosière Group. "Report of the High Level Group on Financial Supervision in the EU." 2009.

The Truth in Securities Act. May 27, 1933.

Thieffry, Gilles. "The Case for a European Securities Commission." In *Regulation Financial Services in the 21st Century*, edited by Eilís Ferran and Charles A.E. Goodhart, 211–34. Oxford/Portland: Hart Publishing, 2001.

United Kingdom of Great Britain and Northern Ireland V European Parliament and Council of the European Union (2014).

United Kingdom V European Commission and Council, ECR I-3771 (2006).

United States General Accounting Office. "Administrative Law Judges – Comparison of SEC and CFTC Programs." 1995.

US Department of the Treasury. "Federal Insurance Office." https://www.treasury.gov/about/organizational-structure/offices/Pages/Federal-Insurance.aspx.

———. "Financial Stability Oversight Council." https://www.treasury.gov/initiatives/fsoc/Pages/home.aspx.

Wymeersch, Eddy. "The Reforms of the European Financial Supervisory System – An Overview." *European Company and Financial Law Review* 7, no. 2 (2010): 240–65.

———. "The European Financial Supervisory Authorities or ESAS." In *Financial Regulation and Supervision: A Post-Crisis Analysis*, edited by Guido Ferrarini, Klaus J. Hopt and Eddy Wymeersch. Oxford: Oxford University Press, 2012.

Yataganas, Xenophon A. *Delegation of Regulatory Authority in the European Union – The Relevance of the American Model*. Jean Monnet Working Paper 03/01. Cambridge: Harvard Law School, 2001.

6

Private Enforcement

6.1 Collective Redress for Retail Investors

6.1.1 Collective Redress for EU Retail Investors at Union Level

Even if the EU normative production penetrates private law,[1] the founding Treaties of the European Union do not provide the Union with a genuine and wide-ranging competence on private law, private enforcement tools, and civil liability proceedings, let alone the establishment of a federal-like jurisdiction. As Professor Micklitz rightly points out, "[u]nder the architecture of the Treaty, the Member States enjoy procedural autonomy. They are free to choose and to determine the appropriate institutions and the remedies."[2] The EU, thus, has never developed its own collective and individual private enforcement mechanisms, and the contractual consequences of a breach of MiFID conduct-of-business rules are still handled by domestic legal orders, with the European Court of Justice choosing not to meddle into the relationship between European public-law conduct-of-business rules and domestic private-law conduct-of-business rules.[3] The following pages, then, are aimed at giving the

© The Author(s) 2018
A. Marcacci, *Regulating Investor Protection under EU Law*,
https://doi.org/10.1007/978-3-319-90297-5_6

reader a short overview of the US securities class action, bearing in mind that a genuine comparison in this regard between the United States and the EU is institutionally impracticable.

However, it is worth noting that in 2013 the European Commission kicked off an initiative[4] that culminated in the adoption of the Recommendation 2013/396/EU of 11 June 2013 concerning "common principles for injunctive and compensatory collective redress mechanisms in the Member States concerning violations of rights granted under Union Law".[5] The Recommendation does not harmonize Members States' systems of group litigations but, instead, invites all Member States to establish domestic collective redresses and provides for a set of principles aimed at promoting a coherent horizontal approach throughout the EU.[6] Chief among such principles are the injunctive relief,[7] the compensatory relief,[8] and the opt-in principle.[9] As of the time of writing, the European Commission is assessing how the Recommendation of 11 June 2013 is being implemented throughout the EU.[10] Once the Commission's assessment is complete, it will be interesting to learn whether and to what extent the invitation and principles put forward by the Recommendation have been received by the Member States.

6.1.2 Collective Redress for US Retail Investors at Federal Level

6.1.2.1 Short Overview of the US Class Action

The first form of group litigation was introduced in the United States in the mid-nineteenth century under the provisions of the Federal Equity Rule 48 promulgated by the US SC,[11] which, for the first time, officially stated that:

> Where the parties on either side are very numerous, and cannot, without manifest inconvenience and oppressive delays in the suit, be all brought before it, the Court in its discretion may dispense with making all of them parties, and may proceed in the suit, having sufficient parties before it to represent all the adverse interests of the plaintiffs and the defendants in the suit properly before it. But in such cases the decree shall be without prejudice to the rights and claims of all the absent parties.[12]

Even if a first step toward a collective redress was taken, Professor Yeazell rightly points out how the Rule made the litigation non-binding on absent parties[13] and the subsequent "series of twists and turns"[14] cases contributed to making group litigation an "oddity",[15] particularly due to the difficulty to figure out the contours of "litigative representation".[16] In order to overcome this situation, in 1912 the US SC promulgated Equity Rule 38, which affirmed that "where the parties were too numerous for joinder, a few could sue or defend on behalf of the rest."[17]

The adoption of the Federal Rules of Civil Procedure in 1938 was the formal turning point because, by promulgating Rule 23, it turned an equity device into a procedural litigation tool.[18] However, the original Rule 23 did not convey any clear and effective instructions and its elusiveness brought about "infrequent, inefficient, and at times, inappropriate uses of the class action".[19] For these reasons, in 1966 Rule 23 was modified by making the opt-out option the default one.[20] Class actions blossomed ever since, and in 2005, Congress adopted the Class Action Fairness Act with the intention of expanding the federal jurisdiction over many large class action claims and avoiding the "forum shopping" phenomenon at the federal level.[21]

The Federal Rule of Civil Procedure 23 contains the details to begin a class action, which can be a class on either side (plaintiffs or defendants).[22] Rule 23 provides four mandatory prerequisites: (1) *Numerosity* ("the class is so numerous that joinder of all members is impracticable"[23]); (2) *Commonality* ("there are questions of law or fact common to the class"[24]); (3) *Typicality* ("the claims or defenses of the representative parties are typical of the claims or defenses of the class"[25]); (4) *Adequacy of Representation* ("the representative parties will fairly and adequately protect the interests of the class"[26]).

Beyond these four mandatory prerequisites, there are two more compulsory characteristics implied in each class action.[27] The first one is the legitimacy to represent a class: "If none of the named plaintiffs purporting to represent a class meets the case or controversy requirement, none may seek relief on behalf of himself or any other member of the class."[28] The second one is that the group gathered as a class must be identifiable so that it is possible for the Court to determine the class membership.[29] Alongside mandatory prerequisites that must be all met, letter (b) of Rule 23 provides that at least one of some other alternative requirements must apply.[30]

As regards the procedures to follow in order to pursue a class action, some steps[31] must be taken. In the pre-trial phase, both plaintiffs and defendants carry out the so-called discovery process, contemplated by Title V of the Rules of Civil Procedure for the United States District Courts.[32] In particular, Rule 26 states that in this phase the "[p]arties may obtain discovery regarding any nonprivileged matter that is relevant to any party's claim or defense."[33]

Subsequently, the court certifies the class by verifying the conditions set forth by Rule 23(a,b), and then, it must appoint both class counsel under Rule 23(g) and the class representative.[34] Then, the members of a class are notified of their rights: they must declare, within a predetermined span of time, whether they wish to opt out—that is, not to be part of a class action.[35] Finally, when all of the necessary communications are sent, the parties can meet and try to find an agreement in order to settle the dispute (however, the settlement can take place even at a previous stage): if no agreement is found, then an actual trial will begin.[36]

6.1.2.2 Specific Characteristics of Securities Class Actions

There are two categories of Securities Class Actions[37]: the first—so-called *non-fraud claims*—is based on Section 11 and Section 12 of the 1933 Securities Act; the second—so-called *securities fraud class actions*—is based on Section 10(b) of the 1934 Securities Exchange Act and its derivative SEC Rule, namely, the SEC Rule 10b-5.[38]

Section 11 of the 1933 Securities Act is entitled "Civil Liabilities on Account of False Registration Statement".[39] Section 11(a) deals with the civil liability connected to the registration statement of a security, and it affirms that any "untrue statement of a material fact or [...omission] to state a material fact"[40] may generate liability on the part of a determined multitude of persons involved in the issuance.[41]

Persons found responsible for false registration statements are subject to pay damages to those investors who have fallen victim to false statements. These investors may recoup "the difference between the amount paid for the security (not exceeding the price at which the security was offered to the public)" (Section 11[e]) and either (1) the value of the security at the time that the lawsuit was brought, or (2) the price at which the plaintiff sold the security before the lawsuit, or (3) the price at which the plaintiff sold the security after the lawsuit but before the judgment.[42] Importantly, Section 11(g) clarifies that the amount of damages recoverable by the investors cannot "exceed the price at which the security was offered to the public".[43]

Concerning the burden of proof on plaintiffs' shoulders, this is not very challenging[44] as they simply need to prove that the registration statement contained an omission or misrepresentation of a necessary information and "that the omission or misrepresentation was material, that is, it would have misled a *reasonable investor* [*our emphasis*] about the nature of his or her investment".[45] Coherently, SEC Rule 12b-2 clarifies that "The term material, when used to qualify a requirement for the furnishing of information as to any subject, limits the information required to those matters to which there is a substantial likelihood that a *reasonable investor* [*our emphasis*] would attach importance in determining whether to buy or sell the security registered."[46] The relevance of material information for reasonable investors is the same theoretical approach adopted by the EU Prospectus legislation as well.

Section 12 of the 1933 Securities Act is entitled "Civil Liabilities Arising in Connection with Prospectuses and Communications".[47] It conveys a case of civil liability which takes place in two different situations: (a) the offer or sale of an unregistered security; (b) the offer or sale of a security by means of a prospectus or oral communication including an untrue statement of a material fact or omitting to state a material fact necessary in order to make the statements not misleading.[48]

Securities fraud class actions are based on Section 10(b) of the 1934 Securities Exchange Act[49] and its derived SEC Rule—the SEC Rule 10b-5[50]—and they play a key role in US securities class actions.[51] Section 10 is entitled "Manipulative and Deceptive Devices," and it establishes the general framework for civil liability of any person who uses or employs manipulative or deceptive devices. It also provides for the secondary regulatory authority of the SEC in this remit so that it can issue its own regulations when "necessary or appropriate in the public interest or for the protection of investors".[52] The SEC Rule 10b-5 was, indeed, adopted under this provision.

The SEC Rule 10b-5 is entitled "Employment of Manipulative and Deceptive Devices" and states that, in connection with the purchase or sale of any security, it is unlawful:

a. "to employ any device, scheme, or artifice to defraud,
b. to make any untrue statement of a material fact or to omit to state a material fact necessary in order to make the statements made, in the light of the circumstances under which they were made, not misleading, or
c. to engage in any act, practice, or course of business which operates or would operate as a fraud or deceit upon any person."[53]

The behaviors expressed in letters a, b, and c are much broader than those envisaged in Sections 11 and 12.[54] However, the main difference between the claims connected to SEC Rule 10b-5 and those arising under Sections 11 and 12 concerns the defendants. Unlike Sections 11 and 12, the SEC Rule 10b-5 applies to any person that "directly or indirectly, by the use of any means or instrumentality of interstate commerce, or of the mails or of any facility of any national securities exchange"[55] engages in the unlawful behaviors.[56] Such characteristics have made the securities fraud class actions relatively easy to activate and, thus, they have been widely used.[57]

In order to make it more difficult for small investors (and, above all, their attorneys) to sue companies operating in financial markets,[58] and with the aim of reducing the "race to the courthouse"[59] of those claims defined as "nonmeritorious"[60] cases, Congress enacted the Private Securities Litigation Reform Act in 1995—the so-called PSLRA.[61] The bill was strongly supported by the financial industry that feared the threat of an increasing number of class actions, particularly those based on securities frauds, and tried to bring to an end the alleged abuses perpetrated by attorneys against listed technology companies and financial audit firms.[62] Whether the PSLRA actually delivered on its promises is subject to various empirical studies.[63]

What the reform formally did was to provide for some special rules and procedures, applicable only to securities class actions. For instance, the PSLRA has introduced stricter rules for the appointment of the plaintiff representative for the entire class—the so-called lead plaintiff—and a more limited use of the discovery process.[64] However, procedurally speaking, even if subject to the PSLRA, the securities class actions—like any other class action—are still governed by the Federal Rule of Civil Procedure 23.

6.2 Out-of-Court Mechanisms for Financial Services Disputes

This section concerns the extrajudicial procedures operating in the European Union and the United States in the field regarding the provision of investment services. Using the words of the European Commission, we can define an extrajudicial procedure as "any method enabling a dispute to be resolved through the intervention of a third party that proposes or imposes a solution. Extrajudicial instruments may be established by public authorities, professionals in the legal sector, professional bodies or civil society organizations (arbitration tribunals, private arbitration centers, mediators, etc.)."[65]

If widely used and effectively deployed, extrajudicial schemes for the resolution of disputes can play an important role in enforcing contracts, in both retail and wholesale markets. In the European telecommunication sector, for instance, Cantero rightly argues that ADR mechanisms contribute to filling the gap in the enforcement of EU rules affecting private relationships.[66] The side effect of this is that ADR mechanisms are used to achieve regulatory objectives and to push for further integration (also at the expense of traditional national rules and principles of contract law), even if divergences across Member States still exist, in particular for retail dispute resolutions.[67] However, this Section will show that the landscape for out-of-court settlement mechanisms in the European (cross-border) retail investment services market looks much less developed (even if it is increasing) and only recently MiFID II has introduced a stronger EU-wide provision for ADR mechanisms in the retail financial services sector. A comparison with the United States proves a lack of EU-wide uniform schemes that EU retail investors can access.

6.2.1 Alternative Dispute Resolution Mechanisms for Investment Services in the EU

The Lisbon Treaty provides the European Union with a larger cooperation competence to adopt civil justice measures. Article 81 of the Treaty on Functioning of the European Union states that: "The Union shall develop judicial cooperation in civil matters having cross-border implications, based on the principle of mutual recognition of judgments and of decisions in extrajudicial cases. Such cooperation may include the adoption of measures for the approximation of the laws and regulations of the Member States."

The Article continues by mentioning the areas in which the EU can base its civil justice legislation—domains such as the cross-border service of judicial and extrajudicial documents, effective access to justice and, most importantly for this book, the development of alternative methods of dispute settlement. Significantly, the new Article seems to provide the EU with the competence to adopt ADR schemes concerning cross-border matters, without prejudice for domestic measures.[68] However, the EU has not used this new cooperation-linked competence yet, and the ADR Directive[69] is still based on Article 114 TFEU.

Prior to the ADR Directive, the entire field of ADRs was handled by the European Commission only through soft-law measures, such as Recommendation 98/257/EC[70] on the principles applicable to the bodies responsible for out-of-court settlement of consumer disputes and Recommendation 2001/310/EC[71] on the principles for out-of-court settlement bodies involved in the consensual resolution of consumer disputes. With the 1998 Recommendation, the European Commission established the "ideal framework" within which all domestic out-of-court settlements of consumer disputes should be built. In essence, this framework was set down through seven basic principles:

1. Principle of independence, meaning that the independence of the decision-making body is ensured so as "to guarantee the impartiality of its actions".[72]
2. Principle of transparency, requiring that appropriate measures are taken in order "to ensure the transparency of the procedure".[73]

3. Adversarial principle, meaning that the procedure to be followed allows all the parties involved "present their viewpoint before the competent body and to hear the arguments and facts put forward by the other party, and any experts' statements".[74]
4. Principle of effectiveness, whereby the effectiveness of the procedure is ensured through measures guaranteeing, among other things, "that the consumer has access to the procedure without being obliged to use a legal representative," and "that the procedure is free of charges or of moderate costs".[75]
5. Principle of legality, referring to how the "decision taken by the body may not result in the consumer being deprived of the protection afforded by the mandatory provisions of the law of the State in whose territory the body is established".[76]
6. Principle of liberty, such that the decision taken by "the body concerned may be binding on the parties only if they were informed of its binding nature in advance and specifically accepted this".[77]
7. Principle of representation, revolving around how the "procedure does not deprive the parties of the right to be represented or assisted by a third party at all stages of the procedure".[78]

The 2001 Recommendation reproduces many of the features of the 1998 Recommendation (impartiality, transparency, effectiveness, and fairness). Furthermore, it englobes all those procedures where a third party facilitates "the resolution of a consumer dispute by bringing the parties together and assisting them, for example by making informal suggestions on settlement options, in reaching a solution by common consent",[79] like a mediation scheme.

Since the entry into force of the Lisbon Treaty, the Commission carried out several studies concerning ADRs in Europe, such as the "Study on the use of Alternative Dispute Resolution in the European Union",[80] the study on "Consumer redress in the EU: consumers' experiences, perceptions and opinions,"[81] and the study on "Cross-border ADR in the European Union" (2011).[82] All these studies led, at the end of 2011, the European Commission to put forward a legislative act which was officially adopted in 2013 as a minimum-harmonization Directive englobing the quality standards (Articles 7, 8, 9, 10, 11) set forth by Recommendations 98/257/

EC and 2001/310/EC: the Directive on Alternative Dispute Resolution for consumer disputes.[83]

In the intention of the Commission, the ADR Directive—still based on the internal market provision of Article 114 TFEU—must "be seen in the context of efforts to improve the functioning of the retail internal market and more particularly to enhance redress for consumers".[84] The aim is to overcome three particular "shortcomings which hinder the effectiveness of ADR: gaps in the coverage, the lack of consumer and business awareness as well as the uneven quality of ADR procedures".[85] The ADR Directive enshrines the Commission's four strategic planks on alternative consumer disputes:

1. *Ensuring that ADR procedures exist for all consumer disputes*, with the inclusion of both online and offline purchases.[86]
2. *Ensuring the adequate provision of information on ADRs*, so that "when disputes arise, consumers must be able to quickly identify which ADR entities are competent to deal with their dispute [...and obtain] information on the competent ADR entity in the main commercial documents provided by the trader and, where a trader has a website, on that website."[87]
3. *Ensuring high quality of ADR entities*, so that the such "entities respect the quality principles of impartiality, transparency, effectiveness and fairness."[88]
4. *Ensuring a public monitoring* of *ADR entities at national level*, with each Member State appointing a competent authority "in charge of monitoring the functioning of ADR entities established on its territory".[89]

A key important aspect of the ADR Directive is that it covers both domestic and cross-border disputes (Article 2) taking place between a provider established in the Union and a consumer resident in the Union, without affecting direct negotiations/judicial attempts at settlement or in-house dispute resolution services established by trader.[90] Furthermore, the Directive fosters cooperation between ADR entities and national authorities enforcing EU Law (Article 17), including "mutual exchange of information on practices in specific business sectors", thus recognizing the importance of cooperation between public and private enforcement mechanisms.

The objective scope of the Directive covers the provision of all services and the sales of all goods—both online and offline—with the exclusion of the so-called non-economic services of general interest,[91] health-care services, and higher education.[92] Investment services provided on both a domestic and cross-border basis are, thus, included. The subjective scope of the Directive concerns complaints submitted by consumers against traders and it excludes complaints filed by traders against consumers or disputes between traders (even if Member States are free to adopt mechanisms for such disputes).[93] Coherently, access should be free of charge for the consumer or, when this is not possible, costs should not exceed a nominal fee (Recital 41).

Interestingly, Recital 7 of the Proposal originally submitted by the Commission had a larger scope as it covered "also complaints submitted by traders against consumers".[94] Evidently, this was perceived as quite a controversial point that could have changed the very nature of ADRs in the EU: giving traders the possibility to "sue" a consumer before an ADR would have definitely helped the former reduce legal costs (and this may be the primary reason behind the Commission's move). However, it could have transformed the grounding philosophy of the ADRs, which were created in order to help consumers obtain a fast and cheap redress.[95]

The ADR Directive directly handles the issue of conflicts of interests. In order to avoid ADR mechanisms morphing into an industry tool, the European lawmaker condemns intrusive instructions from either party or their representatives on the ADR itself (Article 6.1[c]) and it imposes restrictions on the ability of natural persons in charge of dispute resolutions to be employed or remunerated exclusively by the individual trader (Article 2.2[a]). Furthermore, the very same persons can be appointed to the office of a duration which is sufficient to ensure the independence of their actions (Article 6.1[b]) and the remuneration cannot be linked to the dispute outcome (Article 6.1[d]).

Alike to what is laid down by MiFID for conflicts of interests between a service provider and its actual or prospective clients, natural persons in charge of ADR mechanisms must disclose without undue delay potential conflicts of interests to the entity running the ADR. Article 6.1(e) foresees such a duty as an ongoing obligation throughout the unfolding of an

ADR procedure. Coherently, ADR entities must have in place procedures to overcome and mitigate the disclosed conflicts (Article 6.2).

Significantly, ADR awards cannot supersede the protection afforded to the consumer by the applicable Private International Law, in particular, the already mentioned Regulation Rome I.[96] Article 11.1(b) provides that in case of conflict of laws, the law applicable to the sales or services contract must be determined according to Article 6.1/2 of Rome I. Furthermore, the solution adopted by the ADR cannot turn out in depriving the consumers from the protection granted to them by the provisions that cannot be negotiated away according to the laws of the Member State in which the consumer is habitually resident (Article 11.1[c]).

The ADR Directive was soon after ensued by the 2013 Online Dispute Resolution Regulation[97] (ODR). The Regulation establishes a pan-European web-based platform run by the European Commission to help both consumers and traders to resolve their disputes arising from online transactions on goods and services. The platform—accessible since 15 February 2016—works as a smart entry point for consumers who need to submit a dispute: after receiving a claim, the platform forwards it to the national ADR entities communicated by each Member State which will take care of the dispute.[98] The platform also includes out-of-court resolution of disputes that can be initiated by a trader/provider against a consumer, as far as the applicable legislation of the Member State in which the consumer has her/his habitual residence allows so.[99] Online financial services are covered by the ODR platform; for instance, the ADR specialized in financial issues from Belgium is the *Ombudsman en conflits financiers/Ombudsman in financiële geschillen* (Ombudsfin).

As regards financial services, MiFID II Article 75 very importantly provides for the compulsory establishment of ADRs schemes at domestic level handling disputes regarding the provision of investment services and requires that *all* investment firms adhere to such schemes. When looked from the inside of an investment firm, the Compliance Function is again the internal structure that should be in charge of liaising with such ADR bodies. If combined with the responsibility of running and monitoring the internal complaints-handling procedures, the Compliance Function would be in the optimal position to (1) gather information on the complaints submitted by firm's customers, (2) internally solve those very minor infringements, and (3) avoid customers bringing lawsuits before courts by channeling complaints through available ADR schemes.

Coherently with the philosophy of cross-border cooperation-among-authorities pervading the EU law—with the foregoing ODR being an example thereof—Article 75 sets forth that national ADR bodies must actively cooperate with their counterparts in the resolution of cross-border disputes. The strengthened role of ESMA as jointer of domestic authorities (shown in Chap. 5) is confirmed by the fact that it is in charge of drafting a list of all domestic extrajudicial mechanisms.

The Commission's interest in pan-European ADR mechanisms for retail financial services has been recently revamped.[100] Indeed, an already existing project of the European Commission might develop in the coming years into a proto-pan-European ADR scheme for the investment sector: the Consumer Complaints Network for Financial Services, the so-called FIN-NET.[101] This was launched by the European Commission in 2001[102] in order to establish a network of dispute resolution schemes regarding financial services purchased cross-border, with the aim to link the many domestic out-of-court settlement bodies.

The official goal of FIN-NET is to create a pan-European platform where national schemes can cooperate in order "to provide consumers with easy access to out-of-court complaint procedures in cross-border cases. If a consumer in one country has a dispute with a financial services provider from another country, FIN-NET members will put the consumer in touch with the relevant out-of-court complaint scheme and provide the necessary information about it."[103] This is actually useful because in cross-border disputes a customer's complaint is handled by a dispute resolution body operating in the country of origin of the financial services provider, thus making it difficult for the customer to access the scheme.

FIN-NET works through the following steps: (1) the ADR of the Member State where the consumer has her/his habitual residence is contacted by the consumer; (2) the ADR of the consumer home Member State shall decide which ADR in the financial service provider's Member State is competent and, then, inform the consumer accordingly; (3) the files are transferred to the competent ADR either by the consumer or by ADR of the consumer home Member State; (4) the competent ADR in the financial service provider's Member State has the responsibility to carry out the due investigation and adopt the decision/recommendation.[104]

As of July 2017, FIN-NET had sixty members in twenty-seven countries.[105] All of them are national ADR schemes and all of them comply with the principles set out in the ADR Directive and adhere to the Memorandum of Understanding[106] on a Cross-Border Out-of-Court Complaints Network for Financial Services in the European Economic Area.[107] The impact of FIN-NET has increased over time with the amount of cross-border disputes handled by FIN-NET from 2007 to 2015 being quadrupled: from 1041 to 4195.[108] Most of those cases have usually taken place in the banking sector (in particular, payment services), with fewer arising in the insurance and investment sectors.[109] Such a strong increase corroborates the gradually integration trend that EU retail financial services market has been undergoing.

6.2.2 The Arbitration System for Broker-Dealers and Investment Advisers in the United States

The US arbitration system is governed by both state and federal laws. The 1925 Federal Arbitration Act[110] regulates the general framework for arbitrations in the United States and it applies to both state and federal courts. The Act's general principle is that arbitration agreements—which must be in writing as *ad substantiam*—are to be considered "valid, irrevocable, and enforceable", except when there are legal grounds for revoking a contract.[111]

All fifty US states have adopted statutes concerning arbitration procedures[112] with the purpose of giving a steady framework to this extrajudicial mechanism. Particular attention must be paid to the compliance with the due process principle and the confirmation of an arbitration award,[113] which is a very important aspect since it allows arbitration awards to become enforceable as civil judgments.[114] In addition, many states have also adopted the 1955 Uniform Arbitration Act and its successor, the 2000 Revised Uniform Arbitration Act, which aim at harmonizing states' laws dealing with arbitrations.[115] Importantly, the State of New York, where a large part of the US financial business is located, has its own arbitration statute incorporated into Article 75 of the New York Civil Practice Law and Rules.[116] Alongside federal and state legislation, self-regulatory organizations such as the American Arbitration Association (AAA) and, for BDs, the FINRA play a significant role.

Alike many other disputes, those arising from the relationship between investors and their BDs can nowadays be dealt with through arbitration schemes. As it is extensively known, in 1953, with the *Wilko v. Swan*[117] case, the US SC recognized that Section 14 of the 1933 Securities Act provides that "Any condition, stipulation, or provision binding any person acquiring any security to waive compliance with any provision of this title or of the rules and regulations of the Commission shall be void",[118] making it clear that the aim of the 1933 Securities Act's is to "protect the rights of investors".[119] Therefore, although the US SC recognized that the intention of Congress in enacting the 1925 Federal Arbitration Act was to give participants in commercial transactions the opportunity "to secure prompt, economical, and adequate solution of controversies through arbitration if the parties are willing to accept less certainty of legally correct adjustment",[120] it then stated that "the intention of Congress concerning the sale of securities [… was] better carried out by holding invalid such an agreement for arbitration of issues arising under the Act."[121] Following this case, the situation remained stable for around thirty years.

The turning point was the *Shearson/American Express v. McMahon*[122] case that took place in 1987. In this leading case, the US SC held that the anti-waiver provisions of the 1933 Securities Act do not apply to securities disputes arising under the 1934 Exchange Act because of the differences in the language employed by the two statutes of 1930s. Subsequently, in 1989, with the case *Rodriguez de Quijas v. Shearson/American Express Inc.*[123] the US SC effectively overruled its own position in *Wilko v. Swan* by permitting arbitration clauses even for claims arising under the provisions of the 1933 Securities Act.

To figure out the role played by self-regulatory organizations in the field of securities arbitrations, it must be said that brokers and dealers have a duty to arbitrate their disputes simply because they are members of the FINRA, which compels them to use arbitrations instead of court procedures. The FINRA Code of Arbitration Procedure for Customer Disputes, which must be approved by the SEC,[124] requires all FINRA members to use arbitration procedures in disputes if this option is chosen by the customer. This is clearly stated in the Part II General Arbitration Rules 12200—Arbitration Under an Arbitration Agreement or the Rules of FINRA:

"Parties must arbitrate a dispute under the Code if:

- Arbitration under the Code is either: (1) Required by a written agreement, or (2) Requested by the customer;
- The dispute is between a customer and a member or associated person of a member; and
- The dispute arises in connection with the business activities of the member or the associated person, except disputes involving the insurance business activities of a member that is also an insurance company."[125]

Importantly, the above provision clarifies that membership of FINRA only compels FINRA members to bring a claim before an arbiter instead of a court if this is so requested by the customer, and not the other way around. Indeed, in case there is no written arbitration clause, FINRA members' customers can choose civil proceedings before a court over an arbitration procedure.

Unlike BDs who are subject to the mandatory FINRA dispute resolution mechanisms in case of disputes with their investors, IAs are not subject to a similar compulsory procedure and can choose between arbitration and litigation before a court (can also choose to adhere to the FINRA arbitration scheme[126]). Investment advice contracts, indeed, may include an arbitration clause that allows the settlement of disputes through sectorial entities, such as the AAA, and the Judicial Arbitration and Mediation Services—JAMS, which can review claims over alleged breaches of IAs' fiduciary duty. In particular, the Commercial Rules of the AAA can be used as the arbitration framework to apply to disputes arising out or in relation to financial advisory agreements.[127]

Consistently with its investor-friendly purpose, Section 921 of the Dodd-Frank Act has granted the SEC the authority to restrict or prohibit the use of arbitration agreements on the part of BDs and IAs, with the view to overcoming the existing hiatus. However, a potential unification of the arbitration schemes for BDs and IAs might be incomplete without a harmonization of their duties toward customers, namely, the extension of the IAs' fiduciary duty to BDs. Nevertheless, as of July 2017, the general issue of consumer arbitration is still a hot political topic[128] and the SEC has not stepped in on the use of securities arbitration agreements and it is unclear whether it will do so in the near future.[129]

6.3 Lack of the Interplay Between Private and Public Enforcement Mechanisms at EU Level

Professor Moloney rightly points out how private enforcement by individuals plays an important role in the investment service sector:

> Market mechanisms which promote good behaviour by investment firms depend, in part, on the active policing by investors of firm failures, particularly with respect to investment advice. The development of an effective retail investor constituency includes, therefore, the development of a cohort of investors empowered, and sufficiently informed, to monitor investment firms […] and to exercise liability rights, whether contractual or otherwise.[130]

On the same wavelength, Professor Cherednychenko highlights how "neither purely administrative nor purely private mode of enforcement in itself is sufficient to ensure the effectiveness of"[131] investor protection rules, because deterrence-oriented administrative sanctions are complemented by the compensatory nature of private remedies.[132] Public and private enforcers can be separated and still cooperate and co-ordinate each other,[133] but a good hybrid compromise[134] may be the assignment to an administrative agency of the power to choose to either bring a lawsuit before a court or look for administrative fines, as it is the case of the SEC.

Coherently with this approach, the US system has two fully developed legs at the federal level—public and collective private enforcement mechanisms—which are usually conceived as complementary and should be working as such.[135] In particular, regulatory/policy-oriented class actions—namely, those cases filed in order to achieve a policy aim[136]—

should play a role complementary to that played by the SEC through its enforcement efforts.[137] In addition, the SEC can choose to bring civil lawsuits before a court, which amplifies the usage of private enforcement tools. Finally, alongside lawsuits before civil courts, arbitration clauses have been employed with the purpose of lowering the cost of proceedings, for both consumers and service providers.[138]

The complementary interplay between federal public and collective private enforcement tools[139] was clearly expressed by Arthur Levitt, the then chairperson of the SEC, during his 1995 hearing before the US House of Representatives: "[P]rivate actions also provide a "necessary supplement" to the Commission's own enforcement activities by serving to deter securities law violations. Private actions are crucial to the integrity of our disclosure system because they provide a direct incentive for issuers and other market participants to meet their obligations under the securities laws."[140] Importantly, does not only Arthur Levitt imply that the SEC's limited resources to police its supervisees' conduct of business give class actions an essential complementary role[141] but also confirms the disclosure paradigm as the one shaping the US regulatory philosophy.

In class action lawsuit, the role played by attorneys and their law firms is of utmost importance because, with the purpose of earning fees,[142] they organize class actions that, if they were left only to individual initiative, would never concretize due to the small amount of individual damages.[143] Not-for-profit associations can also bring a class action lawsuit before a court but, due to their lack of financial means, their role has a much smaller impact.[144] The cost-recovery relationship explains why class actions have been largely used in the United States: due to the opt-out system, the expected recovery is likely to exceed the costs of the procedures.[145]

Drawbacks of the class actions' supplementary role toward the SEC enforcement activity should not be underestimated though. Professors Correia and Klausner connect such drawbacks to the incentives of the parties involved in a class action and draw up a list of four main maladies[146]: (1) the logic underneath the incentive structure often leads to settlements instead of trials[147]; (2) settlements tend to be financed by the company itself rather than by the officers who have committed violations[148]—whereas the SEC's policy and practice is that to fine single individuals as well[149]; (3) defendants may be induced by settlement incentives to over-pay in order to settle, even in weak cases[150]; (4) plaintiffs' lawyers may be incentivized to file weak cases with the purpose of obtaining over-paid settlements and the related fees.[151] Correia and Klausner then hold that these factors weaken the supplementary role of securities class actions, due to the fact that, to be truly supplementary, class actions should "target serious violations—violations that the SEC would target if it had the resources".[152]

Even if weighing the benefits and drawbacks of the US system of securities class actions is important to avoid any frivolous mythologizing, what strikes the most when drawing parallels between the EU and the US private enforcement procedures is the following: nothing like this exists in Europe at Union level.[153] As seen in the previous chapters, there is no European Contract law providing EU-level private remedies enforceable before civil courts. MiFID I/II is publicly oriented, and consistent with this goal, it only harmonizes sanctioning tools of public supervisors.[154] Similarly, there are no rules on common, EU-wide collective private enforcement mechanisms harmonizing group/class actions at Member States level. However, under the ADR Directive,[155] domestically based ADR entities are subject to the monitoring of domestic public competent authorities, thus establishing an interaction between public enforcers and out-of-court settlement procedures of investor disputes.

Even if the European Union is characterized for having a multilevel structure and the interactions with Member States are crucial to understand its functioning, a comparison with the United States makes it evident what is missing in Europe. It has been properly shown by Della Negra[156] how the increasingly detailed (public-law) EU rules have been influencing the interpretation of national private laws and the related remedies granted thereunder.[157] This trend has been wisely defined as *hybridization*: national private remedies employed to protect EU-derived rights.[158] This finding, however, smoothly reaffirms an unbridgeable gap between the EU and US Union/federal system of securities regulation, namely, that the EU legal system as such—and the EU law of financial services in particular—does not provide for its own private remedies.[159]

The US system of interplay of public and private enforcement mechanisms at the federal level is untransplantable in Europe, even if ESMA itself implicitly admits how important such an interplay is: "In many

Member States private enforcement is even more important than fines and other measures by NCAs. In particular this is true for all duties for investment firms advising clients."[160] Moreover, such an interplay would certainly have an effect on investment firms' internal Compliance Function and how it handles prospective (very) minor infringements concerning retail investor protection through internal complaints-handling procedures.[161]

Concerning ADR schemes, the US arbitration systems for BDs and IAs are incomparably more developed and sophisticated than the one harmonized in Europe by the ADR Directive. As shown above, the Federal Arbitration Act—which rests on contracts rooted in the common-law tradition—provides for uniform federal rules, leaving states some leeway for state-based legislation.[162] On the one hand, the FINRA arbitration regime is "the largest securities dispute resolution forum in the United States".[163] On the other hand, disputes arising out of advisory contracts can rely on the arbitration schemes defined by SROs other than the FINRA, such as the American Arbitration Association. Unfortunately, the different treatment and procedures between BDs and IAs may lead to confusion at the damage of the weaker parties.[164]

Nevertheless, nothing like this exists in Europe. To partially fill the gap with the United States and with a view of further stimulating the trend of moving away from courts[165]—corroborated by the increasing importance of public vis-à-vis private enforcement—the EU Commission is trying to establish harmonized ADR schemes across Europe to be used for minor infringements, run by ADR entities assessed by domestic public authorities. Although insufficient, the approach of the EU Commission reveals an intention already somehow heralded by the ERPL theory: building ADR mechanisms with such a wide leeway to potentially culminate in a Europeanized proto-jurisdiction, particularly if the use of such ADRs becomes sectorially mandatory in the future.

As of today, however, the ADR Directive simply harmonizes domestically based ADR mechanisms, does not directly provide for collective redress,[166] and, importantly, does not "require the participation of traders in ADR procedures to be mandatory or the outcome of such procedures to be binding on traders."[167] The concern of the current EU lawmaker is that making an ADR mechanism mandatory for both consumers and traders would cause harm to the fundamental rights of the parties of access to justice and to their right to seek an effective redress, as established by the Article 47 of the Charter of Fundamental Rights.[168]

As for the (near) future, it is no longer a mere intellectual speculation to hypothesize a Regulation laying down an EU-regulated set of contractual rules specifically drawn up for the digital cross-border market in financial services—adopted, for instance, within the remit of the Capital Market Union—and sectorially superseding the Europeanized Private International Law (Rome I). Within this context, a truly EU opt-in system of voluntary (leaving counterparties the chance to bring action before domestic courts) ADRs specialized in digital cross-border cases might be established by means of a Regulation (at least for b2b transactions as a first step). It would be a sort of a prototype for an EU-wide "jurisdiction" apt to cover an increasing slice of today's wholesales financial transactions.[169] Retailization of such a uniform ADR scheme specialized in digital cross-border cases would likely ensue in case of success in the wholesale market, especially for infringements of minor gravity. However, it should be borne in mind that disputes concerning investment services usually imply greater monetary amounts than those connected to other services such as banking and payments. For this practical reason, domestic civil courts will likely keep playing an important role even in the foreseeable future.

Notes

1. Cherednychenko gives an interesting overview of the ways Member States resist the penetration of EU investor protection law into their domestic private legal regimes. The most striking examples are Luxemburg and Scotland, where the courts have declined to recognize any private law effect to MiFID I rules. Olha O. Cherednychenko, "Financial Consumer Protection in the Eu: Towards a Self-Sufficient European Contract Law for Consumer Financial Services?," *European Review of Contract Law* 10, no. 4 (2014). At 487.
2. Hans-Wolfgang Micklitz, "The Transformation of Enforcement in European Private Law: Preliminary Considerations," *European Review of Private Law* 4 (2015).

3. In the words of the European Court of Justice: "It is for the internal legal order of each Member State to determine the contractual consequences where an investment firm offering an investment service fails to comply with the assessment requirements laid down in Article 19(4) and (5) of Directive 2004/39." *Genil 48 Sl and Comercial Hostelera De Grandes Vinos Sl V Bankinter Sa and Banco Bilbao Vizcaya Argentaria Sa*, EU:C:2013:344 (2013). On this case and regulatory standards as duties in contract law, see the seminal article of Professor Grundmann Stefan Grundmann, "The Bankinter Case on Mifid Regulation and Contract Law," *European Review of Contract Law* 9, no. 3 (2013). At 275–279.
4. "Commission Recommendation 2013/396/Eu—C (2013)3539 [11.06.2013]," (2013).
5. Ibid.
6. European Commission, "Press Release—Commission Recommends Member States to Have Collective Redress Mechanisms in Place to Ensure Effective Access to Justice," (2013).
7. "A legal mechanism that ensures a possibility to claim cessation of illegal behaviour collectively by two or more natural or legal persons or by an entity entitled to bring a representative action (injunctive collective redress)." Point 3(a) of the Recommendation.
8. "A legal mechanism that ensures a possibility to claim compensation collectively by two or more natural or legal persons claiming to have been harmed in a mass harm situation or by an entity entitled to bring a representative action (compensatory collective redress)." Point 3(a) of the Recommendation.
9. "The claimant party should be formed on the basis of express consent of the natural or legal persons claiming to have been harmed." Point 21 of the Recommendation.
10. European Commission, "Call for Evidence on the Operation of Collective Redress Arrangements in the Member States of the European Union," http://ec.europa.eu/newsroom/just/item-detail.cfm?item_id=59539.
11. Michael D. Hausfeld et al., "Antitrust Class Proceedings—Then and Now," in *The Law and Economics of Class Actions*, ed. James Langenfeld (Bingley: Emerald Group Publishing, 2014). At 80.
12. Rule 48 as reported by Joseph Story, *Commentaries on Equity Pleadings, and the Incidents Thereof: According to the Practice of the Courts of Equity, of England and America* (C.C. Little & J. Brown, 1844). At 172. Also reported by Hausfeld et al. At 80.

13. Stephen C. Yeazell, *From Medieval Group Litigation to the Modern Class Action* (New Haven, CT: Yale University Press, 1987). At 221.
14. Ibid. At 224.
15. Ibid. At 224.
16. Ibid. At 224.
17. Ibid. At 225.
18. "The Rule was considered to have refined and substantially restated Equity Rule 38". Columbia Law Review Notes, "Federal Class Actions: A Suggested Revision of Rule 23," *Columbia Law Review* 46, no. 5 (1946). At 820.
19. Nikita Malhotra Pastor, "Equity and Settlement Class Actions: Can There Be Justice for All in Ortiz V. Fibreboard," *American University Law Review* 49, no. 3 (2000). At 786.
20. Nyal D. Deems, "The Cy Pres Solution to the Damage Distribution Problems of Mass Class Actions," *Georgia Law Review* 9, no. 4 (1975). At 893.
21. Paolo Stella, *L'enforcement Nei Mercati Finanziari* (Milano: Giuffré, 2008). At 244.
22. Ibid. At 246.
23. *Rules of Civil Procedure for the United States District Courts—Rule 23.*
24. Ibid.
25. Ibid.
26. Ibid.
27. Stella. At 252–253.
28. *O'shea V. Littleton*, 414 U.S. 488 (1974). Mentioned by Stella At 252.
29. Stella. At 253, mentioning: *Pigford V. Glickman*, 182 FRD 341 (DDC 1998).
30. Stella. At 254.
31. Ibid. At 260–292.
32. "Title V. Disclosures And Discovery"
33. *Rules of Civil Procedure for the United States District Courts—Rule 26*, U.S.C. § 1332(d).
34. Stella. At 273.
35. Ibid. At 277.
36. Ibid. At 277–294.
37. As clearly explained by Stella: ibid. At 296.
38. Ibid. At 296.
39. Section 11, *The Truth in Securities Act*, (May 27, 1933).

40. A "material fact required to be stated therein or necessary to make the statements therein not misleading". Section 11(a), ibid.
41. Section 11(a), ibid.
42. Rewording of the text: Section 11 (e), ibid.
43. Section 11(g), ibid.
44. Stella. At 296.
45. *Kaplan V. Rose*, 49 F.3d 1363 (9th Cir.1994).
46. SEC Rule 12b-2, (*Definitions*).
47. Section 12, *The Truth in Securities Act.*
48. Stella. At 297. Section 12, *The Truth in Securities Act.*
49. Section 10, *The Securities Exchange Act.*
50. *Employment of Manipulative and Deceptive Devices.*
51. Stella. At 298.
52. *The Securities Exchange Act.*
53. *Employment of Manipulative and Deceptive Devices.*
54. Stella. At 298.
55. *Employment of Manipulative and Deceptive Devices.*
56. Stella. At 298.
57. Ibid. At 298.
58. Ibid. At 294.
59. Michael A. Perino, "Did the Private Securities Litigation Reform Act Work?," *University Of Illinois Law Review* 2003 (2003). At 915.
60. Ibid. At 914.
61. *Private Securities Litigation Reform Act.*
62. Stella. At 294; Perino. At 914.
63. Relevant studies are: Perino.—also reported by Stella. (At 357); Marilyn F. Johnson, Karen K. Nelson, and AC Pritchard, "Do the Merits Matter More? The Impact of the Private Securities Litigation Reform Act," ed. Stanford Law and Economics Olin Working Paper No. 249 (Stanford, CA 2002)—also reported by Stella. (At 358); Marilyn F. Johnson, Karen K. Nelson, and AC Pritchard, "Do the Merits Matter More? The Impact of the Private Securities Litigation Reform Act," *The Journal of Law, Economics, & Organization* 23, no. 3 (2007); Stephen J. Choi, "Do the Merits Matter Less after the Private Securities Litigation Reform Act?," ed. NYU Law School—Law and Economics Research Paper Series—Research Paper No. 03-04 (New York, NY 2005); Stephen J. Choi, Karen K. Nelson, and Adam C. Pritchard, "The Screening Effect of the Private Securities Litigation Reform Act," ed.

University of Michigan Law and Economics Olin Working Paper No. 07-008 (Ann Arbor, MI 2007); Stephen J. Choi and Adam C. Pritchard, *Lead Plaintiffs and Their Lawyers: Mission Accomplished, or More to Be Done?—Research Handbook on Shareholder Litigation* (Elgar Publishing, Forthcoming, 2017).

64. Stella. At 299–306.
65. European Commission, "Out-of-Court Settlement of Consumer Disputes," http://europa.eu/legislation_summaries/consumers/protection_of_consumers/l32031_en.htm.
66. Marta Cantero-Gamito, "Dispute Resolution in Telecommunications: A Commitment to out-of-Court," *European Review of Private Law* 25, no. 2 (2012).
67. Ibid.
68. "For consumer dispute resolution, Article 81(2)(e) and (g) TFEU is particularly relevant. Based on this, the EU may adopt measures that facilitate collective and alternative redress mechanisms in order to promote "effective access to justice." This competence is nonetheless generally restricted to cross-border matters, so that Member States procedures may remain unaffected". Iris Benohr, "Consumer Dispute Resolution after the Lisbon Treaty," *Journal of Consumer Policy* 38, no. 1 (2013). At 96.
69. *Directive 2013/11/Eu*. Article 1 of the Directive clearly states that its purpose is that to "contribute to the proper functioning of the internal market by ensuring that consumers can, on a voluntary basis, submit complaints against traders".
70. *Recommendation 98/257/Ec*.
71. *Recommendation 2001/310/Ec*.
72. *Recommendation 98/257/Ec*.
73. Ibid.
74. Ibid.
75. Ibid.
76. Ibid.
77. Ibid.
78. Ibid.
79. *Recommendation 2001/310/Ec*.
80. European Commission, "Study on the Use of Alternative Dispute Resolution in the European Union, Civic Consulting of the Consumer Policy Evaluation Consortium (Cpec)," (Bruxelles 2009).

81. "Consumer Redress in the European Union: Consumers' Experiences, Perceptions and Opinions," (2009).
82. "Cross-Border Adr in the European Union," (2011).
83. *Directive 2013/11/Eu.*
84. *Proposal for a Directive on Alternative Dispute Resolution for Consumer Disputes.*
85. Ibid. At 2.
86. Ibid. At 5.
87. Ibid. At 5.
88. Ibid. At 5.
89. Ibid. At 5.
90. Recital 23, (Article 2.2(b,e,f)), *Directive 2013/11/Eu.* Also: Benohr.
91. Non-economic services are those services not performed for economic consideration. Recital 13, *Directive 2013/11/Eu.*
92. Article 2.2(c,h,i) ibid.
93. Article 2.2(d,g) and Recital 16, ibid.
94. Recital 7 of the *Proposal for a Directive on Alternative Dispute Resolution for Consumer Disputes.*
95. Cristian Silviu Busoi, "Draft Opinion of the Committee on Legal Affairs on the Proposal for a Directive of the European Parliament and of the Council on Alternative Dispute Resolution for Consumer Disputes (Com(2011)0793—C7-0454/2011—2011/0373(Cod))," (Brussels 2012). At 3.
96. *Regulation 593/2008.*
97. *Regulation 524/2013.*
98. The official ODR website: European Commission, "Online Dispute Resolution," https://ec.europa.eu/consumers/odr/main/index.cfm?event=main.home.show&lng=EN.
99. Article 2, *Regulation 524/2013.*
100. "Green Paper on Retail Financial Services: Better Products, More Choice, and Greater Opportunities for Consumers and Businesses, Brussels, 10.12.2015, Com(2015) 630 Final," (2015).
101. European Commission, "Financial Dispute Resolution Network," http://ec.europa.eu/internal_market/fin-net/index_en.htm.
102. "Financial Services: Commission Launches out-of-Court Complaints Network to Improve Consumer Confidence," (Bruxelles 2001).
103. European Banking Authority—EBA, "Personal Finance at the Eu Level—Fin-Net," http://www.eba.europa.eu/consumer-corner/personal-finance-at-the-eu-level.

104. As summarized in: European Commission, "Fin-Net Activity Report 2015," (2015). At 2.
105. European Commission, "About Fin-Net," https://ec.europa.eu/info/business-economy-euro/banking-and-finance/consumer-finance-and-payments/consumer-financial-services/financial-dispute-resolution-network-fin-net/fin-net-network/about-fin-net_en.
106. "Memorandum of Understanding on a Cross-Border out-of-Court Complaints Network for Financial Services in the European Economic Area," (Bruxelles 2001).
107. The European Economic Area (EEA) was established in 1994 by the then European Communities and the European Free Trade Association (EFTA) with the aim of allowing Iceland, Liechtenstein, and Norway to take part to the European Internal Market without being full members of the European Union. *See*: "Proposal for a Regulation of the European Parliament and of the Council Establishing a European Securities and Markets Authority," (September 23, 2009).
108. Commission, "Fin-Net Activity Report 2015." At 5.
109. Ibid. At 5. Note that in 2015 the largest category was "other" with 1612 cases.
110. *Federal Arbitration Act.*
111. "[…] an agreement in writing to submit to arbitration an existing controversy […] shall be valid, irrevocable, and enforceable, save upon such grounds as exist at law or in equity for the revocation of any contract". Ibid.
112. Susan Wiens and Roger Haydock, "Confirming Arbitration Awards: Taking the Mystery out of a Summary Proceeding," *William Mitchell Law Review* 33, no. 4 (2007). Table of Confirmation Procedures, 1319–1328.
113. Ibid.
114. Ibid. At 1294.
115. Uniform Law Commission, "Arbitration Act (2000)," http://www.uniformlaws.org/Act.aspx?title=Arbitration%20Act%20 (2000).
116. *Civil Practice Law and Rules of the State of New York.*
117. *Wilko V. Swan*, 346 U.S. 427 (1953).
118. Section 14, *The Truth in Securities Act.*
119. *Wilko V. Swan.*
120. Ibid.
121. Ibid.
122. *Shearson/American Express V. Mcmahon*, 482 U.S. 220 (1987).

123. *Rodriguez De Quijas V. Shearson/American Express Inc.*, 490 U.S. 477 (1989).
124. *See*: Financial Industry Regulatory Authority—FINRA, "Sec Approves New Nasd Code of Arbitration Procedure," http://www.finra.org/newsroom/2007/sec-approves-new-nasd-code-arbitration-procedure.
125. "Code of Arbitration Procedure for Customer Disputes," http://finra.complinet.com/en/display/display_viewall.html?rbid=2403&element_id=4096&record_id=5174&filtered_tag.
126. "Guidance on Disputes between Investors and Investment Advisers That Are Not Finra Members," https://www.finra.org/arbitration-and-mediation/investment_advisers.
127. See the contractual template on page 381–390 in Katherine Vessenes, *Protecting Your Practice* (New York: Bloomberg Press, 2010).
128. As it is proved by attempted reforms such as the new Arbitration Fairness Act introduced in March 2017, which, if approved, would make a pre-dispute arbitration clause invalid or unenforceable in case it requires the arbitration of a dispute concerning employment, consumer, antitrust, or civil rights. Available at: *H.R.1374—Arbitration Fairness Act of 2017*.
129. On this point: John I. Sanders and Paul J. Foley, "Broker-Dealers and Investments Advisers Exempted from Cfpb's Arbitration Agreement Rule," https://www.lexology.com/library/detail.aspx?g=59c3fe0e-0ebd-449a-b1d5-58d8f762a3c1.
130. Niamh Moloney, "Effective Policy Design for the Retail Investment Services Market: Challenges and Choices Post Fsap "in *Investor Protection in Europe: Corporate Law Making, the Mifid and Beyond*, ed. Guido Ferrarini and Eddy Wymeersch (Oxford: Oxford University Press, 2006). At 425. As also mentioned by Olha O. Cherednychenko, "Public and Private Enforcement of European Private Law in the Financial Services Sector," *European Review of Private Law* 24, no. 4 (2015). At 633–634.
131. "Public and Private Enforcement of European Private Law in the Financial Services Sector." At 640. Important literature too confirms how public and private enforcement complement each other: Charles D. Kolstad, Thomas S. Ulen, and Gary V. Johnson, "Ex Post Liability for Harm Vs. Ex Ante Safety Regulation: Substitutes or Complements?," *American Economic Review* 80, no. 4 (1990); Steven Shavell, "A Model of the Optimal Use of Liability and Safety Regulation," *Rand Journal of Economics* 15, no. 2 (1984); also mentioned by Cherednychenko,

"Public and Private Enforcement of European Private Law in the Financial Services Sector." At 640.
132. "Public and Private Enforcement of European Private Law in the Financial Services Sector." At 641.
133. Ibid. At 641.
134. Professor Cherednychenko too puts forward examples of hybrid forms of enforcement: "[A] hybrid form of enforcement can emerge whereby deterrence and compensation can be pursued by the same authority. Thus, for example, an administrative agency can be entrusted with providing compensation to the aggrieved consumers who have suffered losses as a result of the violation of contract-related supervision standards by financial service providers." Ibid. At 641.
135. In the words of Professor Coffee: "In the United States, public enforcement of law is supplemented by a vigorous, arguably even hyperactive, system of private enforcement." John C. Coffee Jr., "Law and the Market: The Impact of Enforcement," ed. Columbia Law and Economics Working Paper No. 304 (2007). At 17. Professor MacNeil points out how "Private enforcement in the context of the federal securities laws was first recognized in the US in J. I Case Co. v Borak, in which the Supreme Court justified its availability as a necessary supplement to SEC enforcement." Iain MacNeil, "Enforcement and Sanctioning," in *The Oxford Handbook of Financial Regulation*, ed. Niamh Moloney, Eilís Ferran, and Jennifer Payne (Oxford: Oxford University Press, 2015). At 293. Very interestingly, professor Langevoort points out that "in the U.S., a robust system of private securities litigation is a mixed blessing: some, perhaps substantial, level of speculative litigation results, which costs investors and others a considerable amount while benefiting lawyers on both sides considerably. The right balance of incentives is hard to achieve. However, there is a distinct possibility that without the supplement of easily-invoked private actions, public securities enforcement in the U.S. would require much greater resources to be anything near effective." Donald C. Langevoort, "Structuring Securities Regulation in the European Union: Lessons from the U.S. Experience," in *Investor Protection in Europe: Corporate Law Making, the Mifid and Beyond* ed. Guido Ferrarini and Eddy Wymeersch (New York: Oxford University Press, 2006). At 506.
136. Stella. At 237.
137. Professors Correia and Klausner cast doubts on such complementarity: "To supplement SEC enforcement effectively, class actions must target

violations and impose costs on violators consistent with SEC practice and policy. We have analyzed both targeting and penalties associated with class actions in comparison to the targeting and penalties associated with SEC enforcement actions. We find evidence that the targeting of class actions diverges from SEC practice. [...] The supplementation rationale for class actions thus gets tepid support from this analysis." Maria Correia and Michael Klausner, "Are Securities Class Actions "Supplemental" to Sec Enforcement? An Empirical Analysis," in *The Tel Aviv International Conference in Accounting—The Leon Recanati Graduate School of Business Administration* (Tel Aviv 2012). At 44–45.

138. In the words of Professors Wiens and Haydock: "Aided by numerous federal and state judicial decisions and statutes favoring the enforcement of arbitration agreements, more parties are discovering that binding arbitration is an efficient, costeffective, and flexible alternative to litigation." Wiens and Haydock. At 1293–1294.
139. Alongside public and private enforcement mechanisms, also criminal enforcement tools are employed in the US system so that "the prospect of criminal enforcement radically distinguishes securities regulation in the United States from the rest of the world. [...] the [overall] interplay [is, thus, between] SEC enforcement, Department of Justice criminal prosecution, and private class actions". Coffee Jr. At 44.
140. Subcommittee on Telecommunications And Finance Committee on Commerce, *Testimony of Arthur Levitt Concerning Litigation Reform Proposals*, 1995.
141. In the words of Professors Correia and Klausner: "the Supreme Court, Congress, and the SEC have justified securities class actions as "supplemental" to SEC enforcement and necessary because of constraints on the SEC's resources." Correia and Klausner. At 2.
142. An attorney's fees are calculated by the court through two different methods: the so-called POF, substantially based on a percentage of the total amount to be paid by the defendant; and the so-called lodestar, substantially based on the number of hours spent working on the case. Stella. At 353.
143. Ibid. At 239.
144. Ibid. At 239.
145. In the words of Professor MacNeil: "The availability of class actions in the US provides an incentive for private enforcement [...]. For private enforcement to work, the expected recovery must exceed the costs and for that reason the class action in the US, which draws investors who

have suffered loss into litigation unless they opt out, is closely linked with the prevalence of private enforcement in that country and has been instrumental in boosting private monetary sanctions to a level that over some time frames exceeds public enforcement sanctions." MacNeil. At 293.

146. Correia and Klausner. At 10.
147. Ibid. At 10.
148. Ibid. At 10.
149. Ibid. At 44.
150. Ibid. At 10.
151. Ibid. At 10.
152. Ibid. At 10.
153. Even when the domestic level is under scrutiny: "Private litigation is common in the United States and (to a lesser extent) the United Kingdom and other "common-law" jurisdictions. In contrast, the "civil law" countries, such as those of continental Europe, have far less private litigation, and rely more on enforcement by public agencies." Howell E. Jackson and Mark J. Roe, "Public and Private Enforcement of Securities Laws: Resource-Based Evidence," *Journal of Financial Economics* 93, no. 2 (2009). At 232.
154. In the words of Professor Moloney: "Private enforcement is not, however, significantly enhanced under the MiFID II reforms. The EU faces, of course, severe difficulties with respect to the harmonization of private enforcement mechanisms." Niamh Moloney, "Liability of Asset Managers: A Comment," *Capital Markets Law Journal* 7, no. 4 (2012). At 421; Also Federico DellaNegra, "The Private Enforcement of the Mifid Conduct of Business Rules. An Overview of the Italian and Spanish Experiences," *European Review of Contract Law* 10, no. 4 (2014). At 574.
155. ADR Directive, Chap. 5.
156. Federico DellaNegra, "Private Law and Private Enforcement in the Post-Crisis Eu Retail Financial Regulation" (European University Institute, 2017). Also: Mads Andenas and Federico DellaNegra, "Between Contract Law and Financial Regulation: Towards the Europeanisation of General Contract Law," *European Business Law Review* 28, no. 4 (2017).
157. Furthermore, "civil courts have acknowledged the civil effects of financial regulatory law: the infringement of the regulatory standards gives rise to contractual remedies. […] it seems that the private enforcement driven by civil courts remains the most important vehicle to protect investors. In both countries courts do recognize the civil effects of the regulatory law

by interpreting national contract law in order to afford an effective contractual protection to the investors. [...] national contract law, which remains on the shadow of EU securities regulation, is filling the gap left by the legislative and supervisory apathy." DellaNegra, "The Private Enforcement of the Mifid Conduct of Business Rules. An Overview of the Italian and Spanish Experiences." At 579, 592, 594–595.

158. "Private Law and Private Enforcement in the Post-Crisis Eu Retail Financial Regulation."
159. In the words of Della Negra: "EU financial regulatory law is driven by a public-oriented approach and does not provide private law remedies for investors vis-à-vis the investment firms. At EU level, the breach of the conduct of business rules gives rise only to public-administrative sanctions. Whereas supervision and public enforcement are vertically-centralised, private enforcement is horizontally decentralised." "The Private Enforcement of the Mifid Conduct of Business Rules. An Overview of the Italian and Spanish Experiences." At 571.
160. ESMA Securities and Markets Stakeholder Group, "Advice to Esma—Investor Protection Aspects of the Consultation Paper on Mifid Ii and Mifir—Esma/2014/Smsg/035," (2014). At 4. The report also states that: "[...I]n its 2010 Public Consultation, the Commission considered whether to introduce a principle of civil liability of investment services providers. However, this point was not followed up on by the Commission in its proposal. Therefore, the SMSG thinks that it would be helpful to know which role private enforcement (esp. of the suitability doctrine) plays in the Member States." At 4.
161. Concerning transnational private standards on some fields other than financial services, Paul Verbruggen carries out an excellent analysis on how the interplay between public and private enforcement mechanisms pushes firms toward compliance of such standards. Paul Verbruggen, *Enforcing Transnational Private Regulation: A Comparative Analysis of Advertising and Food Safety* (Cheltenham: Edward Elgar, 2014).
162. All fifty US states have adopted statutes concerning arbitration procedures, as shown by the Table of Confirmation Procedures in Wiens and Haydock. At 1319–1328.
163. FINRA, "Guidance on Disputes between Investors and Investment Advisers That Are Not Finra Members".
164. The general confusion generated by the fact that broker-dealers and investment advisers are subject to different regulatory regimes is a key concern raised by the SEC: Securities and Exchange Commission—

SEC, "Study on Investment Advisers and Broker-Dealers" (Washington, DC 2011). At 2.

165. Micklitz. At 508.
166. A brilliant research on collective redresses, regulatory redress techniques, and ADRs in some EU Member States has been carried out by Professor Hodges: Christopher Hodges, "Mass Collective Redress: Consumer Adr and Regulatory Techniques," ibid. 23, no. 5. Ibid.
167. Recital 49, ADR Directive. This is also criticized by Professors Fejős and Willett who rightly claim that: "It is appropriate that the Directive at least does not insist that outcomes are binding on consumers. However, if the aim is consumer access to justice, and if this is understood in a way that is sensitive to consumer needs and vulnerabilities, then it is strongly arguable that outcomes *should* be binding on businesses. There *should* be a final and enforceable outcome, without an option for the business to challenge the decision routinely, based on the substantive outcome. Rather, the business should only be able to challenge the outcome on the very limited grounds of a 'judicial review' type action. [...O]utcomes that are binding on the business have the potential to ameliorate the inherent inequalities between consumers and businesses, giving consumers fast and cost-effective ways to enforce their private law rights." Andrea Fejős and Chris Willett, "Consumer Access to Justice: The Role of the ADR Directive and the Member States," ibid. 24, no. 1 (2016). Ibid. At 45–47.
168. Busoi.
169. On this hypothesis: Antonio Marcacci, "Digitally-Provided Financial Services under Eu Law: Overcoming the Current Patchwork of Europeanized Private International Law and Sectorially-Harmonized National Private Laws," *Studi sull'integrazione europea* 12, no. 3 (2017).

Bibliography

Alces, Kelli A. "Debunking the Corporate Fiduciary Myth." *Journal of Corporation Law* 35 (2009): 240.

Andenas, Mads, and Federico DellaNegra. "Between Contract Law and Financial Regulation: Towards the Europeanisation of General Contract Law." *European Business Law Review* 28, no. 4 (2017): 499–521.

Benohr, Iris. "Consumer Dispute Resolution After the Lisbon Treaty." *Journal of Consumer Policy* 38, no. 1 (2013): 87–110.

Busoi, Cristian Silviu. "Draft Opinion of the Committee on Legal Affairs on the Proposal for a Directive of the European Parliament and of the Council on Alternative Dispute Resolution for Consumer Disputes (COM(2011)0793 – C7-0454/2011 – 2011/0373(COD))." Brussels, 2012.

Cantero-Gamito, Marta. "Dispute Resolution in Telecommunications: A Commitment to Out-of-Court." *European Review of Private Law* 25, no. 2 (2012): 387–420.

Cherednychenko, Olha O. "Financial Consumer Protection in the EU: Towards a Self-Sufficient European Contract Law for Consumer Financial Services?". *European Review of Contract Law* 10, no. 4 (2014): 476–95.

———. "Public and Private Enforcement of European Private Law in the Financial Services Sector." *European Review of Private Law* 24, no. 4 (2015): 621–47.

Choi, Stephen J. *Do the Merits Matter Less After the Private Securities Litigation Reform Act?* Law and Economics Research Paper Series – Research Paper No. 03-04. New York: NYU Law School, 2005.

Choi, Stephen J., and Adam C. Pritchard. *Lead Plaintiffs and Their Lawyers: Mission Accomplished, or More to Be Done? – Research Handbook on Shareholder Litigation*. Cheltenham: Elgar Publishing, 2017.

Choi, Stephen J., Karen K. Nelson, and Adam C. Pritchard. "The Screening Effect of the Private Securities Litigation Reform Act." Economics Olin Working Paper No. 07-008. Ann Arbor, MI: University of Michigan Law, 2007.

Civil Practice Law and Rules of the State of New York.

Coffee, John C., Jr. "Law and the Market: The Impact of Enforcement." Columbia Law and Economics Working Paper No. 304, 2007.

"Commission Recommendation 2013/396/EU – C (2013)3539 [11.06.2013]." 2013.

Correia, Maria, and Michael Klausner. "Are Securities Class Actions "Supplemental" to SEC Enforcement? An Empirical Analysis." In *The Tel Aviv International Conference in Accounting – The Leon Recanati Graduate School of Business Administration*. Tel Aviv, 2012.

Deems, Nyal D. "The Cy Pres Solution to the Damage Distribution Problems of Mass Class Actions." *Georgia Law Review* 9, no. 4 (1975): 893–929.

Definitions.

DellaNegra, Federico. "The Private Enforcement of the MiFID Conduct of Business Rules. An Overview of the Italian and Spanish Experiences." *European Review of Contract Law* 10, no. 4 (2014): 571–95.

———. "Private Law and Private Enforcement in the Post-Crisis EU Retail Financial Regulation." European University Institute, 2017.

Directive 2013/11/EU.

EBA, European Banking Authority. "Personal Finance at the EU Level – Fin-Net." http://www.eba.europa.eu/consumer-corner/personal-finance-at-the-eu-level.

Employment of Manipulative and Deceptive Devices.

European Commission. "Financial Services: Commission Launches Out-of-Court Complaints Network to Improve Consumer Confidence." Bruxelles, 2001a.

———. "Memorandum of Understanding on a Cross-Border Out-of-Court Complaints Network for Financial Services in the European Economic Area." Bruxelles, 2001b.

———. "Consumer Redress in the European Union: Consumers' Experiences, Perceptions and Opinions." 2009a.

———. "Proposal for a Regulation of the European Parliament and of the Council Establishing a European Securities and Markets Authority." September 23, 2009b.

———. "Study on the Use of Alternative Dispute Resolution in the European Union, Civic Consulting of the Consumer Policy Evaluation Consortium (CPEC)." Bruxelles, 2009c.

———. "Cross-Border ADR in the European Union." 2011.

———. "Press Release – Commission Recommends Member States to Have Collective Redress Mechanisms in Place to Ensure Effective Access to Justice." 2013.

———. "Fin-Net Activity Report 2015." 2015a.

———. "Green Paper on Retail Financial Services: Better Products, More Choice, and Greater Opportunities for Consumers and Businesses, Brussels, 10.12.2015, COM(2015) 630 Final." 2015b.

———. "Call for Evidence on the Operation of Collective Redress Arrangements in the Member States of the European Union." http://ec.europa.eu/newsroom/just/item-detail.cfm?item_id=59539.

———. "Online Dispute Resolution." https://ec.europa.eu/consumers/odr/main/index.cfm?event=main.home.show&lng=EN.

———. "About Fin-Net." https://ec.europa.eu/info/business-economy-euro/banking-and-finance/consumer-finance-and-payments/consumer-financial-services/financial-dispute-resolution-network-fin-net/fin-net-network/about-fin-net_en.

———. "Financial Dispute Resolution Network." http://ec.europa.eu/internal_market/fin-net/index_en.htm.

———. "Out-of-Court Settlement of Consumer Disputes." http://europa.eu/legislation_summaries/consumers/protection_of_consumers/l32031_en.htm.

Federal Arbitration Act.

Fejős, Andrea, and Chris Willett. "Consumer Access to Justice: The Role of the ADR Directive and the Member States." *European Review of Private Law* 24, no. 1 (2016): 33–60.

FINRA, Financial Industry Regulatory Authority. "Code of Arbitration Procedure for Customer Disputes." http://finra.complinet.com/en/display/display_viewall.html?rbid=2403&element_id=4096&record_id=5174&filtered_tag.

———. "Guidance on Disputes Between Investors and Investment Advisers that Are Not Finra Members." https://www.finra.org/arbitration-and-mediation/investment_advisers.

FINRA, Financial Industry Regulatory Authority. "SEC Approves New NASD Code of Arbitration Procedure.". http://www.finra.org/newsroom/2007/sec-approves-new-nasd-code-arbitration-procedure.

Genil 48 Sl and Comercial Hostelera De Grandes Vinos Sl V Bankinter Sa and Banco Bilbao Vizcaya Argentaria Sa, EU:C:2013:344, 2013.

Group, ESMA Securities and Markets Stakeholder. "Advice to ESMA – Investor Protection Aspects of the Consultation Paper on MiFID II and MiFIR – ESMA/2014/SMSG/035." 2014.

Grundmann, Stefan. "The Bankinter Case on MiFID Regulation and Contract Law." *European Review of Contract Law* 9, no. 3 (2013): 267–80.

H.R.1374 – Arbitration Fairness Act of 2017.

Hausfeld, Michael D., Gordon C. Rausser, Gareth J. Macartney, Michael P. Lehmann, and Sathya S. Gosselin. "Antitrust Class Proceedings – Then and Now." In *The Law and Economics of Class Actions*, edited by James Langenfeld, 77–133. Bingley: Emerald Group Publishing, 2014.

Hodges, Christopher. "Mass Collective Redress: Consumer ADR and Regulatory Techniques." *European Review of Private Law* 23, no. 5 (2015): 829–73.

Jackson, Howell E., and Mark J. Roe. "Public and Private Enforcement of Securities Laws: Resource-Based Evidence." *Journal of Financial Economics* 93, no. 2 (2009): 207–38.

Johnson, Marilyn F., Karen K. Nelson, and A.C. Pritchard. "Do the Merits Matter More? The Impact of the Private Securities Litigation Reform Act." Stanford Law and Economics Olin Working Paper No. 249. Stanford, CA, 2002.

———. "Do the Merits Matter More? The Impact of the Private Securities Litigation Reform Act." *The Journal of Law, Economics, & Organization* 23, no. 3 (2007): 627–52.

Kaplan V. Rose, 49 F.3d 1363 (9th Cir.1994).

Kolstad, Charles D., Thomas S. Ulen, and Gary V. Johnson. "Ex Post Liability for Harm Vs. Ex Ante Safety Regulation: Substitutes or Complements?". *American Economic Review* 80, no. 4 (1990): 888–901.

Langevoort, Donald C. "Structuring Securities Regulation in the European Union: Lessons from the U.S. Experience." In *Investor Protection in Europe: Corporate Law Making, the MiFID and Beyond*, edited by Guido Ferrarini and Eddy Wymeersch. New York: Oxford University Press, 2006.

MacNeil, Iain. "Enforcement and Sanctioning." In *The Oxford Handbook of Financial Regulation*, edited by Niamh Moloney, Eilís Ferran and Jennifer Payne. Oxford: Oxford University Press, 2015.

Marcacci, Antonio. "Digitally-Provided Financial Services Under EU Law: Overcoming the Current Patchwork of Europeanized Private International Law and Sectorially-Harmonized National Private Laws." *Studi sull'integrazione europea* 12, no. 3 (2017): 569–584.

Micklitz, Hans-Wolfgang. "The Transformation of Enforcement in European Private Law: Preliminary Considerations." *European Review of Private Law* 4 (2015): 491–524.

Moloney, Niamh. "Effective Policy Design for the Retail Investment Services Market: Challenges and Choices Post FSAP". In *Investor Protection in Europe: Corporate Law Making, the MiFID and Beyond*, edited by Guido Ferrarini and Eddy Wymeersch. Oxford: Oxford University Press, 2006.

———. "Liability of Asset Managers: A Comment." *Capital Markets Law Journal* 7, no. 4 (2012): 414–22.

Notes, Columbia Law Review. "Federal Class Actions: A Suggested Revision of Rule 23." *Columbia Law Review* 46, no. 5 (1946): 818–36.

O'shea V. Littleton, 414 U.S. 488 (1974).

Pastor, Nikita Malhotra. "Equity and Settlement Class Actions: Can There Be Justice for All in Ortiz V. Fibreboard." *American University Law Review* 49, no. 3 (2000): 773–821.

Perino, Michael A. "Did the Private Securities Litigation Reform Act Work?". *University Of Illinois Law Review* 2003 (2003): 913–77.

Pigford V. Glickman, 182 FRD 341 (DDC 1998).

Private Securities Litigation Reform Act.

Proposal for a Directive on Alternative Dispute Resolution for Consumer Disputes.

Recommendation 2001/310/Ec.
Recommendation 98/257/Ec.
Regulation 524/2013.
Regulation 593/2008.
Rodriguez De Quijas V. Shearson/American Express Inc., 490 U.S. 477 (1989).
Rules of Civil Procedure for the United States District Courts – Rule 23.
Rules of Civil Procedure for the United States District Courts – Rule 26, U.S.C. § 1332(d).
Sanders, John I., and Paul J. Foley. "Broker-Dealers and Investments Advisers Exempted from CFPB'S Arbitration Agreement Rule." https://www.lexology.com/library/detail.aspx?g=59c3fe0e-0ebd-449a-b1d5-58d8f762a3c1.
SEC, Securities and Exchange Commission. "Study on Investment Advisers and Broker-Dealers." Washington, DC, 2011.
Shavell, Steven. "A Model of the Optimal Use of Liability and Safety Regulation." *Rand Journal of Economics* 15, no. 2 (1984): 271–80.
Shearson/American Express V. Mcmahon, 482 U.S. 220 (1987).
Stella, Paolo. *L'enforcement Nei Mercati Finanziari*. Milano: Giuffré, 2008.
Story, Joseph. *Commentaries on Equity Pleadings, and the Incidents Thereof: According to the Practice of the Courts of Equity, of England and America.* Boston: C.C. Little & J. Brown, 1844.
Subcommittee on Telecommunications And Finance Committee on Commerce. *Testimony of Arthur Levitt Concerning Litigation Reform Proposals*, 1995.
The Securities Exchange Act.
The Truth in Securities Act. May 27, 1933.
Uniform Law Commission. "Arbitration Act (2000)". http://www.uniformlaws.org/Act.aspx?title=Arbitration%20Act%20.
Verbruggen, Paul. *Enforcing Transnational Private Regulation: A Comparative Analysis of Advertising and Food Safety*. Cheltenham: Edward Elgar, 2014.
Vessenes, Katherine. *Protecting Your Practice*. New York: Bloomberg Press, 2010.
Wiens, Susan, and Roger Haydock. "Confirming Arbitration Awards: Taking the Mystery Out of a Summary Proceeding." *William Mitchell Law Review* 33, no. 4 (2007): 1293–329.
Wilko V. Swan, 346 U.S. 427 (1953).
Yeazell, Stephen C. *From Medieval Group Litigation to the Modern Class Action*. New Haven, CT: Yale University Press, 1987.

7

The Compliance Function as Embedder of the Law-on-the-books and as Enforcement-Frontliner

The first pair of chapters of this book show, on the one hand, the increasingly penetrating splinter of EU public-law norms into relationships traditionally governed by private law; and, on the other hand, how the EU tries to reproduce the US approach on investor protection without using contract law but, instead, replacing it with regulatory law. The second pair of chapters delve into enforcement tools and show, on the one hand, how the current EU public enforcement architecture is trying to fill the gap with its American counterpart and, on the other hand, how private enforcement is overlooked (with the exception of ADR mechanisms).

This last chapter is devoted to framing the Compliance Function against this backdrop. Thoughts and reflections are rooted into the professional experience of the author. On such basis, the Compliance Function is defined as the intra-firm embedder of extra-firm rules and enforcement-frontliner for (not only investor protection) infringements that can be solved *within* the firm without going to a court, using an ADR scheme, and/or the imposition of sanctions on the part of public enforcers. As Professor Miller clearly depicts: "[the Compliance Function] is a form of internalized law enforcement which, if it functions effectively, can substitute for much (although not all) of the enforcement activities

© The Author(s) 2018
A. Marcacci, *Regulating Investor Protection under EU Law*,
https://doi.org/10.1007/978-3-319-90297-5_7

provided by the state."[1] The Compliance Function, thus, appears to be designed as the tool to fill the vacuum between the law-on-the-books and the law-in-action *within* the firm.

To give ground to this assertion, this chapter gives an account of what the Compliance Function is and what it does under current transnational and EU soft- and hard-laws. It, then, links the emergence of Compliance with the increasingly penetrating splinter of EU-made public regulatory norms, thus corroborating a key assumption of the ERPL theory. Subsequently, the chapter mirrors the characteristics of public enforcement under the EU law against the features of the Compliance Function, to prove that the latter are patterned after the former.

7.1 The Internal Control System: What "Compliance Function" Means

The Compliance Function is one of the internal control Functions investment firms are required to establish within the framework of the "Three Lines of Defense"[2] system of internal controls,[3] also defined as "internal gatekeepers".[4] The firm's business and operational employees—as part of their main activities—directly execute first-line-of-defense controls—also defined as *line controls*.[5] For instance, a retail investment advisor shall ensure that s/he obeys internal rules and follows internal procedures when providing investment advice to clients. Second-level controls are carried out by internal control functions such as the Compliance Function, the division for the prevention of anti-money laundering, and the Risk Management.[6] Finally, third-level controls are under the responsibility of the Internal Audit: it periodically verifies whether previous controls have been correctly executed.[7]

At transnational level, the first key document dealing with the Compliance Function was the "Compliance and the compliance function in banks"[8] Report issued by the Basel Committee on Banking Supervision in April 2005. Although the Report—defined as "meta-regulatory"[9]—focused on the banking rather than investment services industry, its release chronologically overlaps the adoption of MiFID I in

2004 and is very coherent with the profile of the Compliance Function in investment firms provided by MiFID (see next section).

The April 2005 Report was meant to shape a worldwide meaning of what a Compliance Function is and what it is asked to do. The report—quite detailed, indeed, to be a soft-law[10] document[11]—was adopted with the view to enhancing and spreading sound practices in banking organizations at world level, so that public supervisors would be satisfied with internal policies and procedures, including responsibilization of senior management in terms of capacity to take the necessary remedial actions in case of breaches.[12]

A key reason justifying the establishment of a Compliance Function in banking and financial institutions is, indeed, the difficulties of public supervisors to effectively monitor supervisees due to a lack of technical knowledge and resources. A firm, instead, "has the knowledge and the ability to more effectively perform these tasks. It therefore makes sense for institutions to police themselves—to carry out a compliance operation".[13]

The definition of the "compliance risk" is the key takeaway of the Report. This is defined as the: "risk of legal or regulatory sanctions, material financial loss, or loss to reputation a bank may suffer as a result of its failure to comply with laws, regulations, rules, related self-regulatory organization standards, and codes of conduct applicable to its banking activities (together, "compliance laws, rules and standards")."[14]

Compliance risk is large. However, it is ultimately perceived by Compliance professionals as being linked to administrative fines imposed by public supervisors. Unlike the risk-management function which is substantially focused on analyzing and controlling the level of risk-taking by a financial intermediary, the Compliance Function in investment firms is much more related to conduct-of-business rules, namely, the way a firm behaves with its counterparties and, in particular, with its clients.[15]

The Basel Committee's Report clarifies that the expression "compliance function" is employed to describe the staff executing compliance responsibilities and it is not meant to prescribe a particular governance structure. However, it suggests that in larger, international banks compliance staff should be located through operating business lines and split into group (at holding's company level) and local (at subsidiary level) units, whereas smaller banks may locate the compliance staff into one single unit.

The Report outlines ten principles focused on the responsibilities of the Board of Directors and of a firm's senior management for compliance (who are ultimately responsible for overseeing and the effective management of a bank's compliance risk). It also deals with the characteristics and responsibilities of the Compliance Function; the possibility to outsource specific tasks (provided that these are subject to appropriate oversight by the Head of the Compliance Function); and the relationship with the Internal Audit (compliance risk is to be included in the risk assessment methodology of the Internal Audit Function). Finally, the Report highlights the necessity for international banks to comply with applicable laws and regulations in all jurisdictions in which they lead business.[16]

In particular, a Compliance Function must have the necessary resources to effectively perform its responsibilities and must be independent, for example, have a formal status within the firm, with clear roles and responsibilities different from those of other Functions. Furthermore, it must be led by a formal Head, such as a Chief Compliance Officer responsible for the correct functioning of the entire Function. The compliance staff and their Head should not be in a position to be embroiled in potential conflicts of interests; for instance, remuneration schemes cannot reproduce the performance of the business lines for which a particular Compliance Unit carries out its compliance tasks. Finally, the compliance staff should be granted access to the necessary information in order to execute their tasks on their own initiative and be free to report to senior management on any irregularities or potential breaches.[17]

As regards the Compliance Function responsibilities, the Basel Report outlines the main areas. These are: advice on single legal and regulatory matters; education of internal personnel on specific topics related to compliance issues; identification, assessment, and measurement of the compliance risks associated with a firm's business activities; monitoring and testing of the compliance risk and the reporting thereof to the senior management; liaison with external public (supervisors and lawmakers) and private bodies (self-regulatory associations).

The 2005 Basel Report was ensued by the 2006 IOSCO Report on the "Compliance Function at Market Intermediaries".[18] The IOSCO Report is much more detailed than the Basel Report but it follows the same features. It stems from the then Principle 23—now Principle 31—of the Objectives and Principles of Securities Regulation:

> Market intermediaries should be required to establish an internal function that delivers compliance with standards for internal organization and operational conduct, with the aim of protecting the interests of clients and their assets and ensuring proper management of risk, through which management of the intermediary accepts primary responsibility for these matters.[19]

The IOSCO Report outlines eight principles. The first one is the establishing and definition of a Compliance Function in market intermediaries. Importantly, IOSCO states the Function's key tasks (identify, assess, advise on, monitor, and report on the firm's compliance with regulatory requirements), but it recognizes that the concrete organization of the Function changes[20] on the basis of the firm's "nature, scale and complexity of its business".[21]

The second principle is the "Role of Senior Management and the Governing Authority". The former is responsible for the establishment and maintenance of a Compliance Function and its related procedures in order to "achieve compliance with securities regulatory requirements".[22] The latter is requested to liaise with the Senior Management and obtain information on the actual effectiveness of the firm's Compliance Function, even directly from the Function itself.

The third principle concerns the Function's independence and ability to act. The Function should be granted adequate budget and compensation for its personnel, not be subject to improper influence from the business, and have unrestricted access to both senior management and, in particular, the Governing Authority. Finally, "self-compliance" (when someone carries out compliance assessments on their own business activities) should be avoided.[23]

The fourth principle regards the important point of the Qualification of Compliance Personnel. Given the wide range and different nature of the Function's responsibilities, the personnel should have the necessary skills, and cutting-edge knowledge and expertise. In this regard, different backgrounds (i.e., not only legal or statistical) are needed.[24]

The fifth principle is about the assessment of the effectiveness of the Compliance Function. In practice, this is usually left to the Internal Audit, which assesses the entire control structure of a firm. However, even external parties can be asked to perform an independent review of the Compliance Function on a periodic basis.[25]

The sixth principle concerns the Regulators' Supervision. Public authorities are requested to assess the supervisees' internal Compliance Function and bring enforcement actions in case deficiencies are detected. This implies that public regulators must be endowed with directive examinations and sanctioning powers.[26]

The seventh principle regards cross-border compliance arrangements. This is particularly important for transnational banking and financial institutions. In this case, the Compliance Function cannot only focus on the firm's home jurisdiction but, instead, should be able to identify and assess the regulatory requirements of the jurisdictions where business is undertaken.[27]

The last principle is about the Outsourcing of the Compliance Function. IOSCO does not seem to favor this option even if it does not state that it is "forbidden" (which would not be possible given the soft nature of the document!). However, IOSCO reminds that in case of outsourcing of certain compliance tasks, a firm still retains full legal liability and accountability before the regulator.[28]

7.2 The Compliance Function Under the EU Law of Investment Services

Under the EU law of investment services, the Compliance Function is regulated by both hard- and soft-law measures. Regarding the former, MiFID I, MiFID II, and the 2006 Commission Directive implementing MiFID I, and the brand-new Commission Delegated Regulation 2017/565,[29] provide for a stable legal framework concerning the Compliance Function in investment firms and in banks licensed to perform investment services. The latter, instead, refer to guidelines adopted by the EBA and the ESMA. Significantly, both the Basel Committee 2005 Report and the IOSCO 2006 Report are consistent with the EU approach and, being adopted soon after MiFID I, it is not groundless to assume that the EU lawmaker and the two international standard setters had mutually influenced each other.[30]

Article 13 of MiFID I already provided for a general legal framework on which the "Compliance Function" could legally rest since it stated that an "investment firm shall establish adequate policies and procedures sufficient to ensure compliance of the firm" and "shall have sound [...] internal control mechanisms". The same language has been reproduced by Article 16 of MiFID II on organizational requirements even if its content is much denser and specifically takes into account the potential issues arising from the specific position of an investment firm in the product governance flow, namely, whether it is a manufacturer or a distributor (Chap. 4).

More specifically, the 2006 Commission Directive implementing MiFID I[31] provided for a concrete, detailed set of provisions on organizational requirements and procedures, including the Compliance Function (even if the fashion in which the Compliance Function is concretely organized changes on firm-by-firm basis).[32] In this regard, Article 6 was fully dedicated to Compliance and highlighted that Member States had to require investment firms to "establish, implement and maintain adequate policies and procedures designed to detect any risk of failure by the firm to comply with its obligations" so as to "enable the competent authorities to exercise their powers effectively". Alike what had already been stated by the 2005 Report of the Basel Committee, the compliance measures and procedures should be developed by taking into account the nature and the complexity of the business: the bigger and more complex the business, the larger and more sophisticated its Compliance Function. Public authorities would thus not accept a shallow "window-dressing" that provides appearance of legitimacy of the applicable regulatory requirements,[33] without a concrete embedding of rules into (monitored) internal processes and their gist being absorbed as part of the firm's compliance culture.[34]

The key point was that the 2006 Commission Directive introduced a legally binding requirement on the establishment and maintenance of a permanent and effective Compliance Function tasked with the two key responsibilities concerning MiFID I investment services and the conduct-of-business rules thereof. The first one is the monitoring and regularly assessment of the adequacy and effectiveness of the compliance measures and procedures and the addressing of any deficiencies encountered. The second one is advising and assisting the internal staff responsible for performing investment services and activities for which the firm has been authorized (Article 6.2).

To put the Compliance Function in a position to effectively carry out its tasks, firms were required to: grant the necessary authority, resources, expertise, and access to all relevant information; appoint a chief compliance officer responsible for the entire Function; ensure that compliance staff are not involved in the execution of the services they monitor; make sure that the remuneration policies and schemes for the compliance staff cannot be designed in a way to compromise their objectivity (Article 6.3).

In 2011, the EBA issued its "Guidelines on Internal Governance"[35] for credit institutions and investment firms. In this document, the EBA confirms the necessary establishment of a permanent and effective Compliance Function in each regulated institution and defines, coherently with the 2005 Basel Report, the Compliance risk as "the current or prospective risk to earnings and capital arising from violations or non-compliance with laws, rules, regulations, agreements, prescribed practices or ethical standards".[36]

EBA Guidelines require the adoption and implementation of a compliance policy to be communicated to all staff of the institution, the observance of such policy, and the reporting to the management body (which is usually the Board) of the management of the compliance risk.[37] Furthermore, EBA highlights the importance of the appointment of a person responsible for the entire function (even though this can be calibrated on the basis of the complexity and the size of the institution) and the duty for the Compliance Function to advise the management body.[38] Finally, the European Authority stresses the need to assess possible impacts of any regulatory developments, and verify whether new products and procedures comply with the applicable legal environment.[39]

Within its supervisory convergence responsibility, in 2012 the ESMA issued "Guidelines on certain aspects of the MiFID compliance function requirements".[40] In this document, ESMA designs quite a detailed skeleton of a financial firm's internal Compliance Function with the aim to promote "convergence in the interpretation of, and supervisory approaches to, the MiFID"[41] requirements (thus related to investment services), which reveals the quasi-enforcement nature of the Compliance Function.[42] Importantly, even if the senior management is responsible for a firm's ultimate compliance with the law, the Compliance Function is established to support them in fulfilling this duty.

The Guidelines confirm the approach already set out by the Basel Committee and followed by the EBA, by defining Compliance as the "function within an investment firm responsible for identifying, assessing, advising, monitoring and reporting on the investment firm's compliance risk",[43] which is the risk that an investment firm fails to comply with its obligations. Interestingly, the Guidelines frame the compliance risk within a firm's MiFID-related responsibilities by specifying that it is the risk to comply with MiFID duties "and the respective national laws, as well as the applicable standards set out by ESMA and competent authorities". This is due to the fact that the Guidelines have been adopted within the remit of MiFID, even if the Compliance Function's duties are not limited to the obligations stemming from MiFID and MiFID-related domestic regulations, but they also cover further legislation such as PRIIPs and Prospectus.

A Compliance Function must handle the compliance risk through a proportionality-grounded, risk-based approach, which implies that "non-material risks may receive minimal compliance attention".[44] In so doing, a compliance risk assessment[45] is to be carried out in order to detect those areas where risks are higher, address the focus and the scope of the Function's activities, and balance the correct allocation of the Function's resources. The public regulator should take into account the risk-based approach also in a lenient fashion before enacting sanctions because "[i]mposing penalties on firms is pointless when the firms have done all they could to support compliance and identify wrongdoing: Such a response is unjust, and does not deserve support".[46]

Consistently with what is already set out by the Basel Committee's Report, the IOSCO Report, the 2006 Commission Directive, and the EBA Guidelines, also the ESMA Guidelines confirm the Compliance Function's main responsibilities and key organizational requirements. The former are the adoption and the execution of a monitoring program (including the overseeing of the complaints-handling process); the issuance of reports on the effective compliance within the firm; and the execution of advisory and training activities,[47] from which often derives the task of drafting an internal Code of Conduct/Code of Ethics that outlines the firm's core values.[48] The latter are the appropriate allocation of resources and the Function's permanence, independence, and possibility of outsourcing.[49]

ESMA highlights the importance of the actual monitoring and controlling activity—shaped by the risk-based assessment—as it is where the Compliance Function behaves like an internal "cop" to investigate (both desk-based and on-site) and detect breaches of the applicable laws, in particularly on the part of the operative units executing the so-called first-level controls. This is why an oversight of the internal complaints-handling procedures is very important in order to promote investor protection and overcome those smaller infringements that can be resolved directly within the firm. Furthermore, through the information coming from internal complaints-handling procedures, the Compliance Function can better map where its intervention is necessary and have a deeper effect on employees' behavior with an enhancement of the firm's compliance culture.[50]

The reporting activity—initially addressed to the senior management—is strictly linked to the monitoring and controlling activity. It aims at giving a description of the firm's control environment and a summary of the risks identified, the material breaches detected, and the related remedial actions that the business units are to undertake to mitigate and overcome such risks and breaches. Reporting the proposed remedial actions is particularly important because, on the one hand, these prove the effectiveness of the monitoring activity; and, on the other hand, they may lead to internal disciplinary actions in case the business unit staff involved do not comply.

The advisory and training activity is a cornerstone for the Compliance Function and it is the main means to spread a culture of compliance within a firm. The key pillars of a firm's culture of compliance are often spelled out in a formal Code of Conduct/Code of Ethics written by the Compliance Function itself. In a very regulated and complex market like the one of the provision of investment services, staff working within an investment firm must have the necessary knowledge and awareness not only of the products sold but also of the related legal requirements and ethical values.[51] The Compliance Function, thus, must take care of the business staff's training and advisory needs (and carry out the related assessments) on a regular, ongoing, and even ad hoc basis, and be proactively involved in all strategic decisions and new business models in order to supply compliance expertise and advice, as it is the case in the PG and complaints-handling procedures. Importantly, in case Compliance's recommendations fall unheard, this should be documented. If resistance from the business in terms of regulatory compliance occurs, then it would be cautiously justified for the Compliance staff even to "amplify the threat of regulatory enforcement in order to raise managers' awareness and cooperation".[52]

On the organizational side, the ESMA highlights that the Compliance Function must be effective (being provided with the necessary authority, skilled staff, and budget); permanent (i.e., established as a Function able to perform its tasks on a permanent basis and this should be set out by an ad hoc "compliance policy" lining out competences and responsibilities); and independent (from both the monitored business units and the senior management; protection of whistleblowers[53]).

Effectiveness of the Compliance Function cannot be impaired when all or part of the Function is outsourced. In this regard, ESMA clarifies that even if the outsourcing of the Compliance Function is possible, this does not alter the Function's duties and that the ultimate responsibility rests on a firm's senior management's shoulders and that the firm should be able to monitor whether the outsourced activities are adequately conducted.

The principle of proportionality informs the fashion the Compliance Function is to be built up. Indeed, the actual arrangement of the organizational requirements of the Function may change according to types of investment services provided and the activities executed or the scope and volume of such services and activities. Importantly, ESMA clarifies how an investment institution should avoid combining the compliance function with the Internal Audit, due to the fact that the latter is tasked with overseeing the former and this may compromise Compliance's effectiveness and independence.[54] In a similar fashion, Compliance staff cannot be involved in the activities they monitor.

Furthermore, ESMA clarifies that only smaller investment firms should apply the so-called proportionality exemption[55] and combine the Legal department and Compliance Function as it may yield many conflicts of interest difficult to detect and disentangle.[56] This solution, indeed, is likely to hinder independence in the case of larger and more complex institutions. Importantly, the use of the "proportionality exemption" should be assessed by the competent public authority.

Indeed, the last point worth noting is the power the ESMA requests to be granted to competent public authorities to review the way investment firms organize their internal Compliance Function. This applies not only during a firm's filing for authorization but also in the course of ongoing supervision. A public supervisor must take into account the resources allocated to the Compliance Function, its risk-based methodology approach, and its independence status within the firm.

In 2014, the ESMA published a "Guidelines compliance table"[57] summarizing the intention of the competent authorities to comply with the 2012 Guidelines. More significantly, as of the time of writing, the ESMA is conducting a peer review of the 2012 Guidelines under the Supervisory Convergence Work Programme 2016 (2016 SCWP)[58] in order to assess the degree of incorporation of the Guidelines into the national watchdogs' supervisory practices. This is particularly important to ESMA in order to gain a grounded understanding of how domestic regulators liaise with their supervisees' Compliance Functions given the core position it plays in the correct unfolding of the EU law on investment services (compliance as rule-embedder).

Based on the professional experience of the author, it can be said that do not only regulated supervisees strongly need clarity from regulators in such a period of regulatory blossoming,[59] but also the latter need in-house information from the former's Compliance Function in order "to devise adequate policies and interventions",[60] in a context where more "informal enforcement practices"[61] may be employed. An open dialogue—which is different from a mere lobbying activity, sometimes carried out by an ad hoc advocacy office—between supervisors and supervisees strongly contributes to a more effective implementation of the rules and it is by now accepted by the financial industry as a normal practice.[62] A responsive and reachable regulator would much more easily achieve its enforcement objectives, which should not be the enactment of sanctions but an improvement in the supervisees' conduct of business.[63]

Against this backdrop, the authority-Compliance Function liaison is indispensable. On the one hand, official soft-law documents from and unofficial talks with public regulators "telling" the Compliance Function what it ought to do are very welcome because they de facto reduce the compliance risk (even if the regulatory splinter dramatically increases).

On the other hand, liaising with a responsive and reachable regulator does not mean an ex ante approval of the specific processes and procedures embedding public-law rules within an investment firm (let alone the ex ante approval of single products, which is not even hinted by the MiFID Product Governance itself).[64] It is obvious that public authorities can still sanction an investment firm, regardless of whether they are reachable for regulatory interpretations and clarifications.

It can be said that, on the one hand, supervisees can legitimately ask their regulator for clarity on the interpretation of rules. On the other hand, they should understand that each time a public authority takes a stance on an interpretative issue, it exposes itself to a public reputational risk which, at the end, is a political risk due to the governmental nature of the authority. Based on the professional experience of the author, both the industry and public authorities sometimes seem to lack a "wearing the other's shoes" approach. The industry (first of all, the Compliance Function) should understand that, given the current highly regulated financial markets, it is practically improbable to obtain a clear interpretation of each rule beforehand.[65] Public authorities, on their side, should limit what Professor MacNeil defines as the traditional deterrence-based approach on enforcement and embrace a compliance-based style centered on an open dialogue with the industry.[66]

Not only does a compliance-based approach create a mutual trust relationship that leads supervisors and supervisees to exchange important information, but it is also reassuring for compliance officers. Such a psychological aspect is substantially due to the fact that the Compliance Function staff is aware that their role is to make the firm abide by the law and conform to ethical standards.

The supervisor-supervisee liaison is a key component of the compliance-based style of enforcement. Against this backdrop, the ESMA can indirectly influence the supervisees' Compliance Functions through its efforts on supervisory convergence. When this is partnered with the increasing regulatory leeway of ESMA Single Rulebook under MiFID II,[67] the importance of the European Authority has acquired vis-à-vis European investment firms becomes clearer.

Within this framework, the MiFID II 2017 Commission Delegated Regulation, indeed, makes some significant harmonizing improvements to the features of European firms' Compliance Function, incorporating most of the recommendations put forward by the ESMA in 2012 and definitively abandoning an ineffective "box-ticking" approach.[68] The Compliance Function must now *permanently* monitor and *regularly* assess not only measures and procedures but also policies, that is, internal written rules transposing into a firm's internal procedures the regulatory requirements provided by the law on the provision of investment services, first of all MiFID conduct-of-business rules. This is an example of the rule-embedder role of the Compliance Function.

Furthermore, the top management body,[69] that is, usually the Board, is now responsibilized, and specularly, the Compliance Function is made more independent from the senior management.[70] This is due to the fact that the Compliance Function has now the clearer duty to yearly report to the management body an update on the "implementation and effectiveness of the overall control environment for investment services and activities, on the risks that have been identified and on the complaints-handling reporting as well as remedies undertaken or to be undertaken" (Article 22, 2c). In addition, the Compliance Function must report "on an ad-hoc basis directly to the management body where it detects a significant risk of failure by the firm to comply with its obligations under" MiFID.

This is a move from the previous situation when the ESMA was more leaning toward a strict relationship between the Compliance Function and the senior management mostly due to "different corporate legal structures in Member States".[71] The move toward the Board makes the Compliance Function more independent from the business and reinforces its take on senior management (and its "tone from the top" approach).[72]

Importantly, under MiFID II the complaints-handling procedures are now a key task of the Compliance Function. Indeed, Article 22.2(d) Delegated Regulation puts the Function officially in charge of monitoring the internal complaints-handling processes aimed at addressing minor claims from investors before these go to an ADR scheme or, in the worst-case scenario, before a court. Indeed, Article 22.2 closes by clarifying that in its general controlling and regulatory advising activities, the Function must establish a risk-based monitoring program which takes into account all areas of the firm's investment services and activities, "including relevant information gathered in relation to the monitoring of complaints handling".

Interestingly, investors' complaints are officially viewed by MiFID II Commission Delegated Regulation as a valuable source of relevant information in the context of the Function's general monitoring responsibilities (and, thus, for public authorities when carrying out administrative enforcement investigations).[73] Investors' complaints can be used to test how internal processes and procedures work in practice; to feed and refine the Compliance Function's methodology for setting such internal processes and procedures[74]; and, finally, to permeate the entire firm structure with a culture of investor protection,[75] which should be grounded on the fiduciary duty toward customers.

To be fully effective, the monitoring activity should be theoretically linked to sanctioning powers, but so far the Compliance Function has not formally been endowed with the powers to directly impose sanctions on single employees. Nevertheless, in case a misconduct is detected when carrying out controls, the senior management is to be alerted—and also the management body if the breach is serious—and a remediation measure is often agreed (sometimes with the intervention of the Internal Audit, in its capacity of third-level control Function). Importantly, should the addressees of the remediation measure (persistently) fail to comply with the terms of the measure, then the Human Resources Department would have solid grounds for the adoption of individual disciplinary actions under applicable domestic employment laws. So, although not provided by MiFID, the activity of Compliance Function can indirectly lead to internal sanctions.

Finally, it should be highlighted how the 2004 MiFID I, the 2005 Basel Committee Report, the 2006 Commission Directive, the 2011 EBA Guidelines, the 2012 ESMA Guidelines, the 2014 MiFID II, and the Commission Delegated Regulation 2017/565 substantially put forward the very same leitmotif with little, if no, contradictions. This seems to show that the path paved by the European rulemaker was not only persevered over time, but it has been even shared at transnational level.[76]

A little difference, for instance, is the ESMA's more intransigent take on the possibility to merge the Compliance Function with other internal structures, in particular the Internal Audit Function and the Legal department. The first point has been recently corroborated by Article 24 of the Commission Delegated Regulation 2017/565 that reaffirms that the Audit Function must be independent from any other Functions in order to be in a position to "examine and evaluate the adequacy and effectiveness of the investment firm's systems, internal control mechanisms and arrangements".

The second point is mainly due to the safeguard of the independence of the Compliance Function itself.[77] The Legal department is usually in charge of drafting contractual clauses a client cannot change but to which s/he is asked to agree for the service to be provided. In doing so, the Legal department does not have to be in a position of independence from the business units (those providing the actual services) but it is asked to mitigate/minimize the litigation risk[78] by forecasting prospective lawsuits (even if the actual contractual liability can only stem from single—either individual or collective—civil proceedings). On the contrary, the Compliance Function shall be independent in order to be able to monitor the correct implementation of the regulatory requirements, even those expressed through (public-law) business-of-conduct rules.

However, the boundary is not clear-cut and both offices are asked to cooperate. There are crossing topics where collaboration is necessary. This is the case, for instance, of mandatory information disclosure. Here the Compliance Function shall first analyze the requirements set forth by public regulation and, then, cooperate with the Legal department to ensure such requirements are reflected into the contractual relationship material with customers. Interestingly, information disclosure is clearly linked to litigation risk, and firms may choose a formalistic approach to the former to minimize the latter.[79] To do that, strong cooperation and a similar mindset between the Compliance Function and the Legal department is necessary.

Within the leeway defined by the law, financial firms are free to choose the internal organization that best fits their business. However, generally speaking, the Legal department usually *looks at* the contract itself, trying to mitigate litigation risk—taking into account contractual rules such as those dealing with unfair terms—while meeting the business needs when, for instance, drafting a contract which combines two different services. The Compliance Function must, instead, make sure that investor protection provisions (public-law business-of-conduct and/or product rules) introduced by statutes are always complied with when services and products are being supplied and sold. For this reason, the establishment of the Compliance Function has been provided by MiFID I/II and the Function has been endowed with regulatory advice and monitoring tasks directly the Law.[80]

7.3 The Emergence of the Compliance Function as a Rule-Embedder and Enforcement-Frontliner

Given the booming of rules in the current regulatory era, the importance of Compliance Function profession is augmenting.[81] Chapter 3 offers several concrete examples of when the Compliance Function steps in and what it does to cope with the compliance risk and connected reputational risk. These examples are a mark of how important the Compliance Function has become for European investment firms. Coherently, the profession is becoming increasingly stabilized and organized.[82]

Even if an efficient and forward-looking compliance needs different skills,[83] many compliance employees and officers should have a legal background.[84] This is because compliance employees—especially if they work in transnational financial institutions and were trained in different jurisdictions—can use such background as a lowest common denominator or—to some extent—as lingua franca. When in pan-European banks the holding company's Compliance Function speaks the same language of the controlled companies' Compliance Functions, a common culture of compliance is more easily established and disseminated. Furthermore, legal skills are necessary to understand the changes currently occurring in the European legal landscape.

Legally speaking, MiFID I and—even more so—MiFID II clearly depict the trend transforming rules traditionally belonging to the domestic private-law domain into substantive Europeanized supervisory standards,[85] a trend likely to be corroborated by the new supervisory (product intervention) powers of the ESMA, now able to potentially coordinate its regulatory powers with its enforcement responsibilities. The emergence of the Compliance Function is linked to the emergence of the EU regulatory law.

For instance, MiFID I/II introduce many informative requirements to be conveyed through contractual documents. In the pre-MiFID era, the very same contractual documents were scarcely (if not at all) publicly regulated at EU level and they had to be usually drafted and validated by the internal Legal department (with the support of external law firms, if any). In the post-MiFID era, instead, the Compliance Function has taken over the responsibility to carry out a regulatory analysis of such documents and, then, validate them. This is because contractual documents have become—either directly or indirectly—object of ad hoc public regulation.

As explained in Chaps. 3 and 4, the adoption of MiFID II has marked an expansion of EU law in both qualitative (more detailed norms) and quantitative (a greater deal of provisions) terms, reinforcing the regulatory grip on relationships traditionally governed by private law. Firms are required to abide by efficiency-aimed public-law rules and their internal policies and procedures must be consistent with such rules. The Compliance Function must contribute that nothing is hastily baked since instability at micro level may pose, at macro level, a dire menace to the entire financial system. The effect is twofold: the wider and more detailed the regulation; the broader the responsibility of the Compliance Function and the more residual the role of the traditional Legal department, whose by-now main task[86] is often counseling on and drafting ex ante standardized contracts with a view to removing or, at least, mitigating litigation risk.[87]

The emergence of the Compliance Function at the expenses of the traditional Legal department is, thus, coherent with and corroborates key assumptions of the European Regulatory Private Law Theory. First, it marks the shift in justice paradigm. The old Legal department focuses on the traditional private-law tools, whose justice paradigm is distributive justice.[88] Instead, the recently established Compliance Function focuses on public-law rules aimed at increasing market fairness and efficiency, whose justice paradigm is access justice/*Zugangsgerechtigkeit*.[89] Second, it proves the "merging" of pre-contractual information and contract conclusion through a network of mandatory informational duties embedded in standardized contracts under the monitoring of the Compliance

Function, whose role is to avoid administrative sanctions, thus indirectly improving market functioning.

Importantly, meeting the expectations of a public authority does not necessary imply being protected from civil claims. The two risks—litigation and compliance—belong to two different legal realms: administrative sanctions and contractual liability. Being administratively compliant means designing internal processes and procedures and effectively implementing them according to the expectations of a public enforcer. This may help a firm avoid systemic cases of customers' claims due to the fact that such processes and procedures are geared at saving and promoting customers' welfare.

However, a civil claim may anyhow occur in case of individual misconducts (an employee breaching internal policies); misconducts not covered by existing processes and procedures; or even in cases of conduct compliant with internal policies, which are themselves compliant with the regulatory requirements, but such requirements do not cover circumstances from which civil liability may arise. Thus, the two risks/legal realms stay apart, even if under an increasingly regulatory European private law the litigation risk (lawsuits before civil courts) is gradually embraced by the compliance risk (the risk of financial loss, first of all administrative fines, stemming from non-obedience with laws and regulations). The gauge of the extent to which the two risks can be addressed separately from one another is left to domestic legislation to decide as it mirrors the relationship between private-law remedies on contractual liability and MiFID public-law conduct-of-business. Significantly, the increasing importance of the compliance risk gives grounds to the assertion that enforcement in Europe keeps steadily moving toward public enforcement and away from the judiciary.[90]

The emergence of the Compliance Function seems to corroborate the evidence that public, rather than private, enforcement is privileged by the EU lawmaker due to the position of public supervisors over market players and the possibility they have to implement efficiency-geared policy strategies to navigate intermediaries through the unchartered waters of globalized financial markets. Against this backdrop, the Compliance Function becomes a *quasi-enforcement institution*[91] for very minor infringements in the contemporary plethora populated by several actors—such as regulatory agencies, courts, and ADR bodies created by the current legal landscape.[92]

The "quasi" is due to the fact that the Compliance Function operates *within* a firm but it is—de facto—the first addressee of both the European (*soft*) regulatory production and any prospective enforcement actions coming from NCAs.[93] The "quasi" generates the ambivalence[94] of the Compliance Function, which, on the one hand, must work to morph a firm's culture toward an ethics of compliance. But, on the other hand, it is itself integrated into a firm's already existing bureaucracy. In order to accomplish its mission, the Compliance Function should be able to detach itself from its own internal bureaucracy without losing grip on the business reality. The Compliance Function should create its own subsystem that, autopoietically,[95] makes it a bridge between the inward centers of decision-making and the outward law enforcement mechanisms, ultimately acting as an internalized law enforcement mechanism.[96]

The nature of the Compliance Function as an internalized law enforcement mechanism is clear when it is analyzed vis-à-vis the features used by MiFID to describe public-law enforcement mechanisms. Both public authorities and the internal Compliance Function must be endowed with the necessary capacity and resources to carry out the assigned tasks, following a risk-based approach in assigning resources.[97] Being in a position to investigate and, where necessary, wield sanctioning powers mirrors the Compliance Function's powers to request for information and its duty to report any actual or potential breaches. The outsourcing of specific tasks is possible only when certain strict requirements are met. Finally, independence of supervisory agencies from economic actors in order to avoid conflicts of interest mirrors the independence of the Compliance Function staff vis-à-vis the senior management and business lines on which they carry out their tasks.

For the same reason, a centralized structure under the control of the Chief Compliance Officer is more apt to guarantee the Function's independence, even if working among the business lines also means having a more concrete chance to spread a culture of compliance.[98] However, even a centralized Function can be able to spread a culture of compliance if it is well structured and its personnel are well trained and have a good understanding of the business and of the internal code of ethics and conduct. Indeed, alongside formal attributes, also "informal aspects and personal characteristics will ultimately determine how organisational power is exercised"[99] by the Compliance Function: the stricter the public enforcer, the severer the internal Compliance Function.

The Compliance Function's quasi-enforcement tools have twin nature. On the one hand, the Compliance Function has the responsibilities of identifying, monitoring, measuring, and assessing the compliance risk. This is supervisory function in stricto sensu and the Compliance Function acts as the enforcement-frontliner.[100] On the other hand, the Compliance Function is asked to advise and train those business lines upon which it exercises its monitoring tasks and, often, to liaise with external bodies, that is, industry associations[101] and, above all, public regulators. Similarly, public regulators ought to hear the voice of consumers and that of the industry when planning financial literacy programs[102] and before adopting a new or amending/abrogating existing regulations. This is supervisory function in sensu lato.

A practical example of how the activities of the Compliance Function may reproduce/overlap those of a public enforcement mechanism as provided by the EU Law is the use of investment services contracts to assess compliance with the law. The Compliance Function is required to adopt and oversee the business lines' compliance with the internal policy on the MiFID suitability test to be performed when executing advisory-based investment services. The front-office personnel must correctly execute the test—as framed by internal policies and procedures—and are assessed on these grounds. The result of the test informs the performance of the services contract between the investment service provider and its clients. Similarly, a public enforcer uses contracts stipulated between a client and their service provider to assess the observance of the law on the part of the latter.[103] In both cases a contract and its terms (conduct of business—suitability and appropriateness) are used to assess whether compliance with the law has been achieved or not (administrative enforcement of private law[104]). The following table compares the characteristics of the Compliance Function with those of public supervisors under the EU law (Table 7.1):

In order to monitor complex and intricate markets and due to limited public resources, public supervisors need to be "helped out" by their own supervisees, who very often have the necessary expertise, skills, knowledge, and information on technical issues. The architecture of a financial firm's internal controls should be viewed and interpreted against this

Table 7.1 Public supervisors versus internal compliance function

Public supervisors under MiFID	Internal compliance function under MiFID
Remit and responsibilities specifically granted by and organized under the law.	Establishment provided by the law. Firms de facto have quite a large leeway on how to organize the Compliance Function and its connections to other functions and departments (such as audit and legal).
Independence from external actors.	Independence of the Compliance Function vis-à-vis the business lines on which it carries out its tasks.
Allocation of the necessary capacity and resources.	Allocation of the necessary capacity and resources.
Power to investigate and, where necessary, exercise a wide range of sanctioning powers, such as cease-and-desist orders and pecuniary fines.	Powers to request information and duty to report any actual or potential breaches. There are no sanctioning powers mirroring the ones granted to public authorities, but failure to meet the conditions of the remediation plans set out after a compliance investigation may lead to individual disciplinary actions on the part of the human resources department.
Performing an analysis of possible breaches of applicable regulations.	Responsibilities of identifying, monitoring, measuring, and assessing the compliance risk.
The outsourcing of specific tasks (possible only where certain strict requirements are met).	The outsourcing specific tasks (but the Chief Compliance Officer and the firm are still responsible for the fulfillment of requirements: Outsourcing a task does not imply the outsourcing of the related responsibilities).
Open consultations for the adoption of a new regulation or amendments to an existing one.	Liaison with external bodies, such as industry associations and public regulators (depending on a firm's internal organization, lobbying activities can be carried out by an ad hoc advocacy office. However, the input of the Compliance Function as regulatory expert should always be provided).
Financial literacy programs for investors.	Training and education programs for internal personnel.

backdrop. In particular, the Compliance Function is conceived as the internal office meant to smooth the regulatory kinks out, in order to avoid these are simply smoothed over (and the spirit of regulation is overlooked, with detriment to the firm's compliance culture).

The Compliance Function could be seen as complementary to public enforcement[105]—or gatekeeper[106]—directly implanted *within* a firm, built to address (very) minor infringements on investor protection before these become major infringements. Against this backdrop, the oversight responsibility partially shifts from public agencies toward the shoulders of market participants. This is so for two main reasons: the first one is resource-led—public enforcement is expensive unless (big) fines directly go to the enforcing agencies; the second one is concrete-led—a firm's internal offices are supposed to know better the firm itself and, then, be faster in solving actual or potential breaches.[107] This is representative of the sharing of responsibilities between the enforcement institutions and their changing functions under EU law.[108]

Coherently with this design, MiFID II, on the one hand, requires the Compliance Function to set up and monitor intra-firm complaints-handling procedures for those cases of very minor infringements of investor protection rules that can be resolved within a firm. On the other hand, MiFID II requires Member States to establish ADR schemes (Chap. 6) for minor infringements that cannot be dealt with internally by a firm but are too small to be brought before a court and cannot be resolved through public enforcement due to its punitive/deterrent and non-compensatory nature.[109]

With the increased independence granted to the Compliance Function under MiFID II (report to the Board instead of senior management), the EU lawmaker seems to be aware of the intrinsic conflict of interests[110] of an internal control function designed to fill the vacuum between the law-on-the-books (EU-made public rules) and the law-in-action[111] directly *within* a firm. Should a Compliance Function act as watchdog even if it appears as apparently moving against its own firm's business interests (substantial outsource of public enforcement)? Instead, should it try to re-frame regulatory requirements in an apparent, formal way so that their ripple effects on the business are minimized (formal outsource of public enforcement, with window-dressing[112] risks)? Given its key role in the Product Governance internal processes, should the Compliance Function adopt a conservative approach likely to stifle financial innovation,[113] or should it be audacious and stretch the normative requirements to let innovation flow?

The answer does not only affect the way business is carried out in the financial industry, but it also concerns the penetration of (public) law into a firm's daily activity and business conduct (traditionally belonging to private law). As said above, the more penetrating the ex ante regulation into private-law relationships (and into its ex post remedies by means of courts using EU-originated public rules to interpret national private laws),[114] the more intrusive the role of the Compliance Function (at the expenses of the traditional Legal department).

Furthermore, it could be assumed—but empirical research is needed in this regard—that the higher the risks involved in a financial instrument, the higher the chance of a customer submitting an internal complaint: this is why the responsibility of the Compliance Function has severely increased under MiFID II. The Function is, indeed, in the crossroads between education (with the purpose of spreading a culture of compliance within the firm); Product Governance (at the genesis of financial innovation and aimed at reducing mis-selling cases when the risk profile of a financial instrument does not fit a specific clients cluster); internal complaints-handling processes (for very minor infringement of investor protection rules); and ADR schemes (to solve minor infringements without going before a court). The result is that under MiFID II the Compliance Function is likely to play a key strategic role in investment firms: not being able to solve prospective mis-selling cases or disputes might endanger a firm's reputation and hit its revenues.

It is very difficult to strike a balance between two opposite points: on the hand, the Compliance Function is an internal Function of a firm and it is instinctively incentivized to be profit-oriented. However, on the other hand, its goal is to make the firm compliant with the applicable laws, even if this implies a loss of potential revenues. The ultimate goal of the Compliance Function is to reduce risk at the micro level (avoiding administrative fines for the single investment firm) in order to indirectly stabilize the market at the macro level and, thus, contribute to its efficient functioning. If this is true, then the effective Compliance Function the EU rulemaker has in mind should be placed in a position to curb—when necessary—business profitability from the inside and, eventually, act as a substantial outsourcing of public enforcement.

Notes

1. Geoffrey P. Miller, "The Compliance Function: An Overview," in *Law and Economics Working Papers—Paper 393*, ed. New York University (2014). At 1.
2. Ibid. At 4.
3. The Institute of Internal Auditors provides for a clear picture of the "Three Lines of Defense mode": operational management; Compliance and Risk Management Functions; Internal Audit. The Institute of Internal Auditors, "Iia Position Paper: The Three Lines of Defense in Effective Risk Management and Control," ed. The Institute of Internal Auditors (2013).
4. Iris H-Y Chiu, *Regulating (from) the Inside: The Legal Framework for Internal Control in Banks and Financial Institutions* (London: Bloomsbury Publishing, 2015). At 271.
5. Elisa Dellarosa and Ranieri Razzante, *Il Nuovo Sistema Dei Controlli Interni Della Banca. Riprogettare Il Sistema Dopo Basilea 2, Mifid E Compliance: Riprogettare Il Sistema Dopo Basilea 2, Mifid E Compliance* (Milan: FrancoAngeli, 2010). At 75.
6. Defined by professor Miller as "close cousins". Miller. At 1.
7. Dellarosa and Razzante. At 245. The Internal Audit "is responsible for checking on the entire organization, including senior managers, in order to ensure that policies and procedures are being observed and shortcomings in the organization's internal controls are identified and promptly fixed". Miller. At 4.
8. Basel Committee on Banking Supervision, "Compliance and the Compliance Function in Banks," (2005).
9. "The Basel Committee's framework is meta-regulatory in nature as it provides a high-level framework for the objectives and responsibility of the compliance function, and a skeletal profile of the procedural nature of tasks that the compliance function should undertake." Chiu. At 44.
10. It is not an easy task to categorize "soft-law" measures because several "instruments may be included within this generic term for a number of reasons: (1) they have been articulated in non-binding form according to traditional modes of law-making; (2) they contain vague and imprecise terms; (3) they emanate from bodies lacking international law-making authority; (4) they are directed at non-state actors whose practice cannot constitute customary international law; (5) they lack

any corresponding theory of responsibility; (6) they are based solely upon voluntary adherence, or rely upon non-judicial means of enforcement." Christine Chinkin, "Normative Development in the International Legal System," in *Commitment and Compliance: The Role of Non-Binding Norms in the International Legal System*, ed. Dinah Shelton (New York: Oxford University Press, 2000). At 30.

11. As Professor Chiu states: "The Basel Committee's recommendations in 2005 provided considerable detail as to how the compliance would carry out its responsibilities." Chiu. At 43.
12. Basel Committee on Banking Supervision. At 7.
13. Miller. At 2.
14. Basel Committee on Banking Supervision. A very good definition is also given by the "Risk Management Disclosures 2015" by Deloitte Investment Services Limited: "Compliance risk is the risk of financial loss, including fines and other penalties, which arises from non-compliance with laws and regulations of the state. The risk is limited to a significant extent due to the supervision applied by the Compliance Officer, as well as by the monitoring controls applied by the Company." Deloitte Investment Services Limited—Wealth Advisory Services, "Risk Management Disclosures 2015," (2015).
15. On internal controls other than Compliance (Risk Management, Internal Audit), see: Chiu.
16. Basel Committee on Banking Supervision.
17. Ibid.
18. International Organization of Securities Commissions—IOSCO, "Compliance Function at Market Intermediaries," (Madrid 2006).
19. International Organization of Securities Commissions—IOSCO, "Objectives and Principles of Securities Regulation" (Madrid 2010).
20. Differences in organizational implementation of the Compliance Function have been examined by: Chiu. At 41. Also: Giuliana Birindelli and Paola Ferretti, "Compliance Risk in Italian Banks: The Results of a Survey," *Journal of Financial Regulation and Compliance* 16, no. 4 (2008).
21. IOSCO. At 7.
22. Ibid. At 10.
23. Ibid. At 12.
24. Ibid. At 14.
25. Ibid. At 15.
26. Ibid. At 17.

27. Ibid. At 19.
28. Ibid. At 21.
29. *Commission Delegated Regulation 2017/565/Eu.*
30. On the EU and IOSCO: Antonio Marcacci, "The Eu in the Transnational Financial Regulatory Arena: The Case of Iosco," in *Private Law in the External Relations of the Eu*, ed. Marise Cremona and Hans-Wolfgang Micklitz (Oxford: Oxford University Press, 2016).
31. *Commission Directive 2006/73/Ec.*
32. Even if with reference to the US context, Professor Miller points out that: "distribution of responsibility is often unclear and varies from organization to organization." Miller. At 5.
33. Kimberly Krawiec, "Cosmetic Compliance and the Failure of Negotiated Governance," *Washington University Law Quarterly* 81, no. 2 (2003). At 542. On codes of ethics and mere window-dressing: Christopher Hodges, *Law and Corporate Behaviour: Integrating Theories of Regulation, Enforcement, Compliance and Ethics* (Oxford: Hart Publishing, 2015). At 689.
34. On the same wavelength, Professors Parker and Nielsen state that the "implementation of formal systems alone is not enough if those systems do not promote and connect to a "culture" of compliance within each organization". Christine Parker and Vibeke Lehmann Nielsen, "Corporate Compliance Systems: Could They Make Any Difference?," *Administration & Society* 41, no. 1 (2009). At 27. Similarly, Professor Lenglet states that "Not only because there is usually a point where the compliance officer looks at his own interests as an individual, and cannot go too far in an apparent fulfilment of compliance while bending the spirit of the rules (this would be the point where merely conformist compliance clashes with personal ethics), but also because compliance officers are regulatory pathfinders." Marc Lenglet, "Ambivalence and Ambiguity: The Interpretive Role of Compliance Officers," in *Finance: The Discreet Regulator*, ed. Isabelle Huault and Chrystelle Richard (London: Palgrave Macmillan, 2012). At 72.
35. European Banking Authority—EBA, "Eba Guidelines on Internal Governance," (2011).
36. Ibid. At 43.
37. Ibid. At 43.
38. Ibid. At 43.
39. Ibid. At 43.

40. European Securities and Markets Authority—ESMA, "Final Report—Guidelines on Certain Aspects of the Mifid Compliance Function Requirements—Esma/2012/388," (2012).
41. Ibid. At 23.
42. Professor Miller speaks of a "form of internalized law enforcement". Miller. At 1.
43. ESMA. At 23.
44. Ibid. At 7. Professor Chiu rightly points out that "A risk-based approach may then excuse a firm for ignoring risks of an improbable nature which could become a 'black swan'." Chiu. At 58.
45. ESMA. At 6.
46. Hodges. At 706. Professor Hodges also states that: "Given the existence of multiple sub-units within businesses, each with individual functions, groups of individuals, and sub-cultures, an idea that the behaviour of every internal group can be absolutely controlled so as to conform to every required norm, whether the source of control emanates from an internal or even less—external position, appears highly unlikely." At 507–508.
47. In more details, according to ESMA, a Compliance Function's main responsibilities are to determine which risks must be monitored and/or for which an advice activity is necessary; the adoption of a monitoring program—coherent with the priorities identified by the risk-based approach—covering all areas of the firm's investment activities and services; issuance of reports to senior management describing the implementation and effectiveness of the executed controls, a summary of the identified risks alongside the remedies undertaken; and the advisory obligations, such as providing support for staff training. ESMA.
48. Professor Hodges speaks about core values "which are shared by all members of the workforce [...and] form an ideology that is enduring and able to be applied consistently in different trading and geographical circumstances, whilst operational goals are constantly examined and develop". Hodges. At 508.
49. In more detail, according to ESMA, a Compliance Function's main organizational requirements are: being endowed with the appropriate allocation of resources (depending on the size and complexity of the business); the permanence of the Function (tasks and responsibilities must be performed on a permanent basis); independence (a firm must ensure compliance staff are in a position to act independently when

performing their tasks); possibility of outsourcing (but a firm's senior management must ensure that all the requirements are fulfilled and is held responsible for this). ESMA.

50. In the words of Professors Parker and Nielsen: "[C]ompliance culture can also refer to values, beliefs, and attitudes within an organization that support compliance with the law. This is much more subjective and difficult to measure. We hypothesized that these values would also affect the way compliance is managed in practice and actual compliance behavior." Parker and Nielsen. At 27–28.
51. Professor Hodges rightly points out: "Compliance with the norms of a social system is produced by ethical values and systems. It is not produced directly by rules (laws) and their enforcement. Systems can be risk-based, but behaviour is value-based." This is why the ethical role played why the Compliance Function is important. Hodges. At 699.
52. Sharon Gilad, "Institutionalizing Fairness in Financial Markets: Mission Impossible?," *Regulation & Governance* 5, no. 3 (2011). At 311.
53. In the words of Professor Miller: "Whistleblowers are key to compliance because they come forward with private information about violations." Miller. At 15.
54. ESMA. At 34.
55. Ibid. At 34.
56. On the pros of the separation between Compliance and Legal: Miller. At 9.
57. European Securities and Markets Authority—ESMA, "Guidelines Compliance Table—Esma/2013/923," (2014).
58. "Esma Supervisory Convergence Work Programme 2016—Esma/2016/203," (2016).
59. Professor Hodges states—and the practical experience of the author strongly confirms so—that: "Most businesses expected regulators to provide some help and guidance rather than simply enforcing rules and regulations only." Hodges. At 516.
60. Luca Enriques and Gerard Hertig, "The Governance of Financial Supervisors: Improving Responsiveness to Market Developments," (ECGI—Law Working Paper No. 171/2010, 2010). In their groundbreaking paper on the governance of financial supervisors, Professors Enriques and Hertig highlight the importance of contacts between Regulators and representatives of the regulated industry. In order to reduce the risk of capture, the authors claim that "[f]ull disclosure

about lobbying activities involving supervisory authorities, possibly including periodic disclosure by anyone engaged in lobbying activities, would be useful to discourage excessive familiarity between supervisors and the industry they regulate and allows for public control over this delicate relationships". At 26–27.

61. "If 'informal' means of enforcement suggests going beyond reliance on formal infringement combined with sanctioning, our research shows that all authorities—even the self-consciously more legalistic ones—engage in informal enforcement practices." Yane Svetiev and Annetje Ottow, "Financial Supervision in the Interstices between Private and Public Law," *European Review of Contract Law* 10, no. 4 (2014). At 542.
62. On the basis of the discussions held and the opinions exchanged by the author with his peers.
63. In their seminal article Professors Svetiev and Ottow use the expression of "cooperative implementation" which very well fits the reality of the financial industry. Svetiev and Ottow. At 503.
64. Professor Moloney rightly points out the: "strong implication of regulatory approval which product authorization, in particular, can generate and the related risk that the product provider takes less care in monitoring the product". Niamh Moloney, "Regulating the Retail Markets," in *The Oxford Handbook of Financial Regulation*, ed. Niamh Moloney, Eilís Ferran, and Jennifer Payne (Oxford: Oxford University Press, 2015). At 762.
65. Compliance staff should understand that "The job of policymakers is to devise a system which minimizes total costs of norm enforcement and norm violations. This task cannot be performed scientifically. Lawmakers are not structural engineers. When it comes to designing a compliance system much is done by intuition and guesswork". Miller. At 2.
66. On deterrence-based versus compliance-based: Iain MacNeil, "Enforcement and Sanctioning," in *The Oxford Handbook of Financial Regulation*, ed. Niamh Moloney, Eilís Ferran, and Jennifer Payne (Oxford: Oxford University Press, 2015). At 282–283.
67. As implicitly admitted by ESMA itself at the end of 2016: "The number of legislative mandates in the coming years might be lower than the ones that ESMA had to face in the past with the major reforms to the key financial regulations (MIFID, MAR, etc.). However, ESMA expects to continue to develop the single rulebook activity." European Securities and Markets Authority—ESMA, "2017 Work Programme—Esma/2016/1419," (2016). At 17.

68. On overcoming the box-ticking approach, Professor Hodges states that: "In many businesses, compliance management has been elevated from 'box ticking' so as to provide a paper trail as a defence mechanism against external interference to a very senior function, capable of shutting down non-compliant operations on their own authority." Hodges. At 512.
69. According to MiFID II Article 4.1(36): "'[M]anagement body' means the body or bodies of an investment firm […] which are appointed in accordance with national law, which are empowered to set the entity's strategy, objectives and overall direction, and which oversee and monitor management decision-making and include persons who effectively direct the business of the entity." According to MiFID II Article 4.1(37): "'[S]enior management' means natural persons who exercise executive functions within an investment firm […] and who are responsible, and accountable to the management body, for the day-to-day management of the entity, including for the implementation of the policies concerning the distribution of services and products to clients by the firm and its personnel."
70. Professor Chiu reports that "Some commentators are of the view that the independence of the compliance function may be compromised by accountability to senior management, and advocate that the Chief Compliance Officer should report directly to the Board". *See*: Chiu. At 52–53. Professors Hoffman, Neill, and Stovall clearly opt for compliance officers to "(1) be hired by, (2) be fired by, and (3) report directly to the corporate board of directors rather than company management." W. Michael Hoffman, John D. Neill, and O. Scott Stovall, "An Investigation of Ethics Officer Independence," *Journal of Business Ethics* 78, no. 1–2 (2008). At 87. MiFID II seems to be following this path, already paved by the SEC for mutual funds: "In the case of an investment company, the chief compliance officer will report directly to the fund board." Securities and Exchange Commission—SEC, "Release Nos. Ia-2204—Final Rule: Compliance Programs of Investment Companies and Investment Advisers," (2004).
71. "[A] few respondents […] proposed that only a supervisory board (not senior management) should be able to appoint and replace the compliance officer. ESMA cannot accommodate this suggestion because of the different corporate legal structures in Member States" ESMA. At 13.
72. In this direction, also the Group of Thirty in their 2012 "Toward Effective Governance of Financial Institutions" Report: "It is for the

board of directors to articulate and senior executives to promote a culture that embeds these values from the top to the bottom of the entity. Culture is values brought to life." G30, "Toward Effective Governance of Financial Institutions," (2012). At 25.

73. Article 22.2 of Commission Delegated Regulation 2017/565: "[T]he compliance function shall conduct an assessment on the basis of which it shall establish a risk-based monitoring programme that takes into consideration all areas of the investment firm's investment services, activities and any relevant ancillary services, including relevant information gathered in relation to the monitoring of complaints handling. The monitoring programme shall establish priorities determined by the compliance risk assessment ensuring that compliance risk is comprehensively monitored."
74. In this regard, MiFID-provided intra-firm complaints-handling procedures seem to share a similar connotation with self-enforcement in transnational private regulation where this is used to provide "input for the private regime about the way in which the standards function in practice. Accordingly, enforcement activities are employed as an instrument to test and verify the viability of standards and update the standards when necessary". Paul Verbruggen, *Enforcing Transnational Private Regulation: A Comparative Analysis of Advertising and Food Safety* (Cheltenham: Edward Elgar, 2014). At 299. However, in the transnational private regulation realm, complaints-handling is very often run by extra-firm certification bodies and trade associations. *See*: ibid. At 8, 39, 188, 192.
75. English and Hammond rightly point out that: "Compliance should be able to oversee cultural change and assist with its implementation. Leadership for cultural change must, however, remain firmly with the firm's board and senior management, without which cultural change is unlikely to happen." Stacey English and Susannah Hammond, "Cost of Compliance," (Thomson Reuters, 2016). At 12.
76. On the transnationalization of European Regulatory Private Law, see: Antonio Marcacci, "European Regulatory Private Law Going Global? The Case of Product Governance," *European Business Organization Law Review* 18, no. 2 (2017).
77. An empirical research shows that even before the adoption of MiFID II the Compliance Function was often split from the Legal Department. Paola Musile Tanzi et al., "Managing Compliance Risk after Mifid," *Journal of Financial Regulation and Compliance* 21, no. 1 (2013). At 55.

78. The "litigation risk" can be defined as "the risk of a contracting party that it will be required to enforce its rights by litigation, or defend proceedings brought by a counterparty". Richard Fentiman, *International Commercial Litigation* (Oxford: Oxford University Press, 2010). At 51. Viewed from the prospective of an investment firm, the litigation risk is the likelihood to be brought before a court by one or more of its counterparties/clients. As very well defined by the "Risk Management Disclosures 2015" by Deloitte Investment Services Limited: "Litigation risk is the risk of financial loss, interruption of the Company's operations or any other undesirable situation that arises from the possibility of non-execution or violation of legal contracts and consequentially of lawsuits. The risk is restricted through the contracts used by the Company to execute its operations." Deloitte Investment Services Limited—Wealth Advisory Services.
79. On mandatory disclosure and the risk of litigation: Luca Enriques and Sergio Gilotta, "Disclosure and Financial Market Regulation," in *The Oxford Handbook of Financial Regulation*, ed. Niamh Moloney, Eilís Ferran, and Jennifer Payne (Oxford: Oxford University Press, 2015). At 532.
80. Paul Verbruggen has carried out an excellent analysis on the phenomenon of compliance with private (i.e., predominantly established by private, non-state actors) transnational regulations on fields other than investment services (advertising and food safety), the institutional design of privately run tools to enforce such regulations, and the relationship these tools have with public enforcement mechanisms. Paul Verbruggen highlights how the interplay between public and private enforcement mechanisms pushes firms toward compliance of such standards, for instance, through formal delegation of public regulatory powers or by means of contractual clauses that oblige firms to comply with industry practices codes and SROs' decisions. *See*: Verbruggen. At 149–150). The kind of compliance this book deals with is, instead, an internal Function that investment firms are *legally required* (by MiFID) to establish in order to observe public-law rules on investment services (provided by MiFID itself). This does not mean that if an industry-created rule is officially endorsed by the ESMA or incorporated in ESMA's regulatory standards, then the internal Compliance Functions of European MiFID firms are free to ignore it due to the fact that it was not originally enacted by a public body, but quite the contrary (see also

Verbruggen on increasingly difficult to distinguish between public and private regulation, at 296). However, given the extremely high level of public regulation of the investment services market in the post-crisis Europe, the overlap between public and private regulation is substantially reduced in favor of the former, so that the Compliance Function's focus for investment services is—de facto—almost entirely on public regulation. The landscape in the United States is, instead, different given the role played by SROs in developing the suitability rule and arbitration schemes for broker-dealers (on the differences between the EU and the United States in this regard, see Chaps. 5 and 6). Having said that, further research on the intersections between the post-crisis EU Law of Financial Services and Markets and the transnational public and private regulation covering the same field is worth executing, with particular attention being paid to the normative production of the International Organization of Securities Commission—IOSCO.

81. In the words of Mills and Haines: "As the financial industry grows in complexity, there is a corresponding broadening in the scope of the Compliance function, which also makes it a more interesting area in which to work." Annie Mills and Peter Haines, *Essential Strategies for Financial Services Compliance, 2nd Edition* (Chichester: Wiley, 2015). At 43. Also Miller: "The importance of compliance and the extent of liability for its failure have greatly increased over the past decades." Miller. At 2. On the development of compliance professional in general: "The increased importance of compliance programs has led to the development of compliance professionals. This development is supported by several nonprofit organizations and networks devoted to compliance professionals. [...] Some universities are also starting to offer certificate programs in compliance." Cristie Ford and David Hess, "Can Corporate Monitorships Improve Corporate Compliance?," *Journal of Corporation Law* 34, no. 3 (2009). At 692.
82. Chiu. At 47. Mentioning: Andrew Newton, *The Handbook of Compliance: Making Ethics Work in Financial Services* (Mind into Matter, 2002). At European level, it is worth mentioning the TECC—The European Compliance Conference as the "Europe's leading, international conference for Compliance Professionals" TECC, "The European Compliance Conference—Tecc," http://www.shcog.co.uk/tecc-intro/. The author joined the 2016 edition of the TECC as speaker and Conference Planning Committee Member.

83. In the words of Professor Chiu: "Empirical research carried out in European banks shows that compliance personnel generally have a diverse range of business knowledge and skills." Chiu. At 50. However, English and Hammond state that: "There is a lack of good compliance skills in the marketplace, which has driven up the costs of senior compliance professionals in particular and may in turn make it harder for firms (and indeed regulators) to keep hiring ever more compliance staff." Stacey English and Susannah Hammond, "Cost of Compliance 2016," (Thomson Reuters, 2016). At 6.
84. "Meanwhile, the Compliance Function has a strong connection with law and legal practice; it takes legal training to decipher applicable laws and regulations." John B McNeese, "The Ethical Conflicts of the Hybrid General Counsel and Chief Compliance Officer," *Georgetown Journal of Legal Ethics* 25, no. 3 (2012). At 683.
85. Olha O. Cherednychenko, "Public and Private Enforcement of European Private Law in the Financial Services Sector," *European Review of Private Law* 24, no. 4 (2015). At 626.
86. Even if lawsuits are often handled by external law firms, the Legal department usually exercises a supervisory task.
87. It could be added that a more demanding and complex regulatory framework requires a robust and full-fledged Compliance Function, whose costs can be more easily borne by bigger firms. A very interesting article published on the SEC website and dealing with regulatory compliance costs and related economies of scale benefitting larger firms is the following: C. Steven Bradford, "Does Size Matter? An Economic Analysis of Small Business Exemptions from Regulation," *The Journal of Small & Emerging Business Law* 8, no. 1 (2004).
88. "Most, not all, continental private legal orders enshrine the idea of social justice, understood as distributive justice, which has to be preserved in private law matters, both in contract and in tort law" Hans-Wolfgang Micklitz, "The Visible Hand of European Regulatory Private Law—the Transformation of European Private Law from Autonomy to Functionalism in Competition and Regulation," *Yearbook of European Law* 28, no. 1 (2009). At 9. In addition: "Social Justice and Access Justice in Private Law," in *EUI Working Paper Law 2011/2*, ed. European University Institute (Florence 2011).
89. "Social Justice and Access Justice in Private Law."

90. Hans-Wolfgang Micklitz and Andrea Wechsler, eds., *The Transformation of Enforcement: European Economic Law in Global Perspective* (Oxford: Hart Publishing Limited, 2015). Marta Cantero-Gamito, "Dispute Resolution in Telecommunications: A Commitment to out-of-Court," *European Review of Private Law* 25, no. 2 (2012). At 420.
91. The term "enforcement institution" is employed by Professor Micklitz: Hans-Wolfgang Micklitz, "The Transformation of Enforcement in European Private Law: Preliminary Considerations," *European Review of Private Law* 4 (2015). Professor Miller defines the Compliance Function as "a form of internalized law enforcement". Miller. At 1.
92. In the words of Professor Micklitz: "In the old world of contract and tort, two parties litigated against each other and it was for the courts to decide this interpersonal conflict, that is, if the parties decided to involve courts rather than find a solution outside the court system by way of arbitration. The Europeanization of private law has considerably altered the landscape of law enforcement." Micklitz, "The Transformation of Enforcement in European Private Law: Preliminary Considerations." At 497.
93. However, it is still the firm—either individually or though industry organizations—to *formally* interact with other enforcement actors.
94. Term also used by Lenglet.
95. Professor Hodges on multiple modes of corporate organizations, also mentioning Teubner. Hodges. At 503–506.
96. As rightly pointed out by Professor Miller. Miller.
97. "The risk-based approach is one that emphasises cost-effectiveness, so that resources can be deployed in areas susceptible to the highest risk and therefore used efficiently." Chiu. At 58.
98. "A decentralised structure also provides an opportunity for compliance officers to spread the compliance culture to front line units, embedding the compliance objective within business culture more effectively." Ibid. At 56.
99. Ibid. At 63.
100. Professor Hodges pushes the edge even further: "Both structures and language have historically divided regulation and enforcement (by officials) from compliance (by firms internally). They are the same thing, and should be joined up both functionally, operationally and linguistically. […] It is time that the internal and external functions were regarded as holistic and joined up. They need to operate in partnership.

[...] Regulatory systems should not be thought of as opposing public officials and firms. Both of those groups—but also many other stakeholders—are all integral parts of learning and hence compliance and successful systems." Hodges. At 700–701.

101. For example, the important Association for Financial Markets in Europe (AFME). (https://www.afme.eu/).
102. On financial education initiatives: European Commission, "Review of the Initiatives of the European Commission in the Area of Financial Education," (2011). Examples of these initiatives organized by public authorities can be found in the program launched in 2007 by the Italian Ministry of Education, University and Research (MIUR) and the Bank of Italy called "Financial Education for Schoolchildren". Organisation for Economic Co-operation and Development—OECD, "Italy: Financial Education for Schoolchildren," http://www.financial-education.org/Italy_Financial_Education_for_Schoolchildren.html.
103. On the use of contract terms for public enforcement reasons: Olha O. Cherednychenko, "The Regulation of Retail Investment Services in the Eu: Towards the Improvement of Investor Rights?," *Journal of Consumer Policy* 33, no. 4 (2010). At 410.
104. Hans-Wolfgang Micklitz, "Administrative Enforcement of European Private Law," in *The Foundations of European Private Law*, ed. Roger Brownsword, et al. (Oxford-Portland: Hart Publishing, 2011).
105. As, in a similar fashion, class actions are viewed as "'supplemental' to SEC enforcement and necessary because of constraints on the SEC's resources". Maria Correia and Michael Klausner, "Are Securities Class Actions "Supplemental" to Sec Enforcement? An Empirical Analysis," in *The Tel Aviv International Conference in Accounting—The Leon Recanati Graduate School of Business Administration* (Tel Aviv 2012). At 2.
106. Chiu.
107. As rightly pointed out by Professor Miller: "[A]n external norm enforcer may not have the resources or the ability either to detect violations or to devise an effective system of sanctions. The organization has the knowledge and the ability to more effectively perform these tasks. It therefore makes sense for institutions to police themselves—to carry out a compliance operation." Miller. At 2.
108. Micklitz, "The Transformation of Enforcement in European Private Law: Preliminary Considerations."

109. On the difference between public and private enforcement remedies: Olha O. Cherednychenko, "Public Supervision over Private Relationships: Towards European Supervision Private Law?," ibid. 22, no. 1 (2014).
110. On the role of the Compliance Function, Professor Lenglet rightly raises the point of its ambivalent role. On the one hand, the law mandates the Function's establishment to ensure compliance with the Law; but, on the other hand, it is located within a firm and, thus, it cannot underestimate the firm's interests. In the words of Professor Lenglet: "Compliance officers therefore occupy an ambivalent position in the organization: they are hired by the company, and therefore attached to it 'from the inside', but also perform control and reporting duties required by external regulators." Lenglet. At 63.
111. On a similar wavelength, Professor Lenglet states that "compliance officers contribute to internal regulation of the market by managing the *ambiguity* arising from the encounter between texts and contexts". Ibid. At 61.
112. Krawiec. At 542.
113. On the importance of financial innovation: Emilio Avgouleas, "Regulating Financial Innovation," in *The Oxford Handbook of Financial Regulation* ed. Eilís Ferran, Niamh Moloney, and Jennifer Payne (Oxford: Oxford University Press, 2015). At 679.
114. On the resistance of national laws against the intrusion of European regulatory contract law: Olha O. Cherednychenko, "Financial Consumer Protection in the Eu: Towards a Self-Sufficient European Contract Law for Consumer Financial Services?," *European Review of Contract Law* 10, no. 4 (2014). At 486–491. Also: Federico DellaNegra, "The Private Enforcement of the Mifid Conduct of Business Rules. An Overview of the Italian and Spanish Experiences," ibid.

Bibliography

Auditors. The Institute of Internal. "Iia Position Paper: The Three Lines of Defense in Effective Risk Management and Control." The Institute of Internal Auditors, 2013.

Avgouleas, Emilio. "Regulating Financial Innovation." In *The Oxford Handbook of Financial Regulation*, edited by Eilís Ferran, Niamh Moloney and Jennifer Payne. Oxford: Oxford University Press, 2015.

Basel Committee on Banking Supervision. "Compliance and the Compliance Function in Banks." 2005.

Birindelli, Giuliana, and Paola Ferretti. "Compliance Risk in Italian Banks: The Results of a Survey." *Journal of Financial Regulation and Compliance* 16, no. 4 (2008): 335–51.

Bradford, C. Steven. "Does Size Matter? An Economic Analysis of Small Business Exemptions from Regulation." *The Journal of Small & Emerging Business Law* 8, no. 1 (2004): 1–37.

Cantero-Gamito, Marta. "Dispute Resolution in Telecommunications: A Commitment to Out-of-Court." *European Review of Private Law* 25, no. 2 (2012): 387–420.

Cherednychenko, Olha O. "The Regulation of Retail Investment Services in the EU: Towards the Improvement of Investor Rights?". *Journal of Consumer Policy* 33, no. 4 (2010): 403–24.

———. "Financial Consumer Protection in the EU: Towards a Self-Sufficient European Contract Law for Consumer Financial Services?". *European Review of Contract Law* 10, no. 4 (2014a): 476–95.

———. "Public Supervision Over Private Relationships: Towards European Supervision Private Law?". *European Review of Private Law* 22, no. 1 (2014b): 37–68.

———. "Public and Private Enforcement of European Private Law in the Financial Services Sector." *European Review of Private Law* 24, no. 4 (2015): 621–47.

Chinkin, Christine. "Normative Development in the International Legal System." In *Commitment and Compliance: The Role of Non-Binding Norms in the International Legal System*, edited by Dinah Shelton. New York: Oxford University Press, 2000.

Chiu, Iris H.-Y. *Regulating (from) the Inside: The Legal Framework for Internal Control in Banks and Financial Institutions*. London: Bloomsbury Publishing, 2015.

Commission Delegated Regulation 2017/565/Eu.

Commission Directive 2006/73/Ec.

Correia, Maria, and Michael Klausner. "Are Securities Class Actions "Supplemental" to SEC Enforcement? An Empirical Analysis." In *The Tel Aviv International Conference in Accounting – The Leon Recanati Graduate School of Business Administration*. Tel Aviv, 2012.

DellaNegra, Federico. "The Private Enforcement of the MiFID Conduct of Business Rules. An Overview of the Italian and Spanish Experiences." *European Review of Contract Law* 10, no. 4 (2014): 571–95.

Dellarosa, Elisa, and Ranieri Razzante. *Il Nuovo Sistema Dei Controlli Interni Della Banca. Riprogettare Il Sistema Dopo Basilea 2, MiFID E Compliance: Riprogettare Il Sistema Dopo Basilea 2, MiFID E Compliance*. Milan: FrancoAngeli, 2010.

Deloitte Investment Services Limited – Wealth Advisory Services. "Risk Management Disclosures 2015." 2015.

EBA, European Banking Authority. "EBA Guidelines on Internal Governance." 2011.

English, Stacey, and Susannah Hammond. "Cost of Compliance." Thomson Reuters, 2016.

Enriques, Luca, and Sergio Gilotta. "Disclosure and Financial Market Regulation." In *The Oxford Handbook of Financial Regulation*, edited by Niamh Moloney, Eilís Ferran and Jennifer Payne. Oxford: Oxford University Press, 2015.

Enriques, Luca, and Gerard Hertig. "The Governance of Financial Supervisors: Improving Responsiveness to Market Developments." ECGI – Law Working Paper No. 171/2010, 2010.

ESMA, European Securities. "Guidelines Compliance Table – Esma/2013/923." 2014.

ESMA, European Securities and Markets Authority. "Final Report – Guidelines on Certain Aspects of the MiFID Compliance Function Requirements – Esma/2012/388." 2012.

———. "ESMA Supervisory Convergence Work Programme 2016 – Esma/2016/203." 2016a.

———. "2017 Work Programme – ESMA/2016/1419." 2016b.

European Commission. "Review of the Initiatives of the European Commission in the Area of Financial Education." 2011.

Fentiman, Richard. *International Commercial Litigation*. Oxford: Oxford University Press, 2010.

Ford, Cristie, and David Hess. "Can Corporate Monitorships Improve Corporate Compliance?". *Journal of Corporation Law* 34, no. 3 (2009): 679–738.

G30. "Toward Effective Governance of Financial Institutions." 2012.

Gilad, Sharon. "Institutionalizing Fairness in Financial Markets: Mission Impossible?". *Regulation & Governance* 5, no. 3 (2011): 309–32.

Hodges, Christopher. *Law and Corporate Behaviour: Integrating Theories of Regulation, Enforcement, Compliance and Ethics*. Oxford: Hart Publishing, 2015.

Hoffman, W. Michael, John D. Neill, and O. Scott Stovall. "An Investigation of Ethics Officer Independence." *Journal of Business Ethics* 78, no. 1–2 (2008): 87–95.

IOSCO, International Organization of Securities Commissions. "Compliance Function at Market Intermediaries." Madrid, 2006.

———. "Objectives and Principles of Securities Regulation". Madrid, 2010.

Krawiec, Kimberly. "Cosmetic Compliance and the Failure of Negotiated Governance." *Washington University Law Quarterly* 81, no. 2 (2003): 487–544.

Lenglet, Marc. "Ambivalence and Ambiguity: The Interpretive Role of Compliance Officers." In *Finance: The Discreet Regulator*, edited by Isabelle Huault and Chrystelle Richard. London: Palgrave Macmillan, 2012.

MacNeil, Iain. "Enforcement and Sanctioning." In *The Oxford Handbook of Financial Regulation*, edited by Niamh Moloney, Eilís Ferran and Jennifer Payne. Oxford: Oxford University Press, 2015.

Marcacci, Antonio. "The EU in the Transnational Financial Regulatory Arena: The Case of Iosco." In *Private Law in the External Relations of the EU*, edited by Marise Cremona and Hans-Wolfgang Micklitz. Oxford: Oxford University Press, 2016.

———. "European Regulatory Private Law Going Global? The Case of Product Governance." *European Business Organization Law Review* 18, no. 2 (2017): 305–32.

McNeese, John B. "The Ethical Conflicts of the Hybrid General Counsel and Chief Compliance Officer." *Georgetown Journal of Legal Ethics* 25, no. 3 (2012): 677–94.

Micklitz, Hans-Wolfgang. "The Visible Hand of European Regulatory Private Law – The Transformation of European Private Law from Autonomy to Functionalism in Competition and Regulation." *Yearbook of European Law* 28, no. 1 (2009): 3–59.

———. "Administrative Enforcement of European Private Law." In *The Foundations of European Private Law*, edited by Roger Brownsword, Hans-Wolfgang Micklitz, Leone Niglia and Stephen Weatherill, 563–92. Oxford-Portland: Hart Publishing, 2011a.

———. "Social Justice and Access Justice in Private Law." In *EUI Working Paper Law 2011/2*, Florence: European University Institute, 2011b.

———. "The Transformation of Enforcement in European Private Law: Preliminary Considerations." *European Review of Private Law* 4 (2015): 491–524.

Micklitz, Hans-Wolfgang, and Andrea Wechsler, eds. *The Transformation of Enforcement: European Economic Law in Global Perspective*. Oxford: Hart Publishing Limited, 2015.

Miller, Geoffrey P. "The Compliance Function: An Overview." In *Law and Economics Working Papers – Paper 393*. New York University, 2014.

Mills, Annie, and Peter Haines. *Essential Strategies for Financial Services Compliance*. 2nd ed. Chichester: Wiley, 2015.

Moloney, Niamh. "Regulating the Retail Markets." In *The Oxford Handbook of Financial Regulation*, edited by Niamh Moloney, Eilís Ferran and Jennifer Payne. Oxford: Oxford University Press, 2015.

Newton, Andrew. *The Handbook of Compliance: Making Ethics Work in Financial Services*. London: Mind into Matter, 2002.

OECD, Organisation for Economic Co-operation and Development. "Italy: Financial Education for Schoolchildren." http://www.financial-education.org/Italy_Financial_Education_for_Schoolchildren.html.

Parker, Christine, and Vibeke Lehmann Nielsen. "Corporate Compliance Systems: Could They Make Any Difference?". *Administration & Society* 41, no. 1 (2009): 3–37.

SEC, Securities and Exchange Commission. "Release Nos. Ia-2204 – Final Rule: Compliance Programs of Investment Companies and Investment Advisers." 2004.

Svetiev, Yane, and Annetje Ottow. "Financial Supervision in the Interstices Between Private and Public Law." *European Review of Contract Law* 10, no. 4 (2014): 496–544.

Tanzi, Paola Musile, Giampaolo Gabbi, Daniele Previati, and Paola Schwizer. "Managing Compliance Risk After MiFID." *Journal of Financial Regulation and Compliance* 21, no. 1 (2013): 51–68.

TECC. "The European Compliance Conference – TECC." http://www.shcog.co.uk/tecc-intro/.

Verbruggen, Paul. *Enforcing Transnational Private Regulation: A Comparative Analysis of Advertising and Food Safety*. Cheltenham: Edward Elgar, 2014.

8

Conclusions: The Unbridgeable Gaps with the United States and the Emergence of an Increasingly Self-Sufficient EU Regulatory Investor Protection Law

8.1 The Unbridgeable Gaps with the United States…

From a European perspective, the American system formally looks like the best legal construction to draw parallels from. Nevertheless, a comparison of the two structures of legal protection of retail investors soon brings to the surface the fault lines between the European Union and the United States and uncovers the existing unbridgeable gaps. The following synoptic table summarizes the main points of divergence between the EU and the United States as observed throughout the book (Table 8.1):

Chronologically speaking, the mismatch between the EU and the United States is evident. The US federal legal framework for investor protection was established in the 1930s, whereas the EU—due to obvious historical reasons—started legislating on this topic many decades later. More importantly, the reason which led to the enactment of federal rules was the reaction to the Great Depression and the commonly perceived need to make financial markets more transparent and to prevent frauds.[1] The European legislation in this field, instead, has always been conceived as a tool to establish a unified financial

© The Author(s) 2018

A. Marcacci, *Regulating Investor Protection under EU Law*,
https://doi.org/10.1007/978-3-319-90297-5_8

Table 8.1 EU versus the United States: comparative table

	The United States	EU
Chronology	As of 1930s at the federal level.	Substantially, as of 1990s–2000s after the adoption of the 1985 Commission's internal market white paper and the 1986 single European act.
Financial system	Market-based financial system.	Shift from bank-based to market-based financial system.
Leading paradigms	Disclosure paradigm mitigated by fiduciary duty (for investment advisers) or by SROs-developed conduct-of-business rules (for broker-dealers).	Disclosure paradigm mitigated by: 1. Ex ante public regulation of conduct-of-business rules traditionally governed by private-law 2. Ex ante public regulation of client categorization, 3. Ex ante public regulation of infra-firm processes to avoid mis-selling at the *micro* level, thus contributing to market efficiency at the *macro* level
Enforcement	Full-fledged public and collective private enforcement procedures at the federal level: Interplay between public and private tools. Federal rules on arbitration and industry-developed arbitration schemes.	Reliance on domestic EU-harmonized public enforcement. Infantile public enforcement at the European level. No collective private enforcement procedures at the European level. Light-touch harmonization of domestic ADRs.
Legal instrument	Common-law contract law. Federal/states' securities laws and regulations. SROs' rules.	Ex ante public regulation of private relationships traditionally governed by domestic private laws. No European civil code. [more recently: Increased centralization of detailed (second-level) regulation at EU level, see *sub-section b*]
Justice pattern	Market fairness as leading value.	Shift from social distributive justice enshrined in national private laws toward access justice. [more recently, toward "paternalistic access justice", see *sub-section b*]

market, particularly after the adoption of the Single European Act,[2] by trying to "embed market finance in the single market".[3]

In the United States—a market-based financial system—rules for the protection of investors in securities markets appeared as early as the 1930s. They mainly dealt with disclosure,[4] under the assertion that investors could play an active role and the more informed they are, the more rational investment decisions they (are supposed to) make.[5] In European countries, instead, attention was mainly paid to the banking system, where the "prudent banking saver" could rely on banks' stability, ultimately guaranteed by the state, under the assertion that a bank was a safety net for savings.[6]

Information disclosure is used by both legal systems but it stems from a different landscape, is differently mitigated, and is particularly relied on in the United States.[7] In the United States, disclosure for broker-dealers stems from statutory anti-fraud norms and SROs' rules on business conduct, whereas disclosure for investment advisers hinges upon their common-law fiduciary duty toward their customers.[8] In Europe, rules on disclosure are provided by regulatory law, enter into national private laws, and turn traditionally contract-law tools (contractual and pre-contractual documents on investment services and financial products) into supervisory tools. This can be defined as "administrative enforcement of private law"[9] or "European supervision private law",[10] basically depending on the stress over public enforcement of private law "versus" the European origin of the public instrumental use of private law.

On the same wavelength, disclosure is calibrated on the kind of customer the product is being advised/sold. MiFID I/II supply (public-law) rules on ex ante classification of customers through pre-defined categories, and the level of financial sophistication is realized before a potential investment recommendation takes place. This approach has been refined after the introduction of the Product Governance rules which provide for the establishment of internal processes and procedures managing the mandatory ex ante matching between sub-categories (clusters) of clients with similar features and financial products listed in catalogs according to their complexity and risk profile. The aim of PG's ex ante client-product matching is to overcome and/or mitigate inefficiencies at the *micro* level (mis-selling)[11] with a broader view of contributing to market efficiency at the *macro* level.

In the United States, client classification is "less-binding"[12] than in Europe with firms enjoying a more bottom-up leeway with no duty to inform customers about their categorization.[13] Interestingly, Professor Choi identifies four client categories based on sophistication criteria, which can by and large be compared to the MiFID eligible counterparties (issuer-level investors); professional clients (intermediary-level and aggregate-level investors); and retail clients (unsophisticated investors).[14] However, the US system clearly looks much more flexible than the European one and it is evident that the former more easily adapts to ex post enforcement, whereas the latter is created for ex ante public supervision.

Where the United States and the EU seem to share a regulatory convergence is on institutional investors. Under Article 30 of MiFID II, eligible counterparties are investment firms, credit institutions, insurance companies, UCITS and their management companies, and other financial and governmental institutions. Under Rule 501 of Regulation D[15] accredited investors are banking institutions, investment companies, financial institutions, and other businesses. However, even natural persons when exceeding certain worth thresholds can fall into the accredited investors' category. This is an important difference with MiFID, which would treat these investors as either professional or retail clients.[16]

Another crucial point of divergence between the EU and the United States is, actually, enforcement. The choice and methodology to choose among different enforcement tools or institutions[17] vary largely across jurisdictions, but it is by now obvious that the single market strategy of the EU leverages on public, rather than private, enforcement remedies. The privileging of the coordination of public enforcement procedures over the establishment of EU-wide public enforcement structures and private enforcement remedies can be ascribed to *constitutional* constraints,[18] as shown in Chap. 5. The result is that the difference between the EU and the United States is both in terms of structural public enforcement mechanisms—particularly because Europe does not have a proper "federal" supervisor/enforcer—and in terms of the private enforcement remedies available for supervisors and retail investors—due to the fact that the European Union has neither a federal jurisdiction nor European harmonized class action regimes.[19,20]

In Europe what matters the most is the integration of different financial sectors and the opening up of previously restricted local capital markets. In this framework, coordinated public enforcement rather than private enforcement seems to play the essential role of keeping markets efficient and opening access to operators. To achieve this aim, conduct-of-business rules are mostly used by public authorities as tools to sanction market players for their wrongdoings, thus indirectly affecting the relationship between retail investors and investment services providers.[21] This phenomenon can be perfectly framed in the ERPL theory.

A leading example is provided by the MiFID suitability, restricted only to the very sensitive areas of investment advice and portfolio management (the so-called advisory services). Unlike the US suitability rule, which can be employed in arbitration and private enforcement procedures,[22] MiFID I/II do not set forth any pan-European private remedies around its suitability and all private remedies are left to national legislation and enforced before domestic courts. The result is that MiFID suitability is, de facto, a tool for public enforcement in that it is "directed at ensuring the effective supervision over the compliance by investment service providers".[23]

Coherently with its public-law nature and supervision-leaning goal, the European suitability was introduced in 2004 through a full harmonization Directive. The evolution of the Prospectus legislation offers another clear example of how the EU law introduces and regulates tools that are used for public enforcement. In particular, the June 2017 Regulation mentions the fact that a prospectus can raise civil liability, but it does not address the issue of the harmonization of remedies at EU level. On the one hand, the Prospectus Regulation pushes the Union's competence in civil matters over the edge by delimiting civil liability,[24] but, on the other hand, remedies are still ensured by the Member States.

The evolution of the Prospectus legislation represents a mark of how far the ERPL has gone. It does show not only how deep the EU (public) law has dug into private law relationships but even the reasons justifying such inroads: the need to provide all European retail investors with a sufficiently fair level of disclosure. Nevertheless, even if the boundary has been pushed over the edge, the remedy foreseen by the EU law is still public and contract tools are still used for the administrative enforcement of private law.[25] In addition, the recent amplification in quantitative terms and the increased level of details of ESMA normative production under MiFID II (as shown in Chap. 7) may lead us to wonder whether national courts should/will somehow feel "bound" to use ESMA rules to fill open-ended private law norms.[26] However, this largely depends on the relationship between national private laws and the (EU) public law in each single Member State legal system.

The result is that the interplay between private and public enforcement tools used by the US federal financial supervisor is another telling point where Europe and the United States clearly diverge. Chapter 5 shows that the SEC "has a wide range of sanctions at its disposal"[27] and uses a complex set of public and private enforcement mechanisms to sanction violations of conduct-of-business rules, but conduct-of-business rules can be used also by investors in class actions and SROs' arbitration schemes. In Europe—"where legal centralism, strong public authorities and public ownership have [historically] left little room"[28]—instead, attention is largely focused on giving domestic authorities the powers to enforce conduct-of-business rules (even if Article 75 MiFID II introduces norms on ADRs, as shown in Chap. 6). The same rules, however, are not framed into a pan-European scheme for collective actions, since there is no pan-European class action at all. Coherently with the cooperation-based structure of the EU, it is not the ESMA but domestic supervisors to be entitled to sanction market operators in case of violations. However, since its inception, the ESMA has been gaining enforcement powers and the newly introduced MiFIR product intervention powers might be a boost for a federal-like enforcement mechanism.

Another point of divergence between the United States and the EU—strictly connected to a lack of enforcement interplay—is the reliance on contract law. In the United States, contract law works as a scaffolding onto which specific duties of business conduct are mounted.[29] The European Union, instead, cannot rely on a single common-law tradition and has no proper competence on contract law matters. Since there is no single, unified (or unifying) Civil Code,[30] the EU can only make Member States adapt their national civil codes/contract laws in order to ease private-law, commercial transactions and overcome barriers within the single market.[31] The tool employed is public regulation, which has become more and more penetrating over time: from minimum harmonization Directives to full harmonization Directives to Regulations.[32]

Finally, the EU is trying to reproduce the US market-based financial system by transforming its traditional bank-based system through the adoption of public-law rules.[33] The law contributes to wearing the old "prudent banking saver" with clothes tailored for the rational investor, who is "reasonably well informed and reasonably observant and circumspect"[34] to be able to make efficient investment decisions. The latter much better fits the evolution of the Anglo-American legal system, where "commercial law was needed to manage English trade internationally"[35] and market fairness is a leading value. Within this framework, retail investors are provided with all the information necessary to fully understand the product or service they undertake as if they were "rational maximizers of their own utility".[36] Disclosure as competitive transparency, which has always been the protection tool granted to institutional investors supposed to be able to make rational investment decisions when properly informed, has gradually been extended to reach the retail level. Within this model,[37] "There is no room for social justice as an eminent expression of a social welfare obligation [..., which it] is replaced by [...] 'access justice'—*Zugangsgerechtigkeit*",[38] coherent with the leading value of market fairness. Social distributive justice—developed as a social welfare obligation and embedded in Continental traditions—is viewed as having a curbing effect on the market.

The outcome of the comparison of the European and American structures of legal protection of retail investors shows how the policy choice made by the EU lawmakers— that is, preference of the market-based over the bank-based financial system—(in)directly leads to an attempted but limited Americanization of the EU law that seems to exist only at regulatory philosophy level. Such an attempt is, indeed, strongly incomplete. The EU has neither a single, common contract law nor a federal system of public (the ESMA is still far from being a federal fully fledged law-enforcer and regulator) and, in particular, private enforcement (where only national-based remedies can be employed) mechanisms apt to reproduce at Union level an interplay similar to that characterizing the US federal system.[39]

8.2 ...The Emergence of an Increasingly Self-Sufficient EU Regulatory Investor Protection Law

This book analyzes how the EU regulatory unfolding has, first, introduced regulatory measures aimed at transforming traditional banking savers into retail investors allegedly capable of making rational investment decisions, and, then, mitigated the rationality paradigm through duties on investment service providers (suitability and, in particular, product governance). The underlying factual difference between the traditional prudent banking saver and the legal prototype of the retail investor is the switch from (theoretically) riskless bank deposits to potentially more lucrative but also more risky investments. The model of utility-maximizer investors[40] capable of making rational investment decisions better suits the structure of a market-based financial system.

Within this context, European pieces of legislation first focused on disclosure as a "one-size-fits-all" solution to overcome the information asymmetry between retail investors and investment services providers, with the aim of correcting market failures generated by inefficient decisions and discouraging providers from employing unfair or deceptive practices,[41] which may erode investors' confidence and refrain them from entering financial markets. Since retail investors are thought to have neither the possibility to access the information necessary to understand the risk involved in a recommended investment, nor the time to acquire such information, the law "empowered [them] with information and basic rights [... so that they could be] aware of their responsibilities"[42] and feel ready to operate in securities markets.[43]

Unfortunately, mandatory information disclosure is also likely to generate the "perverse effect".[44] On the one hand, the law provides for written information to be complete, standardized, true, non-misleading, and accurate—as it is very well represented by the PRIIPs KID and the UCITS KIID. But, on the other hand, once this information is formally conveyed, even less sophisticated investors may be presumed to be able to make informed investment decisions with the result that disclosure may "be used against the investor".[45] The side effect of information disclosure is that it does not consider the difficulties arising when non-professional investors manage financial risk in uncertain conditions,[46] the issue of bounded rationality,[47] information overload,[48] and the limited cognitive skills[49] of less sophisticated investors, so that a document such as a security prospectus is likely to turn into a cumbersome hurdle for them.[50] Disclosure has definitely proved to be "a very limited tool given the behavioural weaknesses to which retail investors are vulnerable".[51]

Over time, the European lawmaker has increasingly become aware of the difficulties produced by disclosure for many retail investors,[52] and for this reason the European legislation has gradually introduced tools aimed at mitigating the disclosure paradigm. First of all, MiFID I has introduced the suitability and appropriateness tests that, as shown above, are anyhow used by supervisors as enforcement tools. Such phenomenon has been brilliantly described by Cherednychenko as "European supervision private law" in that it concerns the "regulatory contract-related conduct-of-business rules of EU origin, to be observed by businesses when dealing with their (potential) clients, which forms part of a framework for public supervision over a specified market and is subject to public enforcement".[53]

More recently—and as a post-financial crisis effect[54]—MiFID II has introduced Product Governance which even more strongly mitigates (if not overcomes at all) the disclosure paradigm. PG fully incorporates the issue of investors' cognitive limitations[55] and strongly leads to a responsibilization of the investment firm in terms of avoiding mis-selling cases[56] by designing processes apt to match beforehand a specific investor (belonging to a cluster of investors sharing similar features) with a specific product (belonging to a cluster of products sharing similar risk profiles).

In her seminal 2010 work, Professor Moloney states: "Product design regulation, typically linked to the authorization of the product for public marketing and so associated with segmentation-based regulation, is one of the three arcs of retail market protection along with the regulation of distribution and disclosure."[57] As amply discussed, disclosure has been a feature of European law since the outset, whereas regulation of distribution is already entrenched with MiFID I conduct-of-business and penetrates traditional private-law duties.[58] What MiFID II PG does is to internalize conduct-of-business rules into a firm's internal processes and procedures on a product life-cycle *without* providing for a product-based ex ante pre-approval regime for which public enforcers would be responsible. Within the framework of Product Governance, responsibility rests on the firm's shoulders.[59]

On the one hand, the non-responsibilization of public enforcers automatically leads to a responsibilization of the internal Function in charge of designing such intra-firm processes and procedures, typically the Compliance Function. On the other hand, the investment choice is still formally carried out by the investor,[60] but the involvement of the investment firm to channel such choice is inflated. The shift of responsibilization is twofold but unidirectional: from the authority to the firm (regarding product design and its related internal PG processes and procedures), and from the investor to the firm (regarding investment decision and its related internal processes and procedures). In both cases, the Compliance Function acts as the frontliner.[61]

The concept of justice underpinning this approach is still market fairness or, in the words of the ERPL theory, access justice. Indeed, Product Governance (and product intervention powers) does not overturn the access justice paradigm by recovering the old social distributive justice model. Instead, it *simply* imposes stricter regulatory requirements on firms so that these can guide their own rational clients (allegedly much *less* rational than before) toward efficient investment decisions, in a sort of "paternalistic access justice".[62]

The consequence is twofold. First, a firm—that is, its internal processes and procedures crafted and monitored by the Compliance Function—is de facto (co-)responsible for the right investment choices of its clients up to the point it spurs moral hazard on the part of the investor.[63] Second, too a conservative approach on the part of the manufacturing and, above all, distributing firms—again, under the internal advice released by the Compliance Function—can reduce financial innovation and, prospectively, even competition among market players.[64] Ironically, if access justice was introduced to push the building up and the efficient functioning of a competitive financial market, its latest version—*paternalistic* access justice—may limit the market by curbing innovation and competition.

Furthermore, the instrumental use of traditionally non-public-law tools for supervisory objectives is strongly reaffirmed by Product Governance. A firm's PG internal processes and procedures are indeed used by supervisory authorities to assess whether and to what extent an investment firm has complied with the applicable regulatory requirements. The assumption is that if a firm has set up correct and efficient intra-firm PG processes and procedures, the mis-selling risk is reduced and inefficiencies are overcome or, at least, mitigated at the *micro* level, and the sum of all of the supervisees' efficient PG processes would likely contribute to market efficiency at the *macro* level.

The redress provided by Union law has always been public, and private enforcement has been structurally overlooked.[65] MiFIR product intervention powers reaffirm the importance of public enforcement. Under MiFIR, indeed, ESMA has been granted with enforcement powers to wield in emergency situations, thus for *very major infringements* left culpably uncovered by inert national competent authorities.

Private remedies are still left to Member States. However, PRIIPs now provides for a contractual liability related to the KID (to be, anyhow, construed according to national private laws), and the Prospectus Regulation too defines the limit of civil liability. Furthermore, Article 75 of MiFID II significantly provides for ADRs to be mandatorily established, overcoming Article 53 of MiFID I that simply encouraged the setting up of such mechanisms. Infringements of retail investor protection rules being handled through such ADRs are those supposed to be too serious to be internally resolved by firms, but not that severe to be brought before a court.[66] These can be defined as *minor infringements*. Significantly, the duty introduced under MiFID II to establish ADRs "can be interpreted as a striving towards a self-sufficient EU private legal order".[67]

Notwithstanding such new features, under EU Law of investment services it is still up to public authorities to play the key role in enforcing retail investors' rights. Such authorities should indirectly protect investors by sanctioning firms for violations of public-law conduct-of-business rules and requiring changes on related internal processes and procedures, by—for instance—verifying the correct functioning of investment services providers' internal conciliation schemes designed to handle consumers' complaints. The role of the Compliance Function in this regard has progressively increased as it is the Function that the law charges to fill the vacuum between the law-on-the-books (EU-made public rules) and the law-in-action[68] directly *within* a firm. Traditionally speaking, civil courts had the role to fill the gaps left by open-ended rules of private law.[69] Under

EU law of investment services, the Compliance Function partially plays this role by interpreting and embedding public rules and by monitoring internal complaints-handling procedures that are conceived to address *very minor infringements*, that is, those that a firm can solve internally. Moreover, these procedures are also important because they contribute to gathering significant information on the way the legal relationships between retail investors and investment services providers work in practice—a background activity necessary for the Compliance Function to optimize a firm's internal procedures and for a public authority to fine-tune business-conduct-rules (in)directly affecting investment services contracts.

The result of the combination of an increased role of the Compliance Function and its internal complaints-handling procedures for very minor infringements; the introduction of mandatory ADR mechanisms for minor infringements; and the new product intervention powers of ESMA for very major infringements is that only "average" severe cases of infringements of retail investor protection rules are left to either domestic courts or domestic public enforcement authorities.[70]

Table 8.2[71] takes a snapshot of the current situation in the EU law of investor protection. It depicts, on the one hand, the centralization trend pushed by MiFIR in favor of the ESMA at the expenses of the domestic financial authorities; and, on the other hand, the waving role of the judiciary, that is gradually "outsourced away from the judicial system".[72]

Alongside the fading role of the judiciary, what this table highlights is, first, the absence of a full interplay between private and public enforcement at Union level—which is also the main takeaway of the comparison between the European Union and the United States. Second, the fact that the only key aspect left largely uncovered by the EU law is by-now private remedies. However, new regulations (such as PRIIPs) now provide for a general contractual liability and the possibility for retail investors to claim damages.

Even if public enforcement is clearly favored, it cannot replace private enforcement (due to public budgetary constraints, which is also one of the reasons why the Compliance Function was established).[73] First of all, it is a general understanding that the 2008 crisis clearly showed how vulnerable public enforcement can be if it is not constantly refined.[74] Moreover, through private enforcement mechanisms, it is possible to dig into concrete situations in order to understand whether an investment

Table 8.2 Infringement severity and redress mechanisms

Very minor infringements	Minor infringements	Major infringements	Very major infringements
Complaints-handling procedures set up and monitored by the compliance Function within a financial firm. Such complaints-handling procedures can be assessed by domestic public authorities when carrying out inspections and investigations.	EU-harmonized domestic ADR procedures assessed by domestic public authorities (under the coordination of the ESMA).	Either/both domestic courts or/and domestic public enforcers (with latter's powers being harmonized).	Emergency intervention powers of the ESMA to replace domestic public enforcers. The ECJ interprets European regulatory private law and guides domestic courts without replacing them.[75]

services has actually breached its conduct-of-business rules, has misled a specific customer of its, or has recommended an investment unsuitable for such customer's financial needs and risk profile.

Administrative supervision and enforcement are not in a position to ex ante ensure that investor protection rules are constantly obeyed, thus to achieve zero risk in mis-selling. For this reason, MiFID II has introduced the Product Governance requirements, which are under the monitoring and responsibility of the Compliance Function. However, achieving zero risk in mis-selling is practically impossible for, at least, one good reason: neither public authorities nor firms' internal Compliance Function have the resources to achieve such a result. This is why efficient, ex post private enforcement mechanisms harmonized throughout the EU may be useful.

In addition, as far as retail mass markets are at stake, private collective mechanisms serve retail investors' needs much better than individual mechanisms would. This is due to the fact that clusters of similar retail investors are very likely to experience analogous problems concerning the same recommended investments or, even more likely, suffer from the same abusive (mis)selling practices. The EU lawmaker has recently proved to be particularly sensitive toward the problem of mis-selling practices for clusters of similar retail investors, due to the ripple effects it may have on the financial system as a whole (repeated inefficiencies at the *micro* level can menace stability at the *macro* level).

However, the response provided by MiFID to retail mass-markets issues is still publicly sided. The MiFID Product Governance requirements are, indeed, to be incorporated into an investment firm through a double-ended flow. From the moment a product is manufactured up to the moment it is sold to clusters of similar retail investors, and the other way around in order to detect and resolve mis-selling cases (which can concern an individual client put in the wrong cluster, or the product sold being unfit for the entire specific cluster of clients). Here again, the role played by the Compliance Function is crucial as it has to craft and monitor such a double-faceted procedure and work to mirror an authority's expectations: this is a clear example of the fact that the Compliance Function acts as an internal embedder and watchdog of the regulatory requirements imposed by the EU law.

Although the EU legal system of the protection of investors still relies on domestic private enforcement mechanisms and looks formally far from its completeness as the comparative analysis with its American counterpart shows, when it is viewed from a perspective of an investment firm, it already looks quite close to self-sufficiency. If the standpoint of an investment firm's Compliance Function is taken into account, the EU law produces very detailed norms that are increasingly often either directly applicable to firms or reproduced into domestic texts.

Being in charge of shielding the firm from administrative sanctions (compliance risk), the Compliance Function embeds such EU-produced rules into a firm's internal rule book and crafts and monitors the related internal processes and procedures on the basis of the compliance risk (compliance risk assessment). The very detailed norms produced at EU level are then enforced either by domestic supervisors whose enforcement powers are harmonized under EU law, or, in emergency cases, by the Paris-based European Authority.

Furthermore, the Compliance Function is requested to, first, craft and monitor the EU-introduced complaints-handling procedures and, second, to be the firm's entry point to liaise with the EU-introduced and ESMA-monitored ADRs in the investment services field. Given that the litigation risk (lawsuits before civil courts) is, as said above, usually handled by the

Legal department, from a Compliance's perspective, the EU law on investor protection is de facto complete. This is because the EU law on investor protection produces almost most of the applicable rules—which are directly embedded into a firm via the Compliance Function itself (as the examples exposed in Chap. 3 prove) and harmonizes or directly handles the mechanisms to enforce such rules (mechanisms with which the Compliance Function constantly interacts) (Fig. 8.1):

The centralization trend—started with Lamfalussy, which gathered regulatory functions previously scattered among different nation states[76]—is clear and it is likely to increase in the coming years even if the Treaties remain unchanged. It is possible, thus, to assume that legal framework on ADR mechanisms for investment services will undergo further harmonization in normative terms and that the ESMA will push domestic public authorities toward a stronger convergence. Furthermore, the ESMA's direct enforcement powers are likely to be enhanced in the future, in particular if specific cases were to occur and these were brought before the Court of Justice of the European Union. Alongside this, the ESMA will probably be endowed with further direct supervisory powers in other areas of financial markets law (as already happens for EMIR

Location: Conclusion, part b

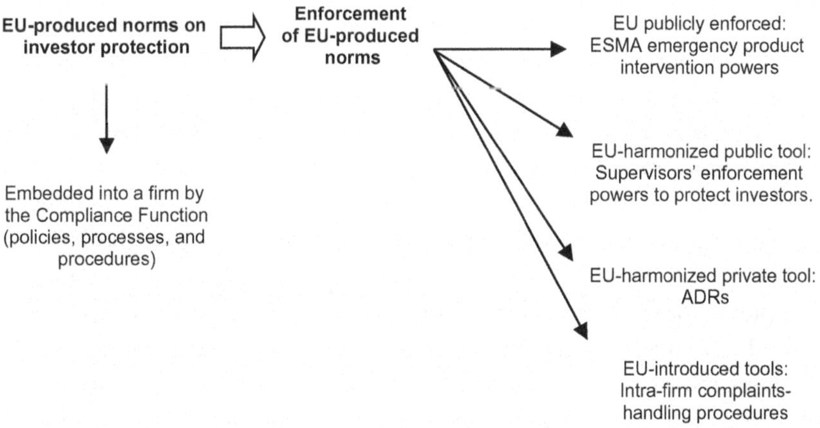

Fig. 8.1 Self-sufficiency of the EU system of investor protection as viewed by an EU-regulated firm

Trading Repository and Credit Rating Agencies) and/or for transactions taking place on a cross-border basis.[77] The result, in either case, would be giving ESMA a more or less direct leveling-out influence on the different Compliance Functions throughout Europe and help the spread of a common regulatory and compliance culture.

Finally, private enforcement is also likely to be eventually addressed by the EU law. The EU lawmaker seems to be coming to the conclusion that public enforcement alone is not enough to achieve the policy goal of market stability and efficiency. In case the Treaties remain unchanged—thus in the current situation that does not allow to formally transplant the US federal interplay of public and private enforcement mechanisms—the EU law may try reshaping domestic (compensation) remedies in a way to make them more coherent with the newly revised paternalistic access justice. As a first step, a prospective revision of the MiFID II will very probably include a civil liability clause like that already provided by the PRIIPs Regulation, altering forever the relationship between EU law of investment services and domestic contract laws.

8.3 Concluding Remarks

At the end of this journey, this book has tried to show how the EU law of investment services—by accompanying the effort to transform a bank-based financial system into a market-based system—initially embraced a regulatory leitmotiv (information disclosure) and a concept of justice (*access justice*) closer to the American tradition rather than to the Continental European one.

However, the comparison carried out in Chaps. 4, 5, and 6 has shown how the European convergence effort is incomplete in that the EU has not been (and is still not) in a position to replicate and accommodate the complexity of the US legal system of investor protection. The latter can, indeed, leverage on a common-law contract law, on federal/state securities laws and regulations, on SROs' rules, and on a complementary interplay of public and private enforcement mechanisms.[78] Even if private enforcement is slowly gaining ground,[79] as of today, the EU law of investment services still basically harmonizes domestic supervisory laws through public-law conduct-of-business rules (which directly/indirectly affect enforcement before domestic courts)[80] and strongly relies on ESMA-coordinated domestic public enforcers.

Additionally, although the increased splinter of EU public-law duties on investment firms (and the bourgeoning of the ESMA Single Rulebook, in particular under MiFID II[81]) has not altered the final goal (construction of an efficient single, market-based financial system), significant changes in Europe concerning the regulatory leitmotiv and justice pattern must be registered. The disclosure paradigm has been so strongly mitigated (if not even overcome) so that part (most?) of the responsibility of an investor's investment choice has shifted on the shoulders of the service provider and its internal Compliance Function, with the result that the *access justice* paradigm has been modified in paternalistic terms to better accommodate the retail investors' limited investment skills.

Nevertheless, the self-sufficiency of the EU law in the area of retail investor protection very much becomes "a matter of degree rather than absolute"[82] if the standpoint of a European investment firm is taken into account. The EU law of investor protection produces its public-law rules and employs, to enforce such rules, either public (increasingly centralized at EU level) rather than private (decentralized at the domestic level) enforcement tools for major infringements, or EU-originated intra-firm complaints-handling procedures for very minor infringements monitored by domestic public authorities. Between the two (public or public-leaning) poles, MiFID II has recently inserted private enforcement through extra-judicial mechanisms for minor infringements of EU investor protection rules (with such ADRs being registered with domestic public enforcers). The picture, thus, looks much more self-sufficient if the standpoint of an EU-regulated firm is considered.

The main divergence between the two standpoints is essentially due to the fact the "EU-US comparative view" formally includes both private and public laws, whereas the *in-action* "within-the-firm view" mostly focuses on regulatory public law, its enforcement by public authorities, and its embeddedness into a firm. As widely shown, the EU legal system is strongly lopsided in favor of public- rather than private-law solutions; this contributes to explaining the increased importance of the Compliance Function (responsible for the observance of public-law rules and of complaints-handling procedures) at the expenses of the traditional Legal department.

Viewed through the lenses of an investment firm, the EU law of investor protection emerges as a *Regulatory Investor Protection Law* that already resembles a self-sufficient system.[83] This *Regulatory Investor Protection Law* has its own principles (similar but autonomous from national private-law systems, as Product Governance proves) and provides for a complete set of rules that stands distinctively from (and replaces old) domestic rules and that directly becomes an apparatus of compliance requirements for MiFID firms upon which public enforcers (both domestic and, now, European) can assess law obedience. Within this context, the Compliance Function becomes the guardian of new *paternalistic access justice* (and the related shift in regulatory leitmotiv, from disclosure to intra-firm proceduralization).

The way forward, that is, the next level of self-sufficiency, is likely to be the width of the EU-centralized public enforcement, specifically whether and to what extent the current centralization toward the European level under MiFIR will remain on paper and whether such new powers granted by MiFIR will be partnered with other pieces of financial services legislation. It is not unreasonable to assume a deepening and acceleration in the centralization trend in the near future, which will result in the EU law wrestling more power away from the domestic level in the investment services field.

Notes

1. Francesco D'Alessandro, *Regolatori Del Mercato, Enforcement E Sistema Penale* (Torino: Giappichelli, 2014). At 406.
2. Hans-Wolfgang Micklitz, "The Visible Hand of European Regulatory Private Law—the Transformation of European Private Law from Autonomy to Functionalism in Competition and Regulation," *Yearbook of European Law* 28, no. 1 (2009). At 18.
3. Niamh Moloney, Eilís Ferran, and Jennifer Payne, "Introduction," in *The Oxford Handbook of Financial Regulation*, ed. Niamh Moloney, Eilís Ferran, and Jennifer Payne (Oxford: Oxford University Press, 2015). At 6.

4. In the words of Professor Avgouleas: "In an attempt to clean up US markets from abuse in the post-1929 crash era, the Roosevelt administration created widespread disclosure regimes for securities issuers and traders by means of the so-called New Deal Statutes: mainly the Securities Act 1933 and the Securities Exchange Act 1934." Emilios Avgouleas, "What Future for Disclosure as a Regulatory Technique? Lessons from Behavioural Decision Theory and the Global Financial Crisis," in *The Future of Financial Regulation*, ed. Iain G MacNeil and Justin O'Brien (Oxford: Hart Publishing, 2010). At 206.
5. On the "rational expectations investor model": Lynn A. Stout, "The Investor Confidence Game," *Brooklyn Law Review* 68, no. 2 (2002).
6. Filippo Zatti, "La Dimensione Costituzionale Della Tutela Del Risparmio. Dalla Tutela Del Risparmio Alla Protezione Dei Risparmiatori/Investitori E Ritorno?," in *Studi in Onore Di Vincenzo Atripaldi*, ed. Marco Benvenuti et al. (Naples: Jovene, 2010).
7. In the words of Professor Tuch: "Generalized comparisons with the US are difficult. Nevertheless, MiFID I imposes a broad-based conflict-'management' obligation, while the US relies more on disclosure and, in some contexts, specific bans." Andrew Tuch, "Conduct of Business Regulation," in *The Oxford Handbook of Financial Regulation*, ed. Niamh Moloney, Eilís Ferran, and Jennifer Payne (Oxford: Oxford University Press, 2015). At 558.
8. Kristina A. Fausti, "A Fiduciary Duty for All," *Duquesne Business Law Journal* 2009–2010, no. 2 (2010). At 187–189.
9. Hans-Wolfgang Micklitz, "Administrative Enforcement of European Private Law," in *The Foundations of European Private Law*, ed. Roger Brownsword, et al. (Oxford-Portland: Hart Publishing, 2011).
10. Olha O. Cherednychenko, "Public Supervision over Private Relationships: Towards European Supervision Private Law?," *European Review of Private Law* 22 no. 1 (2014).
11. On the link between PG and mis-selling: Carmine DiNoia, "Atto Del Governo N. 143 (Mercati Degli Strumenti Finanziari)—Audizione Informale, Commissione Finanze, Camera Dei Deputati," (2017).
12. Tanja Bošković, Caroline Cerruti, and Michel Noël, "Comparing European and U.S. Securities Regulations: Mifid Versus Corresponding U.S. Regulations," in *World Bank Publications*, ed. The World Bank (Washington, DC 2010). At 23.
13. Ibid. At 23.

14. Stephen J. Choi, "Regulating Investors Not Issuers: A Market-Based Proposal "*California Law Review* 88 (2000). At 284–302.
15. SEC Office of Investor Education and Advocacy, "Investor Bulletin: Accredited Investors," Securities and Exchange Commission SEC, https://www.investor.gov/additional-resources/news-alerts/alerts-bulletins/investor-bulletin-accredited-investors.
16. Professor Tuch draws a parallel between US institutional clients and MiFID professional clients. Tuch. At 558.
17. On the general difficulties of choosing which institution is best equipped to implement policy goals, see the seminal contribution by professor Komesar: Neil Komesar, *Imperfect Alternatives: Choosing Institutions in Law, Economics, and Public Policy* (Chicago: University of Chicago Press, 1997).
18. Alongside the connected complexities and the obvious political hurdles. The author would like to thank Federico Della Negra for this point.
19. The book does not mean to mythologize the United States, where the situation is anyhow not perfect. Apart from being very complex (as depicted in Chap. 5), the US system of public enforcement did not fully accomplish its mission when it failed to monitor consolidated supervised entities before 2008. (See: Christopher Cox, "Chairman Cox Announces End of Consolidated Supervised Entities Program," http://www.sec.gov/news/press/2008/2008-230.htm.) In this regard, Professor Tagliabue points out how the Gramm–Leach–Bliley "repealed most of the existing legislation based on a sharp separation between banking, security, and insurance markets, giving origin to a single financial market. The creation of this single financial market, however, was not supported by appropriate regulation of the supervisory bodies, which remained unchanged". Giovanna Tagliabue, "The Role of Controls in the International Financial Crisis," *International Review of Economics* 56, no. 3 (2009). At 312. Furthermore, whether and the extent to which the PSLRA on class actions has actually delivered on its promises is still subject to various empirical studies (see Chap. 6).
20. Very interestingly, "these measures were considered by some as poor, and a review of the criteria is needed in view of substantially substituting the traditional "command and control" regulation with a quasi-market mechanism".
21. Cherednychenko.
22. The mere violation of suitability rule does "not provide an independent basis for private relief" but it may be relevant in SEA Rule 10b-5 actions.

Thomas Lee-Hazen, *Broker-Dealer Regulation in a Nutshell* (Thomson/West, 2003). At 161.

23. Olha O. Cherednychenko, "The Regulation of Retail Investment Services in the EU: Towards the Improvement of Investor Rights?," *Journal of Consumer Policy* 33, no. 4 (2010). At 410.
24. Article 7.5(e): "[C]ivil liability attaches only to those persons who have tabled the summary including any translation thereof, but only where the summary is misleading, inaccurate or inconsistent, when read together with the other parts of the prospectus, or where it does not provide, when read together with the other parts of the prospectus, key information in order to aid investors when considering whether to invest in such securities." *Regulation 2017/1129/Eu.*
25. Micklitz, "Administrative Enforcement of European Private Law."
26. Della Negra argues that "the measures adopted by ESMA in the framework of its investor protection task may enhance the uniform interpretation of contract law across national jurisdictions and strengthen the private enforcement of the MiFID II conduct of business rules, namely by incentivising investors to bring claims for compensation before national courts based on the ESMA's interpretation of the EU law." Federico DellaNegra, "The Effects of the Esma's Powers on Domestic Contract Law," in *Regulating and Supervising European Financial Markets: More Risks Than Achievements*, ed. Mads Andenas and Gudula Diepenbrock (Berlin: Springer, 2016).
27. Iain MacNeil, "Enforcement and Sanctioning," in *The Oxford Handbook of Financial Regulation*, ed. Niamh Moloney, Eilís Ferran, and Jennifer Payne (Oxford: Oxford University Press, 2015). At 297. Professor MacNeil adds that the US "pattern is not replicated across the world, as demonstrated by IOSCO assessments of regulatory systems which show that the lack of effective sanctions is a common weakness of many systems".
28. Tommaso Padoa-Schioppa, "Self Vs. Public Discipline in the Financial Field," in *the London School of Economics* (London 2002).
29. On the same wavelength, professor Tuch highlights how "[t]he general law serves as an important backdrop against which to consider COB regulatory developments." Tuch. At 541.
30. Hans-Wolfgang Micklitz, "The Internal Vs. The External Dimension of European Private Law—a Conceptual Design and a Research Agenda," in *EUI Working Paper Law 2015/35*, ed. European University Institute (Florence 2015).

31. On failures of attempts made in this direction (Draft Common Frame of Reference—DCFR and Common European Sales Law—CESL), see: "The Transformation of Enforcement in European Private Law: Preliminary Considerations," *European Review of Private Law* 4 (2015). At 493–494.
32. On the relationship between full harmonization measures and national private legal orders: Olha O. Cherednychenko, "Financial Consumer Protection in the EU: Towards a Self-Sufficient European Contract Law for Consumer Financial Services?," *European Review of Contract Law* 10, no. 4 (2014).
33. In her seminal work, Eilís Ferran carries out an analysis on the law's role in building an integrated securities market. In particular, Professor Ferran points out: "The recent shift in Continental Europe towards securities market-based financing can be attributed to a range of factors, some of which affected securities markets around the world, some of which were exclusively, or particularly, EU-orientated. [...] The evolving EU processes of political and economic integration also played a significant part in fostering the development of securities market-based financing." Eilís Ferran, *Building an EU Securities Market* (Cambridge: Cambridge University Press, 2004). At 22–23.
34. *Estée Lauder Cosmetics Gmbh & Co. Ohg V Lancaster Group Gmbh*, ECR I–117 (2000).
35. Hans-Wolfgang Micklitz, "Social Justice and Access Justice in Private Law," in *EUI Working Paper Law 2011/2*, ed. European University Institute (Florence 2011). At 6.
36. Peter Cartwright, "Optimal Consumer Protection in Financial Services," in *ECRI/CEPS SEMINAR at the European Credit Research Institute and Centre for European Policy Studies* (Brussels 2001). At 7.
37. On such a legislative approach, it has been argued that consumer law cannot be just a tool to filling up the gaps of a market system: "At stake are elements of the correction of market failures and, additionally, the achievement of fairness to consumers (inter alia) as the economically weaker parties. Consumer protection law has a wide range of forms and objectives." Geraint Howells and Stephen Weatherill, eds., *Consumer Protection Law, 2nd Ed.* (Hants Ashgate, 2005).
38. Hans-Wolfgang Micklitz, "Jack Is out of the Box—the Efficient Consumer-Shopper," *Juridiska Föreningen i Finland* 3, no. 4 (2009). At 422.

39. What might be exported from the American experience in Europe is a harmonized power of public enforcers to bring civil actions against investment firms as an alternative to public enforcement measures through sanctions and fines. However, harmonization of such power at European level might be counterproductive since divergences between Member States may emerge, with the result of creating barriers within the Single Market. This would be due to the different private remedies provided by national civil regimes (on which the EU has no harmonizing powers).
40. Cartwright. At 7.
41. Niamh Moloney, *How to Protect Investors: Lessons from the EC and the UK* (Cambridge: Cambridge University Press, 2010). At 46.
42. These words are used by the World Bank in: World Bank, "Bulgaria Diagnostic Review of Consumer Protection and Financial Capability Vol I," (Washington, DC: Private and Financial Sector Development Department for Europe and Central Asia Region, 2009). At 6.
43. In the words of Professor Moloney: "[E]mpowerment is concerned with equipping and encouraging the retail investor to navigate the financial markets." Moloney. At 53.
44. Tom Van Dyck, "(Opt-out) Intermediation as an Alternative for Ensuring a True Protection for European Retail Investors?," *Catholic University of Leuven (KUL) Working Paper* (2009). At 23. Also Troy A. Paredes, "Blinded by the Light: Information Overload and Its Consequences for Securities Regulation," *Washington University Law Quarterly* 81, no. 2 (2003).
45. Van Dyck. At 24.
46. Daniel Kahneman and Amos Tversky, "Prospect Theory: An Analysis of Decision under Risk "*Econometrica* 47, no. 2 (1979).
47. Bounded rationality implies that economic agents have problems when "formulating and solving complex problems and [when] processing (receiving, storing, retrieving, transmitting information" [Oliver E Williamson, "The Economics of Organization: The Transaction Cost Approach," *American Journal of Sociology* 87, no. 3 (1981)]. Indeed, if the investor is not actually fully rational, the allegedly "enough" information is likely to be either "too much" or even useless. And if one has information that s/he can potentially use but s/he does not know how to use it, then her/his choice will not be the best possible result and this can eventually generate imperfections in her/his own decision-making process (thus transaction costs).

48. In the words of Professors Enriques and Gilotta: "Problems of bounded rationality and information overload (the incapacity of the individual investor to 'handle' large amounts of information) prevent the unsophisticated investor from really benefiting from MD [mandatory disclosure] and may even make matters worse, relative to a situation of less available information." Luca Enriques and Sergio Gilotta, "Disclosure and Financial Market Regulation," in *The Oxford Handbook of Financial Regulation*, ed. Niamh Moloney, Eilís Ferran, and Jennifer Payne (Oxford: Oxford University Press, 2015). At 516.
49. On cognitive biases and other important deviations from full rationality in the financial contexts, see the seminal contribution of professors Nicholas Barberis and Richard Thaler, "Chapter 18: A Survey of Behavioral Finance," in *Handbook of the Economics of Finance—Volume 1, Part B*, ed. George M. Constantinides, Milton Harris, and René Stulz (Amsterdam: Elsevier, 2003).
50. On the perverse effect of mandatory disclosure: Van Dyck. At 23–24.
51. Niamh Moloney, "Regulating the Retail Markets," in *The Oxford Handbook of Financial Regulation*, ed. Niamh Moloney, Eilís Ferran, and Jennifer Payne (Oxford: Oxford University Press, 2015). At 748. Similarly, Professors Svetiev and Ottow state that: "[T]he shift from emphasis on market transparency towards greater supervision of private law areas such as contract development and corporate governance may reflect the observed failures of the disclosure paradigm in financial markets as buttressed by a growing body of research in behavioural economics and finance". Yane Svetiev and Annetje Ottow, "Financial Supervision in the Interstices between Private and Public Law," *European Review of Contract Law* 10, no. 4 (2014). At 502.
52. In the words of professor Moloney: "[the] more conservative investors who dominate in the EC market (typically consumers of investment products which [can be] characterized as prudent 'savers') found disclosures to be complicated, obscure, complex, incomplete, often designed as marketing rather than information documents and insufficiently focused on risk; they relied on advice rather than on personal assessment of disclosure." Moloney, *How to Protect Investors: Lessons from the EC and the UK*. At 294.
53. Cherednychenko, "Public Supervision over Private Relationships: Towards European Supervision Private Law?." At 40.
54. Professor Cherednychenko points out that: "The financial crisis has urged a rethinking of the pre-crisis regulatory philosophy driven by the

consumer empowerment model and the point of no return has probably already been reached." "Freedom of Contract in the Post-Crisis Era: Quo Vadis?," *European Review of Contract Law* 10, no. 3 (2014). At 418.

55. Ibid. At 418–421.
56. DiNoia.
57. Moloney, *How to Protect Investors: Lessons from the EC and the UK.* At 134.
58. Cherednychenko, "Financial Consumer Protection in the EU: Towards a Self-Sufficient European Contract Law for Consumer Financial Services?." Vanessa Mak, "The Consumer in European Regulatory Private Law," in *Tilburg Private Law Working Paper Series No. 05/2015*, ed. Tilburg University (Tilburg 2015).
59. On a similar fashion, Professors Svetiev and Ottow highlight that product intervention "creates uncertainty for firms and shifts on them the responsibility for assessing the likely consumer detriment". Svetiev and Ottow. At 508.
60. Except for the portfolio management service which based on a mandate.
61. The Compliance Function is responsible for the effectiveness of the processes, procedures, and programs it crafts: "[T]he external enforcer needs to monitor the compliance function to ensure that it is faithfully and effectively carried out." Geoffrey P. Miller, "The Compliance Function: An Overview," in *Law and Economics Working Papers—Paper 393*, ed. New York University (2014). At 2.
62. Professor Cherednychenko speaks of "hard paternalism in post-crisis financial services regulation". Cherednychenko, "Freedom of Contract in the Post-Crisis Era: Quo Vadis?." At 418.
63. In the words of Professor Cherednychenko: "Minimising personal responsibility in financial decision-making may remove any incentive for consumers to learn and play an active role in policing financial institutions." Ibid. At 419. In a similar fashion on product intervention, Professor Moloney claims that "product intervention [...] might be regarded as infusing retail market regulation with an overly paternalistic approach which risks limiting investor autonomy and firm innovation". Moloney, "Regulating the Retail Markets." At 763.
64. Cherednychenko, "Freedom of Contract in the Post-Crisis Era: Quo Vadis?." At 419.
65. In the words of Professor Tison: "EU securities law is devised as a system that is not intended to realize enforcement primarily through private litigation and enforcement", Michel Tison, "The Civil Law Effects of Mifid in a Comparative Law Perspective," in *Financial Law Institute Working Paper 2010–05*, ed. Universiteit Gent—Financial Law Institute (Gent 2010). At 17.

66. Within the ADR and private enforcement context, Professor Cherednychenko points out how these mechanisms are likely to add "another layer of rules in an already complex legal matrix for financial services—one consisting of contract-related financial supervision rules, on the one hand, and traditional private law rules, on the other". Olha O. Cherednychenko, "Public and Private Enforcement of European Private Law in the Financial Services Sector," *European Review of Private Law* 24, no. 4 (2015). At 639.
67. Svetiev and Ottow. At 511.
68. On a similar wavelength, Lenglet speaks of "Ambivalence and Ambiguity". Marc Lenglet, "Ambivalence and Ambiguity: The Interpretive Role of Compliance Officers," in *Finance: The Discreet Regulator*, ed. Isabelle Huault and Chrystelle Richard (London: Palgrave Macmillan, 2012). At 61.
69. "In the course of private adjudication, civil courts also played an important role in the development of private law by filling in open-ended private law norms, such as good faith, good morals, or public policy." Public Supervision over Private Relationships: Towards European Supervision Private Law?". *European Review of Private Law* 22, no. 1 (2014): 37–68. At 38.
70. "To put it bluntly, in practice national courts and national regulatory agencies tend to become 'agents' of the European 'principal'." Micklitz, "The Transformation of Enforcement in European Private Law: Preliminary Considerations." At 522.
71. Close to the tables developed by Professor Micklitz in "Administrative Enforcement of European Private Law." At 569 and 587–588.
72. "The Transformation of Enforcement in European Private Law: Preliminary Considerations." At 520.
73. As rightly pointed out by Professor Miller: "[A]n external norm enforcer may not have the resources or the ability either to detect violations or to devise an effective system of sanctions. The organization has the knowledge and the ability to more effectively perform these tasks. It therefore makes sense for institutions to police themselves—to carry out a compliance operation." Miller. At 2.
74. In the United States, for instance, the adoption of the Gramm-Leach-Bliley Act in 1999 "created a significant regulatory gap by failing to give to the SEC or any agency the authority to regulate large investment bank holding companies". Cox.

75. A recent example for the financial services sector is the *Bankinter* case. *Genil 48 Sl and Comercial Hostelera De Grandes Vinos Sl V Bankinter Sa and Banco Bilbao Vizcaya Argentaria Sa.*
76. Professor Brummer argues that this centralization has "made possible a shift in the transatlantic balance of regulatory power". Chris Brummer, *Soft Law and the Global Financial System: Rule Making in the twenty-first Century* (Cambridge; New York: Cambridge University Press, 2012).
77. This is heralded by the words of the European Commission in its recent ESA Consultation Paper: "As the EU is developing the CMU, there is a need to consider how more integrated supervision at EU level can support the development of deeper and more integrated capital markets through more convergent supervisory approaches and outcomes which ensure consistency in the application of capital markets rules and the supervision of market participants. [...]The Five Presidents' Report had previously acknowledged the need to strengthen the supervisory framework through more centralisation of supervision of capital markets in order to ensure the solidity of all financial actors. [...] A possible extension of ESMA's powers could be considered in market segments in which there is a strong need to support more integrated, efficient and well-functioning financial instruments markets [...] or in areas where high integration or intense cross-border activity entail higher cross-border contagion risks to financial stability or market integrity." European Commission, "Public Consultation on the Operations of the European Supervisory Authorities," (2017). At 16–17.
78. "The US approach involves multiple layers of rules, sources of law, and regulators. The product is a complex and often esoteric amalgam of laws." Tuch. At 546.
79. As pointed out by Svetiev and Ottow, the MiFID II obligation to establish ADRs "can be interpreted as a striving towards a self-sufficient EU private legal order". Svetiev and Ottow. At 511.
80. In the words of Professor Micklitz: "[P]ublic administrative law [...] put[s] pressure on private law rules." Micklitz, "The Transformation of Enforcement in European Private Law: Preliminary Considerations." At 516. On the resistance of national laws against the intrusion of European regulatory contract law: Cherednychenko, "Financial Consumer Protection in the EU: Towards a Self-Sufficient European Contract Law for Consumer Financial Services?." At 486–491.
81. As shown by the quantity and quality of ESMA's technical standards.

82. Cherednychenko, "Financial Consumer Protection in the EU: Towards a Self-Sufficient European Contract Law for Consumer Financial Services?."
83. On the degree of self-sufficiency of Financial Consumer Protection in the EU: ibid.

Bibliography

Advocacy, SEC Office of Investor Education. "Investor Bulletin: Accredited Investors." Securities and Exchange Commission SEC. https://www.investor.gov/additional-resources/news-alerts/alerts-bulletins/investor-bulletin-accredited-investors.

Avgouleas, Emilios. "What Future for Disclosure as a Regulatory Technique? Lessons from Behavioural Decision Theory and the Global Financial Crisis." In *The Future of Financial Regulation*, edited by Iain G. MacNeil and Justin O'Brien. Oxford: Hart Publishing, 2010.

Barberis, Nicholas, and Richard Thaler. "Chapter 18: A Survey of Behavioral Finance." In *Handbook of the Economics of Finance – Volume 1, Part B*, edited by George M. Constantinides, Milton Harris and René Stulz. Amsterdam: Elsevier, 2003.

Bošković, Tanja, Caroline Cerruti, and Michel Noël. "Comparing European and U.S. Securities Regulations: MiFID Versus Corresponding U.S. Regulations." In *World Bank Publications*. Washington, DC: The World Bank, 2010.

Brummer, Chris. *Soft Law and the Global Financial System: Rule Making in the 21st Century*. Cambridge/New York: Cambridge University Press, 2012.

Cartwright, Peter. "Optimal Consumer Protection in Financial Services." *ECRI/CEPS SEMINAR at the European Credit Research Institute and Centre for European Policy Studies*. Brussels, 2001.

Cherednychenko, Olha O. "The Regulation of Retail Investment Services in the EU: Towards the Improvement of Investor Rights?". *Journal of Consumer Policy* 33, no. 4 (2010): 403–24.

———. "Financial Consumer Protection in the EU: Towards a Self-Sufficient European Contract Law for Consumer Financial Services?". *European Review of Contract Law* 10, no. 4 (2014a): 476–95.

———. "Freedom of Contract in the Post-Crisis Era: Quo Vadis?". *European Review of Contract Law* 10, no. 3 (2014b): 390–421.

———. "Public Supervision Over Private Relationships: Towards European Supervision Private Law?". *European Review of Private Law* 22, no. 1 (2014c): 37–68.

———. "Public and Private Enforcement of European Private Law in the Financial Services Sector." *European Review of Private Law* 24, no. 4 (2015): 621–47.

Choi, Stephen J. "Regulating Investors Not Issuers: A Market-Based Proposal". *California Law Review* 88 (2000): 279–334.

Cox, Christopher. "Chairman Cox Announces End of Consolidated Supervised Entities Program". http://www.sec.gov/news/press/2008/2008-230.htm.

D'Alessandro, Francesco. *Regolatori Del Mercato, Enforcement E Sistema Penale.* Torino: Giappichelli, 2014.

DellaNegra, Federico. "The Effects of the ESMA'S Powers on Domestic Contract Law." In *Regulating and Supervising European Financial Markets: More Risks Than Achievements*, edited by Mads Andenas and Gudula Diepenbrock. Berlin: Springer, 2016.

DiNoia, Carmine. "Atto Del Governo N. 143 (Mercati Degli Strumenti Finanziari) – Audizione Informale, Commissione Finanze, Camera Dei Deputati." 2017.

Enriques, Luca, and Sergio Gilotta. "Disclosure and Financial Market Regulation." In *The Oxford Handbook of Financial Regulation*, edited by Niamh Moloney, Eilís Ferran and Jennifer Payne. Oxford: Oxford University Press, 2015.

Estée Lauder Cosmetics Gmbh & Co. Ohg V Lancaster Group Gmbh, ECR I–117 (2000).

European Commission. "Public Consultation on the Operations of the European Supervisory Authorities." 2017.

Fausti, Kristina A. "A Fiduciary Duty for All." *Duquesne Business Law Journal* 12, no. 2 (2010): 183–209.

Ferran, Eilís. *Building an EU Securities Market.* Cambridge: Cambridge University Press, 2004.

Howells, Geraint, and Stephen Weatherill, eds. *Consumer Protection Law.* 2nd ed. Aldershot: Hants Ashgate, 2005.

Kahneman, Daniel, and Amos Tversky. "Prospect Theory: An Analysis of Decision Under Risk". *Econometrica* 47, no. 2 (1979): 263–91.

Komesar, Neil. *Imperfect Alternatives: Choosing Institutions in Law, Economics, and Public Policy.* Chicago: University of Chicago Press, 1997.

Lee-Hazen, Thomas. *Broker-Dealer Regulation in a Nutshell.* St. Paul, MN: Thomson/West, 2003.
Lenglet, Marc. "Ambivalence and Ambiguity: The Interpretive Role of Compliance Officers." In *Finance: The Discreet Regulator*, edited by Isabelle Huault and Chrystelle Richard. London: Palgrave Macmillan, 2012.
MacNeil, Iain. "Enforcement and Sanctioning." In *The Oxford Handbook of Financial Regulation*, edited by Niamh Moloney, Eilís Ferran and Jennifer Payne. Oxford: Oxford University Press, 2015.
Mak, Vanessa. "The Consumer in European Regulatory Private Law." In *Tilburg Private Law Working Paper Series No. 05/2015.* Tilburg: Tilburg University, 2015.
Micklitz, Hans-Wolfgang. "Jack Is Out of the Box – The Efficient Consumer-Shopper." *Juridiska Föreningen i Finland* 3, no. 4 (2009a): 417–36.
———. "The Visible Hand of European Regulatory Private Law—The Transformation of European Private Law from Autonomy to Functionalism in Competition and Regulation." *Yearbook of European Law* 28, no. 1 (2009b): 3–59.
———. "Administrative Enforcement of European Private Law." In *The Foundations of European Private Law*, edited by Roger Brownsword, Hans-Wolfgang Micklitz, Leone Niglia and Stephen Weatherill, 563–92. Oxford-Portland: Hart Publishing, 2011a.
———. "Social Justice and Access Justice in Private Law." In *EUI Working Paper Law 2011/2.* Florence: European University Institute. 2011b.
———. "The Internal Vs. The External Dimension of European Private Law—A Conceptual Design and a Research Agenda." In *EUI Working Paper Law 2015/35.* Florence: European University Institute, 2015a.
———. "The Transformation of Enforcement in European Private Law: Preliminary Considerations." *European Review of Private Law* 4 (2015b): 491–524.
Miller, Geoffrey P. "The Compliance Function: An Overview." In *Law and Economics Working Papers – Paper 393.* New York University, 2014.
Moloney, Niamh. *How to Protect Investors: Lessons from the EC and the UK.* Cambridge: Cambridge University Press, 2010.
———. "Regulating the Retail Markets." In *The Oxford Handbook of Financial Regulation*, edited by Niamh Moloney, Eilís Ferran and Jennifer Payne. Oxford: Oxford University Press, 2015.

Moloney, Niamh, Eilís Ferran, and Jennifer Payne. "Introduction." In *The Oxford Handbook of Financial Regulation*, edited by Niamh Moloney, Eilís Ferran and Jennifer Payne. Oxford: Oxford University Press, 2015.

Padoa-Schioppa, Tommaso. "Self Vs. Public Discipline in the Financial Field." In *The London School of Economics*. London: Routledge, 2002.

Paredes, Troy A. "Blinded by the Light: Information Overload and Its Consequences for Securities Regulation." *Washington University Law Quarterly* 81, no. 2 (2003): 417–85.

Regulation 2017/1129/Eu.

Stout, Lynn A. "The Investor Confidence Game." *Brooklyn Law Review* 68, no. 2 (2002): 407–37.

Svetiev, Yane, and Annetje Ottow. "Financial Supervision in the Interstices Between Private and Public Law." *European Review of Contract Law* 10, no. 4 (2014): 496–544.

Tagliabue, Giovanna. "The Role of Controls in the International Financial Crisis." *International Review of Economics* 56, no. 3 (2009): 303–13.

Tison, Michel. "The Civil Law Effects of MiFID in a Comparative Law Perspective." In *Financial Law Institute Working Paper 2010–05*. Gent: Universiteit Gent – Financial Law Institute, 2010.

Tuch, Andrew. "Conduct of Business Regulation." In *The Oxford Handbook of Financial Regulation*, edited by Niamh Moloney, Eilís Ferran and Jennifer Payne. Oxford: Oxford University Press, 2015.

Van Dyck, Tom. "(Opt-out) Intermediation as an Alternative for Ensuring a True Protection for European Retail Investors?". *Catholic University of Leuven (KUL) Working Paper*, 2009.

Williamson, Oliver E. "The Economics of Organization: The Transaction Cost Approach." *American Journal of Sociology* 87, no. 3 (1981): 548–77.

World Bank. "Bulgaria Diagnostic Review of Consumer Protection and Financial Capability, Vol. I." Washington, DC: Private and Financial Sector Development Department for Europe and Central Asia Region, 2009.

Zatti, Filippo. "La Dimensione Costituzionale Della Tutela Del Risparmio. Dalla Tutela Del Risparmio Alla Protezione Dei Risparmiatori/Investitori E Ritorno?". In *Studi in Onore Di Vincenzo Atripaldi*, edited by Marco Benvenuti, et al., 1469–94. Naples: Jovene, 2010.

Index[1]

[1] Note: Page numbers followed by 'n' refer to notes.

© The Author(s) 2018

A. Marcacci, *Regulating Investor Protection under EU Law*,
https://doi.org/10.1007/978-3-319-90297-5

The manufacturer's authorised representative in the EU is Springer
Nature Customer Service Centre GmbH, Europaplatz 3, 69115 Heidelberg,
Germany. If you have any concerns regarding our products, please
contact ProductSafety@springernature.com

Printed and bound by CPI Group (UK) Ltd, Croydon, CR0 4YY
05/10/2026
02228128-0016